Encyclopedia of National Anthems

Edited by Xing Hang

The Scarecrow Press, Inc.
Lanham, Maryland, and Oxford
2003

SCARECROW PRESS, INC.

Published in the United States of America
by Scarecrow Press, Inc.
A wholly owned subsidiary of the Rowman & Littlefield Publishing Group, Inc.
4501 Forbes Boulevard, Suite 200, Lanham, Maryland 20706
www.scarecrowpress.com

PO Box 317
Oxford
OX2 9RU, UK

ISBN 0-8108-4847-3

∞™ The paper used in this publication meets the minimum requirements of
American National Standard for Information Sciences—Permanence of
Paper for Printed Library Materials, ANSI/NISO Z39.48-1992.
Manufactured in the United States of America.

To the citizens of the world. May peace prevail.

Contents

Preface

National anthems encompass a wide variety of music, from folk tunes to religious praises, from patriotic hymns to victory marches. Some songs exalt the beauty of the nation, while others boast a historical event. More than a few are simply brief fanfares without words. Yet, strangely, the uniqueness of each anthem makes them similar because it reflects the cultural and linguistic diversity of the world, and every nation's priceless contribution.

This encyclopedia is an up-to-date collection of national anthems from most of the 193 sovereign countries in the world. Besides providing music sheets arranged for piano, this collection also includes lyrics in the original language of each country along with an English translation, if applicable. Non-Latin texts are also displayed as much as possible, usually coming with a transliterated version in the sheet music so that they can be sung to. Before each anthem, a country fact box and historical background provides facts about the nation itself and a short account of how the song came to be the national anthem. However, the amount of information varies, since more source material is available for some countries than others. Moreover, due to major events such as a change in government or very recent independence, anthems from a couple of nations are unavailable at the time of writing. Two countries—East Timor and Serbia and Montenegro—have been left out of the book because no information could yet be found on them and it is not known whether they have adopted a national anthem or not. East Timor, located in the Indonesian Archipelago, became an independent state in 2002 after a period under United Nations mandate. Serbia and Montenegro changed their name from the Yugoslav Federation in 2003 and is undergoing an overhaul of its national symbols. My apologies for these exclusions or any other insufficiency found within this book.

I would like to thank the various embassies and consulates, governments, on-line sources, and Mr. David Kendall for providing me the lyrics, translations, and background information necessary to compile this collection. Their help has been indispensable. Detailed credits are found in the "Notes" section at the back of this book.

Afghanistan

افغانستان

```
Quick Country Facts
Location: West Asia, Near East
Area: 250,000 sq. mi. (647,500 sq. km.)
Population (2002 est.): 27,755,775
Capital/Largest City: Kabul (pop. 2,450,000)
Languages: Pashtu, Dari, Persian, Tajik
GDP/PPP: $21 billion, $800 per capita
Monetary Unit: Afghani
```

Historical Background

The Taliban government prohibited music and, therefore, had no national anthem. As of yet, it is still unclear which anthem the new government will decide upon.

Anthem Not Available

Albania

Republika e Shqipërisë

(Republic of Albania)

Quick Country Facts
Location: Eastern Europe, Balkan Peninsula
Area: 11,100 sq. mi. (28,750 sq. km.)
Population (2002 est.): 3,544,841
Capital/Largest City: Tiranë (pop. 300,000)
Official Language: Albanian
GDP/PPP: $14 billion, $4,500 per capita
Monetary Unit: Lek

Hymni Kombëtar

(National Anthem)

Lyrics: Aleksandër Stavre Drenova (1872-1947). Music: Ciprian Porumbescu (1853-1883). Adopted: 1912.

Historical Background[1]

This anthem was written by the Albanian poet Asdreni (acronym for Aleksandër Stavre Drenova). Originally entitled "Betimi mi flamur," or "Pledge to the Flag," the hymn was first published as a poem in *Liri e Shqipërisë* (Freedom of Albania), an Albanian-language newspaper in Sofia, Bulgaria, for its issue of 21 April 1912. Later that year it appeared in a volume of collected poems by Asdreni, under the title *Èndra e lot* (Dreams and Tears), published in Bucharest. The official anthem is two verses shorter than the original poem. The music was composed by Romanian songwriter Ciprian Porumbescu.

Albanian Words	English Translation[2]
1	1
Rreth flamurit të përbashkuar,	United around the flag,
Me një dëshirë dhe një qëllim,	With one desire and one goal,
Të gjithë Atij duke iu betuar,	Let us pledge our word of honor
Të lidhim besën për shpëtim.	To fight for our salvation

Prej lufte veç ay largohet,
Që është lindur tradhëtor,
Kush është burrë nuk friksohet,
Po vdes, po vdes si një dëshmor.
(repeat previous two lines)

2
Në dorë armët do t`i mbajmë,
Të mbrojmë Atdheun në çdo vend,
Të drejtat tona ne s`i ndajmë,
Këtu armiqtë s`kanë vend.

Se Zoti vet e tha me gojë,
Që kombe shuhen përmbi dhe,
Po Shqipëria do të rrojë,
Për te, për te luftojmë ne.
(repeat previous two lines)

Only he who is born a traitor
Averts from the struggle.
He who is brave is not daunted,
But falls—a martyr to the cause.
(repeat previous two lines)

2
With arms in hand we shall remain,
To guard our fatherland round about.
Our rights we will not bequeath,
Enemies have no place here.

For the Lord Himself has said,
That nations vanish from the earth,
But Albania shall live on,
Because for her, it is for her that we fight.
(repeat previous two lines)

Albania

Rreth flam - ur - it të për - ba - shku - ar Me një de - shirë dhe një që - llim ___, Të

gjithë At - ij duke iu be - tu - ar ___, Të lid - him be - sën për shpë - tim. Prej

luf - te veç a - y lar - go - - het Që ë - shtë lin - dur tra - dhë - tor ___, Kush ë - shtë bu - rrë

nuk fri - kso - het, Po vdes, po vdes si një dë - shmor ___.

Algeria

الشعبية الجمهورية الجزائرية الديمقراطية

al-Jumhuriya al-Jazairiya ad-Dimuqratiya ash-Shabiya

République Algérienne Démocratique et Populaire

(Democratic and Popular Republic of Algeria)

Quick Country Facts
Location: North Africa
Area: 919,595 sq. mi. (2,381,740 sq. km.)
Population (2002 est.): 32,277,942
Capital/Largest City: Algiers (pop. 1,507,241)
Official Languages: Arabic, French
GDP/PPP: $177 billion, $5,600 per capita
Monetary Unit: Dinar

Qassaman

Nous nous engageons

(The Pledge)

Lyrics: Moufdi Zakaria (1930-1978). Music: Mohamed Fawzi (1918-1966). Adopted: 1963.

Historical Background

"Qassaman" came into being during Algeria's struggle for independence from French colonial rule. Moufdi Zakaria wrote the words to the song in 1955 from the Barberousse Prison in Algiers, where he was incarcerated. These lyrics were then put into music, first by Mohamed Triki in 1956, then by the Egyptian composer Mohamed Fawzi. The anthem was initially performed in July 1957 by Tunisian Radio and Television.

Arabic Words (Transliteration)	French Words	English Translation
1	1	1
Qassaman Binnazilat Ilmahiqat	Par les foudres qui anéantissent,	We swear by the lightning that
Waddimaa Izzakiyat Ittahirat.	Par les flots de sang pur et sans tache,	destroys,
(repeat previous two lines)	Par les drapeaux flottants qui flottent	By the streams of generous blood
Walbonood Illamiaat Ilkhafiqat	Sur les hauts djebel orgueilleux et	being shed.
Filgi bal Ishshamikhat Ish shahiqat	fiers,	By the bright flags that wave,
Nahno Thurna Fa hayaton Aw ma	Nous juron nous être révoltés pour	Flying proudly on the high djebels,
maat.	vivre ou pour mourir,	That we are in revolt, whether to live
Wa Aqadna Alazma An Tahya Algazair	Et nous avons juré de mourir pour que	or to die.
Fashhadoo! Fashhadoo! Fashhadoo!	vive l'Algérie!	We are determined that Algeria should
	Témoignez! Témoignez! Témoignez!	live,
		So be our witness—be
		our witness—be our witness!
2	2	2
Nahno Gondon Fi Sabil Il hakki	Nous sommes des soldats pour la	We are soldiers in revolt for truth
Thorna	justice, révoltés,	And we have fought for our
Wa Ila Isstiqlalina Bilharbi Kumna.	Et pour notre indépendance nous	independence.
Lam Yakon Yossgha Lana Lamma	avons engagé le combat,	When we spoke, nobody listened to
Natakna	Nous n'avons obéi à nulle injonction	us,
Fatta khathna Rannat Albaroodi	en nous soulevant.	So we have taken the noise of
Wazna	Le bruit de la poudre a été notre	gunpowder as our rhythm
Wa Azafna Naghamat Alrashshashi	mesure	And the sound of machine guns as our
Lahna	Et le crépitement des mitrailleuse	melody,
Wa Aqadna Alazma An Tahya Algazair	notre chant favori.	We are determined that Algeria should
Fashhadoo! Fashhadoo! Fashhadoo!	Et nous avons juré de mourir pour que	live,
	vive l'Algérie!	So be our witness—be
	Témoignez! Témoignez! Témoignez!	our witness—be our witness!
3	3	3
Nahno min Abtalina Nadfaoo Gondon	Sur nos héros nous bâtirons une gloire	From our heroes we shall make an
Wa Ala Ashlaina Nassnaoo Magdan.	Et sur nos corps nous monterons à	army come to being,
Wa Ala Arwahena Nassado Khuldan	l'immortalité	From our dead we shall build up a
Wa Ala Hamatina Narfao Bandan.	Sur nos âmes, nous construirons une	glory,
Gabhato Ltahreeri Aataynaki Ahdan	armée	Our spirits shall ascend to immortality
Wa Aqadna Alazma An Tahya Algazair	Et de notre espoir nous lèverons	And on our shoulders we shall raise
Fashhadoo! Fashhadoo! Fashhadoo!	l'étendard.	the standard.
Wa Aqadna Alazma An Tahya Algazair	Front de la Libération, nous t'avons	To the nation's Liberation Front we

Fashhadoo! Fashhadoo! Fashhadoo!	prêté serment Et nous avons juré de mourir pour que vive l'Algérie! Témoignez! Témoignez! Témoignez!	have sworn an oath, We are determined that Algeria should live, So be our witness—be our witness—be our witness!
4 *Sarkhato lawtani min Sah Ilfida* *Issmaoooha Wasstageebo Linnida* *Waktobooha Bidimaa Ilshohadaa* *Waktobooha Libany Ilgeeli ghadan.* *Kad Madadna Laka Ya Magdo Yada*	4 Le cri de la patrie monte des champs de bataille. Ecoutez-le et répondez à l'appel. Ecrivez-le dans le sang des martyrs Et dictez-le aux générations futures. Nous t'avons donné la main, ô gloire, Et nous avons juré de mourir pour que vive l'Algérie! Témoignez! Témoignez! Témoignez!	4 The cry of the Fatherland sounds from the battlefields. Listen to it and answer the call! Let it be written with the blood of martyrs And be read to future generations. Oh, Glory, we have held out our hand to you, We are determined that Algeria should live, So be our witness—be our witness—be our witness!

Algeria

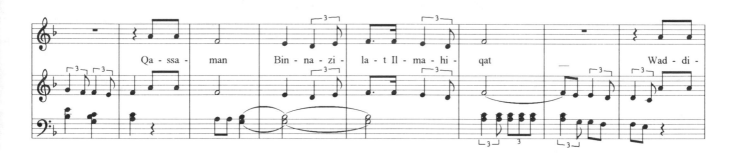

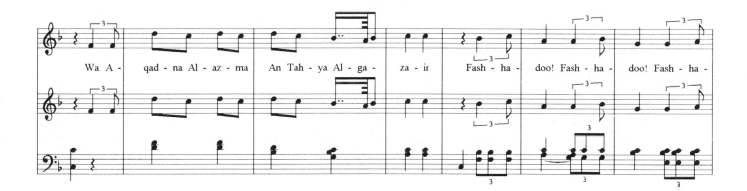

Andorra

Principat d'Andorra

(Principality of Andorra)

```
Quick Country Facts

Location: Western Europe, between Spain and France
Area: 175 sq. mi. (450 sq. km.)
Population (2002 est.): 68,403
Capital/Largest City: Andorra la Vella (pop. 22,390)
Official Language: Catalán
GDP/PPP: $1.3 billion, $19,000 per capita
Monetary Units: French Franc, Spanish Peseta
```

Himne Andorra

(Hymn of Andorra)

Lyrics: D. Joan Benlloch i Vivò (1864-1926). Music: Father Enric Marfany Bons (1871-1942). Adopted: 1914.

Historical Background[1]

Dr. Joan Benlloch i Vivò, Episcopal Co-Prince of Andorra, wrote the words to the national anthem. The music was composed by Father Enric Marfany Bons, a native of Sant Julià de Lòria. The song was first played on 8 September 1921 at the National Sanctuary of the Principality on Andorran National Day to celebrate the anniversary of the coronation of the Jungfrau von Meritxell, Andorra's patron saint.

Catalán Words	English Translation[2]
El gran Carlemany, mon Pare dels alarbs em deslliurà	The great Charlemagne, my father, from the Saracens liberated me,
I del cel vida em donà de Meritxell, la gran Mare,	And from heaven he gave me life of Meritxell the great mother.
Princesa nasquí i Pubilla entre dues nacions neutral	I was born a princess, a maiden neutral between two nations.
Sols resto lúnica filla de l'imperi Carlemany.	I am the only remaining daughter of the Carolingian empire
Creient i lluire onze segles, creient i lliure vull ser.	
Siguin els furs mos tutors i mos Prínceps defensors.	
I mos Prínceps defensors.	

	Believing and free for eleven centuries, believing and free I will be. The laws of the land be my tutors, and my defender princes. My defender princes.

Andorra

El gran Car - le - many, mon Pa - re, dels a - larbs em des - lliu - rà __ I del cel vi - da em

do - nà __ de Me - rit - xell, la gran Ma - re, Prin - ce - sa nasquí i Pu - bi - lla

en - tre dues na - cions neu - tral __ Sols res - to lú - ni - ca fi - lla de l'im - pe - ri Car -

le - ma - ny. Cre - ient i lliu - re on - ze se - gles, cre - ient i lliu - re vull ser __.

Si - guin els furs mos tu - tors __. I mos Prín - ceps de - fen - sors __. I mos Prín - ceps de -

fen - sors __.

Angola

República de Angola

(Republic of Angola)

Quick Country Facts

Location: Southwestern Africa

Area: 481,350 sq. mi. (1,246,700 sq. km.)

Population (2002 est.): 10,593,171

Capital/Largest City: Luanda (pop. 2,000,000)

Official Language: Portuguese

GDP/PPP: $13.3 billion, $1,300 per capita

Monetary Unit: Kwanza

Angola Avante

(Forward Angola)

Lyrics: Manuel Rui Alves Monteiro (b. 1941). Music: Rui Alberto Vieira Dias Mingao (b. 1939). Adopted: 1975.

Portuguese Words	English Translation
1	1
O Pátria, nunca mais esqueceremos	O fatherland, we shall never forget
Os heróis do quatro de Fevereio.	The heroes of the Fourth of February.
O Pátria, nós saudamos os teus filhos	O fatherland, we salute your sons
Tombados pela nossa Independência.	Who died for our independence.
Honramos o passado e a nossa História,	We honor the past and our history
Construindo no Trabalho o Homem novo.	As by our work we build the New Man.
(repeat previous two lines)	(repeat previous two lines)
CHORUS	CHORUS
Angola, avante!	Forward, Angola!
Revolução, pelo Poder Popular!	Revolution through the power of the people!
Pátria Unida, Liberdade,	A united country, freedom,

Um só povo, uma só Nação!	One people, one nation!
(repeat chorus)	(repeat chorus)
2	2
Levantemos nossas vozes libertadas	Let us raise our liberated voices
Para glóriados povos africanos.	To the glory of the peoples of Africa.
Marchemos, combatentes angolanos,	We shall march, Angolan fighters,
Solidários com os poroso primidos.	In solidarity with oppressed peoples.
Orgulhosos lutaremos Pela Paz	We shall fight proudly for peace
Com as forças progressistas do mundo.	Along with the progressive forces of the world.
(repeat previous two lines)	(repeat previous two lines)
CHORUS	CHORUS

Angola

in - do no Tra - bal - ho o Ho - mem no - vo. An - go - la, a - van - te! Re - vo - lu - ção

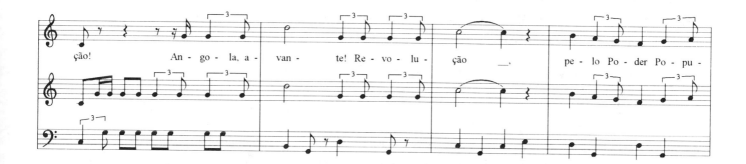

pe - lo Po - der Po - pu - lar ___! Pá - tria U - ni - da, Li - ber - da - de, Um só Po - vo, u - ma só Na -

ção! An - go - la, a - van - te! Re - vo - lu - ção ___, pe - lo Po - der Po - pu -

lar ___! Pá - tria U - ni - da, Li - ber - da - de, Um só Po - vo, u - ma só Na - ção ___!

Antigua and Barbuda

Quick Country Facts

Location: North America, Caribbean Sea

Area: 171 sq. mi. (440 sq. km.)

Population (2002 est.): 67,448

Capital/Largest City: St. John's (pop. 21,514)

Official Language: English

GDP/PPP: $674 million, $10,000 per capita

Monetary Unit: East Caribbean Dollar

Fair Antigua and Barbuda

Lyrics: Novelle Hamilton Richards (1917-1986). Music: Walter Garnet Picart Chambers (b. 1908). Adopted: 1967.

Historical Background[1]

The music was written in 1966 by Mr. Walter Chambers, a church pipe organist and piano tuner. The original lyrics are by Novelle Richards, a unionist, poet, journalist, and author. The song was adopted in 1967, when the islands achieved statehood status within the British Commonwealth. At the time of full independence in 1981, the first verse was modified significantly to include Barbuda.

Words		
1	2	3
Fair Antigua and Barbuda	Raise the standard! Raise it boldly!	God of nations, let Thy blessings
We thy sons and daughters stand,	Answer now to duty's call	Fall upon this land of ours;
Strong and firm in peace or danger	To the service of thy country,	Rain and sunshine ever sending,
To safeguard our native land.	Sparing nothing, giving all;	Fill her fields with crops and flowers;
We commit ourselves to building	Gird your loins and join the battle	We her children do implore Thee,
A true nation brave and free.	'Gainst fear, hate, and poverty,	Give us strength, faith, loyalty,
Ever striving ever seeking	Each endeavoring, all achieving,	Never failing, all enduring
Dwell in love and unity.	Live in peace where man is free.	To defend her liberty.

Antigua and Barbuda

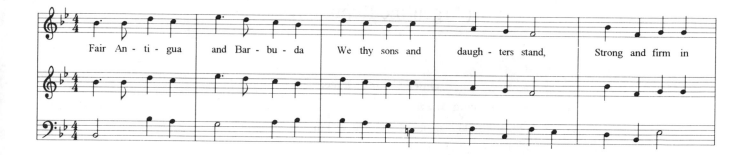

Fair An - ti - gua and Bar - bu - da We thy sons and daugh - ters stand, Strong and firm in

peace or dan - ger To safe guard our na - tive land. We com - mit our - selves to buil - ding

A true na - tion brave and free. E - ver striv - ing e - ver seek - ing Dwell in love and u - ni - ty.

Argentina

República Argentina

(Argentine Republic)

```
Quick Country Facts

Location: South America
Area: 1,072,067 sq. mi. (2,766,890 sq. km.)
Population (2002 est.): 37,812,817
Capital/Largest City: Buenos Aires (pop. 13,250,000)
Official Language: Spanish
GDP/PPP: $391 billion, $10,200 per capita
Monetary Unit: Peso
```

Himno Nacional Argentino

(Argentine National Anthem)

Lyrics: Vincente López y Planes (1785-1856). Music: Blas Parera (1765-c. 1830). Adopted: 1813.

Historical Background

The national anthem of Argentina dates back to the days when the nation had just obtained her independence from Spain. On 22 July 1812, the triumvirate in power at the time decreed that a "march of the homeland" be composed and played at the beginning of theatrical functions and in schools. Vincente López y Planes was put in charge of the words, while Blas Parera composed the music. The Argentine National Assembly officially adopted this song, originally entitled "Marcha Patriótica" ("Patriotic March"), on 11 March 1813. On the night of 25 May of the same year, it was first performed at a patriotic function in a theatre. By 1847, after many changes in the title, the song acquired its current name, "Himno Nacional Argentino."

Although quite effective in stirring up nationalism during the early days of the republic, when resentment against Spain was strong, most of the anthem's verses, which contained hostile references to that country, became outdated as the years passed. In order to update the song to meet modern needs, as well as a symbol of goodwill towards the former mother nation Spain, a decree signed by the president and several ministers was passed in 1900. It stated that "in official or public parties, and in the schools of the state, only the first and last quartets of the national anthem adopted by the National Assembly on 11 March 1813 are to be sung."

Spanish Words	English Translation
Oíd ¡mortales! el grito sagrado	Mortals! Hear the sacred cry;
¡Libertad! ¡Libertad! ¡Libertad!	Freedom! Freedom! Freedom!
oíd el ruido de rotas cadenas	Hear the noise of broken chains.
ved en trono a la noble igualdad.	See noble equality enthroned.
Ya su trono dignísimo abrieron	The United Provinces of the South
las Provincias unidas del Sud,	Have now displayed their worthy throne.
y los libres del mundo responden	And the free peoples of the world reply;
¡al gran Pueblo Argentino Salud!	We salute the great people of Argentina!
(repeat)	(repeat)
y los libres del mundo responden	And the free peoples of the world reply;
¡al gran Pueblo Argentino Salud!	We salute the great people of Argentina!
(repeat previous two lines)	(repeat previous two lines)
CHORUS	CHORUS
Sean eternos los laureles	May the laurels be eternal
Que supimos conseguir.	That we knew how to win.
Coronados de gloria vivamos	Let us live crowned with glory,
O juremos con gloria morir.	Or swear to die gloriously.
(repeat three times)	(repeat three times)

Argentina

O - íd ¡mor- ta - les! el gri - - to sa -

gra - - do ¡Li - ber - tad! ¡Li - ber - tad! ¡Li - ber - tad! o - íd el rui - do de ro - tas ca -

de - nas __ ved en tro - no a la no - ble I - gual - dad. Ya __ su

tro - no dig - ní - si - mo a - brie - ron las Pro - vin - cias u - ni - das del Sud __, y los

li - bres del mun - do res - pon - den ___ ¡al gran pue - blo Ar - gen - ti - no Sa -

lud ___! ¡al gran pue - blo Ar - gen - ti - no Sa - lud! y __ los li - bres del mun - do res -

pon - den ___ ¡al gran pue - blo Ar - gen - ti - no Sa - lud! y __ los li - bres del mun - do res -

pon - den ___ ¡al gran pue - blo Ar - gen - ti - no Sa - lud ___!

Sean e - ter - nos los lau - re - les __ Que su -

pi - mos con - se - guir __. Que su - pi - mos con - se - guir __. Co - ro - na - dos de glo - ria vi -

va - - mos __ O __ ju - re - mos con glo - ria mo - rir. O ju - re - mos con glo - ria mo -

rir. O __ ju - re - mos con glo - ria mo - rir.

Armenia

Հայաստանի Հանրապետության

Haikakan Hanrapetoutioun

(Republic of Armenia)

```
Quick Country Facts
Location: West Asia, Caucasus
Area: 11,500 sq. mi. (29,800 sq. km.)
Population (2002 est.): 3,330,099
Capital/Largest City: Yerevan (pop. 1,226,000)
Official Language: Armenian
GDP/PPP: $11.2 billion, $3,350 per capita
Monetary Unit: Dram
```

Մեր Հայրենիք

Mer Hairenik

(Our Fatherland)

Lyrics: Mikael Ghazari Nalbandian (1829-1866). Music: Barsegh Kanachyan (1885-1967). Adopted: 1991.

Historical Background

The words to the anthem were written by the famous Armenian poet and patriot Mikael Ghazari Nalbandian. The present anthem, adopted 1 July 1991, is a modified version of the original song, which consisted of five clauses. Some of the words have also been changed appropriately to reflect the freedom and independence of the country.

Armenian Words	Armenian Words (Transliteration)	English Translation[1]
1	1	1
Մեր Հայրենիք ազատ, անկախ,	*Mer Hairenik, azad angakh,*	Our fatherland, free and independent,
Որ ապրել է դարեդար,	*Vor abrel eh tareh tar*	That lived from century to century
Իր որդիքը արդ կանչում է	*Ir vor tika art ganchoom eh*	His children are calling
Ազատ, անկախ Հայաստան	*Azad, angakh haiasdan.*	Free independent Armenia.
(repeat previous two lines)	(repeat previous two lines)	(repeat previous two lines)

25

2	2	2
Ահա եղբայր քեզ մի դրոշ,	*Aha yeghpair kez mi trosh,*	Here brother, for you a flag,
Զոր իմ ձեռքով գործեցի	*Zor im tzerkov kordzetzi*	That I made with my hands
Գիշերները ես քուն չեղայ,	*Keeshernera yes koon chega,*	Nights I didn't sleep.
Արտասունքով լուացի	*Ardasoonkov luvatzi.*	With tears I washed it.
(repeat previous two lines)	(repeat previous two lines)	(repeat previous two lines)
3	3	3
Նայիր նրան երեք գոյնով,	*Nayir neran yerek kooynov,*	Look at it, three colors
Նուիրական մեր նշան,	*Nuviragan mer nushan,*	It's our gifted symbol.
Թող փողփողի թշնամու դեմ,	*Togh poghpoghi tushnamoo tem,*	Let it shine against the enemy.
Թող միշտ պանծայ Հայաստան	*Togh meesht bandza Haiastan.*	Let Armenia always be glorious.
(repeat previous two lines)	(repeat previous two lines)	(repeat previous two lines)
4	4	4
Ամենայն տեղ մահը մի է,	*Amenayn degh maha mi eh*	Everywhere death is the same
Մարդը մի անգամ պիտ մեռնե,	*Mart mee ankam bid merni,*	Everyone dies only once
Բայց երանի, որ յուր ազգի	*Paytz yerani vor ir azki*	But lucky is the one
Ազատության կրզոհվի	*Azadootyan ga tzohvi.*	Who is sacrificed for his nation.
(repeat previous two lines)	(repeat previous two lines)	(repeat previous two lines)

Armenia

Mer Hai - ren - ik, a - zad an - gakh, Vor a - brel eh __ ta - reh tar Ir vor ti - ka

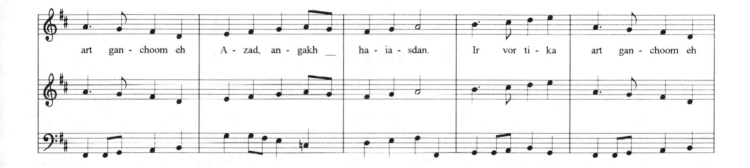

art gan - choom eh A - zad, an - gakh __ ha - ia - sdan. Ir vor ti - ka art gan - choom eh

A - zad, an - gakh __ ha - ia - sdan __ .

Australia

Commonwealth of Australia

Quick Country Facts

Location: Oceania, South Pacific Ocean

Area: 2,966,150 sq. mi. (7,686,850 sq. km.)

Population (2002 est.): 19,546,792

Capital: Canberra (pop. 307,700)

Largest City: Sydney (pop. 3,713,500)

Official Language: English

GDP/PPP: $528 billion, $27,000 per capita

Monetary Unit: Australian Dollar

Advance Australia Fair

Lyrics and Music: Amicus (Peter Dodds McCormick, 1834-1916). Adopted: 1984.

Historical Background[1]

In May 1977 Australians were asked to state a preference for a tune to a national song in a national poll held in conjunction with four referendum questions to amend the Australian Constitution. In June 1977 the following results were announced: "Advance Australia Fair" (2,940,854), "Waltzing Matilda" (1,918,208), "God Save the Queen" (1,257,341), and "Song of Australia" (652,858). After distribution of preferences the final results were: "Advance Australia Fair" (4,415,642) and "Waltzing Matilda" (2,353,617).

In the following year the then Minister for Administrative Services announced that " 'Advance Australia Fair' would be regarded as the people's choice for a national tune and there are no official words for it." In 1984 the government took into account the results of the 1977 referendum for a national tune and announced that two verses (first and third) of "Advance Australia Fair," with amendments to some words, would be the national anthem. (The original lyrics were written in 1878 by Amicus, pen name of Peter Dodds McCormick.) The song was proclaimed as Australia's national anthem by the Governor General on 19 April 1984. In conjunction with this proclamation, the then Prime Minister announced that the royal anthem "God Save the Queen" would be used only in the presence of the Queen or a member of the Royal Family in Australia during official visits.

Words	
1	2
Australians all let us rejoice	Beneath our radiant Southern Cross
For we are young and free;	We'll toil with hearts and hands;
We've golden soil and wealth for toil;	To make this Commonwealth of ours
Our home is girt by sea;	Renowned of all the lands;
Our land abounds in nature's gifts	For those who've come across the seas
Of beauty rich and rare;	We've boundless plains to share;
In history's page, let every stage	With courage let us all combine
Advance Australia Fair.	To Advance Australia Fair.
In joyful strains then let us sing	In joyful strains then let us sing
Advance Australia Fair.	Advance Australia Fair.

Australia

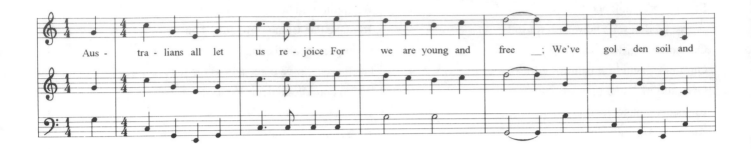

Aus - tra - lians all let us re - joice For we are young and free __; We've gol - den soil and

wealth for toil; Our home is girt by sea __; Our land a - bounds in na - ture's gifts Of beau - ty rich and

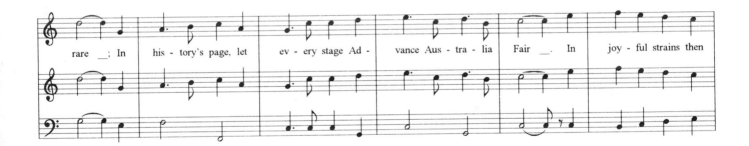

rare __; In his - tory's page, let ev - ery stage Ad - vance Aus - tra - lia Fair __. In joy - ful strains then

let us sing Ad - vance Aus - tra - lia Fair __.

Austria

Republik Österreich

(Republic of Austria)

Quick Country Facts

Location: West Central Europe

Area: 32,375 sq. mi. (83,850 sq. km.)

Population (2002 est.): 8,169,929

Capital/Largest City: Vienna (pop. 1,600,000)

Official Language: German

GDP/PPP: $226 billion, $27,700 per capita

Monetary Unit: Euro

Österreichische Bundeshymne

(Austrian Federal Anthem)

Lyrics: Paula von Preradović (1887-1951). Music: Wolfgang Amadeus Mozart (1756-1791) or Johann Holzer (1753-1818). Adopted: 1947.

Historical Background[1]

On 9 April 1946, the Austrian federal government announced a competition for the text of a new national anthem. It was to be "a song of hymn-like character paying tribute in words and music to the new Austrian federal state and its people both at home and abroad."

Agreement was soon reached on the melody, which was drawn from a masonic cantata (K 623a) by Wolfgang Amadeus Mozart. The work, supposedly dating from the last year of Mozart's life, is now thought by many musicologists to be falsely attributed to Mozart. They believe that evidence points instead to his contemporary, Johann Holzer.

More than 1,800 entries were submitted for the new anthem's text. In the final selection barely thirty remained. These included entries by the distinguished contemporary writers Alexander Lernet-Holenia, Rudolf Henz, and Franz Theodor Csokor. The winner of the first prize would receive 10,000 schillings, a considerable amount in those days.

At the same time, several leading political figures in the cultural field informally contacted other well-known authors with a view to encouraging them to participate in the competition. Fritz Molden, a resistance fighter who later became a journalist and a publisher, recalls that Minister of Education Felix Hurdes persuaded his mother, the writer Paula von Preradović—herself the granddaughter of a Croatian national poet—to submit an entry for the competition. Molden was expressing the widespread views of the age on the issue of a national anthem when he wrote: "The Federal Government had reluctantly concluded that the fine old Haydn anthem, which had survived revolutions and wars and was still being sung with the engaging Kernstock text when I was a boy, could no longer be used. The 'Deutschlandlied,' the anthem of the Third Reich, had employed the same melody, so that the whole world inevitably associated it with Hitler and regarded it as the Nazi hymn." Von Preradović, who was busy working on a new novel, had little time to spare for her entry, and Education Minister Hurdes had to jog her memory several times. When her unaffected, affecting lines did finally reach the jury—made up of literary figures, musicians, and politicians—they awarded her text the highest points. To facilitate the decision, the entries in the final round were read by the popular actor Oskar Werner, who was renowned for his unmistakable voice. On 25 Feburary 1947, the cabinet made a decision declaring the new national anthem to consist of von Preradović's text and the melody from Mozart's masonic cantata.

The text was never published in the official *Legal Gazette* but appeared in the 22 March 1947 issue of the *Die Presse* newspaper. Two weeks earlier the anthem had been played on the radio. It established its popularity relatively fast, although the melody was considerably more complex than that of the Haydn anthem. When Education Minister Hurdes reported to the cabinet on the outcome of the competition, the cabinet passed a motion—at the instigation of the federal president—that in the course of the state treaty negotiations Austria should insist that "Germany be prohibited from using the Haydn anthem because it is a long-standing Austrian cultural asset."

German Words	English Translation
1	1
Land der Berge, Land am Strome,	Land of mountains, land of streams,
Land der Äcker, Land der Dome,	Land of fields, land of spires,
Land der Hämmer, zukunftsreich!	Land of hammers, with a rich future,
Heimat bist du großer Söhne,	You are the home of great sons,
Volk, begnadet für das Schöne,	A nation blessed by its sense of beauty,
Vielgerühmtes Österreich.	Highly praised Austria.
(repeat)	(repeat)
2	2
Heiß umfehdet, wild umstritten	Strongly fought for, fiercely contested,
leigst dem Erdteil du inmitten	You are in the center of the continent
einem starken Herzen gleich.	Like a strong heart,
Hast seit frühen Ahnentagen	You have borne since the earliest days
Hoher Sendung Last getragen	The burden of a high mission,
Vielgeprühtes Österreich.	Much tried Austria.
(repeat)	(repeat)

3	3
Mutig in die neuen Zeiten,	Watch us striding free and believing,
Frei und gläubig sich uns schreiten,	With courage, into new eras,
Arbeistfroh und hoffnungsreich.	Working cheerfully and full of hope,
Einig laß in Brüderchören,	In fraternal chorus let us take in unity
Vaterland, dir Treue schwören,	The oath of allegiance to you, our country,
Vielgeliebtes Österreich.	Our much beloved Austria.
(repeat)	(repeat)

Austria

Azerbaijan

Azərbaycan Respublikası

(Azerbaijani Republic)

Quick Country Facts

Location: West Asia, Caucasus

Area: 33,400 sq. mi. (86,600 sq. km.)

Population (2000 est.): 7,748,163

Capital/Largest City: Baku (pop. 1,713,300)

Official Language: Azerbaijani Turkic

GDP/PPP: $12.9 billion, $1,640 per capita

Monetary Unit: Manat

Dövlət Himni

(National Anthem)

Lyrics: Ahmed Javad (1892-1937). Music: Uzeyir Hajibeyov (1885-1948). Adopted: 1992.

Historical Background[1]

The lyrics for Azerbaijan's national anthem were written in 1919 by Ahmad Javad, a poet who was executed in 1937 for being a "counterrevolutionary." The music was written by composer Uzeyir Hajibeyov. When Azerbaijan regained independence in 1991, it looked back to this earlier period of independence and readopted the same flag and national anthem.

Azerbaijani Turkic Words	English Translation
Azərbaycan, Azərbaycan,	Azerbaijan, Azerbaijan
Ey qəhrəman övladın şanlı vətəni!	Cherished land of valiant sons.
Səndən ötrü can verməyə cümlə hazırız.	We are ready to give our heart and soul for you.
Səndən ötrü qan tökməyə cümlə qadiriz.	All of us can give our blood for you.
Üçrəngli bayrağınla məs'ud yaşa!	Live happily with your three colored banner.
(repeat)	(repeat)

Minlərlə can qurban oldu,	Thousands of souls were sacrificed for you
Sinən hərbə meydan oldu.	Your territory became a fighting arena.
(repeat)	(repeat)
Hüququndan keçən əsgər	Soldiers who deprived themselves of their lives
Hərə bir qəhrəman oldu.	Each of them became a hero.
Sən olasan gülüstan,	May you become a flourishing garden.
Sənə hər an can qurban.	We are ready to give our heart and soul for you.
Sənə bir çox məhəbbət	A thousand and one endearments are in my heart.
Sinəmdə tutmuş məkan.	To raise your banner
Namusunu hifx etməyə,	And protect your honor
Bayrağını yüksəltməyə	All the youth are eager.
Namusunu hifx etməyə.	Cherished land. Cherished land.
Cümlə gənclər müştaqdır.	Azerbaijan! Azerbaijan!
Şanlı vətən, şanlı vətən,	
Azərbaycan, Azərbaycan!	

Azerbaijan

A - zər - bay - can __, A - zər - bay - can, Ey qəh - rə - man öv - la - dın şan - lı və - tə - ni!

Sən - dən öt - rü can ver - mə - yə cüm - lə ha - zı - rız. Sən - dən ö - trü qan tök - mə - yə

cüm - lə qa - di - riz. Ü - çrən - gli bay - ra - ğın - la məs' - ud ya - şa! Ü - çrən - gli bay - ra - ğın - la

məs' - ud ya - şa! Min - lər - lə can qur - ban ol - du, Si - nən hər - bə mey - dan ol - du.

37

Şan - lı və - tən, şan - lı və - tən, A - zər - bay - can, A - zər - bay - can!

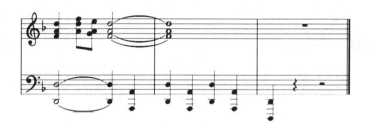

Bahamas

Commonwealth of the Bahamas

Quick Country Facts
Quick Country Facts
Location: North America, West Atlantic Ocean
Area: 5,380 sq. mi. (13,940 sq. km.)
Population (2002 est.): 300,529
Capital/Largest City: Nassau (pop. 171,542)
Official Language: English
GDP/PPP: $5 billion, $16,800 per capita
Monetary Unit: Bahamian Dollar

March on, Bahamaland

Lyrics and Music: Timothy Gibson (1903-1976). Adopted: 1973.

Historical Background

This anthem, written and composed by Timothy Gibson in 1972, was selected as the winning entry in a national competition and adopted 10 July 1973 upon independence.

Words
Words
Lift up your head to the rising sun, Bahamaland;
March on to glory, your bright banners waving high.
See how the world marks the manner of your bearing!
Pledge to excel through love and unity.
Pressing onward, march together to a common loftier goal;
Steady sunward, though the weather hide
The wide and treach`rous shoal.
Lift up your head to the rising sun, Bahamaland;
`Til the road you`ve trod
Lead unto your God.
March on, Bahamaland!

Bahamas

Lift up your head _ to the ris - ing sun, Ba - - ha - ma - land;

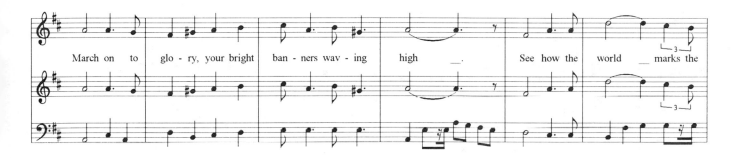

March on to glo - ry, your bright ban - ners wav - ing high _. See how the world _ marks the

man - ner of your _ bear - ing! Pledge to ex - cel _ through love and _ un - i - ty _. Press - ing

on - ward, march to - ge - - ther _ to a com - mon loft - ier goal _; Stead - y sun - ward, though the

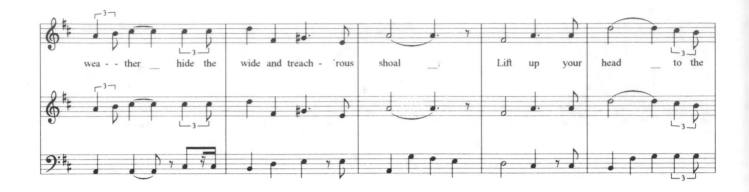

wea - - ther __ hide the   wide and treach - 'rous   shoal __.   Lift   up   your   head __ to the

ris - ing sun Ba - -   ha - ma - land; 'Til the   road you've trod lead un -   to your God, March __   on, Ba - ha - ma -

land __!

Bahrain

دولة البحرين

Dawlat al Bahrain

(State of Bahrain)

Quick Country Facts

Location: West Asia, Middle East

Area: 399 sq. mi. (665 sq. km.)

Population (2002 est.): 656,397

Capital/Largest City: Al-Manamah (pop. 140,401)

Official Language: Arabic

GDP/PPP: $8.4 billion, $13,000 per capita

Monetary Unit: Bahrain Dinar

Bahrainona

(Our Bahrain)

Lyrics: Mohamed Sudqi Ayyash (b. 1925). Adopted: 1971.

Arabic Words (Transliteration)	English Translation
Bahrainona	Our Bahrain,
Baladolaman	Country of security,
Watanol kiram,	Nation of hospitality,
Yahmi Hi maha Amirunal Homam;	Protected by our courageous Amir.
Qamatala Hadyelresalate, Wal Adalati Wal Salam!	Founded on the principles of the message.
A Shat Dawlat al Bahrain	Justice and peace.
(repeat previous five lines)	Long live the State of Bahrain!
	(repeat previous six lines)

Bahrain

Bangladesh

Gana Prajatantri Bangladesh

(People's Republic of Bangladesh)

```
Quick Country Facts
Location: South Asia, Indian subcontinent
Area: 55,598 sq. mi. (144,000 sq. km.)
Population (2002 est.): 133,376,684
Capital/Largest City: Dhaka (pop. 9,600,000)
Official Language: Bangla
GDP/PPP: $230 billion, $1,750 per capita
Monetary Unit: Taka
```

Amar Sonar Bangla

(My Golden Bengal)

Lyrics and Music: Rabindranath Tagore (1861-1941). Adopted: 1972.

Historical Background

In 1905, during the period when Bengal was to be partitioned by the British, the famous Indian national poet Rabindranath Tagore wrote a number of lyrics and set them to music based on folk tunes, especially from *baul* songs, or songs sung by the wandering minstrels of Bengal. "Amar Sonar Bangla" is one of them. It was first sung on 7 August 1905 at the Town Hall in Calcutta where a meeting was held in protest against the Partition of Bengal. In 1971 the first ten lines of this song was chosen as the national anthem of Bangladesh by the provisional government and approved by the national assembly on 13 January 1972.

Bangla Words (Transliteration)	English Translation[1]
Amar sonar Bangla,	My Bengal of gold, I love you.
Ami tomay bhalobashi,	Forever your skies, your air set my heart in tune
Ciradin tomar akas, tomar batas, amar prane	As if it were a flute.
Oma amar prane, bajay basi.	In spring, o mother mine, the fragrance from your mango groves
Sonar Bamla, Ami tomay bhalobasi.	
O ma, Fagune tor amer bane ghrane pagal kare, mari hay,	Makes me wild with joy

45

hay re	Ah, what a thrill!
O ma, Fagune tor amer bane ghrane pagal kare,	
O ma, aghrane tor bhara ksete ki dekhechi	In autumn, O mother mine,
ami ki dekhechi madhur hasi	In the full blossomed paddy fields
Sonar Bangla ami tomay bhalo basi, ki sobha, ki chaya go	I have seen spread all over sweet smiles.
ki sneha,	Ah, what a beauty, what shades, what an affection
ki maya go ki acal bichayecha	And what a tenderness!
bater mule, nadir kule kule.	What a quilt have you spread at the feet of Banyan trees
Ma, tor mukher bani amar kane lage suhar mato,	And along the banks of rivers!
mari hay hay re	
Ma, tor mukher bani amar kane lage suhar mato,	O mother mine, words from your lips
Ma, tor badankhani malin hale, ami nayan,	Are like nectar to my ears.
o ma, ami nayanjale bhasi.	Ah, what a thrill!
Sonar Bangla ami tomay bhalobashi.	If sadness, O mother mine, casts a gloom on your face,
	My eyes are filled with tears!

Bangladesh

ghra - ne ___ pa - gal ka - re ___, ma - ri hay ___, hay ___ re ___

O - ma, Fa - gu - ne tor ___ a - mer ba - ne ghra - ne ___ pa - gal ka - re

___ O ma, a - ghra - ne tor ___ bha - ra kse - te ___ ki de - khe - chi ___ a - mi

ki de - khe - chi ___ ma - dhur ha - si ___ So - nar ___ Bang - - gla ___ a - mi to - may ___

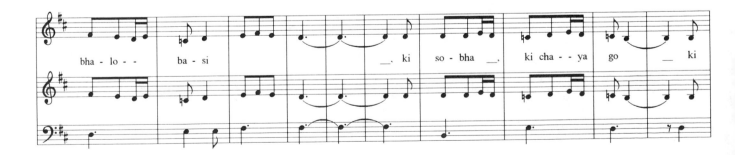

bha - lo - - ba - si ___, ki so - bha ___, ki cha - ya go ___ ki

Barbados

```
┌─────────────────────────────────────────────────┐
│              Quick Country Facts                 │
│  Location: North America, Caribbean Sea          │
│  Area: 166 sq. mi. (431 sq. km.)                 │
│  Population (2002 est.): 276,607                 │
│  Capital/Largest City: Bridgetown (pop. 6,700)   │
│  Official Language: English                      │
│  GDP/PPP: $4 billion, $14,500 per capita         │
│  Monetary Unit: Barbados Dollar                  │
└─────────────────────────────────────────────────┘
```

Barbados National Anthem

Lyrics: Irving Louis Burgie (b. 1926). Music: C. Van Roland Edwards (1912-1985). Adopted: 1966.

Historical Background[1]

When C. Van Roland Edwards composed the music for the Barbadian national anthem in 1966, he was partly blind. Edwards was born in 1912 and had been writing music from his school days as a pupil of St. Peter's Church Boy's School. Although he had no formal training, he had been a member of the British Song society since 1933. Because of his partial blindness he was assisted in his work by his two daughters, Nannette and Eullia. Edwards was known for his compositions "The St. Andrew Murder," "The Goodman Song," and "The Federation Song." He also composed "Welcome to Her Majesty the Queen Elizabeth II," which was sung in the presence of the Queen when she opened the St. Elizabeth School in St. Joseph during the official visit to the island in February 1966. A committee which comprised of Bruce St. John, Frank Collymore, Enid Lynch, George Lamming, Gerald Hudson, and John Fletcher was appointed to oversee the selection of the national anthem. Edwards was awarded $500 for his efforts. He died on 22 April 1985.

In 1967 the music of the national anthem was rearranged. This work was undertaken by Inspector Prince Cave of the Royal Barbados Police Band. He had earlier that year returned from a three-year band masters course at the Royal Military School of Music, Kneller Hall. The anthem was given a more sustained harmony while at the same time retaining the original tune.

The lyrics of the "National Anthem of Barbados" were written in 1966 by Irving Burgie, who was born 1926 in Brooklyn, New York of a Barbadian mother and American father. He served in India and, after his return to the USA, entered the University of Southern California and studied music and performed in many American cities. Burgie has composed works for "Ballad for Bimshire" and "Island in the Sun." He has also written for a number of internationally famous artistes. Among his works is "The West Indian Song Book." He is a life member of the NAACP. Burgie, who is a frequent visitor to Barbados, has instituted the Irving Burgie Literary Award for Barbadian school children.

Words

1

In plenty and in time of need
When this fair land was young,
Our brave forefathers sowed the seed
From which our pride is sprung,
A pride that makes no wanton boast
Of what it has withstood,
That binds our hearts from coast to coast
The pride of nationhood.

CHORUS

We loyal sons and daughters all
Do hereby make it known
These fields and hills beyond recall
Are now our very own.
We write our names on history's page
With expectations great,
Strict guardians of our heritage,
Firm craftsmen of our fate.

2

The Lord has been the people's guide
For past three hundred years.
With Him still on the people's side
We have no doubts or fears.
Upward and onward we shall go,
Inspired, exulting, free,
And greater will our nation grow
In strength and unity.

CHORUS

Barbados

In __ plen - ty and in time of need When this fair land was young __, Our __ brave fore - fa - thers

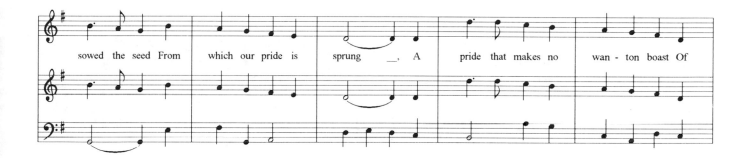

sowed the seed From which our pride is sprung __, A pride that makes no wan - ton boast Of

what it has with - stood __, That binds our hearts from coast to coast The pride of na - tion -

hood __. We loy - al sons and daugh - ters all Do here - by make it known __ These fields and hills be -

53

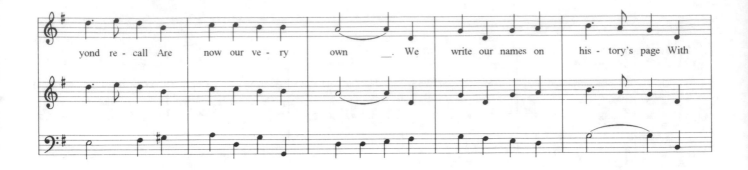

yond re-call Are now our ve-ry own ___. We write our names on his-tory's page With

ex-pec-ta-tions great ___. Strict guard-ians of our he-ri-tage, Firm crafts-men of our fate.

Belarus

Рэспубліка Беларусь

Respublyika Byelarus

(Republic of Belarus)

Quick Country Facts

Location: Eastern Europe
Area: 80,200 sq. mi. (207,600 sq. km.)
Population (2002 est.): 10,335,382
Capital/Largest City: Mensk (pop. 1,666,000)
Official Language: Belarusian
GDP/PPP: $84.8 billion, $8,200 per capita
Monetary Unit: Belarusian Dollar

Гимн

Gimn

Hymn

Lyrics: Mikhas Klimkovich (1899-1954). Music: Nester Sakalouski (1902-1950). Adopted: 1955.

Historical Background[1]

There are several Belarusian patriotic songs, all composed during the first two decades of the twentieth century, that are considered to have been unofficial national hymns. The most widely known is a poem by Yanka Kupala, "Nie pahasnuch zorki u niebie" ("The Stars in the Sky Will Never Darken"). The short-lived Belarusian Democratic Republic had for its anthem the song "My vyjdziem shchylnymi radami" ("Come, We Shall March in Joint Endeavor").

Until 1955, the anthem of the Belarusan SSR, as of the entire Soviet Union, was the Communist Party's official song, the "International." The first proper anthem of the republic, "My—bielarusy" ("We the Belarusians"), in which praise for the Communist Party was sung, was introduced in 1955.

After a long and hard-fought battle, the controversial lyrics have been retained and made official on 2 July 2002.

Belarusian Words

1

Мы, беларусы - мірныя людзі,
Сэрцам адданыя роднай зямлі,
Шчыра сябруем, сілы гартуем
Мы ў працавітай, вольнай сям'і.

2

Слаўся, зямлі нашай светлае імя,
Слаўся, народаў братэрскі саюз!
Наша любімая маці-Радзіма,
Вечна жыві і квітней, Беларусь!

3

Разам з братамі мужна вякамі
Мы баранілі родны парог,
У бітвах за волю, бітвах за долю
Свой здабывалі сцяг перамог!

4

Слаўся, зямлі нашай светлае імя,
Слаўся, народаў братэрскі саюз!
Наша любімая маці-Радзіма,
Вечна жыві і квітней, Беларусь!

5

Дружба народаў - сіла народаў
Наш запаветны, сонечны шлях.
Горда ж узвіся ў ясныя высі,
Сцяг пераможны - радасці сцяг!

6

Слаўся, зямлі нашай светлае імя,
Слаўся, народаў братэрскі саюз!
Наша любімая маці-Радзіма,
Вечна жыві і квітней, Беларусь!

Belarus

Belgium

Royaume de Belgique

Koninkrijk België

(Kingdom of Belgium)

```
Quick Country Facts
Location: Western Europe
Area: 11,781 sq. mi. (30,510 sq. km.)
Population (2002 est.): 10,274,595
Capital/Largest City: Brussels (pop. 949,070)
Official Languages: French, Dutch (Flemish)
GDP/PPP: $297.6 billion, $29,000 per capita
Monetary Unit: Euro
```

La Brabançonne

(The Brabant Song)

Lyrics: Louis-Alexandre Dechet (?-1830) and Charles Rogier (1800-1885). Music: François van Campenhout (1779-1848). Adopted: 1938.

Historical Background

The Belgian national anthem was most likely written by Louis-Alexandre Dechet, better known as Jenneval, toward the end of 1830. An actor at the Théâtre de la Monnaie at Brussels, he joined, on 25 August 1830, the revolution that resulted in the independence of Belgium from the Netherlands. He was killed near Lierre on 18 October of that same year. Before his death, Jenneval composed three versions of the "Chant national belge" ("Belgian National Song"), versions that he adapted to the change of events.

In 1860, the song was adapted again, this time by Prime Minister Charles Rogier, who heavily edited out many violent lyrics addressed by Jenneval to the Dutch Prince of Orange William of Nassau. It is this reproduced version that is still in use today.

As for the music of "La Brabançonne," it was written during the revolutionary days by François van Campenhout. The first performance of the national anthem took place at the Théâtre de la Monnaie at the beginning of October 1830. The primitive partitions were also modified to adapt to the lyrics of Charles Rogier.

However, an official version of "La Brabançonne" does not actually exist. Different commissions have been established to examine the words and melody of the song and establish an official version. Yet all of their efforts had been in vain. Nevertheless, an official circulation of the Ministry of the Interior on 8 August 1921 decreed that only the fourth verse of the text of Charles Rogier should be considered official, in its French and Dutch (Flemish) versions. Today, there still stands a "Monument to the Brabançonne" in Brussels at Surlet de Chokier Plaza. Both the French and Dutch (Flemish) words are engraved there.

French Words	Dutch (Flemish) Words	English Translation
O Belgique, ô mère chérie	O dierbaar België	O beloved Belgium, sacred land of our fathers,
A toi nos cœurs, à toi nos bras	O heilig land der Vadren	Our heart and soul are dedicated to you.
A toi notre sang, ô Patrie	Onze ziel en ons hart zijn U gewijd	Our strength and the blood of our veins we offer,
Nous le jurons tous, tu vivras	Aanvaard ons kracht en het bloed van ons adren	Be our goal, in work and battle.
Tu vivras toujours grande et belle	Wees ons doel in arbeid en in strijd	Prosper, O country, in unbreakable unity,
Et ton invincible unité	Bloei, o land, in eendracht niet te breken	Always be yourself and free.
Aura pour devise immortelle	Wees immer U zelf en ongeknecht	Trust in the word that, undaunted, you can speak:
Le Roi, la Loi, la Liberté	Het woord getrouw, dat ge onbevreesd moogt spreken	For king, for freedom and for law.
(repeat previous two lines)	Voor Vorst, voor Vrijheid en voor Recht	(repeat previous two lines)
Le Roi, la Loi, la Liberté	(repeat previous two lines)	For king, for freedom and for law.
(repeat)	Voor Vorst, voor Vrijheid en voor Recht	(repeat)
	(repeat)	

Belgium

O ___ Bel - gique, ô ___ mè - - re ché - - ri - ___ e A toi ___ nos cœurs, à toi nos
O dier - baar Bel - gië, o heil - ig land der Va - dren, On - ze ziel en ons hart zijn U ge-

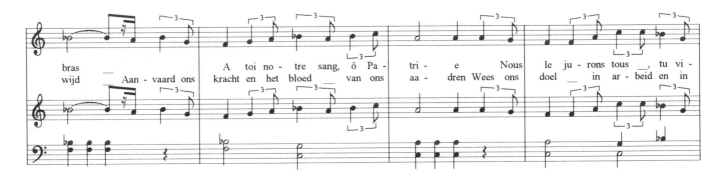

bras ___ Aan - vaard ons A toi no - tre sang, ô Pa - tri - e Nous le ju - rons tous ___, tu vi-
wijd ___ Aan - vaard ons kracht en het bloed ___ van ons aa - dren Wees ons doel ___ in ar - beid en in

vras ___ Tu vi - vras ___ tou - jours grande et bel - le Et ton in - vin - ci - ble u - ni-
strijd ___ Bloei, o land ___ in een - dracht niet te bre - ken Wees im - - mer U zelf en on - ge-

té ___ Au - ra ___ pour de - vise im - mor - tel - le Le Roi, la Loi, la Li - ber-
knecht ___ Het woord ge - trouw, dat ge on - be - vreesd moogt spre - ken Voor Vorst, voor Vrij - heid en voor

60

té,   Au -   ra pour __ de - vise im - mor -   tel - le   Le   Roi, la Loi, la Liber -
Recht   Het woord ge -   trouw dat ge on - be - vreesd moogt   spre - ken   Voor   Vorst, voor Vrij - heid en voor

té __ Le   Roi, la Loi, la Li - ber -   té __ Le   Roi,   la Loi, la Li - ber -   té
Recht __ Voor   Vorst, voor Vrij - heid en voor   Recht __ Voor   Vorst, voor Vrij - heid en voor   Recht __

Belize

Land of the Free

Lyrics: Samuel Alfred Haynes (1898-1971). Music: Selwyn Walford Young (1899-1987). Adopted: 1981.

Historical Background

Samuel Alfred Haynes, who wrote the words to this anthem in 1963, was a black nationalist and an important leader of the 1919 riot against British colonial rule. Hayne's song, originally entitled "Land of the Gods," was put into music in the same year by Selwyn Walford Young. The anthem was adopted when Belize achieved full independence in 1981.

Words

1

O, Land of the free by the Carib Sea,

Our manhood we pledge to thy liberty!

No tyrants here linger, despots must flee

This tranquil haven of democracy

The blood of our sires which hallows the sod,

Brought freedom from slavery oppression's rod,

By the might of truth and the grace of God,

No longer shall we be hewers of wood.

CHORUS

Arise! ye sons of the Baymen's clan,

Put on your armor, clear the land!

Drive back the tyrants, let despots flee
Land of the free by the Carib Sea!

2

Nature has blessed thee with wealth untold,
O'er mountains and valleys where prairies roll;
Our fathers, the Baymen, valiant and bold
Drove back the invader; this heritage hold
From proud Rio Hondo to old Sarstoon,
Through coral isle, over blue lagoon;
Keep watch with the angels, the stars and moon;
For freedom comes tomorrow's noon.

CHORUS

Belize

O, Land of the free by the Ca - rib Sea, Our man - hood we pledge to thy li - ber - ty! No

ty - rants here lin - ger, des - pots must flee This tran - quil ha - ven of de - mo - cra - cy The

blood of our sires which hal - lows the sod, Brought free - dom from slav - ery op - pres - sion's rod, By the

might of truth and the grace of God __. No lon - ger shall __ we be hewers of wood. A - rise __! ye

sons ___ of the Bay - men's clan ___, Put on ___ your ar - mor __,

clear ___ the land __! Drive back ___ the ty - rants _, let des - - pots __

flee Land ___ of the free ___ by the Ca - rib

Sea ___!

Benin

République du Bénin

(Republic of Benin)

Quick Country Facts

Location: West Africa

Area: 43,483 sq. mi. (112,620 sq. km.)

Population (2002 est.): 6,787,625

Capital/Largest City: Porto Novo (pop. 177,660)

Official Language: French

GDP/PPP: $6.8 billion, $1,040 per capita

Monetary Unit: Franc CFA

L'Aube Nouvelle

(The Dawn of a New Day)

Lyrics and Music: Gilbert Jean Dagnon (b. 1926). Adopted: 1960

French Words	English Translation
1	1
Jadis à son appel, nos aïeux sans faiblesse	Formerly, at her call, our ancestors
Ont su avec courage, ardeur, pleins d'allégresse	Knew how to engage in mighty battles
Livrer au prix du sang des combat éclatants.	With strength, courage, ardor, and full of joy,
Accourez vous aussi, bâtisseurs du présent,	But at the price of blood.
Plus forts dans l'unité chaque jour à la tâche,	Builders of present, you too, join forces
Pour la postérité construisez sans relâche.	Each day for the task stronger in unity.
	Build without ceasing for posterity.
CHORUS	CHORUS
Enfants du Bénin, debout!	Children of Benin, arise!
La liberté d'un cri sonore	The resounding cry of freedom
Chante aux premiers feux de l'Aurore;	Is heard at the first light of dawn,
Enfants du Bénin, debout!	Children of Benin, arise!

2

Quand partout souffle un vent de colée et de haine.

Béninois, sois fier, et d'une âme sereine,

Confiant dans l'avenir, regarde ton drapeau!

Dans le vert tu liras l'espoir du renouveau,

De tes aïeux le rouge évoque le courage;

Des plus riches trésors le jaune est le présage.

CHORUS

3

Tes monts ensoleillés, tes palmiers, ta verdure,

Cher Bénin, partout font ta vive parure.

Ton sol offre à chacun la richesse des fruits.

Bénin, désormais que tes fils tous unis

D'un fraternel élan partagent l'espérance

De te voir à jamais heureux dans l'abondance.

CHORUS

2

When all around there blows a wind of anger and hate:

Citizen of Benin be proud, and in a calm spirit

Trusting in the future, behold your flag!

In the green you read hope of spring;

The red signifies the courage of your ancestors:

The yellow foretells the greatest treasures.

CHORUS

3

Beloved Benin, your sunny mountains, palm trees, and green pastures

Show everywhere your brightness;

Your soil offers everyone the richest fruits.

Benin, from henceforth your sons are united

With one brotherly spirit sharing the hope of seeing you

Enjoy abundance and happiness forever.

CHORUS

Benin

68

trui - sez sans re - lâ - che. En - - fants du Bé - nin de - bout ___! La li - ber - té d'un cri so -

no - re Chante aux pre - miers feux de l'Au - ro - re; En - fants du Bé - nin de - bout ___!

Bhutan

Druk-Gyal-Kab

(Kingdom of Bhutan)

Quick Country Facts
Location: South Central Asia
Area: 18,000 sq. mi. (47,000 sq. km.)
Population (2002 est.): 2,094,176
Capital/Largest City: Thimphu (pop. 30,340)
Official Language: Dzongkha
GDP/PPP: $2.5 billion, $1,200 per capita
Monetary Unit: Ngultrum

Royal Anthem

Lyrics: Gyaldun Dasho Thinley Dorji (1914-1966). Music: Aku Tongmi (b. 1913). Adopted: 1953.

Dzongkha Words (Transliteration)	English Translation
Druk tsendhen koipi gyelkhap na	In the Thunder Dragon Kingdom
Loog ye ki tenpa chongwai gyon	Adorned with sandalwood,
Pel mewang ngadhak rinpo chhe	The protector who guards the
Ku jurmey tenching chhap tsid pel	Teachings of the dual system,
Chho sangye ten pa goong dho gyel	He, the precious and glorious ruler,
Bang che kyed nyima shar warr sho.	Causes dominion to spread,
	While his unchanging person abides in constancy.
	As the doctrine of the Lord Buddha flourishes,
	May the sun of peace and happiness
	Shine on the people!

Bhutan

Bolivia

República de Bolivia

(Republic of Bolivia)

Himno Nacional

(National Anthem)

Lyrics: Don José Ignacio de Sanjinés (1786-1864). Music: Leopoldo Benedetto Vincenti Franti (1815-1914). Adopted: 1842.

Historical Background

The verses of the song were written by a poet from Chiquiasca, Don José Ignacio de Sanjinés, and the music was composed by the Italian teacher Leopoldo Benedetto Vincenti in Sucre. This national anthem was first sung at the Municipal Theatre of La Paz to commemorate the fourth anniversary of the Battle of Ingavi on 18 November 1845.

Spanish Words	English Translation
1	1
¡Bolivianos! ¡el hado propicio	Bolivians, a favorable destiny
coronó nuestros votos y anhelo!	Has crowned our vows and longings;
Es ya libre, ya libre este suelo,	This land is free,
ya cesó su servil condición.	Your servile state has ended.
Al estruendo marcial que ayer fuera	The martial turmoil of yesterday
y al clamor de la guerra horroroso,	And the horrible clamor of war

siguen hoy, en contraste armonioso
dulces himnos de paz y de unión.
(repeat previous two lines)

CHORUS
De la Patria, el alto nombre
en glorioso esplendor conservemos
y, en sus aras, de nuevo juremos:
¡Morir antes que esclavos vivir!
(repeat three times)

2

Loor eterno a los bravos guerreros,
cuyo heroico valor y firmeza,
conquistaron las glorias que empieza
hoy Bolivia feliz a gozar.
Que sus nombres el mármol y el bronce
a remotas edades transmitan
y en sonoros cantares repitan:
¡Libertad, Libertad, Libertad!
(repeat previous two lines)

CHORUS

3

Aquí alzó la justicia su trono
que la vil opresión desconoce,
y en su timbre glorioso legose
Libertad, libertad, libertad.
Esta tierra inocente y hermosa
que ha debido a Bolívar su nombre
es la patria feliz donde el hombre
goza el bien de la dicha y la paz.
(repeat previous two lines)

CHORUS

4

Si extranjero poder, algún día,

Are followed today, in harmonious contrast,
By sweet hymns of peace and unity.
(repeat previous two lines)

CHORUS
We have kept the lofty name of our country
In glorious splendor,
And on its altars we once more swear
To die, rather than live as slaves.
(repeat three times)

2

Eternal praise to the brave warriors
Whose heroic valor and firmness
Conquered the glories that now
A happy Bolivia begins to enjoy!
Let their names, in marble and in bronze,
Transmit to remote ages
And in resounding song repeat the call:
Freedom! Freedom! Freedom!
(repeat previous two lines)

CHORUS

3

Here justice raised its throne
That the vile oppression does not know,
And in its glorious tone bequeathed
Liberty, liberty, liberty.
This innocent and beautiful land
That has owed to Bolívar its name
Is the happy homeland where man
Enjoys the good of happiness and peace.
(repeat previous two lines)

CHORUS

4

If, someday, any foreign power

sojuzgar a Bolivia intentare,	Should try to subdue Bolivia,
al destino fatal se prepare	To a fatal destiny must prepare
que amenaza a soberbio agresor.	That pretentious aggressor.
Que los hijos del grande Bolívar	For the children of the great Bolivar
han ya, mil y mil veces, jurado	Have sworn thousands and thousands of times
morir antes que ver humillado,	To die rather than to humiliate
de la Patria el augusto pendón.	The venerable flag of the homeland.
(repeat previous two lines)	(repeat previous two lines)
CHORUS	CHORUS

Bolivia

¡Bo - li - via - nos! ¡el ha - do pro - pi - cio co - ro - nó nues - tros vo - tos y an - he - lo! Es ya

li - bre ya li - bre es - te sue - lo ya ce - só su ser - vil con - di - ción. Al es -

truen - do mar - cial que a - yer fue - ra y al cla - mor de la gue - rra ho - rro - ro - so, si - guen

hoy __, en con - tras - - te ar - mo - nio - - so Dul - ces him - nos de paz __ y __ de u - nión. Si - guen

hoy __ en con - tras - te ar - mo - nio - - so __ Dul - ces him - nos de paz __ y __ de u - nión ____. De la

Pa - tria, el al - to nom - bre En glo - rio - so es - plen - dor __ con - ser - ve - mos Y, en sus

a - - ras, de nue - vo ju - re - mos: ¡Mo - rir an - tes que es - cla - vos vi - vir ____! ¡Mo - rir

an - tes que es - cla - vos vi - vir ____! ¡Mo - rir an - tes que es - cla - vos vi - vir!

Bosnia and Herzegovina

Bosne i Hercegovine

```
┌─────────────────────────────────────────────┐
│            Quick Country Facts                │
│  Location: Eastern Europe, Balkan Peninsula   │
│  Area: 19,741 sq. mi. (51,129 sq. km.)        │
│  Population (2002 est.): 3,964,388            │
│  Capital/Largest City: Sarajevo (pop. 387,876)│
│  Official Language: Bosnian                   │
│  GDP/PPP: $7 billion, $1,800 per capita       │
│  Monetary Unit: Dinar                         │
└─────────────────────────────────────────────┘
```

National Anthem

Music: Dušan Šestic. Adopted: 1999.

Historical Background

On February 10, 1998, the same day the nation's flag was changed, a new anthem was adopted for Bosnia and Herzegovina, one without words, composed by Dušan Šestic.

Bosnia and Herzegovina

Botswana

Republic of Botswana

Fatshe la Rona

Our Country

Lyrics and Music: Kgalemang Tumedisco Motsete (1900-1974). Adopted: 1966.

Historical Background

The words and music of this song were written by Kgalemang Tumedisco Motsete in 1966 and officially adopted in the same year.

Setswana Words	English Words
1	1
Fatshe leno la rona,	Blessed be this noble land,
Ke mpho ya Modimo,	Gift to us from God's strong hand,
Ke boswa jwa borraetsho;	Heritage our fathers left to us,
A le nne ka kagiso.	May it always be at peace.
CHORUS	CHORUS
Tsogang, tsogang! banna, tsogang!	Awake, awake, O men, awake!
Emang, basadi, emang, tlhagafalang!	And women close beside them stand,
Re kopaneleng go direla	Together we'll work and serve
Lefatshe la rona.	This land, this happy land!

2	2
Ina lentle la tumo	Word of beauty and of fame,
La chaba ya Botswana,	The name Botswana to us came.
Ka kutlwano le kagiso,	Through our unity and harmony,
E bopagantswe mmogo.	We'll remain at peace as one.
CHORUS	CHORUS

Botswana

Fat - she le - no la ro - na ___, Ke m - pho ya Mo - di - mo ___, Ke bo - swa jwa bo - r -
Bless - ed be this no - ble land ___, Gift to us from God's strong hand ___, He - ri - tage our fa - thers

ra - e - tsho; A le nne ka ka - gi - so ___. Tso - gang, tso - gang! ban - na, tso - gang! E -
left to us, May it al - ways be at peace ___. A - wake, a - wake, o men, a - wake! And

mang, ba - sa - di, e - mang, tlha - ga - fa - lang! Re ko - pa - ne - leng go di - re - la Le - fat - she
wo - men ___ close be - side ___ them ___ stand, To - ge - ther we'll work ___ and serve This land, this

la ro - na ___.
hap - py land ___!

Brazil

República Federativa do Brasil

(Federative Republic of Brazil)

Quick Country Facts

Location: South America

Area: 3,286,470 sq. mi. (8,511,965 sq. km.)

Population (2002 est.): 176,029,560

Capital: Brasilia (pop. 1,800,000)

Largest City: São Paulo (pop. 17,900,000)

Official Language: Portuguese

GDP/PPP: $1.34 trillion, $7,400 per capita

Monetary Unit: Real

Hino Nacional Brasileiro

(Brazilian National Anthem)

Lyrics: Joaquim Osório Duque Estrada (1870-1927). Music: Francisco Manuel da Silva (1795-1865). Adopted: 1922.

Historical Background[1]

The Brazilian national anthem is sufficient grounds for the fame of its composer, Francisco Manuel da Silva. Through its admirably warm and spirited melody, it took its place as the national anthem before it was accorded any official recognition. Various changes made to it have not distorted its essence, though they have softened its martial tone.

Originally composed in a purely orchestral version for military band, it has been the various texts that have been set to it, especially that of Joaquim Osório Duque Estrada in 1922, which have somewhat spoilt it. The history of the anthem is the subject of controversy. In the view of some, it was composed for Brazilian independence; others believe it was written for the 7th of April and performed on the 13th to a text attributed to Ovídio Saraiva de Carvalho e Silva, in which there are references to "a wise reign" and "a Brazilian monarch," 7 April being taken as the dawn of Brazilian liberty. A third view is that of Souza Pitanga and Ernesto Sena, supported by Alberto Nepomuceno who writes: "In the same year (1841), at perhaps the height of his career, Francisco Manuel composed the anthem to celebrate the coronation of the second Emperor of Brazil, showing himself to be a composer of great merit in this inspired work, which still animates the national soul today."

Decree No. 15671 of 6 September 1922 officially adopted the words of Estrada, written in 1909, the first version of it. Law No. 259 of 1 October 1936 prescribed the version of Leopoldo Miguez for orchestral performance, and the version by Lt. Antonio Pinto Junior of the Federal District Fire Brigades, for military band, in the original key of B Flat; and finally a version in F by Alberto Nepomuceno for singing.

Portuguese Words	English Translation[2]
1	1
Ouviram do Ipiranga às margens plácidas	The peaceful banks of the Ipiranga
De um povo heróico o brado retumbante,	Heard the resounding cry of an heroic people,
E o sol da liberdade, em raios fúlgidos,	And the dazzling rays of the sun of liberty
Brilhou no céu da Pátria nesse instante.	Bathed our country in their brilliant light.
Se o penhor dessa igualdade	If with strong arm we have succeeded
Conseguimos conquistar com braço forte,	In winning a pledge of equality,
Em teu seio ó liberdade,	In thy bosom, O liberty,
Desafia o nosso peito a própria morte!	Our hearts will defy death itself!
Ó Pátria amada	O adored fatherland,
Idolatrada	Cherished and revered,
Salve! Salve!	All hail! All hail!
Brasil de um sonho intenso, um raio vívido,	Brazil, a dream sublime, vivid ray
De amor e de esperança à terra desce	Of love and hope to Earth descends,
Se em teu formoso céu risonho e límpido	Where in your clear, pure, beauteous skies
A imagem do Cruzeiro resplandece	The image of the Southern Cross shines forth.
Gigante pela própria natureza	O country vast by nature,
És belo, és forte, impávido colosso,	Fair and strong, brave and colossus,
E o teu futuro espelha essa grandeza,	Thy future mirrors this thy greatness.
Terra adorada!	O land adored
Entre outras mil	Above all others,
És tu, Brasil,	'Tis thee Brazil,
Ó Pátria amada	Beloved Fatherland!
Dos filhos deste solo és mãe gentil,	Thou art the gentle mother of the children of this soil,
Pátria amada	Beloved land,
Brasil!	Brazil!
2	2
Deitado eternamente em berço esplêndido,	Laid out eternally in the splendor of nature,
Ao som do mar e à luz do céu profundo,	In the sound of the sea and the light of heaven,
Fulguras, ó Brasil, florão da América,	May thou shine, O Brazil, flower of America,
Iluminado ao sol do Novo Mundo!	Illumined by the sun of the New World!

Do que a terra mais garrida	More flowers put forth in thy fair, smiling fields
Teus risonhos lindos campos tem mais flores,	Than in the most gorgeously reputed lands;
"Nossos bosques tem mais vida"	"More life is to be found in the groves"
"Nossa vida" no teu seio "mais amores"	"More love in our lives" in thy embrace.
Ó Pátria amada	O adored fatherland,
Idolatrada	Cherished and revered,
Salve! Salve!	All hail! All hail!
Brasil, de amor eterno seja símbolo	May the star-scattered banner flown by thee,
O lábaro que ostentas estrelado,	Brazil, become the symbol of eternal love,
E diga o verde-louro dessa flâmula	And may the green-gold flag proclaim always
Paz no futuro e glória no passado	Peace in the future and glory in the past
Mas se ergues da justiça a clava forte,	But if the mighty sword of justice drawn forth,
Verás que um filho teu não foge à luta,	You will perceive your children, who adore you,
Nem teme, quem te adora, a própria morte,	Neither fear to fight, nor flee from death itself.
Terra adorada!	O land adored
Entre outras mil	Above all others,
És tu, Brasil,	'Tis thee Brazil,
Ó Pátria amada	Beloved Fatherland!
Dos filhos deste solo és mãe gentil	Thou art the gentle mother of the children of this soil,
Pátria amada	Beloved land,
Brasil!	Brazil!

Brazil

Ou -

vi - ram do I - pi - ran - ga às mar - gens   plá - ci - das De um   po - vo he - rói - co o bra - do re - tum -

ban - te __, E o sol da li - ber - da - de em ra - ios fúl - gi - dos, Bri - lhou no céu da Pá - tria nes - se in -

stan - te __. Se o pe - nhor __ des - sa i - gual - da - de __ Con - se - gui - mos con - quis - tar com bra - ço

for - te __, Em teu sei - o __ ó li - ber - da - de __, De - sa - fi - a o nos - so pei - to a pró - pria

mor - te! Ó Pá - tria a - ma - da I - do - la - tra - da Sal - ve! Sal - ve! Bra -

Brunei Darussalam

Negara Brunei Darussalam

State of Brunei Darussalam

Quick Country Facts
Location: Southeast Asia
Area: 2,226 sq. mi. (5,770 sq. km.)
Population (2002 est.): 350,898
Capital/Largest City: Bandar Seri Begawan
(pop. 52,300)
Official Languages: Malay, English
GDP/PPP: $6.2 billion, $18,000 per capita
Monetary Unit: Brunei Dollar

Allah Peliharakan Sultan

(God Bless the Sultan)

Lyrics: Pengiran Haji Mohamed Yusuf bin Pengrian Haji Andul Rahim (b. 1923). Music: Awang Haji Besar bin Sagap (1914-1988). Adopted: 1951.

Historical Background

This anthem was composed in 1947, almost forty years before independence, when a group of youths decided that the then British protectorate should have a national anthem and chose two of their own to write and compose it.

Malay Words	English Translation
Ya Allah lanjutkanlah Usia	God bless his majesty
Kebawah Duli Yang Maha Mulia	With a long life
Adil berdaulat menaungi nusa	Justly and nobly rule the kingdom
Memimpin rakyat kekal bahagia	And lead our people happily forever
Hidup sentosa Negara dan Sultan	Peacefully be, the kingdom and sultan
Ilahi selamatkan Brunei Darussalam	Lord, save Brunei Darussalam

Brunei

Ya Al - lah lan - jut - kan - lah U - si - a Ke - ba - wah Du - - li Yang Ma -

ha Mu - li - a A - dil ber - dau - lat me - naung - i nu - sa Me - mim - pin rak - - yat ke - kal

baha - gi - a Hi - dup sen - to - sa Ne - ga - ra dan Sul - tan I - la - hi se - la - mat - kan Bru -

nei Da - rus - sa - lam.

Bulgaria

Република България

Republika Bulgaria

Republic of Bulgaria

Quick Country Facts

Location: Eastern Europe, Balkan Peninsula

Area: 42,843 sq. mi. (110,910 sq. km.)

Population (2002 est.): 7,621,337

Capital/Largest City: Sofia (pop. 1,113,674)

Official Language: Bulgarian

GDP/PPP: $50.6 billion, $6,600 per capita

Monetary Unit: Lev

Мила Родино

Mila Rodino

Dear Native Land

Lyrics: Tsevetan Tsvetkov Radoslavov (1863-1931) and Various Writers. Music: Tsevetan Tsvetkov Radoslavov (1863-1931). Adopted: 1964.

Historical Background[1]

This song was originally written and composed by a Bulgarian student in 1885 as he went off to fight in the Serbo-Bulgarian war. Through the years, it has undergone modifications from various writers. The Bulgarian kingdom started using this anthem, until the successor Socialist government replaced it with their own song. "Mila Rodino" was restored in 1964. After the collapse of the Communist bloc, the third verse, which contained references to the Soviet Union, was dropped.

Bulgarian Words	**Bulgarian Words (Transliteration)**	**English Translation**[2]
1	1	1
Горда Стара планина,	*Gorda Stara planina,*	Proud Balkan mountains,
до ней Дунава синей,	*do ney Dunava siney,*	next to them the Danube flows,
слънце Тракия огрява,	*sluntse Trakiya ogryava,*	the sun sheds its light over Thrace,
над Пирина пламеней.	*nad Pirina plameney.*	shining over Pirin.
CHORUS	CHORUS	CHORUS
Мила Родино,	*Mila Rodino,*	Dear native land,
ти си земен рай,	*ti si zemen ray,*	you are paradise on earth,
твойта хубост, твойта прелест,	*tvoyta hubost, tvoyta prelest,*	your beauty and your charm,
ах, те нямат край.	*ah, te nyamat kray!*	ah, they never end.
(repeat chorus)	(repeat chorus)	(repeat chorus)
2	2	2
Паднаха борци безчет	*Padnaha bortsi bezchet*	Many fighters gave their lives
за народа наш любим,	*za naroda nash lyubim,*	for our dear nation,
майко, дай ни мъжка сила	*mayko, day ni muzhka sila*	Mother, give us strength
пътя им да продължим.	*putya im da produlzhim.*	to follow in their steps.
CHORUS	CHORUS	CHORUS

Bulgaria

Gor - da Sta - ra pla - ni - na, Do ney Du - na - va si - ney,

slun - tse Tra - kiya o - - grya - va nad Pi - ri - na pla - men - ey ___ Mi - la Ro - di - no,

1.

ti si ze - men ray ___, tvoy - ta hu - bost, tvoy - ta pre - lest, ah, te nya - mat kray ___

2.

kray ___

Burkina Faso

Quick Country Facts

Location: West Africa

Area: 105,870 sq. mi. (274,200 sq. km.)

Population (2002 est.): 12,603,185

Capital/Largest City: Ouagadougou (pop. 500,000)

Official Language: French

GDP/PPP: $12.8 billion, $1,040 per capita

Monetary Unit: Franc CFA

Ditanyè

(Hymn of Victory)

Lyrics: Thomas Sankara (1949-1987). Adopted: 1984.

Historical Background

Captain Thomas Sankara, the late president of Burkina Faso, wrote the words to this anthem in 1984 during a major revamp of the national symbols and the symbolic change of the country's name from the colonial Upper Volta, reforms that he instituted. On 15 October 1987, Sankara fell prey to violent African politics when he was assassinated by troops loyal to Blaise Campaore—his second-in-command and lifelong friend—the current president of the impoverished African nation.

French Words	English Translation
1	1
Contre la férule humiliante il y a déjà mille ans,	Against the humiliating bondage of a thousand years
La rapacité venue de loin les asservir il y a cent ans.	Rapacity came from afar to subjugate them for a hundred years.
Contre la cynique malice métamorphosée	Against the cynical malice in the shape
En néocolonialisme et ses petits servants locaux	Of neocolonialism and its petty local servants.
Beaucoup flanchèrent et certains résistèrent.	Many gave in and certain others resisted.
Mais les échecs, les succès, la sueur, le sang	But the frustrations, the successes, the sweat, the blood
Ont fortifié notre peuple courageux	Have fortified our courageous people
Et fertilisé sa lutte héroïque.	And fertilized its heroic struggle.

CHORUS

Et une seule nuit a rassemblée en elle

L'histoire de tout un peuple.

Et une seule nuit a déclenché sa marche triomphale

Vers l'horizon du bonheur.

Une seule nuit a réconcilié notre peuple

Avec tous les peuples du monde,

A la conquête de la liberté et du progrès

La patrie ou la mort, nous vaincrons.

2

Nourris à la source vive de la Révolution.

Les engagés volontaires de la liberté et de la paix

Dans l'énergie nocturne et salutaire du 4 août

N'avaient pas que les armes à la main, mais aussi et surtout

La flamme au coeur pour légitimement libérer

Le Faso à jamais des fers de tous ceux qui

Çà et, là en polluaient l'âme sacrée

De l'indépendance, de la souveraineté.

CHORUS

3

Et séant désormais en sa dignité recouvrée

L'amour et l'honneur en partage avec l'humanité

Le peuple du Burkina chante un hymne à la victoire,

A la gloire du travail libérateur, émancipateur.

A bas l'exploitation de l'homme par l'homme!

Hé en avant pour le bonheur de tout homme,

Par tous les hommes aujourd'hui et demain,

Par tous les hommes ici et pour toujours!

CHORUS

4

Révolution populaire notre sève nourricière.

Maternité immortelle du progrès à visage d'homme.

Foyer éternel de démocratie consensuelle,

CHORUS

And one single night has drawn together

The history of an entire people,

And one single night has launched its triumphal march.

Towards the horizon of good fortune.

One single night has brought together our people

With all the peoples of the world,

In the acquisition of liberty and progress.

Motherland or death, we shall conquer.

2

Nourished in the lively source of the revolution,

The volunteers for liberty and peace

With their nocturnal and beneficial energies of the 4th August

Had not only hand arms, but also and above all

The flame in their hearts lawfully to free

Faso forever from the fetters of those who

Here and there were polluting the sacred soul

Of independence and sovereignty.

CHORUS

3

And seated henceforth in rediscovered dignity,

Love and honor partnered with humanity,

The people of Burkina sing a victory hymn

To the glory of the work of liberation and emancipation.

Down with exploitation of man by man!

Forward for the good of every man

By all men of today and tomorrow,

By every man here and always!

CHORUS

4

Popular revolution our nourishing sap.

Undying motherhood of progress in the face of man.

Eternal hearth of agreed democracy,

Où enfin l'identité nationale a droit de cité	Where at last national identity has the right of freedom.
Où pour toujours l'injustice perd ses quartiers,	Where injustice has lost its place forever,
Et où des mains des bâtisseurs d'un monde radieux	And where from the hands of builders of a glorious world
Mûrissent partout les moissons de voeux patriotiques,	Everywhere the harvests of patriotic vows ripen
Brillent les soleils enfin de joie.	And suns of boundless joy shine.
CHORUS	CHORUS

Burkina Faso

98

Burundi

Republika y'UBurundi

République du Burundi

(Republic of Burundi)

Quick Country Facts

Location: South Central Africa

Area: 10,747 sq. mi. (27,830 sq. km.)

Population (2002 est.): 6,373,002

Capital/Largest City: Bujumbura (pop. 300,000)

Official Language: Kirundi, French

GDP/PPP: $4.1 billion, $740 per capita

Monetary Unit: Burundi Franc

Uburundi Bwacu

Cher Burundi

(Beloved Burundi)

Lyrics: Group of writers presided by Jean-Baptiste Ntahokaja (b. 1920). Music: Marc Barengayabo (b. 1934). Adopted: 1962.

Kirundi Words	French Words	English Translation
Burundi Bwacu, Burundi buhire, Shinga icumu mu mashinga, Gaba intahe y'ubugabo ku bugingo. Warapfunywe ntiwapfuye, Warahabishijwe ntiwahababuka,	Cher Burundi, ô doux pays, Prends place dans le concert des nations. En tout bien, tout honneur, accédé à l'indépendance. Mutilé et meurtri, tu es demeuré maître de toi-même.	Beloved Burundi, gentle country, Take your place in the concert of nations, Acceding to independence with honorable intentions. Wounded and bruised, you have remained master of yourself.
Uhagurukana, uhagurukana,	L'heure venue, t'es levé	When the hour came, you arose,

uhagurukana, ubugabo urikukira.	Et fièrement tu t'es hissé au rang des peuples libres.	Lifting yourself proudly into the ranks of free peoples.
Komerwamashyi n'amakungu,	Reçois donc le compliment des nations,	Receive, then, the congratulations of the nations
Habwa impundu nabawe,	Agrée l'hommage de tes enfants.	And the homage of your sons.
Isamirane mu mashinga,	Qu'à travers l'univers retentisse ton nom.	May your name ring out through the universe.
(repeat)		
Burundi bwacu, ragi ry'abasokuru,	Cher Burundi, héritage sacré de nos aïeux,	Beloved Burundi, sacred heritage from our forefathers,
Ramutswa intahe n'ibihugu,	Reconnu digne de te gouverner	Recognized as worthy of self-government,
Ufatanije ishyaka n'ubu hizi;	Au courage tu allies le sentiment de l'honneur.	With your courage you also have a sense of honor.
Vuza impundu wiganzuye uwakuganza uwakuganza.	Chante la gloire de ta liberté reconquise.	Sing the glory of liberty conquered again.
Burundi bwacu. nkoramutima kuri twese,	Cher Burundi, digne objet de notre plus tendre amour,	Beloved Burundi, worthy of our most tender love.
Tugutuye amaboko. umitima n'ubuzima,	A ton noble service nous vouons nos bras, nos cœurs et nos vies.	We vow to your noble service our hands and hearts and lives.
Imana yakuduhaye ikudutungire.	Veuille Dieu, qui nous a fait don de toi,	May God, who gave you to us, keep you for us to venerate,
Horana umwami n'abagabo n'itekane.	Te conserver à notre vénération.	Under the shield of unity,
Sagwa n'urweze, sagwa n'amahoro meza.	Sous l'égide de l'Unité, Dans la paix, la joie et la prospérité.	In peace, joy, and prosperity.

Burundi

ku - ki - ra __. Ko - me - rwa - ma - shyi - n'a - ma - ku - ngu, Ha - bwa i - mpu - ndu n-a - - ba - - we, I -

sa - mi - ra - ne mu ma - shi - nga, i - sa - mi - ra - ne mu ma - shi - nga, Bu - ru - ndi bwa - - cu,

ra - gi ry'a - ba - so - ku - ru, Ra - mu - tswa i - nta - he n'i - bi - hu - gu, U -

fa - ta - ni - je i - shya - ka n'u - bu hi - zi; Vu - za i - mpu - ndu wi - ga - nzu - ye u - wa - ku - ga - nza u -

Cambodia

នៃព្រះរាជាណាចក្រកម្ពុជា

Reacheanachak Kampuchea

Kingdom of Cambodia

Quick Country Facts

Location: Southeast Asia, Indochina Peninsula

Area: 69,884 sq. mi. (181,040 sq. km.)

Population (2002 est.): 12,775,324

Capital/Largest City: Phnom Penh (pop. 900,000)

Official Language: Khmer

GDP/PPP: $18.7 billion, $1,500 per capita

Monetary Unit: Riel

នគររាជ

Nokoreach

Lyrics: Chuon Nat (1883-1969). Adopted: 1941.

Historical Background

The song derives its name from an ancient Khmer kingdom. Its music was adapted from an old folk tune. The country originally adopted this anthem in 1941, but it was replaced after the Communist Khmer Rouge took over in 1976. "Nokoreach" was restored in 1993, when Cambodia became a constitutional monarchy.

Khmer Words	Khmer Words (Transliteration)	French Words
1	1	1
សូមពួកទេព្តា រក្សាមហាក្សត្រយើង	*Som pouk tepda rak sa moha khsath yeung*	Que le ciel protège notre Roi
កោយចានេរុងរឿង កោយថ័យមង្គលា ពីរុក្ស	*Oy ben roung roeung doy chey monkol srey soursdey*	Et lui dispense le bonheur et la gloire
យើងខ្ញុំព្រះអង្គ កូមជ្រកក្រោមម្លប់ព្រះចារម៍		Qu'l règne sur nos cœurs et la sur nos destinées
នៃព្រះនរបតី វង្ស្សក្សត្រាដែលសាងប្រាសាទថ្ម	*Yeung Khnom preah ang som chrok Krom molup preah Baromey*	Celui qui, héritier des Souverains Bâtisseurs
គ្រប់គ្រងដែនខ្មែរ បុរាណថ្កើងថ្កាន		

104

	Ney preah Noropdey vong Khsattra *del sang preah sat thmr* *Kroup Kraung den Khmer borann* *thkoeung thkann.*	Gouverne le fier et vieux Royaume.
2 ស្រាលាឆលីលា កំចាំងកណ្ដាលព្រៃ គួរគោយស្រមយ នឹកដល់យលលក្ដិ មហាគរ ជាតិខ្មែរដូចថ្ម កង់វង្សនៅល្អ វិងប៊ុងជំហរ យើងសង់ឃ្យឹមពរ ភ័ព្ធព្រេងលណាករបល់កម្ពុជា មហារដ្ឋកើតមាន យូរអង្វែងហើយ	**2** *Prasath sela kombang kan dal prey* *Kuor oy srmay noeuk dl yuos sak* *Moha Nokor* *Cheat Khmer dauch Thmar kong* *vong ny lar rung peung chom hor.* *Yeung sang Khim por pheap preng* *samnang robuos Kampuchea.* *Moha rth koeut mieo you ang veanh* *hey.*	**2** Les temples dorment dans la forêt Rappelant la grandeur du Moha Nokor Comme le roc, la race khmère est éternelle Ayons confiance dans le sort du Campuchéa L'mpire qui défie les années.
3 គ្រប់វត្តអារាម ឮតែល្បវល់ពូធមី ស្សគ្រដោយអំណរ វ័ឮកតុណាពុទ្ធលាសនា ស្សរយើងជាអ្នក ថ្យើជាក់ល្បោះស្មោះគ្រ កាមបែបប្បុនគោ កង់តែទេវគោ នឹងជួយជ្រោមព្រែងផ្គត់ផ្គង់ប្រយោជន៍ឱ្យ ដល់ប្រទេសខ្មែរ ជាមហានគរ	**3** *Kroup vath aram lo te so sap thoeur* *Sot doy am nu rom lik koun poth sasna* *Chol yeung chea neak thioeur thiak* *smos smak tam bap donnta* *Kong te thevoda nung chuoy chrom* *chreng phkut phkang pra yoch oy* *Dol prateah Khmer chea* *Moha Nokor.*	**3** Les chants montent dans les pagodes A la gloire de la Sainte foi Bouddhique Soyons fidèles aux croyances de nos pères Ainsi le ciel prodiguera-t-il tous ses bienfaits Au vieux pays khmer, le Moha Nokor.

English Translation

1

Heaven protects our king

And gives him happiness and glory

To reign over our souls and our destinies,

The one being, heir of the sovereign builders,

Guiding the proud old kingdom.

2

Temples are asleep in the forest,

Remembering the splendor of Moha Nokor.

Like a rock the Khmer race is eternal.

Let us trust in the fate of Kampuchea,
The empire which challenges the ages.

3

Songs rise up from the pagodas
To the glory of holy buddhistic faith.
Let us be faithful to our ancestors` belief.
Thus heaven will lavish its bounty
Towards the ancient Khmer country, the Moha Nokor.

Cambodia

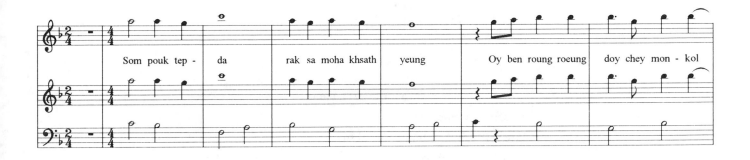

Som pouk tep - da rak sa moha khsath yeung Oy ben roung roeung doy chey mon - kol

___ srey sour - - sdey ___ Yeung Khnom preah ang som chrok Krom molup preah Ba - ro - mey

Ney preah No - rop - dey vong Khsat - tra del sang preah sat thmr Kroup Kraung den

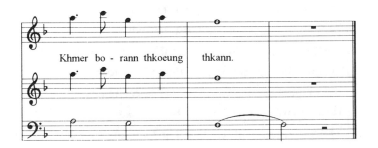

Khmer bo - rann thkoeung thkann.

Cameroon

République de Cameroun

Republic of Cameroon

```
Quick Country Facts
Location: Central Africa
Area: 183,569 sq. mi. (475,440 sq. km.)
Population (2002 est.): 16,184,748
Capital/Largest City: Yaoundé (pop. 730,000)
Official Languages: French, English
GDP/PPP: $26.4 billion, $1,700 per capita
Monetary Unit: Franc CFA
```

Chant de Ralliement

Rallying Song

Lyrics: Student Group and René Jam Afame (1910-1981). Music: René Jam Afame (1910-1981), Samuel Minkio Bamba (b. 1911), and Moïse Nyatte Nko'o (1910-1978). Adopted: 1957.

Historical Background

The song was adopted on an unofficial basis in 1948. It became the official anthem nine years later. In 1978, the lyrics underwent a significant revision.

French Words	English Words
1	1
O Cameroun berceau de nos ancêtres,	O Cameroon, thou cradle of our fathers,
Va, debout et jaloux de ta liberté.	Holy shrine where in our midst they now repose,
Comme un soleil ton drapeau fier doit être,	Their tears and blood and sweat thy soil did water,
Un symbole ardent de foi et d'unité,	On thy hills and valleys once their tillage rose.
Que tous tes enfants du Nord et Sud,	Dear fatherland, thy worth no tongue can tell!
De l'Est à l'Ouest soient tout amour!	How can we ever pay thy due?
Te servir que ce soit le seul but	Thy welfare we will win in toil and love and peace,
Pour remplir leur devoir toujours.	Will be to thy name ever true!

CHORUS

Chère Patrie, terre chérie,
Tu es notre seul et vrai bonheur.
Notre joie, notre vie,
A toi l'amour et le grand honneur.

2

Tu es la tombe où dorment nos pères,
Le jardin que nos aïeux ont cultivé.
Nous travaillons pour te rendre prospère,
Un beau jour enfin nous serons arrivés.
De l'Afrique sois fidèle enfant
Et progresse toujours en paix,
Espérant que tes jeunes enfants
T'aimeront sans bornes à jamais.

CHORUS

CHORUS

Land of promise, land of glory!
Thou, of life and joy, our only store!
Thine be honor, thine devotion,
And deep endearment, for evermore.

2

From Shari, from where the Mungo meanders
From along the banks of lowly Boumba Stream,
Muster thy sons in union close around thee,
Mighty as the Buea Mountain be their team;
Instill in them the love of gentle ways,
Regret for errors of the past;
Foster, for Mother Africa, a loyalty
That true shall remain to the last.

CHORUS

Cameroon

O Ca - me - roun ber - - ceau de nos an - cê - tres, Va, de - bout et ja - loux de ta li - ber -
O Ca - me - roon, thou __ cra - dle of our fa - thers, Ho - ly shrine where in our midst they now re -

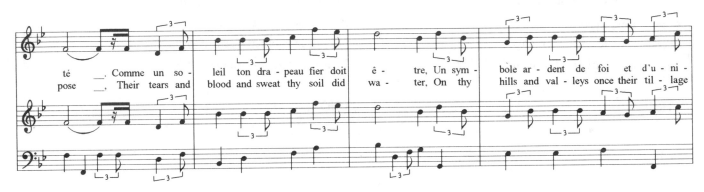

té __. Comme un so - leil ton dra - peau fier doit ê - tre, Un sym - bole ar - dent de foi et d'u - ni -
pose __, Their tears and blood and sweat thy soil did wa - ter, On thy hills and val - leys once their til - lage

té __, Que tous tes en - fants du __ Nord au Sud __, De __ l'Est à l'Ou - est soient tout a -
rose __. Dear fa - ther - land, thy worth __ none can tell __! How __ can we e - - ver pay thy

mour __! Te ser - vir que ce soit le __ seul but peace __, Pour __
due __? Thy wel - fare we will win in toil and love and peace __, Will __

rem - - plir leur de - voir tou - jours __. Chère Pa - tri - e, terre ché - ri - e, Tu
be __ to thy name e - ver true __! Land of pro - mise, land of glo - ry! Thou,

es no - tre seul et vrai bon - heur __. No - tre joie __, no - tre vi - e, A toi l'a -
of life and joy, our on - ly store __! Thine be hon - or, thine de - vo - tion, And deep en -

mour et le grand hon - neur __.
dear - ment, for e - ver - more __.

Canada

Quick Country Facts

Location: North America

Area: 3,851,809 sq. mi. (9,976,140 sq. km.)

Population (2002 est.): 31,902,268

Capital: Ottawa (pop. 1,010,498)

Largest City: Toronto (pop. 4,263,757)

Official Languages: English, French

GDP/PPP: $923 billion, $29,400 per capita

Monetary Unit: Canadian Dollar

O Canada

English Lyrics: Robert Stanley Wier (1856-1926). French Lyrics: Aldolphe-Basile Routhier (1839-1920). Music: Attributed to Calixa Lavallée (1842-1891). Adopted: 1980.

Historical Background[1]

The anthem was written by Calixa Lavallée, "Canada's National Musician," when he was asked to compose the music for a poem written by Judge Adolphe-Basile Routhier. The occasion was the "Congrès national des Canadiens-Français" in 1880, which was being held at the same time as the St. Jean-Baptiste Day celebrations. There had been some thought of holding a competition for a national hymn to have its first performance on St. Jean-Baptiste Day, 24 June, but by January the committee in charge decided there was not enough time, so the lieutenant governor of Quebec, the Honorable Théodore Robitaille, commissioned Judge Routhier to write a hymn and Lavallée to compose the tune. Lavallée made a number of drafts before the tune was greeted with enthusiasm by his musical friends. It is said that in the excitement of success Lavallée rushed to show his music to the Lieutenant Governor without even stopping to sign the manuscript.

The first performance took place on 24 June 1880 at a banquet in the "Pavillon des Patineurs" in Quebec City as the climax of a "Mosaïque sur des airs populaires canadiens" arranged by Joseph Vézina, a prominent composer and bandmaster. Although this first performance of "O Canada" with Routhier's French words was well received on the evening, it does not seem to have made a lasting impression at that time. Arthur Lavigne, a Quebec musician and music dealer, published it without copyright although there was no rush to reprint. Lavallée's obit in 1891 does not mention it among his accomplishments, nor does a biography of Judge Routhier published in 1898. French Canada is represented in the 1887 edition of the University of Toronto song book by "Vive la canadienne," "A la claire fontaine," and "Un canadien errant."

English Canada in general probably first heard "O Canada" when school children sang it when the duke and duchess of Cornwall (later King George V and Queen Mary) toured Canada in 1901. Five years later, Whaley and Royce in Toronto published the music with the French text and a translation into English made by Dr. Thomas Bedford Richardson, a Toronto doctor. The Mendelssohn Choir used the Richardson lyrics in one of their performances about this time and Judge Routhier, and the French press complimented the author. In 1908 *Collier's Weekly* inaugurated its Canadian edition with a competition for an English text to Lavallée's music. It was won by Mercy E. Powell McCulloch, but her version did not take. Since then many English versions have been written for "O Canada." Poet Wilfred Campbell wrote one. So did Augustus Bridle, a Toronto critic. Some were written for the 1908 tercentenary of Quebec City. One version became popular in British Columbia. However, the version that gained the widest currency was made in 1908 by Robert Stanley Weir, a lawyer and at the time Recorder of the City of Montreal. This is the version that was published in an official form for the Diamond Jubilee of Confederation in 1927, and has since been generally accepted in English-speaking Canada.

Many musicians have made arrangements of "O Canada" but there appears to be a scarcity of recordings suitable for various purposes. By the time World War I broke out in 1914, "O Canada" was the best-known patriotic song in Canada, edging out "The Maple Leaf Forever" and others less well-known today. In 1924, the association of Canadian Clubs passed a unanimous resolution recommending the Weir version as suitable for use at club meetings. Since then the Canadian Authors Association has endorsed it and in 1958 the Native Sons of Canada found in favor of it. In 1927, an official version of "O Canada" was authorized for singing in Canadian schools and for use at public functions.

On 27 July 1942, the prime minister, William Lyon Mackenzie King, was asked if he did not think this an appropriate time for proclaiming a national anthem. He replied that "There are times and seasons for all things and this time of war when there are other more important questions with which parliament has to deal, we might well continue to follow what has become the custom in Canada in recent years of regarding 'God Save the King (Queen)' and 'O Canada' each as national anthems and entitled to similar recognition." He said further that this was his opinion, his government's opinion and he had no doubt it was the opinion of most people in the country. Some years later, his successor as prime minister, Louis St-Laurent, made a similar statement.

In 1964, a government resolution authorized the formation of a special joint committee to consider the status of "God Save the Queen" and "O Canada." On 31 January 1966, Prime Minister Lester B. Pearson placed a notice of motion on the order paper "that the government be authorized to take such steps as may be necessary to provide that 'O Canada' shall be the National Anthem of Canada while 'God Save the Queen' shall be the Royal Anthem of Canada. On 15 March of the following year, the special joint committee "unanimously recommends that the government be authorized to adopt forthwith the music for 'O Canada' composed by Lavallée as the music of the National Anthem of Canada with the following notation added to the sheet music: With dignity, not too slowly. 'God Save the Queen' was found to be in the public domain as the Royal Anthem of Canada, but for 'O Canada' the committee deemed it "essential to take such steps as necessary to appropriate the copyright to the music providing that it shall belong to Her Majesty in right of Canada for all time. This provision would also include that no other person shall be entitled to copyright in the music or any arrangements or adaptations thereof." The committee recommended further study of the lyrics.

It discarded an otherwise acceptable bilingual version as being difficult for other ethnic groups in Canada to accept. It suggested keeping the first verse of the original French version and using the first verse of the Weir English version with minor changes—that is replacing two of the "Stand on guard" phrases with "From far and wide" and "God keep our land." There was no trouble with the music copyright that had by now descended to Gordon V. Thompson. They were willing to sell for \$1, but the heirs of Judge Weir objected to the changes in the original version. Since Judge Weir died in 1926, the Weir version would not come into public domain until 1976. There was some doubt that the Weir family had legal grounds for objection since Thompson apparently held copyright on both music and English words. However the committee preferred to settle the matter amicably if at all possible. The Government acquired the rights from G. V. Thompson in 1970.

On 28 Feburary 1972, the Secretary of State of Canada, Gérard Pelletier, presented a bill in the House of Commons proposing the adoption of "O Canada" as the National Anthem of Canada. The recommendations of the 1967 study in Parliament are incorporated in the bill, which did not receive further study in Parliament and died on the order paper. The same legislation was reintroduced by Mr. Pelletier's successors at further sessions of Parliament; no action was ever taken. On 18 June 1980, Pelletier's successor Francis Fox presented a bill, similar to previously presented bills on "O Canada," fulfilling a promise made earlier in the House that "O Canada" be proclaimed as Canada's national anthem as soon as possible in this year of the centenary of the first rendition. The bill was unanimously accepted by the House of Commons and the Senate on June 27; royal assent was given the same day. On 1 July, the governor general, His Excellency the Right Honorable Edward Schreyer, proclaimed the Act respecting the National Anthem of Canada, thus making "O Canada" an official symbol of the country. A public ceremony was held at noon on Parliament Hill in front of thousands of Canadians. Descendants of Weir and Routhier were on the official platform, as well as Jean-Pierre Côté, the successor of Robitaille.

French Words	English Words
O Canada, terre de nos aïeux,	O Canada! Our home and native land!
Ton front est ceint de fleurons glorieux.	True patriot love in all thy sons command.
Car ton bras sait porter l'épée,	With glowing hearts we see thee rise,
Il sait porter la croix.	The true north strong and free!
Ton histoire est une épopée	From far and wide,
Des plus brillants exploits.	O Canada! We stand on guard for thee.
Et ta valeur, de foi trempée,	God keep our land glorious and free!
Protégera nos foyers et nos droits	O Canada! We stand on guard for thee
(repeat)	(repeat)

Canada

et nos droits Pro - té - ge - ra nos foy - ers et nos droits ___.
guard for thee, O Ca - na - da! we stand on guard for thee ___.

Cape Verde

República de Cabo Verde

Republica di Cabo Verde

(Republic of Cape Verde)

```
Quick Country Facts
Location: West Africa, middle of East Atlantic Ocean
Area: 1,557 sq. mi. (4,033 sq. km.)
Population (2002 est.): 408,760
Capital/Largest City: Praia (pop. 61,797)
Languages: Portuguese, Criuolo
GDP/PPP: $581 million, $1,450 per capita
Monetary Unit: Cape Verdean Escudo
```

Cântico da Liberdade

(Song to Liberty)

Historical Background

This anthem was adopted to replace the previous one, which had been the same as that of Guinea-Bissau, after Cape Verde officially renounced its once cherished goal of unification with Guinea-Bissau.

Portuguese Words	English Translation[1]
CHORUS	CHORUS
Canta, irmão	Sing, brother
canta meu irmão	Sing, my brother
que a Liberdade é hino	For freedom is a hymn
e o Homem a certeza.	And man a certainty.

VERSE	VERSE
Com dignidade, enterra a semente	With dignity, bury the seed
no po da ilha nua:	In the dust of the naked island:
No despenhadeiro da vida	In life is precipice
a esperança e do tamanho	Hope is as big as the sea
do mar que nos abraça.	Which embraces us.
Sentinela de mares e ventos perseverante	Unwavering sentinel of the seas and winds
entre estrelas e o Atlântico	Between the stars and the Atlantic Ocean
entoa o cântico da Liberdade.	Sing the chant of freedom.
CHORUS	CHORUS

Music Sheet Not Available

Central African Republic

République Centrafricaine

Quick Country Facts

Location: Central Africa

Area: 241,313 sq. mi. (622,984 sq. km.)

Population (2002 est.): 3,642,739

Capital/Largest City: Bangui (pop. 66,824)

Official Language: French

GDP/PPP: $4.6 billion, $1,300 per capita

Monetary Unit: Franc CFA

La Renaissance

(The Revival)

Lyrics: Barthélémy Boganda (1910-1959). Music: Herbert Pepper (b. 1912). Adopted: 1960.

Historical Background

The music to this anthem was written in 1958 by French ethnomusicologist Herbert Pepper, who composed numerous works of original African music. One of his tunes also became the national anthem of Senegal. That same year, Barthélémy Boganda, the first president of the nation, wrote the words.

French Words	English Translation
VERSE	VERSE
O Centrafrique, ô berceau des Bantous!	Oh! Central Africa, cradle of the Bantu!
Reprends ton droit au respect, à la vie!	Take up again your right to respect, to life!
Longtemps soumis, longtemps brimé par tous,	Long subjugated, long scorned by all,
Mais de ce jour brisant la tyrannie,	But, from today, breaking tyranny's hold.
Dans le travail, l'ordre et la dignité	Through work, order and dignity
Tu reconquiers ton droit, ton unité	You reconquer your rights, your unity,
Et pour franchir cette étape nouvelle,	And to take this new step
De nos ancêtres la voix nous appelle.	The voice of our ancestors calls us.

CHORUS	CHORUS
Au travail dans l'ordre et la dignité	To work! In order and dignity,
Dans le respect du droit dans l'unité	In the respect for rights and in unity,
Brisant la misère et la tyrannie,	Breaking poverty and tyranny,
Brandissant l'étendard de la Patrie.	Holding high the flag of the fatherland.

Central African Republic

121

voix __ nous ap - pel - le. Au tra - vail dans l'ordre et la di - gni - té, Dans le res - pect du

droit dans l'u - ni - té, Bri - sant la mi - sè - re et la ty - ran - nie, Bran - diss - ant l'é - ten -

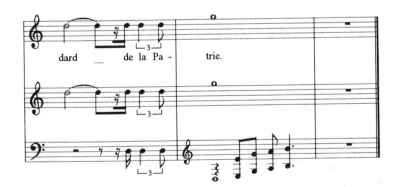

dard __ de la Pa - trie.

Chad

République du Tchad

Jumhuriyat Tashad

(Republic of Chad)

Quick Country Facts

Location: Central Africa

Area: 495,752 sq. mi. (1,284,000 sq. km.)

Population (2002 est.): 8,997,237

Capital/Largest City: N'Djamena (pop. 529,555)

Official Language: French, Arabic

GDP/PPP: $8.9billion, $1,030 per capita

Monetary Unit: Franc CFA

La Tchadienne

(The Song of Chad)

Lyrics: Louis Gidrol (b. 1922) and student group. Music: Paul Villard (1899-1986). Adopted: 1960.

Historical Background

The words of this song were written by Louis Gidrol and a group of students in 1960 to the music of Paul Villard. The anthem was adopted in celebration of Chad's independence from French colonial rule.

French Words	English Translation
CHORUS	CHORUS
Peuple Tchadien, debout et à l'ouvrage!	People of Chad, arise and take up the task!
Tu as conquis ta terre et ton droit;	You have conquered the soil and won your rights;
Ta liberté naîtra de ton courage.	Your freedom will be born of your courage.
Lève les yeux, l'avenir est à Toi	Lift up your eyes, the future is yours.
VERSE	VERSE
O mon Pays, que Dieu te prenne en garde,	Oh, my Country, may God protect you,

Que tes voisons admirent tes enfants.	May your neighbors admire your children.
Joyeux, pacifique, avance en chantant,	Joyful, peaceful, advance as you sing,
Fidèle à tes anciens qui te regardent.	Faithful to your fathers who are watching you.
CHORUS	CHORUS

Chad

Peu - ple Tcha - dien __, de - bout et à l'ou - vra - ge!

Tu as con - quis __ ta terre et ton droit; Ta li - ber - té __ naî - tra de ton cou - ra - ge.

Lè - ve les yeux, l'a - ve - nir est à Toi. O mon Pa - ys

__, que Dieu te prenne en gar - de Que tes voi - sins ad - mi -

Chile

República de Chile

(Republic of Chile)

```
               Quick Country Facts
Location: South America
Area: 292,132 sq. mi. (756,950 sq. km.)
Population (2002 est.): 15,498,930
Capital/Largest City: Santiago (pop. 5,400,000)
Official Language: Spanish
GDP/PPP: $153 billion, $10,000 per capita
Monetary Unit: Peso
```

Himno Nacional de Chile

(National Song of Chile)

Lyrics: Eusebio Lillo (1826-1910) and Bernardo de Vera y Pintado (1789-1826). Music: Ramón Carnicer (1789-1855). Adopted: 1941.

Historical Background

The first national anthem of Chile was composed by Manuel Robles and written by the poet Bernardo de Vera y Pintado. Historians believe that the song was initially performed either during the celebrations of September 1819 or in the Domingo Arteaga Theatre on 20 August 1820. The second anthem was composed, by petition, by Ramón Carnicer, a Spanish songwriter exiled in England at the time because of his liberal beliefs. The music made its debut at the Arteaga Theatre on 23 December 1828 in a concert of the philharmonic society. Years later, in 1847, the Chilean Government ordered the young poet Eusebio Lillo to write a new text to Carnicer's words, thus replacing the original lyrics of de Vera y Pintado, which contained violent references against Spain. Today, the chorus and fifth verse of Lillo's poem make up the official national anthem of Chile.

Spanish Words	English Translation
VERSE	VERSE
Puro, Chile, es tu cielo azulado,	Chile, your sky is a pure blue,
Puras brisas te cruzan también,	Pure breezes blow across you,
Y tu campo de flores bordado,	And your field, embroidered with flowers,
Es la copia feliz del Edén.	Is a happy copy of Eden.
Majestuosa es la blanca montaña	Majestic is the snow-covered mountain
Que te dio por baluarte el Señor	That was given to you by the Lord as a bastion,
(repeat)	(repeat)
Y ese mar que tranquilo te baña,	And the sea that tranquilly washes your shore
Te promete futuro esplendor.	Promises future splendor for you.
(repeat previous two lines)	(repeat previous two lines)
CHORUS	CHORUS
Dulce Patria recibe los votos	Gentle homeland, accept the vows
Con que Chile en tus aras juró	Given, Chile. on your altars,
Que, o la tumba serás de los libres,	That you be either the tomb of the free
O el asilo contra la opresión.	Or a refuge from oppression.
(repeat previous two lines three times)	(repeat previous two lines three times)
O el asilo contra la opresión.	Or a refuge from oppression.
(repeat)	(repeat)

Chile

Pu - ro, Chi - le, es tu cie -

lo a - zu - la - - do, Pu - ras bri - - sas __ te cru - - zan __ tam - bién __ , Y tu cam - - po de flo - -

res bor - da - - do, Es la co - pia fe - liz del E - dén. Ma - jes - tuo - sa es la blan - - -

ca mon - ta - - ña   Que te dio por ba - luar - - te el Se - ñor __   Que te dio por ba - luar - -

te el __ Se - ñor   Y e - se mar __ que tran - qui - - lo te ba - ña,   Te pro - me - te fu - tu - -

ro es - plen - dor __ . Y __   e - - se mar __ que tran - qui - - lo __ te ba - ña, Te __

pro - - me - te __ fu - tu - ro   es - - plen - dor.   Dul -   ce Pa -   tria

Chile

la o - pre - sión ___.   O el a - si - lo con - tra   la o - pre - sión ___.

O el a - si - lo con - tra   la o - pre - sión.

China

中华人民共和国

Zhonghua Renmin Gongheguo

(People's Republic of China)

Quick Country Facts

Location: East Asia

Area: 3,750,000 sq. mi. (9,600,000 sq. km.)

Population (2002 est.): 1,284,303,785

Capital: Beijing (pop. 10,260,000)

Largest City: Shanghai (pop. 13,900,000)

Official Language: Mandarin Chinese

GDP/PPP: $6 trillion, $4,600 per capita

Monetary Unit: Renminbi Yuan

义勇军进行曲

Yiyongjun Jinxingqu

(March of the Volunteers)

Lyrics: Tian Han (1898-1968). Music: Nie Er (1912-1935). Adopted: 1949.

Historical Background[1]

The words to the national anthem were written by Tian Han, and its music was set by Nie Er in 1935. Originally known as the "March of the Volunteers," it was the theme song of *Sons and Daughters in Times of Turmoil*, a film that depicted how Chinese intellectuals marched bravely to the front in the War of Resistance against Japan during World War II.

Sonorous, militant, and inspiring, the song describes the wrath of the Chinese people against imperialist aggression and their determination to protect their motherland against foreign invaders. The song immediately swept the nation, and in 1949 it was submitted as a candidate for the national anthem. Many people liked the idea, and it was adopted on 27 September of that year on a provisional basis. However, it was not until thirty-three years later that this status changed; in 1982, the "March of the Volunteers" was officially named the national anthem by the National People's Congress.

Chinese Words	Chinese Words (Transliteration)	English Translation[2]
起来！不愿做奴隶的人们！	*Qilai! Bu yuan zuo nuli de renmen,*	Arise, ye who refuse to be slaves;
把我们的血肉筑成我们新的长城！	*Ba women de xuerou zhu cheng*	With our very flesh and blood
中华民族到了最危险的时候，	*women xin de Changcheng!*	Let us build our new Great Wall!
每个人被迫着发出最后的吼声。	*Zhonghua Minzu dao liao zui weixian*	The peoples of China are in the most
起来！起来！起来！	*de shihou,*	critical time,
我们万众一心，	*Meige ren beipo zhe fa chu zuihou de*	Everybody must roar their defiance.
冒着敌人的炮火前进！	*housheng!*	Arise! Arise! Arise!
冒着敌人的炮火前进！	*Qilai, qilai, qilai!*	Millions of hearts with one mind,
前进！	*Women wanzhongyixin,*	Brave the enemy`s gunfire,
前进！	*Mao zhe diren de paohuo qianjin!*	March on!
进！	*Mao zhe diren de paohuo qianjin!*	Brave the enemy`s gunfire,
	Qianjin!	March on! March on!
	Qianjin!	March on
	Jin!	On!

China

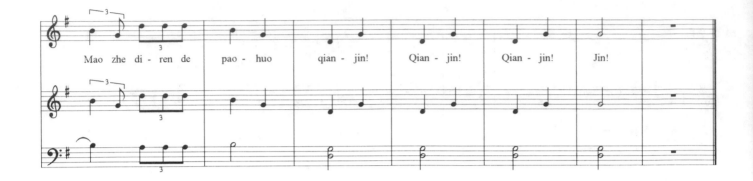

Mao zhe di - ren de   pao - huo   qian - jin!   Qian - jin!   Qian - jin!   Jin!

China, Republic of

中華民國

Zhonghua Minguo

Quick Country Facts

Location: East Asia

Area: 13,895 sq. mi. (35,980 sq. km.)

Population (2002 est.): 22,548,009

Capital and Largest City: Taipei (pop. 7,900,000)

Official Language: Mandarin Chinese

GDP/PPP: $386 billion, $17,200 per capita

Monetary Unit: New Taiwan Dollar

三民主義

Sanmin Zhuyi

(Three People's Principles)

Lyrics: Sun Yat-sen (1866-1925). Music: Cheng Maoyun (1900-1957). Adopted: 1930.

Historical Background[1]

The words of this national anthem were first delivered as an exhortation at the opening ceremony of the Whampoa Military Academy in Guangzhou on 16 June 1924 by Dr. Sun Yat-sen, founder of the Republic of China. The Three People's Principles in his speech referred to his political philosophy of people's government, people's rights, and people's livelihood. This exhortation was designated as the Kuomintang's (KMT) party song in 1928, after which the KMT then publicly solicited contributions for a tune to fit the words. The melody submitted by Cheng Maoyun was the undisputed winner out of 139 contenders.

In the late 1920s and early 1930s, the ministry of education held two separate competitions for lyrics for a national anthem, using the KMT party song in the meantime as a temporary anthem. However, none of the entries reviewed were deemed appropriate, so Sun's composition was finally adopted as the official national anthem of the Republic of China in 1937. The piece was honored as the world's best national anthem at the 1936 Berlin Olympics.

In 1949, after the Communists took over Mainland China, the Kuomintang government retreated to the island of Taiwan, where the song continues to serve as the national anthem to this day.

Chinese Words	Chinese Words (Transliteration)	English Translation
三民主義，吾黨所宗。	*San Min Zhuyi, wu dang suo zong,*	Three People's Principles, our aim shall be,
以建民國，以進大同。	*Yi jian minguo, yi jin datong,*	To found a free land, world peace be our stand.
咨爾多士，爲民前鋒。	*Zier duo shi, wei min qianfeng,*	Lead on comrades, vanguards ye are,
夙夜匪懈，主義是從。	*Suye feixie, zhuyi shi cong,*	Hold fast your aim, by sun and star,
矢勤矢勇，必信必忠。	*Shi qin shi yong, bi xin bi zhong,*	Be earnest and brave, your country to save,
一心一德，貫徹始終！	*Yi xin yi de, guanche shizhong!*	One heart, one soul, one mind, one goal!

China, Republic of

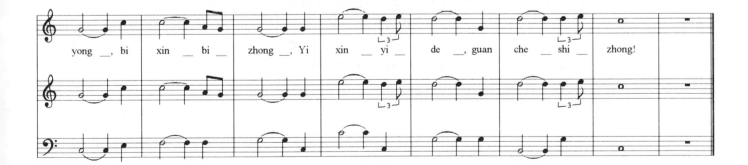

Colombia

República de Colombia

(Republic of Colombia)

Himno Nacional

(National Anthem)

Lyrics: Rafael Núñez (1825-1894). Music: Oreste Sindici (1837-1904). Adopted: 1920.

Historical Background

The Colombian national anthem resulted from a grand idea by José Domingo Torres, a Bogotá comedian. Driven by love for his country and theatrical music, he decided to push for the creation of a national anthem. He requested his close friend, the Italian opera teacher Oreste Sindici, to compose the music to an inspirational poem by then-President Rafael Núñez commemorating the city of Cartagena. Although reluctant at first, Sindici was at last persuaded through the joint efforts of his wife and Torres. On 11 November 1887, the song was sung for the first time in public at an improvised music hall in the old building of the public school where Sindici taught. The following month, on 6 December, the first official appearance was made in front of the Palace of San Carlos. In 1920, the song was adopted as the national anthem by the Colombian Congress. Jose Rozo Contreras, Director of the National Band, later made an official transcription of the anthem in 1946.

Spanish Words (First Two Verses, 11 Total)	English Translation (First Two Verses, 11 Total)
CHORUS	CHORUS
¡Oh gloria inmarcesible!	Oh unfading glory!
¡Oh Júbilo inmortal!	Oh immortal joy!
En surcos de dolores	In furrows of pain
¡El bien germina ya!	Good is already germinating.
(repeat)	(repeat)
(repeat chorus without repeats)	(repeat chorus without repeats)
1	1
¡Cesó la horrible noche!	The fearful night came to an end,
La libertad sublime	Liberty sublime
Derrama las auroras	Is spreading the dawns
De su invencible luz.	Of its invincible light.
La humanidad entera,	The whole of humanity,
Que entre cadenas gime,	Which is groaning under chains,
Comprende las palabras	Understands the words
Del que murió en la cruz.	Of the One who died on the Cross.
CHORUS	CHORUS
2	2
INDEPENDENCIA grita	INDEPENDENCE, cries
El mundo americano;	The American world;
Se baña en sangre de héroes	In heroes' blood is bathing
La tierra de Colón.	The land of Columbus.
Pero este gran principio:	But this great principle:
EL REY NO ES SOBERANO,	THE KING IS NOT SOVEREIGN,
Resuena, y los que sufren	Resounds, and those who suffer
Bendicen su pasión.	Praise the passion in it.
CHORUS	CHORUS

Colombia

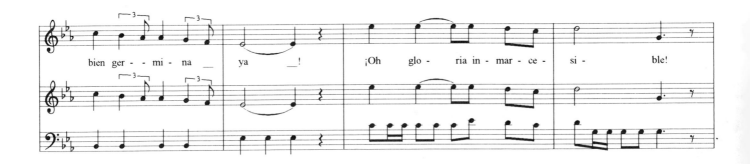

Oh Jú - bi - lo in - mor - tal __! En __ sur - cos __ de do - - lo - res __ El __

bien ger - - mi - na __ ya __! Ce - só la ho - rri - ble __ no - che! La li - ber - tad __ su - -

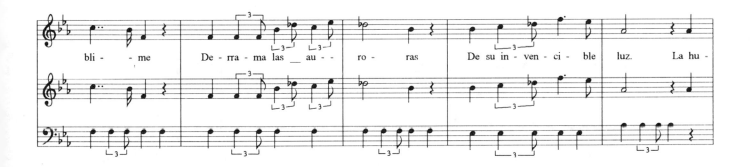

bli - - me De - rra - ma las __ au - - ro - ras De su in - ven - ci - ble luz. La hu -

ma - ni - dad en - te - ra, Que en - tre ca - de - nas gi - me, Com -

gi - me, Com - pren - de las pa - la - bras Del que mu - rió en la cruz __.

¡Oh glo - ria in - mar - ce - si - ble! ¡Oh Jú - bi - lo in - mor -

tal __! En sur - cos de do - lo - res ¡El bien ger - mi - na __ ya __! ¡El __

bien ger - mi - na ya __! ¡Oh glo - ria in - mar - ce - si - ble!

¡Oh Jú - bi - lo in - mor - tal ___! En ___ sur - cos ___ de do - - lo - res ___ ¡El ___

bien ger - - mi - na   ya   ___.

Comoros

Jumhuriyat al-Qumur al-Itthadiyah al-Islamiyah

République Fédérale Islamique des Comores

(Federal Islamic Republic of the Comoros)

Quick Country Facts

Location: Eastern Africa, Middle of Indian Ocean

Area: 690 sq. mi. (2,170 sq. km.)

Population (2002 est.): 614,382

Capital/Largest City: Moroni (pop. 23,432)

Official Languages: Arabic, French, Shikomoro

GDP/PPP: $424 million, $710 per capita

Monetary Unit: Franc CFA

Udzima wa ya Masiwa

(The Union of the Great Islands)

Lyrics: Said Hachim Sidi Abderemane (b. 1942). Music: Kamildine Abdallah (1943-1982) and Said Hachim Sidi Abderemane (b. 1942). Adopted: 1978.

Shikomoro Words	French Words	English Translation
I béramu isi pépéza	Au faîte le Drapeau flotte	The flag is flying,
i nadi ukombozi piya	Appelle a là Liberté totale.	Announcing complete independence;
i daula ivénuha	La nation apparaît,	The nation rises up
tasiba bu ya i dini voya trangaya hunu	Force d'une même religion au sein	Because of the faith we have
Komoriya	des Comores.	In this our Comoria.
Narikéni na mahaba ya huveindza ya	Vivons dans l'amour réciproque dans	
Masiwa	nos îles.	
Yatruwasiwa Komoro damu ndzima	Les Comoriens issue de même sang,	Let us always have devotion
wasiwa Komoro dini ndzima	Nous embrassons la même idéologie	To love our great islands,
Ya masiwa radzali wa	religieuse.	We Comorians are of one blood,

ya masiwa yarileya	Les îles où nous somme nés!!	We Comorians are of one faith.
Mola né ari sayidiya	Les îles qui nous ont prodigués la	On these islands we were born,
Narikéni ha niya	bonne éducation.	These islands brought us up.
riveindzé uwataniya	Dieu y a apporté son aide.	May God always help us;
Mahaba ya dine na duniya.	Conservons notre unité pour l'amour	Let us always have the firm resolve
	de la patrie,	To love our fatherland,
	Amour pour la religion	Love our religion and the world.
	Et pour l'évolution.	
		The flag is flying,
I béramu isi pépéza	Au faîte le Drapeau flotte	From the Sixth of July;
rang mwési sita wa Zuiye	Depuis le 6 du mois de Juillet	The nation rises up
i daula ivénuha	La nation apparaît,	Our islands are lined up.
zisiwa zatru zi pangwi ha	Les îles devenues souveraines;	Maori and Anzuan, Moheli and
Maoré na Nzuani, Mwalina Ngaziya	Maore, N'Dzouani, Mouwali et	Gazidja,
Narikéni na mahaba.	N'Gazidja.	Let us always have devotion
ya huveindzar ya masiwa.	Gardons notre amour pour les îles.	To love our great islands.

Comoros

I béra- mu i-si pé-pé- za i na-di ukom-bo-zi pi-ya i dau- la i-vé-nu-

ha ta- si-ba bu ya i di- ni vo-ya tra-nga- ya hu-nu Ko-mo-ri- ya Na-ri-ké-

ni na ma-ha- ba ya hu-vein-dza ya Ma-si- wa Ya-tru

wa-si- wa Ko- mo- ro da-mu ndzi- ma wa-si- wa Ko-mo- ro di-ni ndzi- ma

148

Ya ma - si - wa ra - dza - li wa

ya ma - si - wa ya - ri - le - ya   Mo - la né a - ri sa - yi - di - ya

Na - ri - ké - ni ha ni - ya   ri - vein - dzé uwa - ta - ni ya   Ma - ha - ba ya di - ne na du - ni -

ya ___. I béra - mu i - si pé - pé - za ___ ra - ng mwési si - ta wa Zui - ye ___ i

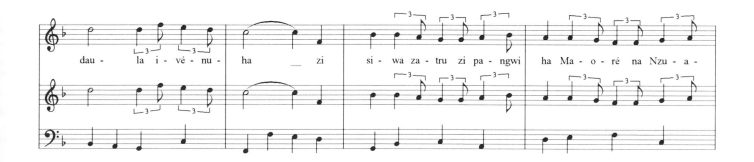

dau - la i - vé - nu - ha ___ zi si - wa za - tru zi pa - ngwi ha Ma - o - ré na Nzu - a -

Congo (Brazzaville)

République du Congo

(Republic of the Congo)

Quick Country Facts

Location: West Central Africa

Area: 132,046 sq. mi. (342,000 sq. km.)

Population (2002 est.): 2,958,448

Capital/Largest City: Brazzaville (pop. 937,580)

Official Language: French

GDP/PPP: $2.5 billion, $900 per capita

Monetary Unit: Franc CFA

La Congolaise

(Song of Congo)

Lyrics: Kimbangui Levent. Music: François Jacques Tondra. Adopted: 1962.

Historical Background

This anthem was adopted in 1962, after the country obtained independence from France. It was replaced nine years later when Congo switched to a socialist form of government. The song was restored in 1991.

French Words	English Translation
1	1
En ce jour, le soleil se lève	On this day the sun rises
Et notre Congo resplendit	And our Congo stands resplendent.
Une longue nuit s'achève	A long night is ended,
Un grand bonheur a surgi	A great happiness has come.
Chantons tous avec ivresse	Let us all, with wild joyfulness, sing
Le chante de la liberté.	The song of freedom.
CHORUS	CHORUS
Congolais debout fièrement partout	Arise, Congolese, proud every man,

Proclamons l'union de notre nation	Proclaim the unity of our nation.
Oublions ce qui nous divise	Let us forget what divides us
Soyons plus unis que jamais	And become more united than ever.
Vivons pour notre devise	Let us live our motto:
Unité, Travail, Progrès.	Unity, work, progress.
(repeat previous two lines)	(repeat previous two lines)

2

Des forêts jusqu'à la savane	From the forest to the bush,
Des savanes jusqu'à la mer	From the bush to the ocean,
Un seul peuple une seule âme	One people, one soul,
Un seul cœur ardent et fier	One heart, ardent and proud.
Luttons tous tant que nous sommes	Let us all fight, every one of us,
Pour notre vieux pays noir.	For our black country.

CHORUS

CHORUS

3

Et s'il nous faut mourir en somme	And if we have to die,
Qu'importe puisque nos enfants	What does it really matter? Our children
Partout pourront dire comme	Everywhere will be able to say how
On triomphe en combattant	Triumph comes through battle,
Et dans le moindre village	And in the smallest village
Chantent sous nos trois couleurs.	Sing beneath our three colors.

CHORUS

CHORUS

Congo (Brazzaville)

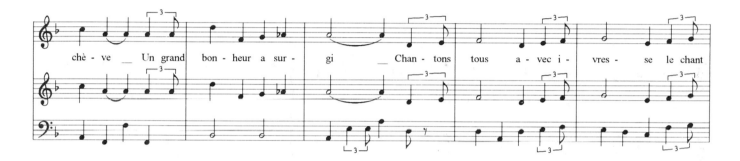

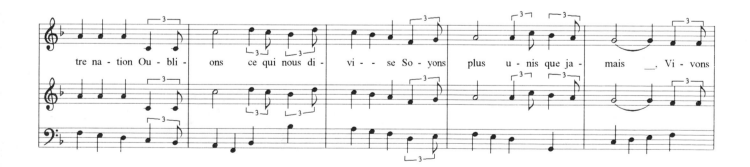

pour   no - tre de -   vi - - - se   U - ni -   té, Tra - vail, Pro -   grès ___ . Vi - vons pour   no - tre de -

vi - - - se U - ni -   té, Tra - vail, Pro -   grès ___ !

Congo (Kinshasa)

République Démocratique du Congo

(Democratic Republic of the Congo)

Quick Country Facts

Location: West Central Africa

Area: 905,365 sq. mi. (2,345,410 sq. km.)

Population (2002 est.): 55,225,478

Capital/Largest City: Kinshasa (pop. 6,050,000)

Official Language: French

GDP/PPP: $32 billion, $590 per capita

Monetary Unit: Congolese Franc

Debout Congolais

(Arise Congolese)

Lyrics: J. Lutumba. Music: S. Boka.

French Words	English Translation
Debout Congolais	Arise, Congolese, united by fate,
(repeat)	United in the struggle for independence,
Unis par le sort	Let us hold up our heads, so long bowed,
Unis dans l'effort pour l'indépendance	And now, for good, let us keep moving boldly ahead, in
Dressons nos fronts	peace.
Longtemps courbés	Oh, ardent people, by hard work we shall build,
Et pour de bon	In peace, a country more beautiful than before.
Prenons	Countrymen, sing the sacred hymn of your solidarity,
Le plus bel élan	Proudly salute the golden emblem of your sovereignty,
Dans la paix	Congo.
Ô peuple ardent	Blessed gift (Congo) of our forefathers (Congo),
Par le labeur	Oh (Congo) beloved country (Congo),
Nous bâtirons un pays plus beau qu'avant	We shall people your soil and ensure your greatness.
Dans la paix	(30th June) Oh gentle sun (30th June) of 30th June,

155

Citoyens,	(Sacred day) Be witness
Entonnez,	(Sacred day) Of the immortal oath of freedom
L'hymne sacré de notre solidarité	That we hand on to our children for ever.
Fièrement	
Saluez	
L'emblème d'or de votre souveraineté	
Congo	
Don béni, Congo	
Des aïeux, Congo	
O pays, Congo	
Bien aimé, Congo	
Nous peuplerons ton sol	
Et nous assurerons ta grandeur	
Trente juin, ô doux soleil	
Trente juin, du trente juin	
Jour sacré, sois le témoin	
Jour sacré de l'immortel serment de liberté	
Que nous léguons	
A notre postérité	
Pour toujours.	

Congo (Kinshasa)

157

Costa Rica

República de Costa Rica

(Republic of Costa Rica)

Quick Country Facts
Location: Central America
Area: 19,652 sq. mi. (51,100 sq. km.)
Population (2002 est.): 3,834,934
Capital/Largest City: San José (pop. 315,909)
Official Language: Spanish
GDP/PPP: $31.9 billion, $6,700 per capita
Monetary Unit: Colón

Himno Nacional

(National Anthem)

Lyrics: José Maria Zeledón Brenes (1877-1949). Music: Manuel María Gutiérrez (1829-1887). Adopted: 1949.

Historical Background[1]

In 1852, the governments of the United States and the United Kingdom accredited, for the first time, their diplomatic representatives in Costa Rica. President Juan Rafael Mora wanted to host a welcome ceremony for the two missions. Since Costa Rica did not have a national anthem at that time, Mora requested Manuel María Gutiérrez, Director of the Costa Rican National Army Orchestra, to compose the music of the national anthem to be performed at the welcome ceremony. The music of the national anthem was first played at the presidential palace (Casa de Gobierno) on 11 June 1852 at midnight. The music does not have a military connotation since it was composed to welcome two diplomatic missions. Instead, it evokes an act of union, solidarity, and peaceful agreements among nations. It conveys a patriotic feeling through which the country shows its identity and peaceful nature.

In 1903 there was a public contest for all Costa Rican citizens who wanted to write the national anthem. José María Zeledón Brenes won that contest. The anthem was sung and played for the first time on 15 September 1903.

In 1949 those words and music became the official national anthem. The words address the "campesinos"—farm workers—of the early twentieth century who laid the foundation of Costa Rica's democracy and development. They lived in the countryside, cultivated crops, raised horses and cattle. The greatness of "campesinos" was not based on their possessions but on the way they handled daily matters and conducted themselves. The blue sky and the fields were enough to find meaning in their lives. The hopes and dreams of Costa Rican people of that time depended on not only the future, strengthened by the efforts and success of the present, but also on the preservation of the traditions passed through generations.

Spanish Words	English Translation[2]
¡Noble patria! tu hermosa bandera	Noble country, our lives
expresión de tu vida nos da	Are revealed in your flying flag;
bajo el límpido azul de tu cielo	For in peace, white and pure, we live tranquil
blanca y pura descansa la paz	Beneath the clear limpid blue of your sky.
En la lucha tenaz, de fecunda labor	And their faces are ruddy with hard work
que enrojece del hombre la faz	In the fields beneath the life giving sun.
conquistaron tus hijos labriegos, sencillos	Though your sons are but farm workers, their labors
eterno prestigio, estima y honor	eternal
(repeat)	Esteem, renown, and honor have won.
	(repeat)
¡Salve oh tierra gentil!	Hail, oh land of our birth!
¡Salve oh madre de amor!	Hail, oh gracious land we love!
Cuando alguno pretenda tu gloria manchar	If an enemy seeking to slander you or
verás a tu pueblo valiente y viril	Harms your name, then we will abandon our farms
la tosca herramienta en arma trocar.	And arise with fervor to take up our arms.
¡Salve, oh patria! tu pródigo suelo	Oh, sweet country, our refuge and shelter;
dulce abrigo y sustento nos da	How fertile your life giving soil!
bajo el límpido azul de tu cielo	May your people contended and peaceful
¡vivan siempre el trabajo y la paz!	Unmolested continue their hard work.

Costa Rica

gos, sen - ci - llos e - ter - no pres - ti - gio, es - ti - ma y ho - nor e - ter - no pres - ti - gio, es - ti -

ma y ho - nor ¡Sal - ve oh tie - rra gen - til __! ¡Sal - ve oh ma -

dre de a - mor ___! Cuan - do al - gu - no pre - ten - da tu glo - ria man - char __ ve - rás

a tu pue - blo va - lien - te y vi - ril la __ tos - ca he - rra - mien - ta en ar - - ma tro - car.

Costa Rica

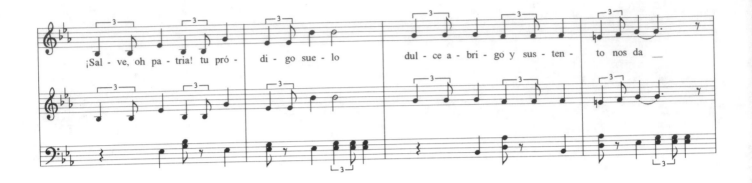

¡Sal - ve, oh pa - tria! tu pró - di - go sue - lo   dul - ce a - bri - go y sus - ten - to nos da

ba - jo el lím - pi - do a - zul   de tu cie - lo   ¡vi - van siem - pre el tra - ba - jo y la paz!

Côte d'Ivoire

République de la Côte d'Ivoire

(Republic of Côte d'Ivoire)

```
Quick Country Facts
Location: West Africa
Area: 124,502 sq. mi. (322,460 sq. km.)
Population (2002 est.): 16,804,784
Capital: Yamoussoukro (pop. 106,786)
Largest City: Abidjan (pop. 2,797,000)
Official Language: French
GDP/PPP: $25.5 billion, $1,550 per capita
Monetary Unit: Franc CFA
```

L'Abidjanaise

(Song of Abidjan)

Lyrics: Mathieu Ekra (b. 1917) with Joachim Bony. Music: Abbé Pierre Marie Pango (b. 1926). Adopted: 1960.

French Words	English Translation
VERSE	VERSE
Salut ô terre d'espérance	We salute you, o land of hope
Pays de l'hospitalité	Country of hospitality;
Tes légions remplies de vaillance	Your legions full of bravery
Ont relevé ta dignité	Have enhanced your dignity.
Tes fils chère Côte d'Ivoire	Dear Côte d'Ivoire, your sons,
Fiers artisans de ta grandeur	Proud builders of your greatness,
Tous rassemblés pour ta gloire	All together and for your glory,
Te bâtiront dans le bonheur.	Shall, in joy, build you up.
CHORUS	CHORUS
Fiers Ivoiriens, le pays nous appelle	Proud Ivorians
Si nous avons dans la paix ramené la liberté	The country needs us.

Notre devoir sera d'être un modèle De l'espérance promise à l'humanité En forgeant unis dans la foi nouvelle La patrie de la vraie fraternité.	If, in peace we have Brought liberty back, Our duty is to be a model Of the hope promised to humanity, In forging united in the new faith The fatherland of true brotherhood.

Côte d'Ivoire

Sa - lut ô ter - re d'es - pé - ran - ce Pa - ys de l'hos - pi - ta - li - té

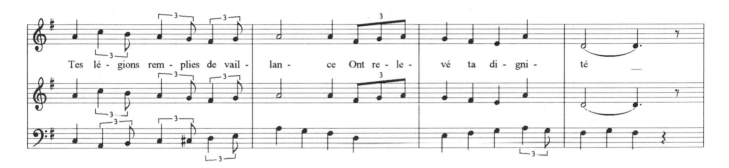

Tes lé - gions rem - plies de vail - lan - ce Ont re - le - vé ta di - gni - té

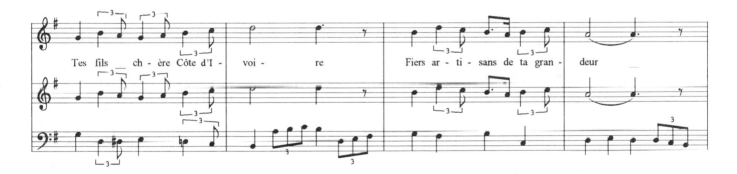

Tes fils ch - ère Côte d'I - voi - re Fiers ar - ti - sans de ta gran - deur

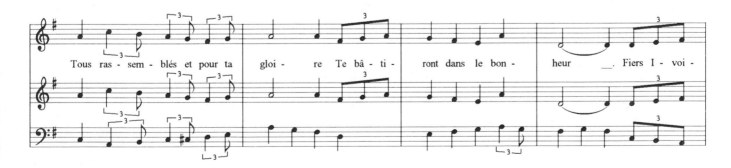

Tous ras - sem - blés et pour ta gloi - re Te bâ - ti - ront dans le bon - heur __. Fiers I - voi -

riens, le pa - ys nous ap - pel - - le Si __ nous a - vons dans la paix ra - me - né la li - ber - té No - tre de -

voir se - - ra d'être un mo - dè - - le De l'es - pé - ran - ce __ pro - mise à l'hu - ma - ni - té En for - geant

u - nis __ dans la foi nou - vel - - le La pa - trie de la vraie fra - ter - ni - té __

Croatia

Republike Hrvatske

(Republic of Croatia)

```
Quick Country Facts
Location: Eastern Europe, Balkan Peninsula
Area: 21,829 sq. mi. (56,542 sq. km.)
Population (2002 est.): 4,390,751
Capital/Largest City: Zagreb (pop. 930,753)
Official Language: Croatian
GDP/PPP: $38.9 billion, $8,800 per capita
Monetary Unit: Kuna
```

Lijepa naša domovino

(Our Beautiful Homeland)

Lyrics: Antun Mihanović (1796-1861). Music: Josip Runjanin (1821-1878). Adopted: 1891.

Historical Background[1]

The words to the Croatian national anthem were written by Antun Mihanović. They were first printed in *Danica* (*The Morning Star*) magazine in 1835, under the title "Hrvatska domovina" ("Croatian Homeland"). The music was composed later (1840s) by Josip Runjanin, a Croatian Serb, on the basis of Donizetti's "O sole piu ratto" from the opera "Lucia di Lammermoor." Later, in 1861, the score went through some minor changes done by V. Lichtenegger. In 1891 the song was first sung as the national anthem at an exhibition held by the Croatian-Slavonian Economic Society in Zagreb. It was readopted a year before Croatia achieved independence from Yugoslavia in December 1990. Only the first and last verses are used officially.

Croatian Words	English Translation[2]
1	1
Lijepa naša domovino,	Beautiful is our homeland,
Oj junačka zemljo mila,	Oh so fearless, oh so gracious,
Stare slave djedovino,	Our fathers' ancient glory,
Da bi vazda sretna bila!	May God bless you, live forever!

Mila, kano si nam slavna,	Yes, you are our only glory,
Mila si nam ti jedina,	Yes, you are our only treasure,
Mila, kuda si nam ravna,	We love your plains and valleys,
Mila, kuda si planina!	We love your hills and mountains.
2	2
Teci, Savo Dravo, teci	Sava, Drava, keep on flowing,
Nit ti Dunaj silju gubi,	Danube, do not lose your vigor,
Sinje more, svijetu reci:	Deep blue sea go tell the whole world,
Da svog narod Hrvat ljubi,	That a Croat loves his homeland.
Dok mu njive sunce grije,	When his fields are kissed by sunshine,
Dok mu hrastje bura vije,	When his oaks are whipped by wild winds,
Dok mu mrtve grob sakrije,	When his dear ones go to heaven,
Dok mu živo srce bije!	Still his heart beats for Croatia!

Croatia

Cuba

República de Cuba

(Republic of Cuba)

Quick Country Facts
Location: North America, Caribbean Sea
Area: 42,843 sq. mi. (110,860 sq. km.)
Population (2002 est.): 11,224,321
Capital/Largest City: Havana (pop. 2,241,000)
Official Language: Spanish
GDP/PPP: $25.9 billion, $2,300 per capita
Monetary Unit: Peso

La Bayamesa

(The Bayamo Song)

Lyrics and Music: Pedro Figueredo (1818-1870). Adopted: 1902.

Historical Background

The national anthem of Cuba, formerly known as "Llamado Himno de Bayamo" ("Rallying Hymn of Bayamo"), was the work of lawyer and musician Pedro Figueredo. After composing the music in 1867, he wrote the lyrics on 20 October 1868, when rebel troops struggling against Spanish rule, of which he was an active member, occupied his hometown Bayamo, only to be driven out days later. The song was sung for the first time that same year.

Spanish Words	English Translation
VERSE	VERSE
Al combate corred Bayameses	Hasten to battle, men of Bayamo,
Que la patria os contempla orgullosa;	For the homeland looks proudly to you.
No temáis una muerte gloriosa	You do not fear a glorious death,
Que morir por la patria es vivir.	Because to die for the country is to live.

CHORUS	CHORUS
En cadenas vivir es vivir.	To live in chains
En afrenta y oprobio sumido.	Is to live in dishonor and ignominy.
Del clarín escuchad el sonido,	Hear the clarion call,
¡A las armas valientes corred!	Hasten, brave ones, to battle!
(repeat chorus)	(repeat chorus)

Cuba

Al com- ba- te co- rred Ba- ya-

me- ses Que la Pa- tria os con- tem- pla or- gu- llo- sa; No te- máis u- na

muer- te glo- rio- sa Que mo- rir por la pa- tria es vi- vir. En ca- de- nas vi-

vir, es vi - vir. En a - fren - ta y o - pro - bio su - mi - do __. Del cla - rín es - cu -

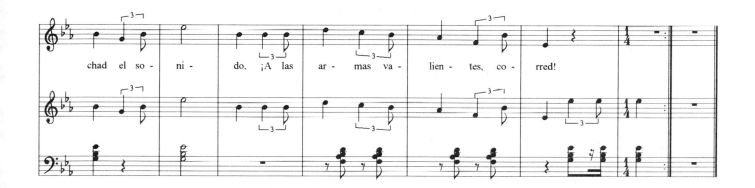

chad el so - ni - do, ¡A las ar - mas va - lien - tes, co - rred!

Cyprus

Κυπριακή Δημοκρατία

Kypriaki Dimokratia

Kibris Cumhuriyeti

(Republic of Cyprus)

Quick Country Facts

Location: Western Asia, Mediterranean Sea

Area: 3,572 sq. mi. (9,250 sq. km.)

Population (2002 est.): 767,314

Capital/Largest City: Nikosia (pop. 186,400)

Official Language: Greek, Turkish

GDP/PPP: $11 billion, $12,000 per capita

Monetary Unit: Cyprus Pound

Ύμνος εις την Ελευθερίαν

Ymnos eis tin Eleftherian

(Hymn to Freedom)

Lyrics: Dionysios Solomos (1798-1857). Music: Nikolaos Mantzaros (1795-1872). Adopted: 1960.

Historical Background[1]

Cyprus has the same national anthem as Greece. It is based on the "Hymn to the Freedom," a large—158 strophes—poem written by the poet Dionysios Solomos, from Zakynthos Island, in 1823. The song was inspired by the Greek Revolution of 1821 against the Ottoman Empire. During 1828, the eminent musician from Kerkyra Island Nikolaos Mantzaros composed the music for Solomos's hymn. In 1960, after Cyprus gained independence, the Greeks on the island, anticipating union with Greece, adopted this anthem. Recently, the government considered a new anthem but met with furious opposition on the part of the Greek Cypriots and disapproval from the Turks in the northern part of the country.

Greek Words (First Verse, 158 Total)	Greek Words (Transliteration, First Verse, 158 Total)	English Translation (First Verse, 158 Total) [2]
Σε γνωρίζω από την κόψη	*Se gnoriso apo tin kopsi.*	We knew thee of old,
του σπαθιού την τρομερή,	*Tou spathiou tin tromeri,*	Oh, divinely restored,
σε γνωρίζω από την όψη	*Se gnoriso apo tin opsi*	By the lights of thine eyes
που με βία μετράει τη γη.	*Pou me via metra tin yi.*	And the light of thy sword
Απ' τα κόκαλα βγαλμένη	*Ap' ta kokala vialmeni*	From the graves of our slain
των Ελλήνων τα ιερά,	*Ton Ellinon ta iera,*	Shall thy valor prevail
και σαν πρώτα ανδρειωμένη,	*Ke san prota andriomeni,*	As we greet thee again-
χαίρε, ω χαίρε, Ελευθεριά!	*Haire, o haire, Eleftheria!*	Hail, liberty! Hail!
(repeat previous two lines two times)	(repeat previous two lines two times)	(repeat previous two lines two times)

Cyprus

Se gno- ri- so a- po tin kop- si. Tou spa- thiou tin tro- me- ri, Se- gno-

ri- so a- po tin op- si Pou me via me- tra tin yi. Ap' ta ko- ka- la vial-

me- ni Ton El- li- non ta ie- ra, Ke san prota an- dri- o- me- ni, Hai- re, o

hai- re, E- lef- th- ria! Ke san prota an- dri- o- me- ni, hai- re, o hai- re, E- lef- the-

ria __! Ke san prota an - dri - o - me - ni, Hai - re, o hai - re, E - lef - the - ria __!

Czech Republic

České Republiky

```
┌─────────────────────────────────────────────┐
│            Quick Country Facts                │
│                                               │
│  Location: Central Europe                     │
│  Area: 30,464 sq. mi. (78,866 sq. km.)        │
│  Population (2000 est.): 10,256,760           │
│  Capital/Largest City: Prague (pop. 1,215,771)│
│  Official Language: Czech                     │
│  GDP/PPP: $155.9 billion, $15,300 per capita  │
│  Monetary Unit: Koruna                        │
└─────────────────────────────────────────────┘
```

Kde domov můj?

(Where Is My Home?)

Lyrics: Josef Kajetán Tyl (1808-1856). Music: František Jan Škroup (1801-1862). Adopted: 1919.

Historical Background[1]

The music to the anthem was composed by František Jan Škroup, a main Revivalist composer of Czech music, and, especially, Czech opera. From 1827 to 1860 he worked as a conductor in the Stavovské theatre. His biggest successes were the singspiel "Dráteník" ("Tinker") and the operas "Oldrich," "Bozena," and "Libušin snatek" ("Marriage of Libuše"). This song was taken from the first stanza of the opera Fidlovačka, which was written by Josef Kajetán Tyl and performed in 1834. It became the first part of the Czechoslovak state anthem after the country's liberation in 1918. Upon dissolution of Czechoslovakia on 1 January 1993, the song became the anthem of the new Czech Republic.

Czech Words	English Translation
Kde domov můj, kde domov můj?	Where is my home, where is my home?
Voda hučí po lučinách,	Water bubbles across the meadows,
bory šumí po skalinách,	Pinewoods rustle among crags,
v sadě skví se jara květ,	The garden is glorious with spring blossom,
Zemský ráj to na pohled;	Paradise on earth it is to see.
a to je ta krásná země,	And this is that beautiful land,
země česká, domov můj.	The Czech land, my home.
(repeat)	(repeat)

Czech Republic

Kde __ do - mov můj? Kde __ do - mov můj __? Vo - da hu - čí __ po lu - či - nách __, bo - ry

šu - - mí __ po __ ska - li - nách __, v sa - dě skví __ se ja - ra květ __, Zem - ský ráj __ to na po -

hled __; a to je ta krá - - sná ze - - mě __, ze - mě če - ská __, do - mov můj __. Ze - mě

če - ská __, do - mov můj __!

Denmark

Kongeriget Danmark

(Kingdom of Denmark)

```
                    Quick Country Facts
Location: Northern Europe, Scandinavia
Area: 16,833 sq. mi. (43,094 sq. km.)
Population (2002 est.): 5,368,854
Capital/Largest City: Copenhagen (pop. 1,339,395)
Official Language: Danish
GDP/PPP: $155.5 billion, $29,000 per capita
Monetary Unit: Krone
```

Der er et Yndigt Land

(A Lovely Land Is Ours)

Lyrics: Adam Gottlob Oehlenschläger (1779-1850). Music: Hans Ernst Krøyer (1798-1879).

Historical Background[1]

Denmark is in the peculiar situation that it actually has two officially recognized national anthems. To celebrate the country itself, the Danes use "Der er et yndigt land." The text of this national anthem was written by the Danish poet Adam Gottlob Oehlenschläger in 1820 and the melody was composed by Hans Ernst Krøyer in 1823. It has been used since 1844.

Danish Words	English Translation[2]
1	1
Der er et yndigt land,	I know a lovely land
det står med brede bøge	With spreading, shady beeches
nær salten østerstrand;	Near Baltic's salty strand;
(repeat)	(repeat)
det bugter sig i bakke, dal,\	Its hills and valleys gently fall,

det hedder gamle Danmark,
og det er Frejas Sal
(repeat)

2
Der sad i fordums tid
de harniskklædte kæmper,
udhvilede fra strid;
(repeat)
så drog de frem til fjenders mén
nu hvile deres bene
bag højens bautasten
(repeat)

3
Det land endnu er skønt,
thi blå sig søen bælter,
og løvet står så grønt;
(repeat)
og ædle kvinder, skønne mø'r
og mænd og raske svende
bebo de danskes øer
(repeat)

4
Hil drot og fædreland!
Hil hver en danneborger,
som virker, hvad han kan!
(repeat)
Vort gamle Danmark skal bestå,
så længe bøgen spejler
sin top i bølgen blå
(repeat)

Its ancient name is Denmark,
And it is Freya's hall
(repeat)

2
There in the ancient days
The armored Vikings rested
Between their bloody frays
(repeat)
Then they went forth the foe to face,
Now found in stone-set barrows,
Their final resting place
(repeat)

3
This land is still as fair,
The sea is blue around it,
And peace is cherished there.
(repeat)
Strong men and noble women still
Uphold their country's honor
With faithfulness and skill
(repeat)

4
Praise king and country with might
Bless every Dane at heart
For serving with no fright
(repeat)
The Viking kingdom for Danes is true
With fields and waving beeches
By a sea so blue
(repeat)

Denmark (De er et yndigt land)

Kong Christian Stod ved Højen Mast

(King Christian Stood by Tow'ring Mast)

Lyrics: Johannes Ewald (1743-1781). Music: Friedrich Kuhlau (1786-1832).

Historical Background[3]

"Kong Kristian" is also a national anthem but it is mostly considered the anthem of the Danish royal family. It is used in connection with state visits, naval visits, military sport arrangements and events in which a member of a foreign or the Danish Government is present. The text was written by Johannes Ewald in 1780, and the melody used presently was composed by Friedrich Kulau in 1828. The national anthem dates approximately from 1830.

Danish Words	English Translation[4]
1	1
Kong Kristian stod ved højen mast	King Christian stood by tow'ring mast,
i røg og damp;	In mist and smoke.
hans værge hamrede så fast,	His sword was hammering so fast,
at gotens hjelm og hjerte brast.	Through Gothic helm and brain it passed
Da sank hvert fjendtligt spejl og mast	Then sank each hostile stern and mast
i røg og damp.	In mist and smoke
Fly, skreg de, fly, hvad flygte kan!	"Fly!" shouted they, "fly, he who can,
hvo står for Danmarks Kristian	Who stands 'gainst Denmark's Christian
(repeat)	(repeat)
i kamp?	in fray?"
2	2
Niels Juel gav agt på stormens brag.	Niels Juel observ'd the tempest's blow:
Nu er det tid.	"Now! For your life!"
Han hejsede det røde flag	Aloft he bade the red flag go,
og slog på fjenden slag i slag.	And stroke on stroke he dealt the foe.
Da skreg de højt blandt stormens brag:	They cried then tro' the tempest's blow:
Nu er det tid!	"Now! For your life!
Fly, skreg de, hver, som véd et skjul!	Fly!" cried they all, "for shelter fly!
hvo kan bestå mod Danmarks Juel	For who can Denmark's Juel defy
(repeat)	(repeat)
i strid?	in strife?"
3	3
O, Nordhav! Glimt af Wessel brød	North Sea, a glimpse of Wessel rent

din mørke sky.

Da ty'de kæmper til dit skød;

thi med ham lynte skræk og død.

Fra vallen hørtes vrål, som brød

den tykke sky.

Fra Danmark lyner Tordenskjold;

hver give sig i himlens vold

(repeat)

og fly!

4

Du danskes vej til ros og magt,

sortladne hav!

Modtag din ven, som uforsagt

tør møde faren med foragt

så stolt som du mod stormens magt,

sortladne hav!

Og rask igennem larm og spil

og kamp og sejer før mig til

(repeat)

min grav!

Thy murky sky!

Then champions to thine arms were sent;

Terror and Death glared where he went;

From the waves was heard a wail that rent

Thy murky sky:

From Denmark thunders Tordenskiol',

"Let each to Heaven commend his soul,

(repeat)

And fly!"

4

Thou path of Danes to praise and might,

Black-surging sea!

Receive thy friend, who feels no fright,

But faces danger with despite,

As proud as thou the tempest's might,

Black-surging sea!

And lead me brisk thro' din and rave,

And fright and vict'ry to my grave

(repeat)

in thee.

Denmark (Kong Kristian Stod ved Højen Mast)

Djibouti

Jumhouriyya Djibouti

(Republic of Djibouti)

Quick Country Facts

Location: Northeast Africa

Area: 8,878 sq. mi. (23,000 sq. km.)

Population (2002 est.): 472,810

Capital/Largest City: Djibouti (pop. 395,000)

Languages: Arabic, French, Somali, Afar

GDP/PPP: $586 million, $1,400 per capita

Monetary Unit: Djibouti Franc

National Anthem

Lyrics: Aden Elmi (b. 1950). Music: Abdi Robleh (b. 1945). Adopted: 1977.

Transliteration	English Translation
Hinjinne u sara kaca	Arise with strength; for we have raised our flag,
Calankaan haraad iyo	The flag which has cost us dear
Haydaar u mudateen.	With extremes of thirst and pain.
Hir cagaarku qariyayiyo	Our flag, whose colors are the everlasting green of the earth,
Habkay samadu tahayoo	
Xiddig dhi igleh hoorshoo	The blue of the sky, and white, the color of peace;
Cadaan lagu hadheeyaay.	And the center the red star of blood.
Maxaa haybad kugu yall.	Oh flag of ours, what a glorious sight!

Djibouti

187

Dominica

Commonwealth of Dominica

Quick Country Facts
Location: North America, Caribbean Sea
Area: 290 sq. mi. (754 sq. km.)
Population (2000 est.): 70,158
Capital/Largest City: Roseau (pop. 15,853)
Languages: English, French patois
GDP/PPP: $262 million, $3,700 per capita
Monetary Unit: East Caribbean Dollar

Isle of Beauty, Isle of Splendor

Lyrics: Wilfred Oscar Morgan Pond (1912-1985). Music: Lemuel McPherson Christian (b. 1913). Adopted: 1967.

Historical Background

This song was adopted when Dominica achieved statehood status within the British Commonwealth in 1967 and retained upon independence in 1978.

Words		
1	2	3
Isle of beauty, isle of splendor,	Dominica, God hath blest thee	Come ye forward, sons and daughters
Isle to all so sweet and fair,	With a clime benign and bright,	Of this gem beyond compare.
All must surely gaze in wonder	Pastures green and flowers of beauty	Strive for honor, sons and daughters,
At thy gifts so rich and rare.	Filling all with pure delight,	Do the right, be firm, be fair.
Rivers, valleys, hills and mountains,	And a people strong and healthy,	Toil with hearts and hands and voices.
All these gifts we do extol.	Full of godly, rev'rent fear.	We must prosper! Sound the call,
Healthy land, so like all fountains,	May we ever seek to praise Thee	In which ev'ry one rejoices,
Giving cheer that warms the soul.	For these gifts so rich and rare.	"All for Each and Each for All."

Dominica

Isle of ___ beau - ty, isle of ___ splen - dor, Isle to all so sweet and

fair ___, All must ___ sure - ly gaze in ___ won - der At thy gifts so rich and rare ___.

Ri - vers ___, val - leys, hills and ___ moun - tains, All these gifts we do ex - - tol. Heal - thy ___ land, so

like all ___ foun - tains, Giv - ing ___ cheer that warms the soul.

189

Dominican Republic

República Dominicana

```
Quick Country Facts

Location: North America, Hispaniola

Area: 18,704 sq. mi. (48,730 sq. km.)

Population (2002 est.): 8,721,594

Capital/Largest City: Santo Domingo (pop. 2,100,000)

Official Language: Spanish

GDP/PPP: $50 billion, $5,800 per capita

Monetary Unit: Peso
```

Himno Nacional

(National Anthem)

Lyrics: Emilio Prud'homme (1856-1932). Music: José Reyés (1835-1905). Adopted: 1934.

Historical Background

The original idea for this song came from José Reyés, who was inspired by a copy of the Argentine national anthem published in the Parisian magazine *The American*. Reyés believed that his country should also have its own national song. So, in 1883, he invited his friend Emilio Prud'homme to write the lines while composing the music himself. The first versions of Prud'homme's verses appeared on 16 August of that year in *El Eco de la Opinion*, a magazine of Santo Domingo. The next day, the song was played during a celebration of the national press at the Logia Esperanza. It was well received by the public and, gradually, its fame spread. In 1897, the periodical *El Teléfono* published a revised edition of Prud'homme's verses, made by the author himself, since the first version was written when he was an inexperienced 27 year old.

Acting on a motion by deputy Rafael García Martinez, the National Congress adopted a resolution on 7 June 1897 to give the song official status. However, President Ulises Heureaux refused to sign it into law, probably because of Prud'homme's disagreement with his dictatorial government. It was not until 30 May 1934 that the president of the Dominican Republic, Rafael Leonidas Trujillo Molina, by means of Law number 700, adopted officially this song as the national anthem.

Spanish Words (First Two Verses of Six)	English Translation (First Two Verses of Six)
1	**1**
Quisqueyanos valientes, alcemos	Brave men of Quisqueya,
Nuestro canto con viva emoción,	Let us sing with strong feeling
Y del mundo a la faz ostentemos	And let us show to the world
Nuestro invicto, glorioso pendón.	Our invincible, glorious banner.
¡Salve! el pueblo que, intrépido y fuerte.	Hail, O people who, strong and intrepid,
A la guerra a morir se lanzó,	Launched into war and went to death!
Cuando en bélico reto de muerte	Under a warlike menace of death,
Sus cadenas de esclavo rompió.	You broke your chains of slavery.
2	**2**
Ningún pueblo ser libre merece	No country deserves to be free
Si es esclavo, indolente y servil;	If it is an indolent and servile slave,
Si en su pecho la llama no crece	If the call does not grow loud within it,
Que templó el heroísmo viril.	Tempered by a virile heroism.
Mas Quisqueya la indómita y brava	But the brave and indomitable Quisqueya
Siempre altiva la frente alzará,	Will always hold its head high,
Que si fuere mil veces esclava	For if it were a thousand times enslaved,
Otras tantas ser libre sabrá.	It would a thousand times regain freedom.

Dominican Republic

Quis - que - ya - nos va - lien - tes, al - ce - mos Nues - tro can - to __ con vi - va e - mo -

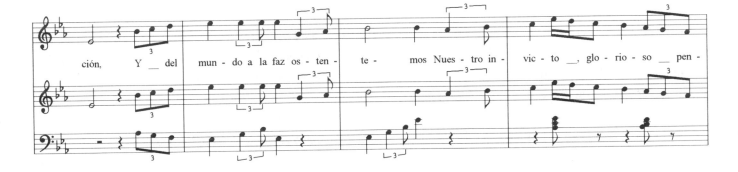

ción, Y __ del mun - do a la faz os - ten - te - mos Nues - tro in - vic - to __, glo - rio - so __ pen -

dón __. ¡Sal - ve! el pue - blo que, in - tré - pi - do y fuer - te. A la gue - rra a mo - rir se lan -

zó __, Cuan - do en bé - li - co re - to de muer - te Sus ca - de - nas de es - cla - vo rom -

tan - tas ser li - bre sa - brá

Ecuador

República del Ecuador

(Republic of Ecuador)

```
Quick Country Facts
Location: South America
Area: 106,822 sq. mi. (283,560 sq. km.)
Population (2002 est.): 13,447,494
Capital: Quito (pop. 1,500,000)
Largest City: Guayaquil (pop. 2,000,000)
Official Language: Spanish
GDP/PPP: $39.6 billion, $3,000 per capita
Monetary Unit: Sucre
```

Salve, O Patria

(Hail, O Fatherland)

Lyrics: Juán León Mera (1832-1894). Music: Antonio Neumane (1818-1871). Adopted: 1948.

Historical Background

The text of the national anthem is a poem that was written by the Ecuadorian writer and essayist Juán León Mera in 1865. It was set to music by Antonio Neumane the following year. The poem itself consists of seven verses. In highly formal settings, the second and third verses are played, with the second verse repeated at the end. In informal settings, only the second verse is used.

Spanish Words	English Translation
CHORUS	CHORUS
¡Salve oh Patria, mil veces!	Hail, oh Fatherland! A thousand times, hail!
¡Oh Patria, gloria a ti! ¡Gloria a ti!	Glory unto thee! With peace and joy,
Y a tu pecho, tu pecho rebosa	Your breast swells, and thy glorious face
Gozo y paz, y a tu pecho rebosa;	Shines brighter than the sun.
Y tu frente, tu frente radiosa	
Mas que el sol contemplamos lucir.	

(repeat previous two lines)

1

Los primeros los hijos del suelo
Que el soberbio; el Pichincha decora
Te aclamaron por siempre señora
Y vertieron su sangre por ti.
Dios miró y aceptó el holocausto,
Y esa sangre fue germen fecundo
De otros héroes; que atónito el mundo
Vio en tu torno a millares surgir.
a millares surgir.
(repeat)

CHORUS

2

De estos héroes al brazo de hierro
Nada tuvo invencible la tierra,
Y del valle a la altísima sierra
Se escuchaba el fragor de la lid;
Tras la lid la victoria volaba.
Libertad tras el triunfo venía.
Y al león destrozado se oía,
De impotencia y despecho rugir.
y despecho rugir.
(repeat)

CHORUS

(repeat 1)

1

The first children of this land,
Which mantles supreme, Pichincha
As their motherland, they forever acclaimed
And shed their blood for thee.
God saw, and accepted this holocaust,
And their blood was the fertile seed
For other heroes who the astonished world,
Would see, by the thousands rally unto thee.

CHORUS

2

For these steel armed heroes
Nothing in the land was invincible
And from the valley to the high Sierra
Could the clamor of the struggle be heard;
After the struggle, victory came flying.
And freedom followed on victory's heel.
And the toppled lion could be heard,
As it roared in impotence and vanity.

CHORUS

(repeat 1)

Ecuador

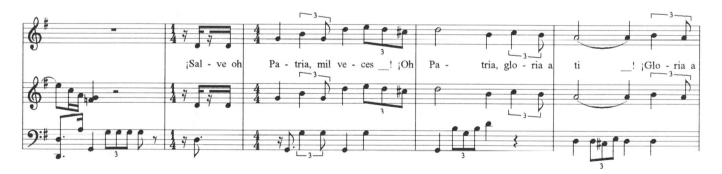

¡Sal - ve oh Pa - tria, mil ve - ces __! ¡Oh Pa - tria, glo - ria a ti __! ¡Glo - ria a

ti __! Y a tu pe - cho, tu pe - cho __ re - bo - sa Go - zo y paz, y a tu pe - cho __ re -

197

bo - sa; Y tu fr* - te __, tu fren - te ra - dio - sa Mas que el sol con - tem - pla - mos lu -

cir. Y tu fren - te, tu fren - te ra - dio - sa Mas que el sol con - tem - pla - mos lu -

cir. Los pri - me - ros los hi - jos del sue - lo Que el so - ber - bio; el Pi - chin - cha de -

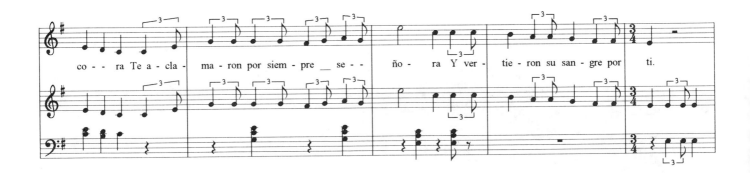

co - ra Te a - cla - ma - ron por siem - pre __ se - ño - ra Y ver - tie - ron su san - gre por ti.

Dios mi - ró y a - cep - tó el ho - lo - ca - - us - to, Y e - sa san - gre fue ger - - men fe -

cun - - do De o - tros hé - roes que a - tó - ni - to el mun - - do Vio en tu tor - no a mi - lla - res sur -

gir. a mi - lla - res sur - gir. a mi - lla - res sur -

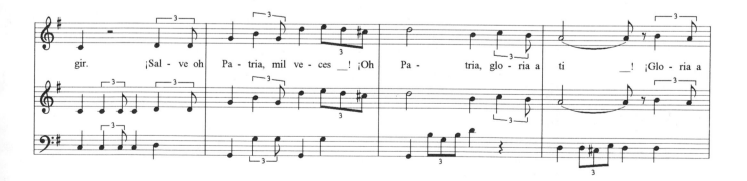

gir. ¡Sal - ve oh Pa - tria, mil ve - ces __! ¡Oh Pa - tria, glo - ria a ti __! ¡Glo - ria a

ti!   Y a tu   pe - cho, tu pe - cho __ re -   bo -   sa   Go - zo y   paz, y a tu pe - cho __ re -

bo -   sa;   Y tu   fren - te __, tu fren - te ra - dio -   sa   Mas que el   sol con - tem - pla - mos lu -

cir __.   Y tu   fren - te, tu fren - te ra -   dio -   sa   Mas que el   sol con - tem - pla - mos lu -

cir.

Egypt

جمهورية مصر العربية

Jumhuriyah Misr al-Arabiyah

(Arab Republic of Egypt)

```
Quick Country Facts
Location: Northeast Africa, Middle East
Area: 386,900 sq. mi. (1,001,450 sq. km.)
Population (2002 est.): 70,712,345
Capital/Largest City: Cairo (pop. 14,350,000)
Official Language: Arabic
GDP/PPP: $258 billion, $3,700 per capita
Monetary Unit: Egyptian Pound
```

بلادى

Biladi

(My Homeland)

Lyrics and Music: Sayed Darwish (1892-1923). Adopted: 1979.

Historical Background[1]

The words and music to the national anthem of Egypt were written by Sayed Darwish, one of the pioneers of Arabic music and a leader of the modern Egyptian renaissance at the turn of the previous century. As a vanguard of innovation, he liberated music from its obsolete forms. During his lifetime, Darwish wrote many patriotic songs and maintained close ties with early leaders of the national movement for independence in the Middle East, like Saad Zaghloul and Mustapha Kamel Artatürk. In fact, the words of Egypt's national anthem were derived from one of Kamel's most famous speeches.

Arabic Words	Arabic Words (Transliteration)	English Translation[2]
بلادى بـــــلادى بـــلادى	*Biladi Biladi Biladi*	My homeland, my homeland, my hallowed land,
لـــك حـــبى وفـــــؤادى	*Laki Hubbi Wa Fuadi*	Only to you, is my due hearty love at command.
(repeat previous two lines)	(repeat previous two lines)	(repeat previous two lines)
مصر يـــــا أم البـــــلاد	*Misr Ya Umm Al Bilad*	Mother of the great ancient land,
أنـــت غـــــايتى والمـــراد	*Inti Ghayati Wal Murad*	My sacred wish and holy demand,
وعلى كـــــل العبـــــاد	*Wa 'Ala Kul Il 'Ibad*	All should love, awe and cherish thee.
كم لديلـــــك مـن أيـــاد	*Kam Lineelik Min Ayadi.*	Gracious is thy Nile to humanity.
بلادى بـــــلادى بـــلادى	*Biladi Biladi Biladi*	My homeland, my homeland, my hallowed land,
لـــك حـــبى وفـــــؤادى	*Laki Hubbi Wa Fuadi*	Only to you, is my due hearty love at command.

Egypt

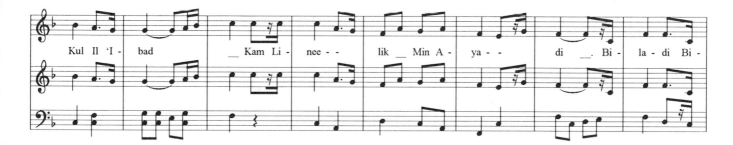

203

Egypt

la - di __ Bi - la - - di La - ki Hu - bbi __ Wa Fu - a - - di

El Salvador

República de El Salvador

(Republic of El Salvador)

```
Quick Country Facts
Location: Central America
Area: 8,260 sq. mi. (21,040 sq. km.)
Population (2002 est.): 6,353,681
Capital/Largest City: San Salvador (pop. 972,810)
Official Language: Spanish
GDP/PPP: $28.4 billion, $4,600 per capita
Monetary Unit: Colón
```

Himno Nacional

(National Anthem)

Lyrics: Juan José Cañas (1826-1918). Music: Juan Aberle (1846-1930). Adopted: 1953.

Historical Background

The music to this anthem was composed by Juan Aberle, an Italian songwriter who came to El Salvador during the late nineteenth century to direct an orchestral group. The words were written by General Juan José Cañas. The two cooperated in producing this work at the recommendation of presidential doctor Rafael Zaldívar. The song was sung for the first time on 15 September 1879 in front of the old National Palace in the capital San Salvador by a group of schoolchildren.

Spanish Words	English Translation
CHORUS	CHORUS
Saludemos la patria orgullosos	Let us salute the motherland,
De hijos suyos podernos llamar;	Proud to be called her children.
Y juremos la vida animosos,	To her well-being let us swear
Sin descanso a su bien consagrar.	Boldly and unceasingly to devote our lives.
(repeat previous four lines)	(repeat previous four lines)
Consagrar, consagrar, consagrar, consagrar.	Our lives, our lives, our lives, our lives.

1	**1**
De la paz en la dicha suprema,	Of peace enjoyed in perfect happiness,
Siempre noble soñó El Salvador;	El Salvador has always nobly dreamed.
Fue obtenerla su eterno problema,	To achieve this has been her eternal proposition,
Conservarla es su gloria mayor.	To keep it, her greatest glory.
Y con fe inquebrantable el camino	With inviolable faith, she eagerly follows
Del progreso se afana en seguir	The way of progress
Por llenar su grandioso destino,	In order to fulfill her high destiny
Conquistarse un feliz porvenir.	And achieve a happy future.
Le protege una férrea barrera	A stern barrier protects her
Contra el choque de ruin deslealtad,	Against the clash of vile disloyalty,
Desde el día que en su alta bandera	Ever since the day when her lofty banner,
Con su sangre escribió: ¡LIBERTAD!	In letters of blood, wrote "FREEDOM,"
¡Escribió libertad! ¡escribió libertad!	Wrote "freedom," wrote "freedom."
CHORUS	CHORUS
2	**2**
Libertad es su dogma, es su guía,	Freedom is her dogma and her guide;
Que mil veces logró defender;	A thousand times she has defended it,
Y otras tantas de audaz tiranía	And as many times has she repelled
Rechazar el odioso poder.	The hateful power of atrocious tyranny.
Dolorosa y sangrienta es su historia,	Her history has been bloody and sad,
Pero excelsa y brillante a la vez;	Yet at the same time sublime and brilliant,
Manantial de legítima gloria,	A source of legitimate glory
Gran lección de espartana altivez.	And a great lesson in Spartan pride.
No desmaya en su innata bravura,	Her innate bravery shall not waver:
En cada hombre hay un héroe inmortal	In every man there is an immortal hero
Que sabrá mantenerse a la altura	Who knows how to maintain the level
De su antiguo valor proverbial.	Of the proverbial valor of old.
Valor proverbial, valor proverbial.	Valor of old, valor of old.
CHORUS	CHORUS
3	**3**
Todos son abnegados y fieles	All are self-denying and faithful
Al prestigio del bélico ardor	To the tradition of warlike ardor
Con que siempre segaron laureles	With which they have always reaped fame
De la patria salvando el honor.	By saving the motherland's honor.

Respetar los derechos extraños	To respect the rights of others
Apoyarse en la recta razón	And base her actions on right and justice
Es para ella, sin torpes amaños	Is for her, without infamous intrigue,
Su invariable, más firme ambición.	The constant and most firm ambition.
Y en seguir esta línea se aferra	And in following this line she persists,
Dedicando su esfuerzo tenaz,	Dedicating her tenacious efforts
En hacer cruda guerra a la guerra:	In giving hard battle for battle;
Su ventura se encuentra en la paz.	Her happiness is found in peace.
En la paz, en la paz.	In peace, in peace.
CHORUS	CHORUS

El Salvador

Sa - lu - de - mos la pa - tria or - gu - llo - sos De hi - jos su - - yos po - der - nos lla - mar __; Y ju - re - mos la vi - da a - ni - mo - sos, Sin des - -

can - so a su bien con - sa - grar.

Sa - lu - de - mos la pa - tria or - gu - llo - sos De hi - jos su - - yos po - der - nos lla - mar ___; Y ju - re - mos la vi - da a - ni - mo - sos, Sin des - - can - so a su bien ___ con - sa - grar.

Con - - sa - grar, con - sa -

grar,   con - sa - grar,   con - sa - grar

De la   paz   en la di - cha su -   pre - - ma, Siem - - pre

no - - ble __ so - ñó El Sal - va -   dor __;   Fue ob - te -   ner -   la su e - ter - no pro -

ble - -   ma, Con - - ser -   va -   la es su glo -   ria ma -   yor.   Y con

fe in - que - bran - ta - - ble el ca - mi - no __ Del pro - gre - so se a - fa - na en se - guir en se - guir Por lle -

nar __ su gran - dio - - so des - ti - no __, Con - quis - tar - - se un fe - liz __ por - ve -

nir. Le pro - te - - ge u - na fé - rrea ba - rre - - ra Con - tra el

cho - - que de ruin des - leal - tad, Des - de el dí - - a que en su al - ta ban -

de - - - ra Con su san - - gre es - cri - bió __: ¡LI - BER - TAD __! ¡Es - cri - bio __ li - ber -

tad __! ¡es - cri - bio __ li - ber - tad!

Sa - lu - de - mos la pa - tria or - gu - llo - sos De hi - jos

su - - yos po-der- nos lla - - mar __; Y ju - re - mos la vi-da a - ni - mo - sos, Sin des - -

can - - so a su bien con - - sa - grar.

Sa - lu - de - mos la Pa - tria or-gu - llo - sos De hi - jos

su - - yos po-der- nos lla- mar __; Y ju - re - mos la vi-da a - ni -

mo - sos,   Sin des -   can - so a   su bien ___ con - sa-   grar.

Con - sa -   grar,   con - sa -

grar,   con - sa- grar,   con - sa -   grar.   ___.

Equatorial Guinea

República de Guinea Ecuatorial

(Republic of Equatorial Guinea)

Quick Country Facts

Location: West Africa and Gulf of Guinea

Area: 10,380 sq. mi. (28,051 sq. km.)

Population (2002 est.): 498,144

Capital/Largest City: Malabo (pop. 30,418)

Official Languages: Spanish, French

GDP/PPP: $1.04 billion, $2,100 per capitab

Monetary Unit: Franc CFA

Himno Nacional

(National Anthem)

Lyrics: Atanasio Ndongo Miyono. Adopted: 1968.

Spanish Words	English Translation
Caminemos pisando las sendas	Let us tread the paths
De nuestra inmensa felicidad.	Of our great happiness.
En fraternidad, sin separación,	In brotherhood, undivided,
¡Cantemos Libertad!	Let us sing for freedom!
Tras dos siglos de estar sometidos,	Behind us are two centuries
Bajo la dominación colonial,	Of colonial domination.
En fraterna unión, sin discriminar,	In brotherly unity, without discrimination,
¡Cantemos Libertad!	Let us sing for freedom!
¡Gritamos Viva, Libre Guinea!	Let us shout: Long live Guinea!
Y defendamos nuestra Libertad.	Let us defend our freedom.
Cantemos siempre, Libre Guinea,	Always singing of our free Guinea,
Y conservemos siempre la unidad.	Let us keep united.
¡Gritamos Viva, Libre Guinea!	Let us shout: Long live Guinea!
Y defendamos nuestra Libertad.	Let us defend our freedom.

Cantemos siempre, Libre Guinea, Y conservemos, Y conservemos La independencia nacional. (repeat previous two lines two times)	Always singing of our free Guinea, Let us keep our nation independent. (repeat)

Equatorial Guinea

Ca - mi - ne - mos pi - san - do las sen - das De nuestra in - men - sa fe - li - ci - dad ___.

En fra - ter - ni - dad, sin se - pa - ra - ción, ¡Can - te - mos Li - ber - tad ___! Tras dos

si - glos de es - tar so - me - ti - dos, Ba - jo la do - mi - na - ción co - lo - ni - al ___,

En fra - ter - na u - nión, sin dis - cri - mi - nar, ¡Can - te - mos Li - ber - tad ___! ¡Gri - ta - mos

Vi - va ___, Li - bre Gui - ne - a ___! Y de - fen - da - mos nues - tra Li - ber - tad ___. Can - te - mos

siem - pre ___, Li - bre Gui - ne - a ___, Y con - ser - ve - mos siem - pre la u - ni - dad ___. ¡Gri - ta - mos

Vi - va ___, Li - bre Gui - ne - a ___! Y de - fen - da - mos nues - tra Li - ber - tad ___. Can - te - mos

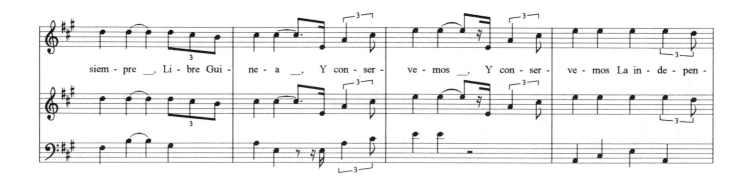

siem - pre ___, Li - bre Gui - ne - a ___, Y con - ser - ve - mos ___, Y con - ser - ve - mos La in - de - pen -

den - cia na - cio - nal ___. Y con - ser - ve - mos ___, Y con - ser - ve - mos La in - de - pen -

den - cia na - cio - nal ___.

Eritrea

ሃገረ ኤርትራ

Hagare Ertra

دولة ارتريا

Dewlet Eritrea

(State of Eritrea)

Quick Country Facts
Location: Northeastern Africa
Area: 45,754 sq. mi. (121,320 sq. km.)
Population (2002 est.): 4,465,651
Capital/Largest City: Asmara (pop. 400,000)
Official Languages: Tigrinya, Arabic
GDP/PPP: $3.2 billion, $740 per capita
Monetary Unit: Birr

Eritrean National Anthem

Lyrics: Solomon Tsehaye Beraki (b. 1956). Music: Isaac Abraham Meharezghi (b. 1944) and Aron Tekle Tesfatsion (b. 1963).

Tigrinya Words	Tigrinya Words (Transliteration, First Verse of Two)	English Translation[1]
1	1	1
ኤርትራ ኤርትራ ኤርትራ	*Ertra, Ertra, Ertra,*	Eritrea, Eritrea, Eritrea,
በዓል ደማ አናልቀስ ተደምሲሱ	*Beal dema'nalkese tedem sisu,*	The barbarian enemy humiliatingly
መስዋእታ ብሓርነት ተደሲሱ	*Meswaeta bharnet tdebisu.*	defeated
(repeat previous three lines)	(repeat stanza)	(repeat stanza)
በዓል ደማ አናልቀስ ተደምሲሱ	*Beal dema'nalkese tedem sisu,*	The barbarian enemy humiliatingly
መስዋእታ ብሓርነት ተደሲሱ	*Meswaeta bharnet tdebisu.*	Defeated

2	2	2
መዋእል ነኺሳ'ብ ዕላማ ትእምርቲ ጽንዓት ኮይኑ ስማ ኤርትራ'ዛ ሓበን ወጹዓት ኣመሰኪራ ሓቂ ከምትዕወት	*Mewael nekhisa'b elame* *Temrti tsnat koynu sma,* *Ertra za haben wtsuat,* *Ameskira haki kem tewet.*	And martyrdom has paid for freedom. Decades of devotion for purpose Your name became challenger, miraculous Eritrea, comfort for the oppressed Proved that truth can win after all.
CHORUS ኤርትራ ኤርትራ ኤርትራ ኣብ ዓስም ጨቢጣቶ ግቡእ ክብራ	CHORUS *Ertra, Ertra, Ertra* *Abalem chebitato gbue kbra.*	CHORUS Eritrea, Eritrea, Eritrea A sovereign state on earth after all.
(repeat 2)	(repeat 2)	(repeat 2)
CHORUS	CHORUS	CHORUS
(repeat 1)		(repeat 1)
3 ናጽነት ዘምጽአ ልዑል ሩኒሕ ንህንጸ ንልምዓት ክስርሕ ሰልጣነ ክነልብላ ግርማ ሕጽሪ`ለና ግርምጃ ክንሰልማ		3 Dedication that led to liberation Will build up and make her green We shall honor her with progress We have a word to her to embellish.
CHORUS		CHORUS
(repeat 3)		(repeat 3)
CHORUS		CHORUS

Eritrea

222

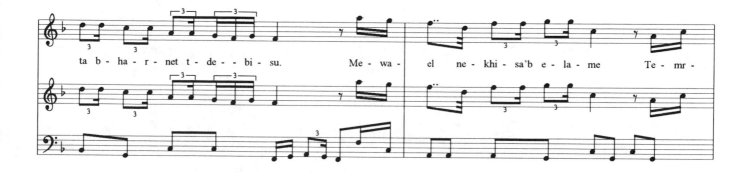

ta b - ha - r - net t - de - - bi - su.   Me - wa - el ne - khi - sa'b e - la - me   Te - mr -

ti tsn - at koy - nu s - - ma,   E - rt - ra za ha - ben w - tsu - at,   A - mes -

ki - ra ha - ki kem te - wet.   E - rt - ra,   E - rtra,   E - rtra

Ab - a - lem che - bi - ta - to gbue kb - ra.   Me - wa - el ne - khi - sa'b e - la - me   Te - mr -

ti tsn - at koy - nu s - ma,   E - rt - ra za ha - ben w - tsu - at,   A - mes - ki - ra ha - ki kem te - wet.   E - rt -

ra,   E - rt - ra,   E - rtra,   Ab - a - lem che - bi - ta - to gbue kb - ra.

Estonia

Eesti Vabariik

(Republic of Estonia)

Quick Country Facts

Location: Eastern Europe, Baltic Sea

Area: 17,666 sq. mi. (45,226 sq. km.)

Population (2002 est.): 1,415,681

Capital/Largest City: Tallinn (pop. 471,608)

Official Language: Estonian

GDP/PPP: $15.2 billion, $10,900 per capita

Monetary Unit: Kroon

Mu Isamaa, mu Õnn ja Rõõm

(My Native Land, My Pride and Joy)

Lyrics: Johann Voldemar Jannsen (1819-1900). Music: Fredrik Pacius (1809-1891). Adopted: 1920.

Historical Background[1]

The Estonian national anthem is a choral-like melody arranged by Fredrik Pacius, a Finnish composer of German origin, in 1843. In Estonia, Johann Voldemar Jannsen's lyrics were set to this melody and sung at the first Estonian Song Festival in 1869. It gained in popularity during the growing national movement. In Finland, it first became popular only as a students' song but soon also became more widely accepted. When both Estonia and Finland became independent after the First World War, this identical melody with different words was recognized as the national anthem by both nations. Officially, Estonia adopted it in 1920, after the war of independence.

During the decades of the Soviet occupation of Estonia, the melody was strictly forbidden and people were sent to Siberia for singing it. However, even during the worst years the familiar tune could be heard over Finnish radio, every day at the beginning and end of the program. Thus, it could never be forgotten. With the restoration of Estonian independence, the national anthem has, of course, been restored, too.

Estonian Words	English Translation[2]
1	**1**
Mu isamaa, mu õnn ja rõõm,	My native land, my joy, delight,
kui kaunis oled sa!	How fair thou art and bright!
Ei leia mina iial teal	And nowhere in the world all round
See suure laia ilma peal,	Can ever such a place be found
mis mul nii armas oleks ka,	So well beloved as I love thee,
kui sa, mu isamaa!	My native country dear!
2	**2**
Sa oled mind ju sünnitand	My little cradle stood on thy soil,
ja üles kasvatand;	Whose blessings ease my toil.
sind tänan mina alati	With my last breath my thanks to thee,
ja jään sull' truuiks surmani,	For true to death I'll ever be,
mul kõige armsam oled sa,	O worthy, most beloved and fine,
mu kallis isamaa!	Thou, dearest country mine!
3	**3**
Su üle Jumal valvaku,	May God in Heaven thee defend,
mu armas isamaa!	My best, my dearest land!
Ta olgu sinu kaitseja	May He be guard, may He be shield,
ja võtku rohkest õnnista,	Forever may He bless and wield
mis iial ette võtad sa,	O graciously all deeds of thine,
mu kallis isamaa!	Thou dearest country mine!

Estonia

Mu i - sa - maa, mu õnn ja rõõm, kui kau - nis o - led sa! Ei lei - a mi - na

ii - al teal See suu - re lai - a il - ma peal, mis mul nii ar - mas o - leks ka, kui sa, mu i - sa-

maa ___ !

Ethiopia

Federal Democratic Republic of Ethiopia

Quick Country Facts

Location: Northeastern Africa

Area: 446,952 sq. mi. (1,127,127 sq. km.)

Population (2002 est.): 67,673,031

Capital/Largest City: Addis Ababa (pop. 2,200,186)

Official Language: Amharic

GDP/PPP: $46 billion, $700 per capita

Monetary Unit: Birr

National Anthem

Lyrics: Dereje Melaku Mengesha (b. 1957). Music: Solomon Lulu Mitiku (b. 1950). Adopted: 1992.

Amharic Words (Transliteration)	English Translation
Yazegennat Keber Ba-Ityopp'yachen S'anto	Respect for citizenship is strong in our Ethiopia;
Tayya Hezbawinnat Dar Eskadar Barto.	National pride is seen, shining from one side to another.
Lasalam Lafeteh Lahezboch Nas'annat;	For peace, for justice, for the freedom of peoples,
Ba'ekkulennat Bafeqer Qomanal Ba'andennat.	In equality and in love we stand united.
Masarata S'enu Sabe'enan Yalsharen;	Firm of foundation, we do not dismiss humanness;
Hezboch Nan Lasera Basera Yanoren.	We are peoples who live through work.
Denq Yabahel Madrak Ya'ahuri Qers Balabet;	Wonderful is the stage of tradition, mistress of proud heritage.
Yatafat'ro S'agga Ya'akuri Qers Balabet;	
Ennet'abbeqeshallan Allabben Adara;	Mother of natural virtue, mother of a valorous people.
Ityopp'yachchen nuri Ennam Banchi Ennekura!	We shall protect you—we have a duty;
	Our Ethiopia, live! And let us be proud of you!

Ethiopia

Fiji

Viti

Sovereign Democratic Republic of the Fiji Islands

Meda Dau Doka

National Anthem of Fiji

Lyrics: Michael Francis Alexander Prescott (b. 1928). Adopted: 1970.

Historical Background

The Fijian anthem is based on an old traditional song. It was adopted in 1970.

Fijian Words	English Words
1	1
Meda dau doka ka vinakata na vanua	Blessing grant oh God of nations on the isles of Fiji
E ra sa dau tiko kina na savasava	As we stand united under noble banner blue
Rawa tu na gauna ni sautu na veilomani	And we honor and defend the cause of freedom ever
Biu na i tovo tawa savasava	Onward march together, God bless Fiji.
CHORUS	CHORUS
Me bula ga ko Viti Ka me toro ga ki liu	For Fiji, ever Fiji, let our voices ring with pride.
Me ra turaga vinaka ko ira na i liuliu	For Fiji ever Fiji her name hail far and wide,
Me ra liutaki na tamata	A land of freedom, hope and glory to endure what ever
E na veika vinaka	befall.

Me oti kina na i tovo ca	May God bless Fiji Forevermore!
2 Me da dau doka ka vinakata na vanua E ra sa dau tiko kina na savasava Rawa tu na gauna ni sautu na veilomani Me sa biu na i tovo tawa yaga CHORUS **3** Bale ga vei kemuni na cauravou e Viti Ni yavala me savasava na vanua Ni kakua ni vosota na dukadukali Ka me da sa qai biuta vakadua CHORUS	**2** Blessing grant oh God of nations on the isles of Fiji Shores of golden sand and sunshine, happiness and song Stand united, we of Fiji, fame and glory ever Onward march together, God bless Fiji. CHORUS

Fiji

Me - da dau do- ka ka vi - na- ka - ta na va nu - a E ra sa dau ti - ko ki - na
Bless - ing grant oh God of na - tions on the isles of Fi - ji __ As we stand u - ni - ted un - der

na sa - va - sa- va __ Ra - wa tu na gau - na - ni ni sau - tu vei - lo - ma ni __
no - ble ban - ner blue __ And we hon - or and de - fend the cause of free - dom e - ver __

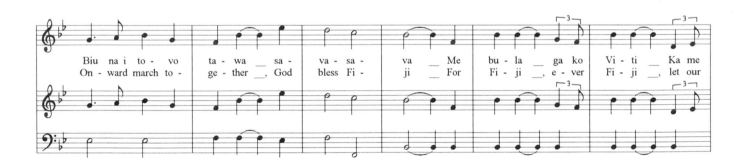

Biu na i to - vo ta - wa sa- va - sa va Me bu - la __ ga ko Vi - ti __ Ka me ra
On - ward march to - ge - ther __, God bless Fi - ji __ For Fi - ji __, e - ver Fi - ji __, let our

to - ro ga ki liu __ Me ra tu - ra ga vi- na - ka ko i - ra na i liu - liu Me ra
voi - ces ring with pride __. For Fi - ji e - ver Fi - ji __ her name hail far and wide, A land of

liu - taki __ na ta - ma - ta __ E na vei - ka vi - na - ka Me o - ti ki - na __ na i
free - dom __, hope and glo - ry __ to en - dure what - ev - er be - fall. May God bless Fi - ji __ For -

to - vo ca
e - ver - more!

Finland

Suomen Tasavalta

Republiken Finland

(Republic of Finland)

Quick Country Facts

Location: Western Europe, Scandinavia

Area: 130,558 sq. mi. (337,030 sq. km.)

Population (2000 est.): 5,183,545

Capital/Largest City: Helsinki (pop. 515,765)

Official Languages: Finnish, Swedish

GDP/PPP: $136.2 billion, $26,200 per capita

Monetary Unit: Euro

Maamme

Vårt land

(Our Land)

Finnish Lyrics: Paavo Eemil Cajander (1846-1913). Swedish Lyrics: Johan Ludvig Runeberg (1804-1877). Music: Fredrik Pacius (1809-1891). Adopted: 1848.

Historical Background[1]

The Finnish national anthem, with words by Johan Ludvig Runeberg and music by Fredrik Pacius, was first performed in 1848 by students celebrating Flora Day (13 May) in a meadow belonging to Kumtähti Manor in Helsinki. Johan Ludvig Runeberg, headmaster of Porvoo (Borgå) Lyceum, had written the original text in Swedish, "Vårt land" ("Our Land"), two years earlier. The poem was published in autumn 1846 as the prologue to Runeberg's "Fänrik Ståls sägner" ("Tales of Ensign Stål"), a collection of thirty-five heroic ballads set in the days of the War of Finland in 1808-1809. As a result of this war, Sweden ceded Finland to Russia in the 1809 Treaty of Hamina. Runeberg's aim was to stir Finnish patriotic feeling with his epic. He is said to have been inspired to write "Vårt land" by Mihaly Vörösmarty's "Szózat," the Hungarian national anthem published in 1836.

Until well into the twentieth century, Finns responded strongly to the idealistic and political idealism of "Fänrik

Ståls sägner" and "Vårt land." Runeberg was promptly elevated to the status of "national poet." He was a conservative and moderate nationalist and loyal to the powers that be. The main concern of the authorities was to prevent the emergence of radical ideas; the revolutionary spirit of the Marseillaise was finding some support in Finland at the time. "Vårt land" helped appease the patriotic yearnings of the students, and the bloodshed seen in other parts of Europe was averted in Finland.

Several composers had already attempted to set Runeberg's lofty poem before Pacius, a German-born composer and music lecturer at the University of Helsinki, but his was the first version to gain widespread popularity. The composer himself conducted the university choir in a slow, majestic first performance, andante maestoso, which moved the crowd to tears. Pacius's tune was later also adopted for "Mu isamaa" ("My Country"), the Estonian national anthem from 1920 to 1940 and again since 1990.

The historians like to say that Finland was born on Flora's Day, 13 May 1848. Fredrik Cygnaeus, chairman of the student body at the University of Helsinki, made the main speech at the celebration, concluding with the toast "To Finland." At the end the audience, several hundred strong, jubilantly joined in with "Vårt land." For the first time, the idea of a distinct Finnish national identity had been put forward. "Vårt land" rapidly won general acceptance as an expression of patriotic sentiment, especially after Paavo Eemil Cajander published his polished Finnish translation ("Maamme") toward the end of the 19th century.

Finnish Words	Swedish Words	English Translation[2]
1	1	1
Oi maamme Suomi, synnyinmaa,	Vårt land, vårt land, vårt fosterland,	Our land, our land, our fatherland,
Soi, sana kultainen!	Ljud högt, o dyra ord!	Sound loud, O name of worth!
Ei laaksoa ei kukkulaa,	Ej lyfts en höjd mot himlens rand,	No mount that meets the heaven's
Ei vettä, rantaa rakkaampaa	Ej sänks en dal, ej sköljs en strand,	band.
Kuin kotimaa tää pohjoinen,	Mer älskad än vår bygd i nord,	No hidden vale, no wave-washed
Maa kallis isien.	Än våra fäders jord.	strand.
		Is loved, as is our native North.
		Our own forefathers' earth.
2	2	2
Sun kukoistukses kuorestaan	Din blomning, sluten än i knopp,	Thy blossom, in the bud laid low,
Kerrankin puhkeaa;	Skall mogna ur sitt tvång;	Yet ripened shall upspring.
Viel' lempemme saa nousemaan,	Se, ur vår kärlek skall gå opp	See! From our love once more shall
Sun toivos, riemus loistossaan,	Ditt ljus, din glans, din fröjd, ditt	grow
Ja kerran laulus, synnyinmaa,	hopp,	Thy light, thy joy, thy hope, thy glow!
Korkeemman kaiun saa.	Och högra klinga skall en gång	And clearer yet one day shall ring
	Vår fosterländska sång.	The song our land shall sing.

Finland

Oi maam - me Suo - mi, syn - nyin - maa, Soi sa - na kul - tai - nen! Ei laak - so - a ___, ei ___
Vårt land, vårt land, vårt fos - ter - land, Ljud högt, o dy - ra ord! Ej lyfts en höjd ___ mot ___

kuk - ku - laa, Ei vet - tä, ran - taa ___ rak - kaam - paa ___ Kuin ko - ti - maa tää poh - joi - nen, Maa
him - lens rand, Ej sänks en dal ___, ej ___ sköljs en strand ___, Mer äls - kad än vår bygd i nord, Än

kal - lis i - si - en.
vå - ra fä - ders jord.

France

République Française

(French Republic)

```
┌─────────────────────────────────────────────┐
│              Quick Country Facts              │
│ Location: Western Europe                      │
│ Area: 211,208 sq. mi. (547,030 sq. km.)       │
│ Population (2002 est.): 59,765,983            │
│ Capital/Largest City: Paris (pop. 10,150,000) │
│ Official Language: French                     │
│ GDP/PPP: $1.54 trillion, $25,700 per capita   │
│ Monetary Unit: Euro                           │
└─────────────────────────────────────────────┘
```

La Marseillaise

(The Song of Marseille)

Lyrics and Music: Claude Joseph Rouget de Lisle (1760-1836). Adopted: 1795.

Historical Background[1]

The French national anthem was not written in Marseille, but in Strasbourg, in the fever of the Revolution, on 24 April 1792, by Claude Joseph Rouget de Lisle. At a banquet in honor of the officers who were to take part in France's campaign against Austria, Captain Rouget de Lisle was commissioned to write a marching song for the soldiers leaving for the front. It was originally known as the "War Song of the Army of the Rhine." The tune quickly spread throughout France, thanks mainly to a student from Montpellier, François Mireur, who obtained a score of the anthem. He sang it at the end of a banquet that the city of Marseille was giving in honor of the 500 volunteers about to depart for Paris. The volunteers also sang it as they entered Paris in July 1792. The song aroused great enthusiasm in the capital and became known as the "Marseillaise."

Declared the national anthem on 14 July 1795, then banned under the Empire and the Restoration, "La Marseillaise" was reinstated by the July Revolution of 1830. Hector Berlioz orchestrated the music, dedicating his composition to Rouget de Lisle. The Third Republic (1879) established it as the French national anthem, and in 1887 an "official version" was adopted by the ministry of war following the recommendation of a specially-appointed commission. Its status was reaffirmed in the 1946 and 1958 Constitutions. In 1974, the newly elected President Giscard d'Estaing wanted the performance of the work to reflect its origins more closely and ordered it to be played at a slower

237

tempo. The version played at official ceremonies today, however, is still adapted from the 1887 version.

French Words (First and Sixth Verses, Seven Total)	English Translation (First and Sixth Verses, Seven Total)
1	1
Allons enfants de la Patrie,	Arise children of the motherland,
Le jour de gloire est arrivé!	Our day of glory has arrived!
Contre nous de la tyrannie!	Over us, the bloodstained banner
L'étendard sanglant est levé	Of tyranny holds sway!
(repeat)	(repeat)
Entendez-vous dans nos campagnes	Oh, do you hear there in our fields
Mugir ces féroces soldats?	The roar of these ferocious soldiers?
Ils viennent jusque dans vos bras.	Who came right here in our midst
Egorger vos fils et vos compagnes!	To slaughter our sons and wives.
CHORUS	CHORUS
Aux armes citoyens!	To arms, oh citizens!
Formez vos bataillons!	Form up in serried ranks!
Marchons! marchons!	March on, march on!
Qu'un sang impur	May their impure blood
Abreuve nos sillons!	Flow in our fields!
6	6
Amour sacré de la Patrie,	Sacred love of country,
Conduis, soutiens nos bras vengeurs	Lead and support our avenging arms
Liberté, Liberté chérie	Freedom, dear freedom,
Combats avec tes défenseurs!	Fight along with those who defend you.
(repeat)	(repeat)
Sous nos drapeaux, que la victoire	Under our flags, may victory
Accoure à tes mâles accents	Follow your manly accents;
Que tes ennemis expirants	May your dying enemies
Voient ton triomphe et notre gloire!	See your triumph and our glory!
CHORUS	CHORUS

France

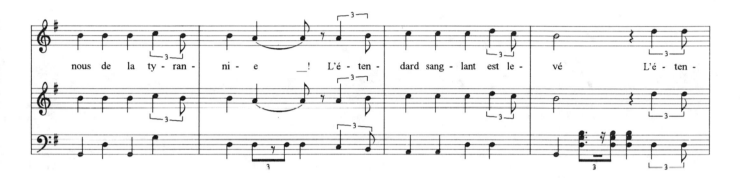

France

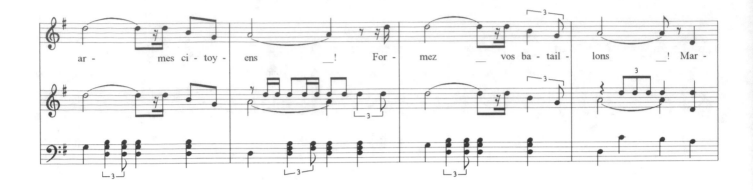

ar - mes ci - toy - ens ____! For - mez ____ vos ba - tail - lons ____! Mar -

chons ____! mar - chons ____! Qu'un sang im - pur ____ A - breu - ve nos sil -

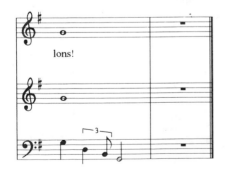

lons!

Gabon

République Gabonaise

(Gabonese Republic)

```
Quick Country Facts
Location: West Africa
Area: 103,346 sq. mi. (267,667 sq. km.)
Population (2002 est.): 1,233,353
Capital/Largest City: Libreville (pop. 419,596)
Official Language: French
GDP/PPP: $6.7 billion, $5,500 per capita
Monetary Unit: Franc CFA
```

La Concorde

(The Concord)

Lyrics and Music: Georges Aleka Damas (1902-1982). Adopted: 1960.

French Words	English Translation
CHORUS	CHORUS
Uni dans la Concorde et la fraternité,	United in concord and brotherhood,
Eveille-toi Gabon, une aurore se lève,	Awake, Gabon, dawn is at hand.
Encourage l'ardeur qui vibre et nous soulève!	Stir up the spirit that thrills and inspires us!
C'est enfin notre essor vers la félicité.	At last we rise up to attain happiness.
(repeat)	(repeat)
1	1
Eblouissant et fier, le jour sublime monte	Dazzling and proud, the sublime day dawns,
Pourchassant à jamais l'injustice et la honte.	Dispelling for ever injustice and shame.
Qu'il monte, monte encore et calme nos alarmes,	May it still advance and calm our fears,
Qu'il prône la vertu et repousse les armes.	May it promote virtue and banish warfare.
CHORUS	CHORUS

2

Oui que le temps heureux rêvé par nos ancêtres
Arrive enfin chez nous, réjouisse les êtres,
Et chasse les sorciers, ces perfides trompeurs.
Qui semaient le poison et répandaient la peur.

CHORUS

3

Afin qu'aux yeux du monde et des nations amies
Le Gabon immortel reste digne d'envie,
Oublions nos querelles, ensemble bâtissons
L'édifice nouveau au quel tous nous rêvons.

CHORUS

4

Des bords de l'Océan au cœur de la forêt,
Demeurons vigilants, sans faiblesse et sans haine!
Autour de ce drapeau, qui vers l'honneurs nous mène,
Saluons la Patrie et chantons sans arrêt!

CHORUS

2

Yes, may the happy days of which our ancestors dreamed
Come for us at last, rejoicing our hearts,
And banish the sorcerers, those perfidious deceivers
Who sowed poison and spread fear.

CHORUS

3

So that, in the eyes of the world and of friendly nations,
The immortal Gabon may maintain her good repute,
Let us forget our quarrels, let us build together
The new structure of which we all have dreamed.

CHORUS

4

From the shores of the Ocean to the heart of the forest,
Let us remain vigilant, without weakness and without
hatred!
Around this flag which leads us to honor,
Let us salute the Fatherland and ever sing!

CHORUS

Gabon

U - ni ___ dans la Con - corde et ___ la ___ fra - ter - ni - té, E -

veil - le- toi Ga - bon ___, une au - ro- re se lè - ve, En - cou - ra - ge l'ar - deur ___ qui vibre et nous sou -

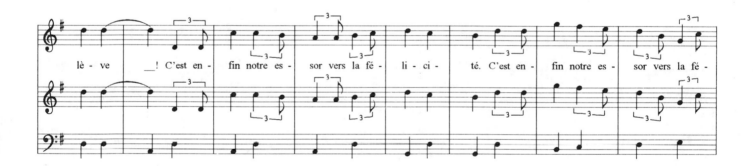

lè - ve ___! C'est en - fin notre es - sor vers la fé - li - ci - té. C'est en - fin notre es - sor vers la fé -

li - ci- té. E - blou - is - sant et fier, le jour su - bli - me monte

Pour - chas - sant à ja - mais l'in - jus - tice et la hon - te __. Qu'il mon -

te, monte en - co - re et cal - me nos a - lar - mes, Qu'il prô - ne la ver - tu

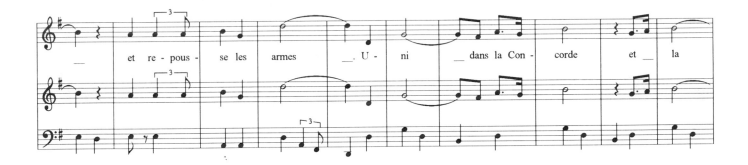

et re - pous - se les armes __. U - ni __ dans la Con - corde et __ la

fra - ter - ni - té, E - veil - le - toi Ga - bon __, une au - ro - re se lè - ve, En -

cou - ra - ge l'ar - deur ___ qui vibre et nous sou - lè - ve ___! C'est en - fin notre es - sor vers la fé - li - ci -

té. C'est en - fin notre es - sor vers la fé - li - ci - té.

The Gambia

Republic of The Gambia

Quick Country Facts
Location: West Africa
Area: 4,093 sq. mi. (11,300 sq. km.)
Population (2002 est.): 1,455,842
Capital/Largest City: Banjul (pop. 44,188)
Official Language: English
GDP/PPP: $2.5 billion, $1,770 per capita
Monetary Unit: Dalasi

For The Gambia, Our Homeland

Lyrics: Virginia Julie Howe (b. 1927).   Music: Jeremy Frederick Howe (b. 1929). Adopted: 1965.

Historical Background

The anthem of this country was adapted from a traditional Mandinka song by Jeremy Frederick Howe in 1964.

Words
For The Gambia, our homeland
We strive and work and pray,
That all may live in unity,
Freedom and peace each day.
Let justice guide our actions
Towards the common good,
And join our diverse peoples
To prove man's brotherhood.
We pledge our firm allegiance,
Our promise we renew;
Keep us, great God of nations,
To The Gambia ever true.

The Gambia

true.

Georgia

საქართველოს

Sakartvelo

Quick Country Facts

Location: West Asia, Caucasus

Area: 26,900 sq. mi. (69,700 sq. km.)

Population (2002 est.): 4,960,951

Capital/Largest City: Tbilissi (pop. 1,279,000)

Official Language: Georgian

GDP/PPP: $15 billion, $3,100 per capita

Monetary Unit: Lari

დიდება

Dideba

(Praise)

Lyrics and Music: Kote Potskhverashvili (1889-1959). Adopted: 1991.

Georgian Words	Georgian Words (Transliteration)	English Translation
1 დიდება ზეციო კურთხეულს, დიდება ქვეყნად სამოთხეს, ტურფა იევრსა, დიდება ძმობას, ერთობას, დიდება თავისუფლებას, დიდება სამარადისო ქართველ მხნე ერსა!	1 *Dideba zetsit kurtheuls,* *Dideba kvehnad samotkhes,* *Turpha iversa.* *Dideba dzmobas, ertobas.* *Dideba tavisuplebas,* *Dideba samaradiso* *Kartulmkhne ersa!*	1 Praise be to the heavenly Bestower of Blessings, Praise be to paradise on earth, To the radiant Georgians, Praise be to brotherhood and to unity, Praise be to liberty, Praise be to the everlasting, lively Georgian people!
2 დიდება ჩვენსა სამშობლოს დიდება ჩვენი სიცოცხლის	2 *Dideba chvensa samshoblos,* *Dideba chveni sitsotskhlis,*	2 Praise be to our fatherland, Praise be to the great and bright aim

მიზანს დიადსა;	*Mizans diadsa;*	of our lives;
ეაშა ტრფობასა, სიყვარულს,	*Vasha trphobasa, sikvaruls,*	Hail, O joy and love,
ეაშა შეებასა, სიხარულს,	*Vasha shvebasa, siharuls,*	Hail helpfulness and happiness,
სალამი ჯეშმარიტების	*Salami chesh maritebis,*	Greetings to the truth, that light of
შჟქ-განთიადსა!	*Shuk gantiadsa!*	dawn!

Georgia

Di - de - ba zet - sit kurt - he - uls, Di - de - ba kveh - nad sa - mot - khes, Tur - pha i - ver - sa

Di - de - ba dzmo - bas, er - to - bas Di - de - ba ta - vi - su - ple - bas,

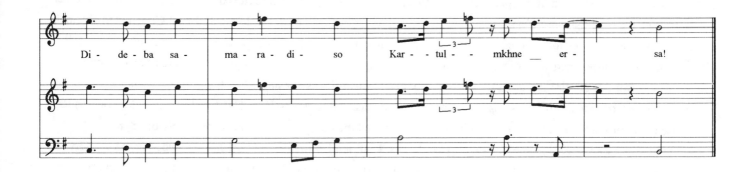

Di - de - ba sa - ma - ra - di - so Kar - tul - mkhne er - sa!

Germany

Bundesrepublik Deutschland

(Federal Republic of Germany)

```
Quick Country Facts
Location: West Central Europe
Area: 137,826 sq. mi. (357,021 sq. km.)
Population (2002 est.): 83,251,851
Capital/Largest City: Berlin (pop. 3,471,418)
Official Language: German
GDP/PPP: $2.184 trillion, $26,600 per capita
Monetary Unit: Euro
```

Lied der Deutschen

(Song of Germany)

Lyrics: August Heinrich Hoffmann von Fallersleben (1798-1874). Music: Franz Joseph Haydn (1732-1809). Adopted: 1922.

Historical Background[1]

The "official" name of the German national anthem is "Lied der Deutschen," or, simply, the "Deutschlandlied." The song is often called "Deutschland über Alles," simply because those are the opening words of the first stanza. It is virtually unknown today that the expression "über alles," or "over all," refers not to the conquest or enslavement of other countries or the establishment of German hegemony over other peoples but, rather, to a call for all Germans to abandon their concept of being a subject or citizen of this or that principality or region (such as Bavaria or Prussia) and to realize the common bond they had with one another by simply being German. This concept was considered "revolutionary" at the time the words were written in 1841, since loyalty to "Germany" was considered by the princelings and kings of the disunited Reich (divided into forty-plus separate states) to be disloyal to themselves. This "all-German" idea was suspect because it was also associated with the rising middle classes and their suppressed Frankfurt assembly of 1848.

The song's words were penned by the teacher August Heinrich Hoffmann von Fallersleben, who had been a fervent supporter of German unity and republican government, and, who, because of his activities on behalf of these causes, was forced to flee to the North Sea island of Heligoland, where the verses were actually written. The music is taken from the String Quartet in C major (the Kaiser-Quartet), Op. 76, 3 of Franz Joseph Haydn, composed in 1797. It was officially ignored during most of the Second Reich (1871 to 1918), which had no official anthem as such. The "Deutschlandlied's" real popularity began with World War I, when it was sung on the battlefield by young soldiers from every Gau of the Reich who were thrown together against a common foe. Ironically, the song did not become the official national anthem until declared so by President Ebert of the Weimar Republic in March 1922.

Not surprisingly, during the next European War, the words "über alles" were ruthlessly exploited by Allied propagandists. Banned after 1945 by the victors, the "Deutschlandlied" is again the German national anthem, but only the third stanza is used. The first stanza is absolutely *verboten*, since it refers to the traditional ethnographic boundaries of Germany ("from the Maas [in Belgium] to the Memel [between the present day Kaliningrad area of Russia and Lithuania], from the Etsch [on the Austro-Italian border] to the Belt [in Denmark]"). Likewise, the propagandistic mistranslation of the words "über alles" has now become accepted "truth," thus precluding their use.

After the fall of the Berlin Wall, proposals were made to combine the hymns of the Federal Republic of Germany and the German Democratic Republic (GDR, the anthem of which was an officially commissioned postwar piece by the communist poet Johannes R. Becher and leftist composer Hans Eisler) to create a "unified" national anthem. At that point, musicologists made the ironic discovery that, in terms of rhythm and meter, the words of the former GDR's anthem "Auferstanden aus Ruinen" (perhaps not accidentally) fit the musical score of the "Deutschlandlied" perfectly!

German Words	English Translation[2]
Einigkeit und Recht und Freiheit	Unity and right and freedom
Für das deutsche Vaterland.	For the German fatherland;
Danach laßt uns alle streben,	Let us all pursue this purpose
Brüderlich mit Herz und Hand.	Brotherly with heart and hand.
Einigkeit und Recht und Freiheit	Unity and right and freedom
Sind des Glückes Unterpfand.	Are the pledge of happiness.
Blüh' im Glanze dieses Glückes,	Flourish in this blessing's glory,
Blühe deutsches Vaterland.	Flourish, German fatherland.
(repeat previous two lines)	(repeat previous two lines)

Germany

Ein - ig- keit und Recht und Frei - - heit Für das deut - sche Va - ter - - land. Da - nach laßt uns

al - le stre - - ben, Brü - der - lich mit Herz und __ Hand. Ein - ig - keit und Recht und Frei - - heit

Sind des Glück - es Un - ter - - pfand. Blüh' im Glan - - ze die - ses Glück - - es,

Blü - he __ deut - - sches __ Va - ter - - land __.

Ghana

Republic of Ghana

Quick Country Facts

Location: West Africa

Area: 92,100 sq. mi. (239,460 sq. km.)

Population (2002 est.): 20,244,154

Capital/Largest City: Accra (pop. 949,100)

Official Language: English

GDP/PPP: $39.4 billion, $1,980 per capita

Monetary Unit: Cedi

Hail the Name of Ghana

Lyrics: Government Committee. Music: Phillip Gbeho (1905-1976). Adopted: 1957.

Historical Background

This anthem was written by a government committee in 1957, when the country gained independence from Britain. The lyrics were changed in 1966, when a coup overthrew the former government.

Words

1

God bless our homeland Ghana,

And make our nation great and strong,

Bold to defend for ever

The cause of freedom and of right;

Fill our hearts with true humility,

Make us cherish fearless honesty,

And help us to resist oppressors' rule

With all our will and might for evermore.

(repeat previous two lines)

Hail to thy name, O Ghana,

To thee we make our solemn vow:

Steadfast to build together

2

A nation strong in unity;

With our gifts of mind and strength of arm,

Whether night or day, in mist or storm,

In ev'ry need, whate'er the call may be,

To serve thee, O Ghana, now and evermore.

(repeat previous two lines)

3

Raise high the flag of Ghana

And one with Africa advance;

Black star of hope and honor

To all who thirst for liberty;

Where the banner of Ghana freely flies,

May the way to freedom truly lie;

Arise, arise, O sons of Ghanaland,

And under God march on for evermore!

(repeat previous two lines)

Ghana

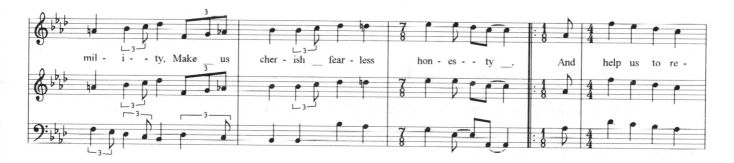

Greece

Ελληνική Δημοκρατία

Elliniki Dimokratia

(Hellenic Republic)

Quick Country Facts

Location: Southern Europe, Balkan Peninsula

Area: 50,961 sq. mi. (131,940 sq. km.)

Population (2002 est.): 10,645,343

Capital/Largest City: Athens (pop. 3,000,000)

Official Language: Greek

GDP/PPP: $201.1 billion, $19,000 per capita

Monetary Unit: Drachma

Ύμνος εις την Ελευθερίαν

Ymnos eis tin Eleftherian

(Hymn to Freedom)

Lyrics: Dionysios Solomos (1798-1857). Music: Nikolaos Mantzaros (1795-1872). Adopted: 1960.

Historical Background[1]

The Greek anthem is based on the "Hymn to the Freedom," a large—158 strophes—poem written by Dionysios Solomos, a distinguished poet from Zakynthos Island. It was inspired by the Greek Revolution of 1821 against the Ottoman Empire. During 1828, the eminent musician from Kerkyra Island, Nikolaos Mantzaros, composed the music for Solomos's hymn. Although King Othon (Otto) decorated both of them for their work (1845 and 1849), he did not think (or, maybe, did not want) to replace the Royal Anthem of that time with the Solomos/Mantzaros hymn. The former anthem was a musical derivative from the German one, with a text glorifying Othon.

After the overthrow of the dynasty, the new King George I and the Greek establishment decided to neglect the fashion of that time—to use the royal anthems also as national—and looked for a clearly Greek work, both with respect to the poetry and the music. The "Hymn to the Freedom" was readily there—extremely popular since the Revolution times, often recited or sung during patriotic meetings and celebrations. "Eleftheria"—the Freedom—is a female word and also a popular female name in Greece. Solomos's Eleftheria is not as erotic and earthly as the Delacroix Liberty. It rather reminds one of an exiled ancient goddess, which Solomos identifies with Greece itself. A majestic and demanding goddess, an object of respect and admiration rather than of belief and passion. She has to be imperative, as the poet reviews the whole history of the Greek Revolution, comments on the negative attitude of the Great Forces, describes the pains and the offerings of the rebels, criticizes their dissensions, calls for unanimity and consolidation—always pointing to Eleftheria—the major human value.

The Greek Anthem was written by a man of only twenty-five years. The Greeks deeply love and respect their emotionally youthful anthem. The unusual 6/4 tempo of the Mantzaros music points clearly to the most manly traditional dance of the Greeks.

Greek Words (First Verse, 158 Total)	Greek Words (Transliteration, First Verse, 158 Total)	English Translation (First Verse, 158 Total) [2]
Σε γνωρίζω από την κόψη	*Se gnoriso apo tin kopsi.*	We knew thee of old,
του σπαθιού την τρομερή,	*Tou spathiou tin tromeri,*	Oh, divinely restored,
σε γνωρίζω από την όψη	*Se gnoriso apo tin opsi*	By the lights of thine eyes
που με βία μετράει τη γη.	*Pou me via metra tin yi.*	And the light of thy sword
Απ' τα κόκαλα βγαλμένη	*Ap' ta kokala vialmeni*	From the graves of our slain
των Ελλήνων τα ιερά,	*Ton Ellinon ta iera,*	Shall thy valor prevail
και σαν πρώτα ανδρειωμένη,	*Ke san prota andriomeni,*	As we greet thee again-
χαίρε, ω χαίρε, Ελευθεριά!	*Haire, o haire, Eleftheria!*	Hail, liberty! Hail!
(repeat previous two lines two times)	(repeat previous two lines two times)	(repeat previous two lines two times)

Greece

Se gno- ri- so a- po tin kop- si. Tou spa- thiou tin tro- me- ri, Se gno-

ri- so a- po tin op- si Pou me via me- tra tin yi. Ap' ta ko- ka- la vial-

me- ni Ton El- li- non ta ie- ra, Ke san prota an- dri- o- me- ni, Hai- re, o

hai- re, E- lef- th- ria! Ke san prota an- dri- o- me- ni, hai- re, o hai- re, E- lef- the-

ria ____! Ke san prota an - dri - o - me - ni, Hai - re, o hai - re, E - lef - the - ria ____!

Grenada

Quick Country Facts
Location: North America, Caribbean Sea
Area: 133 sq. mi. (344 sq. km.)
Population (2002 est.): 89,211
Capital/Largest City: St. George's (pop. 4,439)
Official Language: English
GDP/PPP: $424 million, $4,750 per capita
Monetary Unit: East Caribbean Dollar

Hail! Grenada

Lyrics: Irva Merle Baptiste (b. 1924). Music: Louis Arnold Masanto Jr. (b. 1938). Adopted: 1974.

Words
Hail! Grenada, land of ours,
We pledge ourselves to thee,
Heads, hearts and hands in unity
To reach our destiny.
Ever conscious of God,
Being proud of our heritage,
May we with faith and courage
Aspire, build, advance
As one people, one family.
God bless our nation.

Grenada

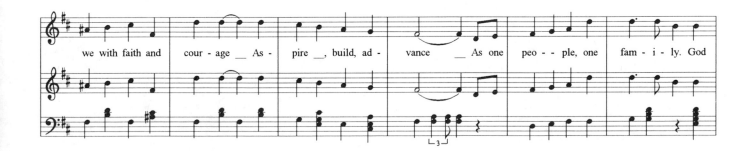

bless our na -   -   tion.

Guatemala

República de Guatemala

(Republic of Guatemala)

Quick Country Facts

Location: Central America

Area: 42,042 sq. mi. (108,890 sq. km.)

Population (2002 est.): 13,314,079

Capital/Largest City: Guatemala City (pop. 1,150,452)

Official Language: Spanish

GDP/PPP: $48.3 billion, $3,700 per capita

Monetary Unit: Quetzal

Himno Nacional

(National Anthem)

Lyrics: José Joaquín Palma (1844-1911). Music: Rafael Alvarez Ovalle (1860-1948). Adopted: 1896.

Historical Background

The music to the Guatemalan anthem came into being as a result of a competition held by the government after the Future Literary Society failed to find a suitable composition to the lyrics of the "Popular Hymn," written by the famous poet Ramon P. Molina. The composer Rafael Alvarez Ovalle won the competition, and, thus, his music and Molina's verses became an unofficial anthem used by the government during important occasions for many years. It was not until 1896, during the administration of General Reina Barrios, that a new contest was held for both the music and the words. Ovalle's former composition was chosen unanimously by the panel. The author of the winning words refused to disclose his name, and remained anonymous until 1911, when it was discovered that he was the Cuban poet José Joaquín Palma.

The new national anthem was first performed at the Teatro Colón on Sunday night, 14 March 1897, as part of the Central American Exhibition. In 1934, during the dictatorial reign of Jorge Ubico, the anthem was modified by José María Bonilla Ruano, who greatly embellished some verses while smoothing out others. The change went into effect by executive decree on 26 July 1934.

Spanish Words (First Verse and Chorus, 4 Verses and Choruses Total)	English Translation (First Verse and Chorus, 4 Verses and Choruses Total)
1	1
¡Guatemala feliz! que tus aras no profane jamás el verdugo; ni haya esclavos que laman el yugo ni tiranos que escupan tu faz.	Fortunate Guatemala! May your altars Never be profaned by cruel men. May there never be slaves who submit to their yoke, Or tyrants who deride you.
Si mañana tu suelo sagrado lo amenaza invasión extranjera, libre al viento tu hermosa bandera a vencer o a morir llamará.	If tomorrow your sacred soil Should be threatened by foreign invasion, Your fair flag, flying freely in the wind, Will call to you: Conquer or die.
CHORUS 1 Libre al viento tu hermosa bandera a vencer o a morir llamará; que tu pueblo con ánima fiera antes muerto que esclavo será.	CHORUS 1 Your fair flag, flying freely in the wind, Will call to you: Conquer or die; For your people, with heart and soul, Would prefer death to slavery.

Guatemala

ña - na tu sue - lo sa - gra - - do lo a - me - na - za in - va - sión ex - tran - je - ra, li - bre al

vien - to tu her - mo - sa ban - de - - ra a ven - cer o a mo - rir __ lla - ma - rá ___. Li - bre al

vien - to tu her - mo - sa ban - de - - ra a ven - cer o a mo - rir lla - ma - rá ___; que tu

pue - blo con á - ni - ma fie - - ra an - tes muer - to que es - cla - vo se - rá ___.

Guinea

République de Guinée

(Republic of Guinea)

Quick Country Facts

Location: West Africa

Area: 94,925 sq. mi. (245,857 sq. km.)

Population (2002 est.): 7,775,065

Capital/Largest City: Conakry (pop. 1,508,000)

Official Language: French

GDP/PPP: $15 billion, $1,970 per capita

Monetary Unit: Guinean Franc

Liberté

(Liberty)

Music: Fodeba Keita (1925-1970).

French Words	English Translation
Peuple d'Afrique!	People of Africa!
Le Passé historique!	The historic past!
Que chante l'hymne de la Guinée fière et jeune	Sing the hymn of a Guinea proud and young
Illustre épopée de nos frères	Illustrious epic of our brothers
Morts au champ d'honneur en libérant l'Afrique!	Who died on the field of honor while liberating Africa!
Le peuple de Guinée prêchant l'unité	The people of Guinea, preaching unity,
Appelle l'Afrique.	Call to Africa.
Liberté! C'est la voix d'un peuple	Liberty! The voice of a people
Qui appelle tous ses frères a se retrouver.	Who call all her brothers to find their way again.
Liberté! C'est la voix d'un peuple	Liberty! The voice of a people
Qui appelle tous ses frères de la grande Afrique.	Who call all her brothers of a great Africa.
Bâtissons l'unité africaine dans l'indépendance retrouvée.	Let us build African unity in a newly found independence!

Guinea

Guinea-Bissau

República da Guiné-Bissau

(Republic of Guinea-Bissau)

Quick Country Facts

Location: West Africa

Area: 13,948 sq. mi. (36,120 sq. km.)

Population (2002 est.): 1,345,479

Capital/Largest City: Bissau (pop. 200,000)

Languages: Portuguese, Portuguese Criolo

GDP/PPP: $1.2 billion, $900 per capita

Monetary Unit: Guinea-Bissau Peso

É Patria Amada

(This Is Our Beloved Country)

Lyrics and Music: Amilcar Lopes Cabral (1924-1973). Adopted: 1975.

Historical Background

The words and music to this song were written in 1963 by the famous revolutionary Amilcar Lopes Cabral, who struggled for the independence of Guinea-Bissau and Cape Verde.

Portuguese Words	English Translation
1	1
Sol, suor e o verde e mar,	Sun, sweat, verdure and sea,
Séculos de dor e esperança!	Centuries of pain and hope;
Esta é a terra dos nossos avós!	This is the land of our ancestors.
Fruto das nossas mãos,	Fruit of our hands,
Da flôr do nosso sangue:	Of the flower of our blood,
Esta é a nossa pátria amada.	This is our beloved country.
CHORUS	CHORUS
Viva a Pátria gloriosa!	Long live our glorious country!

Floriu nos céus a bandeira de luta.	The banner of our struggle
Avante, contra o jugo estrangeiro!	Has fluttered in the skies.
Nós vamos construir	Forward, against the foreign yoke!
Na pátria imortal	We are going to build
A paz e o progresso!	Peace and progress
(repeat previous three lines)	In our immortal country!
	(repeat previous three lines)
2	2
Ramos do mesmo tronco,	Branches of the same trunk,
Olhos na mesma luz:	Eyes in the same light;
Esta é a força da nossa união!	This is the force of our unity!
Cantem o mar e a terra	The sea and the land,
A madrugada e o sol	The dawn and the sun are singing
Que a nossa luta fecundou!	That our struggle has borne fruit!
CHORUS	CHORUS

Guinea-Bissau

Sol, su - or e o ver - de e mar __,

Sé - cu - los de dor e es - peran - ça! Es - ta é a ter - ra dos nos - sos a - vós! Fru - to das nos - sas mãos __,

Da flôr do nos - so san - gue: Es - ta é a nos - sa pá - tria a - ma - da. Vi - va a pá - tri - a glo - ri -

o - sa! Flo - riu nos céus a ban - dei - ra de lu - ta. A - van - te, con - tra o

ju - go es - tran - gei - ro! Nós va - mos cons - tru - ir Na pá - tria i - mor - tal A paz e o pro - gres - so! Nós

va - mos cons - tru - ir Na pá - tria i - mor - tal A paz e o pro - gres - so!

Guyana

Co-operative Republic of Guyana

Quick Country Facts

Location: South America

Area: 83,000 sq. mi. (214,970 sq. km.)

Population (2000 est.): 698,209

Capital/Largest City: Georgetown (pop. 248,500)

Official Language: English

GDP/PPP: $2.5 billion, $3,600 per capita

Monetary Unit: Guyana Dollar

National Anthem of Guyana

Lyrics: Archibald Leonard Luker (1917-1971). Music: Robert Cyril Gladstone Potter (1899-1981). Adopted: 1966.

Historical Background

This song was written by Archibald Leonard Luker in 1965 with music composed by Robert Cyril Gladstone Potter in 1966. It was adopted one month before Guyana obtained independence.

Words

1

Dear land of Guyana, of rivers and plains,

Made rich by the sunshine, and lush by the rains.

Set gemlike and fair, between mountains and sea,

Your children salute you, dear land of the free.

2

Green land of Guyana, our heroes of yore,

Both bondsmen and free, laid their bones on your shore.

This soil so they hallowed, and from them are we,

All sons of one mother, Guyana the free.

3

Great land of Guyana, diverse though our strains,

We are born of their sacrifice, heirs of their pains.

And ours is the glory their eyes did not see,

One land of six peoples, united and free.

4

Dear land of Guyana, to you will we give,

Our homage, our service, each day that we live.

God guard you, Great Mother, and make us to be

More worthy our heritage, land of the free.

Guyana

Dear land of Guy - a - na __, of ri - vers __ and plains __, Made rich by the sun - - shine and

lush __ by the rains __. Set __ gem - like and fair __ be - tween moun - - tains and sea __, Your

child - ren sa - lute you, dear land __ of the free.

Haiti

République d'Haïti

Repiblik Dayti

(Republic of Haiti)

La Dessalinienne

(The Song of Dessalines)

Lyrics: Justin Lhérisson (1873-1907). Music: Nicolas Geffrard (1871-1930). Adopted: 1904.

Historical Background[1]

This anthem was written and composed in 1904 under the government of Nord Alexis to celebrate the centenary of Haiti's independence. The title of the song was named after Jean-Jacques Dessalines, the founding father of Haiti.

French Words	English Translation[2]
1	1
Pour le Pays, pour les Ancêtres,	March on! For ancestors and country,
Marchons unis, marchons unis,	United march, united march;
Dans nos rangs point de traîtres!	Loyal subjects all remain,
Du sol soyons seuls maîtres.	And lords of our domain
Marchons unis, marchons unis,	United march, March on!
Pour le Pays, pour les Ancêtres.	United march for ancestors and country,
Marchons, marchons, marchons unis,	March on, united march, march on!

Pour le Pays, pour les Ancêtres.

Unite for ancestors and country!

2

Pour les Aïeux, pour la Patrie
Bêchons joyeux, bêchons joyeux;
Quand le champ fructifie,
L'âme se fortifie.
Bêchons joyeux, bêchons joyeux,
Pour les Aïeux, pour la Patrie.
Bêchons, bêchons, bêchons joyeux,
Pour les Aïeux, pour la Patrie.

2

For sacred soil, for sires of old,
We gladly toil, we gladly toil.
When teem field and wold
The soul is strong and bold.
We gladly toil, we gladly toil,
For sacred soil, for sires of old.
We gladly, gladly, gladly toil,
For sacred soil, for sires of old.

3

Pour le Pays et pour nos Pères,
Formons des Fils, formons des Fils,
Libres, forts et prospères,
Toujours nous serons frères,
Formons des Fils, formons des Fils,
Pour le Pays et pour nos Pères.
Formons, formons, formons des Fils,
Pour le Pays et pour nos Pères.

3

For land we love, and sires of old
We give our sons, give our sons.
Free, happy, and bold,
One brotherhood we'll hold.
We give our sons, we give our sons
For land we love, and sires of old.
We give, we give, we give our sons
For land we love, and sires of old.

4

Pour les Aïeux, pour la Patrie,
O Dieu des Preux! O Dieu des Preux!
Sous ta garde infinie,
Prends nos droits, notre vie,
O Dieu des Preux, O Dieu des Preux,
Pour les Aïeux, pour la Patrie.
O Dieu, O Dieu, O Dieu des Preux,
Pour les Aïeux, pour la Patrie.

4

For those who gave, for country all,
God of the brave, God of the brave,
To thee, O God, we call;
Without thee we must fall,
God of the brave, God of the brave.
For those who gave, for country all.
O God, O God, O God of the brave
For those who gave, for country all.

5

Pour le Drapeau, pour la Patrie,
Mourir est beau! mourir est beau!
Notre passé nous crie:
Ayez l'âme aguerrie.
Mourir est beau, mourir est beau
Pour le Drapeau, pour la Patrie!

5

For flag on high, for Native land
'Tis fine to die, 'tis fine to die.
Our traditions demand
Be ready, heart and hand,
'Tis fine to die, 'tis fine to die
For flag on high, for native land.

Mourir, mourir, mourir est beau Pour le Drapeau, pour la Patrie!	'Tis fine, 'tis fine, 'tis fine to die, For flag on high, for native land.

Haiti

Pour le Pa - ys, pour les An - cê - tres, Mar - chons u - nis, mar - chons u - nis ___, Dans nos

rangs point de traî - tres ___ ! Du sol soy - ons seuls maî - tres. Mar - chons u - nis, mar -

chons u - nis, Pour le Pa - ys, pour les An - cê - tres ___. Mar - chons, mar - chons, mar - chons u - nis,

Pour le Pa - ys, pour les An - cê - tres.

Honduras

República de Honduras

(Republic of Honduras)

```
Quick Country Facts
Location: Central America
Area: 43,872 sq. mi. (112,090 sq. km.)
Population (2002 est.): 6,560,608
Capital/Largest City: Tegucigalpa (pop. 1,500,000)
Official Language: Spanish
GDP/PPP: $17 billion, $2,600 per capita
Monetary Unit: Lempira
```

Himno Nacional

(National Anthem)

Lyrics: Augusto Constancio Coello Estevez (1884-1941). Music: Carlos Hartling (1869-1920). Adopted: 1915.

Historical Background

This anthem was written by the Honduran statesman Augusto Constancio Coello Estevez in 1903. The music was composed that same year by Carlos Hartling, a military band director of German origin. On 15 November 1915, during the administration of Dr. Alberto Membreño, the song was declared the national anthem by Decree No. 42.

Spanish Words (First and Seventh Verses, 7 Total)	English Translation (First and Seventh Verses, 7 Total)
CHORUS	CHORUS
Tu bandera, tu bandera es un lampo de cielo	Your flag is a splendor of sky
Por un bloque, por un bloque de nieve cruzado;	Crossed with a band of snow;
Y se ven en su fondo sagrado	And there can be seen, in its sacred depths,
Cinco estrellas de pálido azul;	Five pale blue stars.
En tu emblema, que un mar rumoroso	In your emblem, which a rough sea
Con sus ondas bravías escuda,	With its wild waves protects,
De un volcán, de un volcán tras la cima desnuda,	Behind the bare summit of a volcano,
Hay un astro, hay un astro de nítida luz.	A star brightly shines.

1

India virgen y hermosa dormías
De tus mares al canto sonoro,
Cuando echada en tus cuencas de oro
El audaz navegante te halló;
Y al mirar tu belleza extasiado,
Al influjo ideal de tu encanto,
La orla azul de tu espléndido manto
Con su beso de amor consagró.

CHORUS

7

Por guardar ese emblema divino
Marcharemos, ¡oh patria!, a la muerte;
Generosa será nuestra suerte
Si morimos pensando en tu amor.
Defendiendo tu santa bandera,
Y en sus pliegues gloriosos cubiertos,
Serán muchos, Honduras, tus muertos,
Pero todos caerán con honor!

CHORUS

1

Like an Indian maiden you were sleeping,
Lulled by the resonant song of your seas,
When, set in your golden valleys,
The bold navigator found you;
And on seeing, enraptured, your beauty,
And feeling your enchantment,
He dedicated a kiss of love to the blue hen
Of your splendid mantle.

CHORUS

7

To guard this sacred emblem
We shall march, oh fatherland, to our death;
Our death will be honored
If we die thinking of your love.
Having defended your holy flag,
And shrouded in its glorious folds,
Many, Honduras, shall die for you,
But all shall fall in honor.

CHORUS

Honduras

Tu ban - de - - ra, tu ban - de - - ra es un lam - po de cie - lo ___ Por un

blo - - que, por un blo - - que, de ___ nie - ve cru - - za - do ___; Y se ven en su fon - do sa -

gra - do Cin - co es - tre - llas de pá - li - do a - zul; En tu em - ble - ma que un mar ru - mo -

ro - so ___ Con sus on - das bra - ví - as es - cu - da ___, De un vol - cán ___, de un vol -

cán _____ tras la ci - ma des - nu - da _____, Hay un as - - tro, hay un as - - tro de _____

ní - ti - da luz _____. In - dia vir - gen y her - mo - sa dor - mí - as _____ De tus

ma - res al can - to so - no - ro _____, Cuan - do e - cha - da en tus cuen - cas de o - ro El au - -

daz na - ve - gan - - te te ha - lló; Y al mi - rar tu be - lle - za ex - ta - si - a - do, Al in - -

flu - jo i - de - al de tu en - can - to _____, La or - la a - zul de tu es -

plén - di - do ___ man - to ___ Con su be - so de a - mor con - sa - gró. Tu ban -

de - - ra, tu ban - de - - ra es un lam - po de cie - lo ___ Por un blo - que, por un

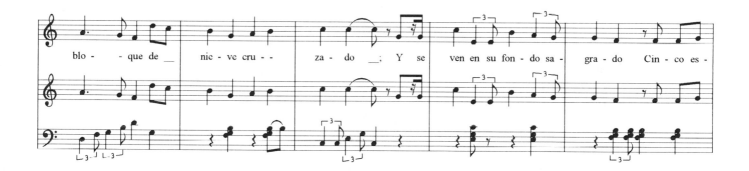

blo - - que de ___ nie - ve cru - - za - do ___; Y se ven en su fon - do sa - gra - do Cin - co es -

tre - llas de pá - li - do a - zul; En tu em - ble - ma que un mar ru - mo - ro - so ___ Con sus

on - - das bra - ví - - as es - cu - da ___, De un vol - cán ___, de un vol - cán ___ tras la

ci - - ma des - nu - da ___, Hay un as - - tro, hay un as - - tro de ___ ní - - ti - da

luz ___.

Hungary

Magyar Köztársaság

(Republic of Hungary)

Quick Country Facts

Location: Central Europe

Area: 35,919 sq. mi. (93,030 sq. km.)

Population (2000 est.): 10,075,034

Capital/Largest City: Budapest (pop. 2,008,546)

Official Language: Magyar

GDP/PPP: $134.7 billion, $13,300 per capita

Monetary Unit: Forint

Himnusz

(National Anthem)

Lyrics: Ferenc Kölcsey (1790-1838). Music: Ferenc Erkel (1810-1893). Adopted: 1844.

Historical Background[1]

The text of the Hungarian national anthem was written in 1823 by Ferenc Kölcsey, one of the great poets of the age of reform. It was first published in 1828 under the title "Hymn."

The music was composed by the composer and conductor Ferenc Erkel in 1844, when he won a contest to compose the national anthem. It was first performed in the National Theater in Pest in 1844 but only adopted officially as the national anthem in 1903. The "Hymn" has eight stanzas, although only the first is normally played or sung on official occasions.

Magyar Words	English Translation[2]
1	1
Isten, áldd meg a magyart	O my God, the Magyar bless
Jó kedvvel, bőséggel,	With Thy plenty and good cheer!
Nyújts feléje védő kart,	With Thine aid his just cause press,
Ha küzd ellenséggel;	Where his foes to fight appear.
Bal sors akit régen tép,	Fate, who for so long didst frown,

Hozz rá víg esztendőt,	Bring him happy times and ways;
Megbünhödte már e nép	Atoning sorrow hath weighed down
A multat s jövendőt!	Sins of past and future days.

2

Őseinket felhozád	By Thy help our fathers gained
Kárpát szent bércére,	Kárpát's proud and sacred height;
Általad nyert szép hazát	Here by Thee a home obtained
Bendegúznak vére.	Heirs of Bendegúz, the knight.
S merre zúgnak habjai	Where're Danube's waters flow
Tiszának, Dunának,	And the streams of Tisza swell,
Árpád hős magzatjai	Árpád's children, Thou dost know,
Felvirágozának.	Flourished and did prosper well.

3

Értünk Kunság mezein	For us let the golden grain
Ért kalászt lengettél,	Grow upon the fields of Kún,
Tokaj szőlővesszein	And let nectar's silver rain
Nektárt csepegtettél.	Ripen grapes of Tokay soon.
Zászlónk gyakran plántálád	Thou our flags hast planted o'er
Vad török sáncára,	Forts where once wild Turks held sway;
S nyögte Mátyás bús hadát	Proud Vienna suffered sore
Bécsnek büszke vára.	From King Mátyás' dark array.

4

Hajh, de bűneink miatt	But, alas! for our misdeed,
Gyúlt harag kebledben,	Anger rose within Thy breast,
S elsújtád villámidat	And Thy lightnings Thou didst speed
Dörgő fellegedben,	From Thy thundering sky with zest.
Most rabló mongol nyilát	Now the Mongol arrow flew
Zúgattad felettünk,	Over our devoted heads;
Majd töröktől rabigát	Or the Turkish yoke we knew,
Vállainkra vettünk.	Which a free-born nation dreads.

5

Hányszor zengett ajkain	Oh, how often has the voice
Ozman vad népének	Sounded of wild Osman's hordes,
Vert hadunk csonthalmain	When in songs they did rejoice
Győzedelmi ének!	O'er our heroes' captured swords!

Hányszor támadt tenfiad	Yea, how often rose thy sons,
Szép hazám kebledre,	My fair land, upon thy sod,
S lettél magzatod miatt	And thou gavest to these sons,
Magzatod hamvvedre!	Tombs within the breast they trod!

6

Bújt az üldözött s felé
Kard nyúl barlangjában,
Szerte nézett s nem lelé
Honját a hazában,
Bércre hág és völgybe száll,
Bú s kétség mellette,
Vérözön lábainál,
S lángtenger fölötte.

6

Though in caves pursued he lie,
Even there he fears attacks.
Coming forth the land to spy,
Even a home he finds he lacks.
Mountain, valego where he would,
Grief and sorrow all the same
Underneath a sea of blood
While above a sea of flame.

7

Vár állott, most kőhalom,
Kedv és öröm röpkedtek,
Halálhörgés, siralom
Zajlik már helyettek.
S ah, szabadság nem virúl
A holtnak véréből,
Kínzó rabság könnye hull
Árvánk hő szeméből!

7

'Neath the fort, a ruin now,
Joy and pleasure erst were found,
Only groans and sighs, I trow,
In its limits now abound.
But no freedom's flowers return
From the spilt blood of the dead,
And the tears of slavery burn,
Which the eyes of orphans shed.

8

Szánd meg isten a magyart
Kit vészek hányának,
Nyújts feléje védő kart
Tengerén kínjának.
Bal sors akit régen tép,
Hozz rá víg esztendőt,
Megbünhödte már e nép
A multat s jövendőt!

8

Pity, God, the Magyar, then,
Long by waves of danger tossed;
Help him by Thy strong hand when
He on grief's sea may be lost.
Fate, who for so long did frown,
Bring him happy times and ways;
Atoning sorrow hath weighed down
All the sins of all his days.

Hungary

Iceland

Lýoveldio Ísland

(Republic of Iceland)

```
Quick Country Facts
Location: Northwest Europe, Atlantic Ocean, Scandinavia
Area: 39,709 sq. mi. (103,000 sq. km.)
Population (2000 est.): 279,384
Capital/Largest City: Reykjavík (pop. 103,036)
Official Language: Icelandic
GDP/PPP: $7.7 billion, $27,100 per capita
Monetary Unit: Icelandic Króna
```

Lofsöngur

(Song of Praise)

Lyrics: Matthías Jochumsson (1835-1920). Music: Sveinbjörn Sveinbjörnsson (1847-1926). Adopted: 1874.

Historical Background[1]

The Icelandic national anthem was in origin a hymn written for a particular occasion; it probably did not occur to either the poet or the composer that there might be in store for it the destiny of becoming a national anthem, for more than a generation elapsed before this came about.

The year 1874 marked the millenary anniversary of the settlement in Iceland of the first Norseman, Ingólfur Arnarson. In the summer of that year there were celebrations throughout the country to commemorate this event, the chief ceremonies being held at Thingvellir, the place of assembly of the ancient parliament of the people ("Althingi"), and in Reykjavík. It was for this occasion that the hymn was written, hence the words "Iceland's thousand years," which recur in all three verses, compare with the title of the original edition of the poem and the music (Reykjavík, 1874), which was "A Hymn in Commemoration of Iceland's Thousand Years."

By an order in council of the 8 September 1873 it was decreed that services should be held in all Icelandic churches to commemorate the millenary anniversary of the first settlement in Iceland, and it was left to the Bishop of Iceland to decide upon a day and the choice of a text for the service. In the autumn of the same year, Bishop Pétur Pétursson announced that the day for the service was to be 2 August and the chosen text Psalm 90, vv. 1-4 and 12-17. This decision led to the Icelandic national anthem being composed and its theme was suggested by the chosen text.

About the same time as the bishop's letter was sent out, the Rev. Matthías Jochumsson set off on the third of his eleven trips abroad. He was the son of a poor farmer with a large family and did not go to school until a comparatively late age, by the aid of people who had been impressed by his talent. After graduating from the Theological School in Reykjavík, he took orders and was appointed to a small living in the neighborhood of the town. This he resigned in the autumn of 1873, whilst in a state of mental distress over the loss of his second wife and being, at the time, as so often in his early life, torn by an inner religious struggle. For the next few years he was editor of the oldest weekly periodical in Iceland, afterwards resuming his office as clergyman, and held two *maj*, or livings, successively until the turn of the century when he became the first Icelander to receive a pension from the Icelandic Parliament, which he held for the remaining twenty years of his life. Matthías Jochumsson was one of the most comprehensive, inspired, eloquent, yet prolific and uneven major Icelandic poets of any age. He was best known and will be longest remembered for the finest of his own poems and for his masterly translations of various major works of world literature, and for his many and spirited essays and letters. More than anyone else he had earned the honored title of "Icelandic national poet." The poem was written in Great Britain during the winter of 1873-1874, the first verse in Edinburgh, the remaining two, which, however, Jochumsson himself never estimated highly, in London. At that time only a decade had passed since he had attracted nationwide notice by his poetry, and yet another ten years went by before a separate volume of poems by him was to appear.

The composer of the tune was Sveinbjörn Sveinbjörnsson; his lot was very different from that of Jochumsson. He was the son of one of the highest officials in the country—the president of the Superior Court of Justice—and spent the greater part of his life abroad. He took a degree in divinity and later became the first Icelander to make music his career. He had finished a five years' musical education in Copenhagen, Edinburgh, and Leipzig and had just settled down as a music master and pianist in Edinburgh when Jochumsson came there in the autumn of 1873 to stay with him, for they were old school friends despite a twelve years' difference in age. When he had finished the opening verse of the hymn, Matthías showed it to Sveinbjörnsson, and in his autobiography we find the following description of this scene: "After studying the words carefully, Sveinbjörnsson professed his inability to set them to music; during the course of the winter I wrote repeatedly, pressing him to attempt the hymn. And at length, in the spring, the music arrived, reaching us at home just in time for the national celebrations." Sveinbjörnsson lived in Edinburgh for most of the remainder of his life, except the last eight years, which he spent in Winnipeg, Reykjavík, and Copenhagen, where he died, sitting at his piano. From the time he wrote the tune for the national anthem until the end of his life he continued to compose different kinds of music. Among his works are to be found a number of excellent tunes written for Icelandic poems, in spite of the fact that he was most of the time in little direct contact with his native people; indeed he became earlier known as a composer in Britain than in his mother country, although his compositions are more in the style of Scandinavian than English music. Among the small band of Icelandic composers he was both among the pioneers and among those who had attained the greatest heights.

Neither the words nor the melody of the anthem seem however to have attracted particular attention when it was sung by the choir during the commemoration services in the Cathedral at Reykjavík on Sunday, 2 August, 1874. On that day there were sung seven commemorative poems that Jochumsson had been commissioned to write, most of them composed in the course of a single day—such could be his speed in writing poetry. But the anthem was one of the few poems he wrote for the celebrations of his own accord. From all parts of Iceland people flocked to the ceremony and dignitaries came from various European countries and from America. From Denmark came King Christian IX, the first of its sovereigns ever to visit the country. On this occasion he presented to his people a constitution containing important new reforms (such as the granting of legislative power and partial control over financial affairs). This was one of the stages in the gradual recovery of national independence which had been lost 1262-64; next came home rule (an Icelandic minister in charge of Icelandic affairs resident in Reykjavík) in 1904; fourteen years later Iceland became a sovereign state in union with Denmark (the king of Denmark being also king of Iceland); and, finally, came the foundation of a republic (with an Icelandic president) on 17 June 1944.

While independence was still a thing of the distant future, there was no question of there being a national anthem in the usual sense. However, when Icelanders wished to sing in praise of their motherland, place of honor was during the nineteenth century given to "Eldgamla Ísafold" by Bjarni Thorarensen (1786-1841), written in Copenhagen, probably during 1808-1809. But there were two reasons why this could not become established as the national anthem despite its general popularity. One was that apart from the first and final verses the poet's nostalgia finds expression there in taunts against Denmark, where the poet was then living. A weightier reason, however, was that it was sung to the tune of the British national anthem—although set originally, it seems, to a tune by Du Puy. During the last quarter of the nineteenth century, the song was often sung in public by choral societies. But it was not until during the period between home rule and independence, that is, from 1904-1918, that it became established by tradition as the national anthem.

When sovereignty was officially proclaimed, it was played as the national anthem of Iceland at the ceremony, and such it has remained ever since. The Icelandic Government acquired the ownership of the copyright of the melody, which formerly had been held by a Danish music-publishing firm in 1948, and that of the words in 1949. Still, undeniably the song has its drawbacks as a national anthem. True, Icelanders do not much object to the poem on account of its being more in the manner of a hymn than a patriotic song. But the melody ranges over so wide a compass that it is not within everyone's power to sing. People, therefore, often turn to other patriotic songs when they wish to sing in praise of their country, and, especially, popular during the last few decades have been "Íslandsvisur" ("Ég vil elska mitt land") by Jón Trausti (penname of Gudmundur Magnússon 1873-1918) sung to a tune by the Rev. Bjarni Thorsteinsson (1861-1938), and "Ísland ögrum skorið," a verse from a poem by Eggert Ólafsson (1726-1768); the melody was by Sigvaldi Kaldalóns (1881-1946). But neither these nor others have succeeded in ousting the "Lofsöngur" from its place as the national anthem.

Icelandic Words	English Translation[2]
1	1
Ó, guð vors lands! Ó, land vors guð,	Our country's God! Our country's God!
Vér lofum þitt heilaga, heilaga nafn,	We worship Thy name in its wonder sublime.
Úr sólkerfum himnanna hnýta þér krans	The suns of the heavens are set in thy crown
þínir herskarar, tímanna safn.	By thy legions, the ages of time!
Fyrir þér er einn dagur sem þúsund ár	With Thee is each day as a thousand years,
og þúsund ár dagur, ei meir:	Each thousand of years, but a day.
eitt eilífðar smáblóm með titrandi tár,	Eternity's flow'r, with its homage of tears,
sem tilbiður guð sinn og deyr.	That reverently passes away.
Íslands þúsund ár,	Iceland's thousand years!
(repeat)	(repeat)

Eitt eilífðar smáblóm með titrandi tár,	Eternity's flow'r, with its homage of tears,
sem tilbiður guð sinn og deyr.	That reverently passes away.

2

Ó, guð, ó, guð! Vér föllum fram	Our God, our God, we bow to Thee,
og fórnum þér brennandi, brennandi sál,	Our spirits most fervent we place in thy care.
guð faðir, vor drottinn frá kyni til kyns,	Lord, God of our fathers from age unto age,
og vér kvökum vort helgasta mál.	We are breathing our holiest prayer.
Vér kvökum og þökkum í þúsund ár,	We pray and we thank Thee a thousand years
því þú ert vort einasta skjól.	For safely protected we stand;
Vér kvökum og þökkum með titrandi tár,	We pray and we bring Thee our homage of tears
því þú tilbjóst vort forlagahjól.	Our destiny rest in Thy hand.
Íslands þúsund ár,	Iceland's thousand years
(repeat)	(repeat)
voru morgunsins húmköldu, hrynjandi tár,	The hoarfrost of morning which tinted those years,
sem hitna við skínandi sól.	Thy sun rising high, shall command!

3

Ó, guð vors lands! Ó, lands vors guð!	Our country's God! Our country's God!
Vér lifum sem blaktandi, blaktandi strá.	Our life is a feeble and quivering reed;
Vér deyjum, ef þú ert ei ljós það og líf,	We perish, deprived of Thy spirit and light
sem að lyftir oss duftinu frá.	To redeem and uphold in our need.
Ó, vert þú hvern morgun vort ljúfasta líf,	Inspire us at morn with Thy courage and love,
vor leiðtogi í daganna þraut	And lead through the days of our strife!
og á kvöldin vor himneska hvíld og vor hlíf	At evening send peace from Thy heaven above,
og vor hertogi á þjóðlífsins braut.	And safeguard our nation through life.
Íslands þúsund ár,	Iceland's thousand years!
(repeat)	(repeat)
verði gróandi þjóðlíf með þverrandi tár,	O, prosper our people, diminish our tears
sem þroskast á guðsríkis braut.	And guide, in Thy wisdom, through life!

Iceland

Ó, guð vors lands! Ó, land vors guð, Vér lof - - um þitt heil - ag - a, heil - - ag - a nafn, Úr sól - kerf - um himn - ann - a hný - - ta þér krans þín - ir her - skar - ar, tím - ann - a safn __. Fyr - ir þér er einn dag - ur sem þús - und __ ár og þús - und ár dag - ur, ei meir __: eitt ei - lífð - ar smá blóm með titr - and - i tár, sem til - bið - ur guð sinn og deyr __. Ís - lands

þús - und ár, Ís - lands þús - sand ár ___, Eitt ei - lífð - ar smá - blóm með titr - and - i tár, sem

til - bið - ur guð sinn og deyr ___.

India

भारत

Bharat

Republic of India

Quick Country Facts

Location: South Asia, Indian subcontinent

Area: 1,229,737 sq. mi. (3,287,590 sq. km.)

Population (2002 est.): 1,045,845,226

Capital: New Delhi (pop. 11,500,000)

Largest City: Mumbai (pop. 17,850,000)

Official Languages: Hindi, English

GDP/PPP: $2.66 trillion, $2,540 per capita

Monetary Unit: Rupee

जन गण मन

Jana-Gana-Mana

(Thou Art the Ruler of All Minds)

Lyrics and Music: Rabindranath Tagore (1861-1941). Adopted: 1950.

Historical Background[1]

The anthem, composed originally in Bengali by Rabindranath Tagore, was adopted in its Hindi version by the Constituent Assembly as the national anthem of India on 24 January 1950. It was first sung 27 December 1911 at the Calcutta session of the Indian National Congress. The complete song consists of five stanzas. Playing time of the full version is approximately fifty-two seconds. A short version consisting of first and last lines of the stanza (playing time approximately twenty seconds) is also played on certain occasions. The lyrics were rendered into English by Tagore himself.

Hindi Words	Hindi Words (Transliteration)	English Translation[2]
जन गण मन अधिनायक जय हे	*Jana-gana-mana-adhinayaka, jaya he*	Thou art the rulers of the minds of all people,
भरत भाग्य विधाता	*Bharata-bhagya-vidhata*	Dispenser of India's destiny.
पंजाढा सिंधु गुजरात मराठा	*Punjab-Sindhu-Gujarata-Maratha*	Thy name rouses the hearts of Punjab,
द्रविड़ उत्क्ल वंग	*Dravida-Utkala-Banga*	Sind, Gujarat and Maratha,
विंध्य हिमाचल यमुना गंगा	*Vindhya-Himachala-Yamuna-Ganga*	Of the Dravida and Orissa and
उच्छ्ल जलधि तरंग	*Uchchala-Jaladhi-taranga*	Bengal;
तव शुभ नामे जागे	*Tava shubha nama se jage*	It echoes in the hills of the Vindhyas
तव शुभ आशिष मागे	*Tava shubha ashish maange*	and Himalayas,
गाहे तव जय गाथा	*Gaye tava jaya-gatha*	Mingles in the music of Yamuna and
जन गण मंगल दायक जय हे	*Jana-gana-mangala-dayaka jaya he*	Ganga and is chanted by
भरत भाग्य विधाता	*Bharata-bhagya-vidhata*	The waves of the Indian Sea.
जय हे जय हे जय हे	*Jaya he, jaya he, jaya he*	They pray for thy blessings and sing thy praise.
जय जय जय जय हे	*Jaya jaya jaya, jaya he!*	The saving of all people waits in thy hand,
		thou dispenser of India's destiny,
		Victory, victory, victory to thee.

India

ye ta-va ja-ya- ga - tha __ Ja - na- ga- na- man- ga - la- da- ya- ka ja - ya he

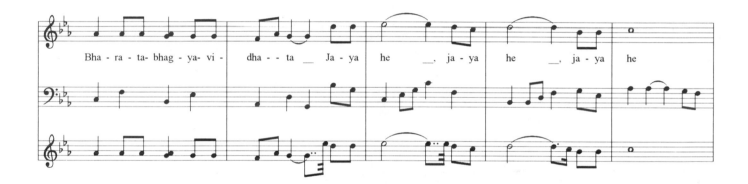

Bha - ra - ta- bhag - ya- vi- dha - ta __ Ja- ya he __, ja- ya he __, ja- ya he

Ja - ya ja - ya ja - ya ja - ya, he __!

Indonesia

Republik Indonesia

(Republic of Indonesia)

```
                    Quick Country Facts
Location: Southeast Asia
Area: 729,000 sq. mi. (1,919,440 sq. km.)
Population (2002 est.): 231,328,092
Capital/Largest City: Jakarta (pop. 12,300,000)
Official Language: Bahasa Indonesia
GDP/PPP: $687 billion, $3,000 per capita
Monetary Unit: Rupiah
```

Indonesia Raya

(Great Indonesia)

Lyrics and Music: Wage Rudolf Supratman (1903-1938). Adopted: 1949.

Historical Background[1]

The song was composed in 1928 during Dutch colonial rule of the islands. "Divide and rule" was the policy of the day, which deliberately aggravated language, ethnic, cultural, and religious differences amongst the people. The birth of "Indonesia Raya" marked the beginning of the Indonesian nationalist movements. The song was first introduced by its composer, Wage Rudolf Supratman, at the second All Indonesian Youth Congress on 28 October 1928 in Batavia, now Jakarta. There, Indonesian youth of different backgrounds resolutely pledged allegiance to one native land, Indonesia, and one unified language, the Indonesian language. Soon the national song gained popularity. It was echoed at political rallies, where people stood in solemn observance. The song seriously aroused national consciousness throughout the archipelago.

Bahasa Indonesia Words	English Translation[2]
VERSE	VERSE
Indonesia tanah airku.	Indonesia, our native country,
Tanah tumpah darahku.	Our place of birth,
Disanalah aku berdiri.	Where we all arise to stand guard
Jadi pandu ibuku.	Over this our motherland:
Indonesia kebangsaanku.	Indonesia our nationality,
Bangsa dan tanah airku.	Our people and our country.
Marilah kita berseru:	Come then, let us all exclaim
"Indonesia bersatu!"	Indonesia united.
Hiduplah tanahku.	Long live our land,
Hiduplah negeriku.	Long live our state,
Bangsaku. Rakyatku semuanya.	Our nation, our people, and all
Bangunlah jiwanya.	Arise then, its spirit,
Bangunlah badannya	Arise, its bodies
Untuk Indonesia Raya!	For Great Indonesia.
CHORUS	CHORUS
Indonesia Raya, merdeka, merdeka	Indonesia the Great, independent and free.
Tanahku, negeriku yang kucinta	Our beloved country.
Indonesia Raya, merdeka, merdeka	Indonesia the Great, independent and free.
Hiduplah Indonesia Raya.	Long live Indonesia the Great!

Indonesia

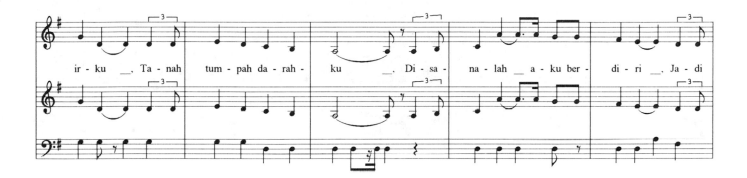

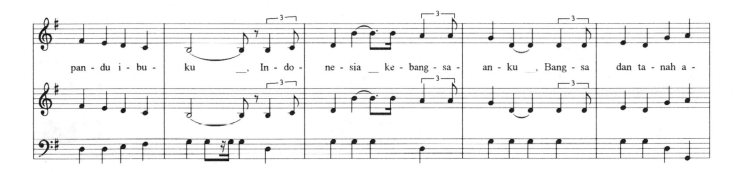

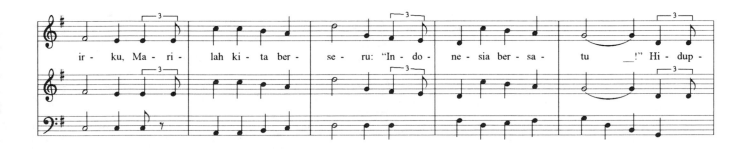

Iran

جمهوري اسلامي ايران

Jomhoori-e-Islami-e-Iran

(Islamic Republic of Iran)

Quick Country Facts

Location: West Asia, Near East

Area: 636,293 sq. mi. (1,648,000 sq. km.)

Population (2000 est.): 66,622,704

Capital/Largest City: Tehran (pop. 10,400,000)

Official Language: Farsi Persian

GDP/PPP: $456 billion, $7,000 per capita

Monetary Unit: Rial

سرود جمهوري اسلامي ايران

Sorood-e-Jomhoori-e-Islami-e-Iran

(National Anthem of the Islamic Republic of Iran)

Music: Hassan Riahi (b. 1945). Adopted: 1990.

Farsi Persian Words (Transliteration)	English Translation
Sar Zad Az Ufuq Mihr-i Hawaran	Upwards on the horizon rises the Eastern Sun,
Furug-i Dida-yi Haqq-Gawaran	The sight of the true religion.
Bahman-Farci Iman-i Mast	Bahman—the brilliance of our faith.
Payamat Ay Imam Istiqal,	Your message,
Azadi-naqs-i Gan-i Mast	O Imam,
Payanda Mani Wa Gawidan	Of independence and freedom
Jomhoori-e-Islami-e-Iran	Is imprinted on our souls.
	O Martyrs!
	The time of your cries of

	Pain rings in our ears.
	Enduring, continuing, eternal,
	The Islamic Republic of Iran.

Iran

Iraq

جمهورية العراق

al-Jumhouriya al-'Iraqia

Republic of Iraq

Quick Country Facts

Location: West Asia, Middle East

Area: 167,920 sq. mi. (437,072 sq. km.)

Population (2002 est.): 24,001,816

Capital/Largest City: Baghdad (pop. 4,850,000)

Official Language: Arabic

GDP/PPP: $59 billion, $2,500 per capita

Monetary Unit: Iraqi Dinar

Historical Background[1]

In September 2000, Saddam Hussein directed Iraq's poets to come up with a new national anthem because he concluded that the current one was too heavy going. He believed they should "prepare an anthem which could be sung with enthusiasm by fighters on the battlefield, by the valiant men of anti-aircraft defense, by people at work, and by women going about their business." Saddam, quoted on Radio Free Europe, said that the words of the new anthem must be "short, so they may be sung on joyous occasions and not only during challenging times." He did not mention whether the current anthem would be dropped in favor of the new song. "We could have more than one anthem; the choice will be made after the new theme is put to music."

Anthem Not Available

Ireland

Poblacht na hÉireann

Republic of Ireland

```
Quick Country Facts
Location: Western Europe, British Isles
Area: 27,136 sq. mi. (70,280 sq. km.)
Population (2002 est.): 3,883,159
Capital/Largest City: Dublin (pop. 1,056,666)
Official Languages: Irish Gaelic, English
GDP/PPP: $111.3 billion, $28,500 per capita
Monetary Unit: Euro
```

Amhrán na bhFiann

The Soldier's Song

Irish Gaelic Lyrics: Liam O'Rinn. English Lyrics: Peadar Kearny (1883-1942). Music: Peadar Kearney and Patrick Heeney (1881-1911). Adopted: 1926.

Historical Background[1]

The Irish national anthem is "Amhrán na bhFiann" or "The Soldier's Song," written in 1907 by Peadar Kearney, an uncle of writer Brendan Behan, who together with Patrick Heeney also composed the music. It was first published in the newspaper *Irish Freedom* in 1912 but was not widely known until it was sung both at the GPO during the Easter Rising of 1916 and, later, at various camps where republicans were interned. "Amhrán na bhFiann" consisted of three stanzas and a chorus. The chorus was formally adopted as the National Anthem in 1926, displacing the earlier Fenian anthem, "God Save Ireland." An official Irish translation by Liam O'Rinn came later. A section of the national anthem (consisting of the first four bars followed by the last five) is also the Irish presidential salute.

Irish Gaelic Words	English Words
Sinne Fianna Fáil,	Soldiers are we, whose lives are pledged to Ireland
Atá fé gheall ag Éirinn,	Some have come from a land beyond the wave,
Buidhean dár sluagh tar rúinn do ráinig chughainn:	Sworn to be free,
Fámhóidh bheith saor,	No more our ancient sireland

Sean-tír ár sinnsear feasta
Ní fágfar fá'n tiorán ná fá'n tráil;
Anocht a theigeamh sa bhearna baoghail,
Le gean ar Ghaeil chun báis nó saoil
Le gunna sgréach fá lámhach na piléar.
Seo Libh canaídh amhrán na bhFiann.

Shall shelter the despot or the slave;
Tonight we man the Bearna Baoghal [gap of danger]
In Erin's cause come woe or weal;
'Mid cannon's roar and rifle's peal
We'll chant a soldier's song.

Ireland

Sin - ne Fian - na Fáil _, A - tá fé gheall ag Éi - rinn, Buidhean dár
Sol - - diers are we _, whose lives are pledged to Ire - land Some have

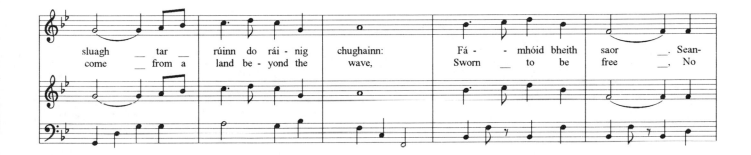

sluagh _ tar rúinn do rái - nig chughainn: Fá - - mhóid bheith saor _. Sean-
come _ from a land be - yond the wave, Sworn _ to be free _, No

tír ár sin - sear feas - ta Ní fág - far fá'n tior - án ná fá'n tráil _; A -
more our an - cient sire - land Shall shel - ter the des - pot or the slave _; To -

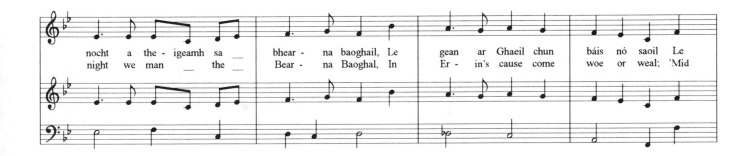

nocht a the - igeamh sa _ bhear - na baoghail, Le gean ar Ghaeil chun báis nó saoil Le
night we man _ the _ Bear - na Baoghal, In Er - in's cause come woe or weal; 'Mid

gun - na ___ sgréach fá lám - hach na ___ piléar __. Seo Libh can - aídh amh - rán na bhFiann __.
can - non's ___ roar and ri - - fles __ peal __ We'll chant __ a sol - dier's song __.

Israel

מדינת ישראל

Medinat Israel

دولة إسرائيل

Daulat Isra'il

State of Israel

Quick Country Facts

Location: West Asia, Middle East

Area: 8,020 sq. mi. (20,770 sq. km.)

Population (2002 est.): 5,842,454

Capital/Largest City: Tel Aviv (pop. 355,900)

Languages: Hebrew, Arabic, English

GDP/PPP: $122 billion, $19,000 per capita

Monetary Unit: Shekel

התקוה

Hatikvah

(The Hope)

Lyrics: Naphtali Herz Imber (1856-1909). Music: Samuel Cohen or Nissan Belzer. Adopted: 1948.

Historical Background[1]

"Hatikvah," the Israeli national anthem, was never officially adopted. It has been attributed to Naphtali Herz Imber, but the song that is sung today bears little resemblance to the original poem written in 1878 and published in 1886. The poem was first published under the title of "Tikvatenu" ("Our Hope") in Imber's *Barkai*. The inspiration for the poem is said to have been the founding of the city of Petach Tikvah (Gateway of Hope) in Israel. Its themes were possibly influenced by Polish patriotic songs. In 1882, Imber went to Rishon L'Zion, where "Tikvatenu" was received with enthusiasm. Samuel Cohen, who was living there at the time, put the poem to music based on an old

Moldavian-Romanian folk song, "Carul cu Boi" ("Cart and Oxen"). The Moldavian-born Cohen did not receive credit due to lack of a copyright on the melody.

The wording went through a number of modifications over the years, reflecting changes of nationalistic ideas and customs. The words "Where David once lived" became "Zion and Jerusalem" in the chorus. The poem was cut to two verses and the chorus and the call was to be "a free nation in our own land," not just to "live in the land of our fathers." The accent was switched to the Sephardic pronunciation. The melody was also corrected to fit the cadence and syllable stress of the new version. These changes can be traced through the various printed editions of the work such as the one from the Hebrew Publishing Company of 1909.

The first competition for the national anthem of a Jewish nation was announced in *Die Welt*, a German newspaper, in 1898. Another contest was called for by the Fourth Zionist Congress in the year 1900, but no song was officially chosen. In 1901, one of the sessions of the Fifth Zionist Congress in Basel, Switzerland, ended with the singing of "Hatikvah" (still called "Tikvatenu"). It was not until 1905 that the song was sung by all the delegates present at the Seventh Zionist Congress.

Imber died in 1909 in New York and his remains were reinterred at the Mt. Herzl cemetery in Jerusalem in 1953.

Hebrew Words	Hebrew Words (Transliteration)	English Translation[2]
כל עוד בלבב פנימה	*Kol od balevav p'nimah*	As long as deep in the heart,
נפש יהודי הומיה	*Nefesh Yehudi homiyah*	The soul of a Jew yearns,
ולפאתי מזרח קדימה	*Ulfa'atey mizrach kadimah*	And forward to the East
עין לציון צופיה	*Ayin l'tzion tzofiyah*	To Zion, an eye looks.
עוד לא אבדה תקותנו	*Od lo avdah tikvatenu*	Our hope will not be lost,
התקוה בת שנות אלפים	*Hatikvah bat shnot alpayim*	The hope of two thousand years,
להיות עם חופשי בארצנו	*L'hiyot am chofshi b'artzenu*	To be a free nation in our land,
ארץ ציון וירושלים	*Eretz Tzion v'Yerushalayim*	The land of Zion and Jerusalem.
(repeat previous two lines)	(repeat previous two lines)	(repeat previous two lines)

Israel

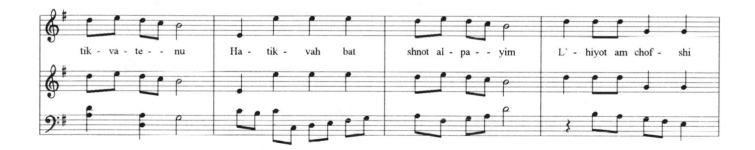

b' - - art - - ze - nu __ E - retz Tzi - on v'Ye - ru - sha - la - - yim __.

Italy

Repubblica Italiana

(Italian Republic)

```
Quick Country Facts
Location: Southern Europe
Area: 116,500 sq. mi. (301,230 sq. km.)
Population (2002 est.): 57,715,625
Capital/Largest City: Rome (pop. 2,693,383)
Official Language: Italian
GDP/PPP: $1.438 trillion, $25,000 per capita
Monetary Unit: Euro
```

Inno di Mameli

(Hymn of Mameli)

Lyrics: Goffredo Mameli (1827-1849). Music: Michele Novaro (1822-1885). Adopted: 1946.

Historical Background[1]

Michele Novaro composed the music of the Italian anthem in 1847 to words by the young poet Goffredo Mameli. The words of the anthem were meant to call to mind past battles for freedom waged by the Lombard towns, the Florentine republic, the Genoese, together with the young Balilla, against the Austrians; and the Sicilians against the French in the so-called Sicilian Vespers. The focus of all inspirations to freedom was Rome, the Rome that, in another poem, Mameli called "city of memories, city of hope."

The song, known as "L'inno di Mameli," has been the national anthem of the Republic of Italy since 1946. Between 1861, the year when Italy became a united nation, and 1946, the official anthem was the "March of the House of Savoia." On 23 November 1847 Mameli went to take the anthem to his musician friend, Michele Novaro. Overnight, the enthused musician composed the music, and the next day, in Genoa, Mameli brought back the words and music to his companions. A few days later, on 1 December, "Fratelli d'Italia" was played for the first time at a popular assembly. The tune began to run like wildfire throughout the peninsula. It was on everyone's lips, in defiance of the Austrian, Bourbon, and Papal police.

There is still another and equally romantic story of the circumstances of the anthem's composition. On the evening of 8 September 1847, in the house of the American consul, there was talk of the uprisings of the day. Many of the guests clustered about Mameli and urged him to write a new song. On the spot he improvised a few lines, and, later in the night, at home, wrote the rest. A few days later a painter friend took the poem to Turin and read it aloud at the evening party given by a nobleman, Lorenzo Valerio, who was also a benefactor in the realm of music and musicians. The composer Novaro, enthused in his turn, tried out a few notes on the piano and then, too, went home to compose the sequel. The anthem was sung for the first time the next day by a group of political exiles in the Cafè della Lega Italiana of Turin.

Italian Words	English Translation[2]
1	1
Fratelli d'Italia	Italian brothers,
L'Italia s'è desta	Italy has arisen,
Dell'elmo di Scipio	With Scipio's helmet
S'è cinta la testa.	Binding her head.
Dov'è la Vittoria?	Where is victory?
Le porga la chioma;	Let her bow down,
Chè schiava di Roma	For God has made her
Iddio la creò.	The slave of Rome.
(repeat verse)	(repeat verse)
CHORUS	CHORUS
Stringiamoci a coorte,	Let us gather in legions,
Siam pronti alla morte:	Ready to die!
(repeat)	(repeat)
Italia chiamò!	Italy has called!
(repeat chorus)	(repeat chorus)
2	2
Noi siamo da secoli	We for centuries
Calpesti e derisi,	Have been downtrodden and derided,
Perchè non siam popolo,	Because we are not a people,
Perchè siam divisi;	Because we are divided.
Raccolgaci un'unica	Let one flag, one hope
Bandiera, un speme;	Bring us together;
Di fonderci insieme;	The hour has struck
Già l'ora suonò.	For us to join forces.
(repeat verse)	(repeat verse)
CHORUS	CHORUS

<table>
<tr><td>

3

Uniamoci, amiamoci;

L'unione e l'amore

Rivelano ai popoli

Le vie del Signore:

Giuriamo far libero

Il suolo natío;

Uniti per Dio

Chi vincer ci può?

(repeat verse)

CHORUS

4

Dall'Alpi a Sicilia

Dovunque è Legnano

Ogni uom di Ferruccio:

Ha il cuor e la mano.

I bimbi d'Italia

Si chiamano Balilla:

Il suon d'ogni squilla

I vespri suonò.

(repeat verse)

CHORUS

5

Son giunchi che piegano

Le spade vendute:

Già l'Aquila d'Austria

Le penne ha perdute.

Il sangue d'Italia

E il sangue polacco

Bevè col Cosacco

Ma il cor le bruciò.

(repeat verse)

CHORUS

</td><td>

3

Let us unite and love one another;

For union and love

Reveal to peoples

The way of the Lord

Let us swear to free

Our native soil;

If we are united under God,

Who can conquer us?

(repeat verse)

CHORUS

4

From the Alps to Sicily,

Everywhere it is Legnano;

Every man has the heart

And hand of Ferruccio.

The children of Italy

Are all called Balilla,

Every trumpet blast

Sounds the (Sicilian) Vespers.

(repeat verse)

CHORUS

5

Mercenary swords

Are feeble reeds,

And the Austrian eagle

Has lost his plumes.

This eagle that drunk the blood

Of Italy and Poland,

Together with the Cossack,

But this has burned his gut.

(repeat verse)

CHORUS

</td></tr>
</table>

Italy

schia - - va ___ di Ro - - ma Id - di - o la ___ cre - - ò ___.

Fra - tel - li d'I - ta - lia L'I - ta - lia s'è des - ta Dell' el - mo di Sci - pio S'è cin - ta la

tes - ta. Dov'è ___ la Vit - to - ria? Le por - ga la chio - ma; Chè schia - va di Ro - ma Id - dio la cre -

ò. String - iam - oci a co - or - te, Siam pronti al - la mor - te: Siam pronti al - la mor - te: l'I - ta - lia chia -

mò. String – iam – oci a co – or – te, Siam pronti al – la mor – te: Siam pron – ti al – la mor – te: l'I – ta – lia chia –

mò.

Jamaica

```
Quick Country Facts
Location: North America, Caribbean Sea
Area: 4,411 sq. mi. (10,991 sq. km.)
Population (2002 est.): 2,680,029
Capital/Largest City: Kingston (pop. 104,000)
Languages: English, Jamaican Creole
GDP/PPP: $9.8 billion, $3,700 per capita
Monetary Unit: Jamaican Dollar
```

National Anthem

Lyrics: Reverend Hugh Braham Sherlock (b. 1905). Music: Robert Charles Lightbourne (1909-1995). Adopted: 1962.

Historical Background

The Jamaican national anthem was written by Hugh Braham Sherlock with music composed by Robert Charles Lightbourne. Originally, the lyrics and music had nothing to do with each other until Mapletoft Poulle (1923-1951) blended them to form the present song. It was selected upon independence from Great Britain in 1962.

Words	
1	2
Eternal Father bless our land	Teach us true respect for all
Guide us with Thy mighty hand.	Stir response to duty's call.
Keep us free from evil powers	Strengthen us the weak to cherish
Be our light through countless hours	Give us vision lest we perish
To our leaders, Great Defender,	Knowledge send us Heavenly Father
Grant true wisdom from above	Grant true wisdom from above
Justice, truth be ours forever,	Justice, truth be ours forever,
Jamaica, land we love.	Jamaica, land we love.
Jamaica, Jamaica, Jamaica, land we love.	Jamaica, Jamaica, Jamaica, land we love.

Jamaica

E - ter - nal Fa - ther bless our land Guide us with Thy migh - ty hand. Keep us free from

e - vil pow - ers Be our light through count - less hours To our lead - ers, Great De - fen - - der,

Grant true wis - dom from __ a - bove Just - ice, truth be ours for - ev - er, Ja - mai - - ca, land we

love __. Ja - mai - ca __, Ja - mai - ca __, Ja - mai - - ca, land we love.

Japan

日本国

Nippon Koku

Quick Country Facts

Location: East Asia

Area: 145,874 sq. mi. (377,835 sq. km.)

Population (2002 est.): 126,974,628

Capital/Largest City: Tokyo (pop. 34,750,000)

Official Language: Japanese

GDP/PPP: $3.55 trillion, $28,000 per capita

Monetary Unit: Yen

君が代

Kımıgayo

(His Majesty's Reign)

Lyrics: Ancient Poem. Music: Hayashi Hiromori (1831-1896). Adopted: 1999.

Historical Background[1]

It is not certain who wrote the words to Japan's national anthem, "Kimigayo." However, they were first found in a poem contained in two anthologies of Japanese thirty-one-syllable *waka*, namely, the tenth-century *Kokin Wakashu* and the 11th-century *Wakan Roeishu*. From very early times, the poem was recited to commemorate auspicious occasions and at banquets celebrating important events. The words were often put to music with melodies typical of such vocal styles as *yokyoku* (sung portions of *Noh* performances), *kouta* (popular songs with *shamisen* accompaniment), *joruri* (dramatic narrative chanting with *shamisen* accompaniment), *saireika* (festival songs), and *biwauta* (songs with *biwa* accompaniment). The words were also used in fairy tales and other stories and even appeared in the Edo-period popular fiction known as *Ukiyo-zoshi* and in collections of humorous *kyoka* (mad verse).

In 1869 the British military band instructor John William Fenton, who was then working in Yokohama, learned that Japan lacked a national anthem and told the members of Japan's military band about the British national anthem "God Save the King." Fenton emphasized the necessity of a national anthem and proposed that he would compose the music if someone would provide the words. The band members, after consulting with their director, requested Artillery Captain

Oyama Iwao (1842-1916) from present-day Kagoshima Prefecture, who was well versed in Japanese and Chinese history and literature, to select appropriate words for such an anthem. (Oyama later became army minister and a field marshal.) Fenton put his own music to the "Kimigayo" words selected by Oyama from a *biwauta* titled "Horaisan," and the first "Kimigayo" anthem was the result.

The melody was, however, completely different from the one known today. It was performed, with the accompaniment of brass instruments, during an army parade in 1870, but it was later considered to be lacking in solemnity, and it was agreed that a revision was needed. In 1876, Osamu Yusuke (later known as Nakamura Yusuke), the director of the Naval Band, submitted to the Navy Ministry a proposal for changing the music, and on the basis of his proposal it was decided that the new melody should reflect the style used in musical chants performed at the imperial court. In July 1880, four persons were named to a committee to revise the music. They were Naval Band director Nakamura Yusuke; Army Band director Yotsumoto Yoshitoyo; the court director of *gagaku* (Japanese court music) performances, Hayashi Hiromori; and a German instructor under contract with the navy, Franz Eckert. Finally a melody produced by Hayashi Hiromori was selected on the basis of the traditional scale used in *gagaku*. Eckert made a four-part vocal arrangement, and the new national anthem was first performed in the imperial palace on the Meiji Emperor's birthday, 3 November 1880.

On 9 August 1999, the Japanese Diet passed a bill which officially adopted the "Kimigayo" as the national anthem of Japan, despite protests from neighboring Asian countries, which claim that the song is a symbol of Japanese imperialism.

Japanese Words	Japanese Words (Transliteration)	English Translation[2]
君が代は 千代に八千代にさざれ 石の巌となりて 苔の生すまで	*Kimi gayo wa* *Chiyo ni yachiyo ni sazare* *Ishi no iwao to nari te* *Koke no musu made*	Thousands of years of happy reign be thine; Rule on, my lord, till what are pebbles now By age united to mighty rocks shall grow Whose venerable sides the moss doth line.

Japan

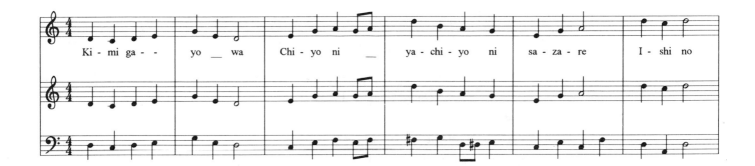

Jordan

المملكة الأردنية الهاشمية

al-Mamlaka al-Urduniya al-Hashemiyah

(Hashemite Kingdom of Jordan)

Quick Country Facts

Location: West Asia, Middle East

Area: 34,573 sq. mi. (92,300 sq.km.)

Population (2002 est.): 5,307,470

Capital/Largest City: Amman (pop. 963,490)

Official Language: Arabic

GDP/PPP: $22.8 billion, $4,300 per capita

Monetary Unit: Jordanian Dinar

عـاش المليـك

A-sha-l Maleek

(Long Live the King)

Lyrics: Abdul-Mone'm al-Rifai (1917-1985). Music: Abdul-Qader al-Taneer (1901-1957). Adopted: 1946.

Arabic Words	Arabic Words (Transliteration)	English Translation
عـاش المليـك عـاش المليـك ساميا مقامه خافقات في المعالي أعلامـه	*A-sha-al Maleek* *(repeat)* *Sa-Mi-yan-ma-qa mu-hu* *Kha-fi-qa-tin fil ma-ali* *a-lam m-hu*	Long live the King! Long live the King! His position is sublime, His banners waving in glory supreme.

Jordan

Kazakhstan

Қазақстан Республикасы

Kazakstan Respublikasy

(Republic of Kazakhstan)

Quick Country Facts

Location: Central Asia

Area: 1,049,000 sq. mi. (2,717,300 sq. km.)

Population (2002 est.): 16,741,519

Capital: Astana (pop. 280,200)

Largest City: Almaty (pop. 1,200,000)

Official Languages: Kazak, Russian

GDP/PPP: $98.1 billion, $5,900 per capita

Monetary Unit: Tenge

Мамлекеттик Гимни

Mamlekettik Gimni

(National Anthem)

Lyrics: Muzafar Alimbayev (b. 1923), Kadyr Myrzaliyev, Tumanbai Moldagaliyev, and Zhadyra Daribayeva. Music: Mukan Tulebayev (1913-1960), Eugeny Brusilovsky (1905-1981), and Latif Khamidi.

Kazak Words	Kazak Words (Transliteration)	English Translation
1	1	1
Жаралған намыстан қаһарман халықпыз,	*Zharalghan namystan qaharman khalyqpyz*	We are a valiant people, sons of honor,
Азаттық жолында жалындап Жаныппыз	*Azattyk zholynda zhalyndap Zhanypyz*	We've sacrificed everything to gain our freedom.
Тағдырдың тезінен, тозақтың өзінен	*Tagdyrdin tezinen, tozaktyn (o-umlaut) zinen*	Emerging from malicious grip of fate, from hell of fire,
Аман-сау қалыппыз, аман-сау	*Aman-saw kalyppyz, aman-saw*	We scored a victory of glory and

330

қалыппыз.	*kälyppyz.*	success.
CHORUS	**CHORUS**	**CHORUS**
Еркіндік қыраны, шарықта,	*Erkindik kyrany, sharykta*	Soar high up in the sky, oh, the eagle of freedom,
Елдікке шақырып тірлікте!	*Eldikke shakyryp tirlikte!*	Call up to harmony, agreement and Accord!
Алыптың қуаты—халықта,	*Alyptyn kuaty--khalykta,*	Since the hero's might and strength is in the nation,
Халықтың қуаты—бірлікте!	*Khalyktyn kuaty—birlikte!*	Just as the unity is nation's razing sword.
2	**2**	**2**
Ардақтап анасын, құрметтеп данасын,	*Ardaktan anasyn, kyrmetten danasyn,*	While honoring and respecting our mothers
Бауырға басқанбыз баршаның баласын.	*Bauyrga baskanbyz barshanyn balasyn.*	The cream of our raising nation
Татулық достықтың киелі бесігі—	*Tatulyk dostyktyn kieli besigi!*	We welcomed all ill-starred and struck by ruin
Мейірбан Ұлы Отан, қазақтың даласы!	*Meyirban Uly Otan, Kazakhtyn dalasy!*	Our homeland, the steppe, a sacred cradle
		Of friendship and accord
		Gave all a shelter and a hearty refuge!
CHORUS	**CHORUS**	**CHORUS**
3	**3**	**3**
Талайды өткердік, өткенге салауат,	*Talaydy otkerdin, otkenge salauat,*	We've overcome the hardships
Келешек ғажайып, келешек ғаламат!	*Keleshek gazhayyp keleshek galamat!*	Let the past serve as a bitter lesson
Ар-ождан, ана тіл, өнеге салтымыз,	*Ar-ozhdan, ana til onege-saltymyz,*	But we face a radiant future ahead
Ерлік те, елдік те ұрпаққа аманат!	*Erlik te, eldik te urlakka amanat!*	We bequeath our sacred legacy
		Implying our mother tongue
		And sovereignty, valor and traditions
		So dearly cherished by our forefathers
		As true mandate to future generations.
CHORUS	**CHORUS**	**CHORUS**

Kazakhstan

Kenya

Jamhuri ya Kenya

Republic of Kenya

```
Quick Country Facts
Location: Central Africa
Area: 224,960 sq. mi. (582,650 sq. km.)
Population (2002 est.): 31,138,735
Capital/Largest City: Nairobi (pop. 2,000,000)
Official Languages: Kiswahili, English
GDP/PPP: $31 billion, $1,000 per capita
Monetary Unit: Kenyan Shilling
```

Wimbo wa Taifa

National Anthem

Lyrics: Group of Citizens. Music: Traditional Melody. Adopted: 1963.

Historical Background

The Kenyan national anthem was written by a national committee of five songwriters to a tune based on traditional music. It was adopted in 1963, the year of independence.

Kiswahili Words	English Words
1	1
Ee Mungu nguvu yetu	O God of all creation,
Ilete baraka kwetu	Bless this our land and nation.
Haki iwe ngao na mlinzi	Justice be our shield and defender,
Natukae na udugu	May we dwell in unity,
Amani na uhuru	Peace and liberty.
Raha tupate na ustawi.	Plenty be found within our borders.
2	2
Amkeni ndugu zetu	Let one and all arise

Tufanye sote bidii	With hearts both strong and true.
Nasi tujitoe kwa nguvu	Service be our earnest endeavor,
Nchi yetu ya Kenya	And our Homeland of Kenya,
Tunayoipenda	Heritage of splendor,
Tuwe tayari kuilinda.	Firm may we stand to defend.
3	3
Natujenge taifa letu	Let all with one accord
Ee, ndio wajibu wetu	In common bond united,
Kenya istahili heshima	Build this our nation together,
Tuungane mikono	And the glory of Kenya,
Pamoja kazini	The fruit of our labor
Kila siku tuwe nashukrani.	Fill every heart with thanksgiving.

Kenya

Ee Mu-ngu ngu-vu ye-tu __ I-lete ba-ra-ka kwe-tu __
O God of all cre-a-tion __, Bless this our land and na-tion __.

Haki i-we nga-o na mli-nzi __ Na-tu-kae na u-du-gu A-mani na u-hu-ru
Justice be our shield and de-fen-der __, May we dwell in __ un-ity __, Peace and __ liber-ty.

Ra-ha tu-pa-te na u-sta-wi __.
Plen-ty be found with-in our bor-ders __.

Kiribati

Aia Maneaba ni Maroro Kain Kiribati

Republic of Kiribati

```
Quick Country Facts
Location: Oceania, Pacific Ocean
Area: 292 sq. mi. (811 sq. km.)
Population (2002 est.): 96,335
Capital/Largest City: Tarawa (pop. 25,154)
Official Languages: English, I-Kiribati
GDP/PPP: $79 million, $840 per capita
Monetary Unit: Australian Dollar
```

Teirake Kaini Kiribati

(Stand, Kiribati)

Lyrics and Music: Urium Tamuera Ioteba (1910-1988). Adopted: 1979

I-Kiribati Words	English Translation
1	1
Teirake kaini Kiribati,	Stand up, Kiribati!
Anene ma te kakatonga,	Sing with jubilation!
Tauraoi nakon te nwioko,	Prepare to accept responsibility
Ma ni buokia aomata,	And to help each other!
Tauaninne n te raoiroi,	Be steadfastly righteous!
Tangiria aoma ta nako.	Love all our people!
Tauaninne n te raoiroi,	(repeat previous two lines)
Tangiria aomata.	
2	2
Reken te kabaia ma te rau	The attainment of contentment
Ibuakoia kaain abara	And peace by our people
Bon reken te nano ae banin	Will be achieved when all

Ma te i-tangitangiri naba.
Ma ni wakina te kab'aia,
Ma n neboa i eta abara.
Ma ni wakina te kab'aia,
Ma n neboa abara.

3
Ti butiko ngkoe Atuara
Kawakinira ao kairika
Nakon taai aika i maira.
Buokira ni baim ae akoi.
Kakabaia ara Tautaeka
Ma ake a makuri iai.
Kakabaia ara Tautaeka
Ma aomata ni bane.

Our hearts beat as one,
Love one another!
Promote happiness and unity!
(repeat previous two lines)

3
We beseech You, O God,
To protect and lead us
In the days to come.
Help us with Your loving hand.
Bless our Government
And all our people!
(repeat previous two lines)

Kiribati

Tei - ra - ke kai - ni Ki - ri - ba - ti, A - ne - ne ma te ka - - ka - to - nga, Tau - ra - oi na - kon te

nwi - o - ko, Ma ni bu - o - ki - a ao - ma - ta, Ta - ua - ni - nne n te __ ra - oi - roi

__, Ta - ngi - ri - a ao - ma ta na - ko __. Ta - ua - ni - nne n te __ ra - oi - roi, Ta - ngi - ri - a

ao - ma - ta __.

338

Korea, North

조선민주주의인민공화국

Choson Minjuju-i Inmin Konghwa-guk

Democratic People's Republic of Korea

Quick Country Facts

Location: East Asia

Area: 46,768 sq. mi. (120,540 sq. km.)

Population (2002 est.): 22,224,195

Capital/Largest City: Pyongyang (pop. 2,741,260)

Official Language: Korean

GDP/PPP: $22 billion, $1,000 per capita

Monetary Unit: Won

애국가

Aeguk-ga

(Patriotic Song)

Lyrics: Pak Se Yong (1902-1989). Music: Kim Won Gyun (b. 1917). Adopted: 1947.

Historical Background[1]

The Democratic People's Republic of Korea (DPRK) has all along used the "Patriotic Song," its national anthem, which was created in Juche 36 (1947), for half a century. The song is the symbol of solemnity, noble feelings, national pride, and honor. It is a source of the patriotism and optimistic emotion of the Korean people. The song was created thanks to the Great Leader Comrade Kim Il Sung. Just after Korea's liberation from the Japanese colonial rule he gave creators a direction for the creation of the national anthem and gave concrete guidance as regards the conception of words, content, appearance, and depiction of the song. The song written by Pak Se Yong and composed by Kim Won Gyun under his guidance reflected the ideas and emotions of the people of a new Korea.

The song that was played on the day when the DPRK was founded with due ceremony on 9 September 1948 has served as the national anthem of socialist Korea for 50 years. The Koreans like to sing the song very much. In Korea where the song is sung as the first item of the radio program at dawn the leader, the party, the army and the people move as one in response to the song. The Korean people are working hard to exalt the dignity and honor of the country and build a prosperous country, singing the song. The great achievements and praiseworthy deeds that can be witnessed in their everyday life are based on the idea of the song. In Korea, led by the Dear Leader Comrade Kim Jong Il, who is attaching importance to the Juche character and the national character, the song will remain the eternal national anthem of Kim Il Sung's Korea.

Korean Words	Korean Words (Transliteration)	English Translation
1	1	1
아침은 빛나라 이 강산 은금의 자원도 가득한 삼천리 아름다운 내 조국 반만년 오랜 력사에 찬란한 문화로 자라난 슬기론 인민의 이 영광 몸과 맘 다 바쳐 이 조선 길이 받드세 (repeat previous four lines)	*A ch'im un pinnara, i kangsan Ungum e, chawon do kaduk han Samch'olli, arumdaun nae choguk, Panmannyon oraen ryoksa e. Ch'allan han munhwa ro charanan Sulgiroun inmin ui i yonggwang. Momgwa mam ta pach'yo, i, Choson Kiri pattuse.* (repeat previous four lines)	Let morning shine on the silver and gold of this land, Three thousand leagues packed with natural wealth. My beautiful fatherland. The glory of a wise people Brought up in a culture brilliant With a history five millennia long. Let us devote our bodies and minds To supporting this Korea forever. (repeat previous four lines)
2	2	2
백두산 기상을 다 안고 근로의 정신을 깃들어 진리로 뭉쳐진 억센 뜻 온 세계 앞서 나가리 솟는 힘 노도도 내밀어 인민의 뜻으로 선 나라 한 없이 부강하는 이 조선 길이 빛내세 (repeat previous four lines)	*Paektusan Kisang ul ta anko. Kullo ui chongsin un kitturo. Chilli ro mungch'yo jin oksen ttut On segye apso nagari. Sonnun him nodo do naemiro, Inmin ui ttus uro son nara. Han opsi pugang hanun I Choson kiri pinnaese.* (repeat previous four lines)	The firm will, bonded with truth, Nest for the spirit of labor, Embracing the atmosphere of Mount Paektu, Will go forth to all the world. The country established by the will of the people, Breasting the raging waves with soaring strength. Let us glorify forever this Korea, Limitlessly rich and strong. (repeat previous six lines)

Korea, North

A ch'im un pin na ra i kang-san Un— gum e, cha— won do ka- duk han Sam-

ch'ol li, a- rum-da un nae cho-guk, Pan— man nyon ora- en ryok-sa e. Ch'al-

lan han mun- hwa ro cha- ra- nan Sul— gi- roun in-min ui i yong-gwang. Mom——

gwa mam ta pa- ch'yo, i, Cho-son Kir i __ pat- tu—— se __.

Korea, South

대한민국

大韓民國

Taehan Min'guk

(Republic of Korea)

Quick Country Facts

Location: East Asia

Area: 38,031 sq. mi. (98,480 sq. km.)

Population (2002 est.): 48,324,000

Capital/Largest City: Seoul (pop. 19,850,000)

Official Language: Korean

GDP/PPP: $931 billion, $19,400 per capita

Monetary Unit: Won

애국가

愛國歌

Aeguk-ga

(Patriotic Song)

Lyrics: Yun Ch'i-ho (1865-1946) or An Ch'ang-ho (1878-1938). Music: Ahn Eak-tae (1905-1965).

Historical Background[1]

It is generally believed that the words of what is now the Republic of Korea's national anthem, which means, literally, "Song of Love of Country," were written toward the end of the nineteenth century either by Yun Ch'i-ho, a politician, or by An Ch'ang-ho, an independence leader and educator. Initially, "Aeguk-ga" was sung to the Scottish folk tune "Auld Lang Syne." During Japanese colonial rule (1910-1945), the song was banned, but overseas Koreans continued to sing it, expressing their yearnings for national independence. In 1937, Ahn Eak-tae, an internationally noted Korean musician based in Spain, composed the music for "Aeguk-ga." His work was officially adopted by the

342

Provisional Korean Government (1919-1945) in Shanghai, China. "Aeguk-ga" was sung at a ceremony celebrating the founding of the Republic of Korea Government on 15 August 1948, following national liberation in 1945.

Korean Words	Korean Words (Transliteration)	English Translation[2]
1 동해물과 백두산이 마르고 닳도록 하느님이 보우하사 우리 나라 만세	1 *Donghae mulgwa Baekdusani mareugo daltorok* *Haneunimi bouhasa urinara manse.*	1 Until the East Sea's waves are dry, Baek-du-san worn away, God watch o'er our land forever! Our Korea hail!
CHORUS 무궁화 삼천리 화려강산 대한사람 대한으로 길이 보전하세	CHORUS *Mugunghwa samcheolli hwaryeogangsan* *Daehan saram Daehan euro giri bojeonhase*	CHORUS Rose of Sharon, thousand miles of beautiful mountain and rivers! Guarded by her people, ever may Korea stand!
2 남산 위에 저 소나무 철갑을 두른 듯 바람 서리 불변함은 우리 기상일세	2 *Namsan wie jeo sonamu cheolgabeul dureundeut* *Baram seori bulbyeonhameun uri gisangilse*	2 Like that South Mountain armored pine, standing on duty still, Wind or frost, unchanging ever, be our resolute will.
CHORUS	CHORUS	CHORUS
3 가을 하늘 공활한데 높고 구름 없이 밝은 달은 우리 가슴 일편단심일세	3 *Gaeul haneul gonghwalhande nopgo gureum eopsi* *Balgeun dareun uri gaseum ilpyeondansimilse*	3 In autumn's arching evening sky, crystal, and cloudless blue, Be the radiant moon our spirit, steadfast, single and true.
CHORUS	CHORUS	CHORUS
4 이 기상과 이 맘으로 충성을 다하여 괴로우나 즐거우나 나라 사랑하세	4 *I gisanggwa i mameuro chungseongeul dahayeo* *Goerouna jeulgeouna nara saranghase*	4 With such a will, such a spirit, loyalty, heart and hand, Let us love, come grief, come gladness, this, our beloved land!
CHORUS	CHORUS	CHORUS

Korea, South

Dong - hae __ mul - gwa Baek - du - san - i

ma - reu - go dal - to - rok __ Ha - neu - nim - i bo - u - ha - sa u - ri - na - ra man -

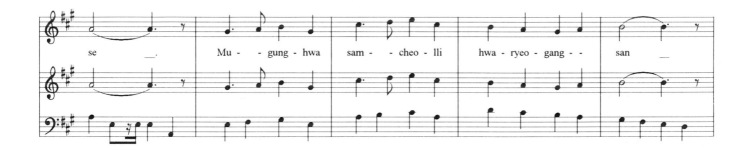

se __. Mu - gung - hwa sam - cheo - lli hwa - ryeo - gang - - san __

Dae - han sa - ram Dae - han __ eu - ro gi - ri bo - jeon - ha - se __.

Kuwait

دولة الكويت

Dowlat al-Kuwait

(State of Kuwait)

```
Quick Country Facts
Location: West Asia, Middle East
Area: 6,880 sq. mi. (17,820 sq. km.)
Population (2002 est.): 2,111,561
Capital/Largest City: al-Kuwait (pop. 151,060)
Official Languages: Arabic, English
GDP/PPP: $30.9 billion, $15,100 per capita
Monetary Unit: Kuwaiti Dinar
```

النشيد الوطني

Al-Nasheed Al-Watani

(National Anthem)

Lyrics: Ahmad Mushari Al-Adwani (1923-1992). Music: Ibrahim Nasir Al-Soula (b. 1935). Adopted: 1978.

Historical Background[1]

The Kuwaiti national anthem was written by the poet Mushari Al-Adwani after the proclamation of independence and was broadcast for the first time on 25 February 1978. The music was composed by Ibrahim Nasir Al-Soula and arranged by Ahmad Ali. The national salute consists of the first six bars of the anthem.

Arabic Words (Transliteration)	English Translation[2]
1	1
Watanil Kuwait Salemta Lilmajdi	Kuwait, Kuwait, Kuwait,
Wa Ala Jabeenoka Tali-Ossadi	My country,
Watanil Kuwait	May you be safe and glorious!
(repeat)	Your face bright,

Watanil Kuwait Salemta Lilmajdi.	(repeat) Your face bright with majesty, Kuwait, Kuwait, Kuwait, My country.
2 *Ya Mahda Abaa-il Ola Katabou* *Sefral Khloudi Fanadati Shohobo* *Allaho Akbar Ehnahom Arabo* *Talaat Kawakebo Jannatil Kholdi* *Watanil Kuwait Salemta Lilmajdi.*	2 Oh cradle of ancestry, Who put down its memory, With everlasting symmetry, Showing all eternity, Those Arabs were heavenly, Kuwait, Kuwait, Kuwait, My country.
3 *Bourekta Ya Watanil Kuwaita Lana* *Sakanan Wa Eshta Alal Mada Watana* *Yafdeeka Horron Fi Hemaka Bana* *Sarhol Hayati Be Akramil Aydi* *Watanil Kuwait Salemta Lilmajdi.*	3 Blessed be My country, A homeland for harmony, Warded by true sentry, Giving their souls aptly, Building high its history, Kuwait, Kuwait, Kuwait, My country.
4 *Nahmeeka Ya Watani Wa Shahidona* *Sharoul Hoda Wal Haqqo Ra-Edona* *Wa Amirona Lil Ezzi Qa-Edona* *Rabbol Hamiyati Sadqol Waadi* *Watanil Kuwait Salemta Lilmajdi.*	4 We're for you, my country, Led by faith and loyalty, With its prince equally, Fencing us all fairly, With warm love and verity, Kuwait, Kuwait, Kuwait, My country, In peace live, in dignity.

Kuwait

Kyrgyzstan

Кыргыз Республикасы

Kyrgyz Respublikasy

Кыргызской Республики

Kyrgyzkoy Respubliki

(Kyrgyz Republic)

Quick Country Facts

Location: Central Asia

Area: 76,000 sq. mi. (198,500 sq. km.)

Population (2002 est.): 4,822,166

Capital/Largest City: Bishkek (pop. 631,000)

Official Languages: Kyrgyz, Russian

GDP/PPP: $13.5 billion, $2,800 per capita

Monetary Unit: Som

Мамлекеттик Гимни

Mamlekettik Gimni

(National Anthem)

Lyrics: Zh. Kadikova and Sh. Kulueva. Music: N. Davlyesova, K. Moldovasanova. Adopted: 1992.

Historical Background

The anthem was adopted on 18 December 1992 by the Supreme Soviet of the Kyrgyz Republic, after the country left the Union of Soviet Socialist Republics (USSR). A Russian translation became an official part of the song after it was declared an official language along with Kyrgyz.

Kyrgyz Words	Kyrgyz Words (Transliteration)	Russian Words	Russian Words (Transliteration)
1	1	1	1
Ак монгулуу аска-зоолор, талаалар, Элибиздин жаны менен барабар. Сансыз кылым Ала-Тоосун мекендеп, Сактап келди биздин ата-бабалар.	*Ak monguluu aska yoolor, talaalar, Elibizdin zhany menen barabar, Sansyz kyldym Ala-Toosun mekendep, Saktap kaldy bizdin ata-babalar!*	Высокие горы, долины, поля— Родная, заветная наша земля. Отцы наши жили среди Ала-Тоо, Всегда свою родину свято храня.	*Vysokie gory, doliny, polia, Rodnaia, zavetnaia nasha zemlia, Otsy nashi zhili sredi Ala-Too Vsegda svoiu rodinu sviato khrania.*
CHORUS Алгалагын кыргыз эл, Азаттыктын жолунда. Оркундой бер, осо бер, Оз тагдырын колунда.	CHORUS *Algai ber, kyrgyz el, Azattyktyn zholunda, Orkundoi ber, oso ber, Oz tagdyrdyn kolunda!*	CHORUS Вперед, кыргызский народ, Путем свободы вперед! Взрастай, народ, расцветай, Свою судьбу созидай!	CHORUS *Vpered, kyrgzskii narod, Putem svobody vpered Vzrastai, narod rastsvetai, Svoiu sud'bu sozidai.*
2 Байыртадан буткон муноз элиме, Достуруна даяр дилин берууго. Бул ынтымак эл бирдигин ширетип, Бакыт нурун тогот кыргыз жерине.	2 *Baiyrtadan butkon munoz elime, Dostoruna daiar dilin beruugo, Bul yntymak el birdigin shiretip, Beikuttuktu beret kyrgyz zherine.*	2 Извечно народ наш для дружбы открыт, Единство и дружбу он в сердце хранит. Земля Кыргызстана, родная страна Лучами согласия озарена.	2 *Izvechno narod nash dlia druzby otkryt Edinstvo i druzhbu on v serdtse khranit Zemlia Kyrgyzstana rodnaia strana Luchami soglasia ozarena.*
CHORUS	CHORUS	CHORUS	CHORUS
3 Аткарылып элдин умут-тилеги, Желбиреди эркиндиктин желеги. Бизге жеткен ата салтын, мурасын,	3 *Atkarylyp eldin umut, tilegi, Zhelbiredi erkindiktin zheligi, Bizge zhetken ata saltyn, murasyn,*	3 Мечты и надежды отцов сбылись. И знамя свободы возносится ввысь. Наследье отцов наших Передадим	3 *Mechty i nadezhdy naroda sbylis' I znamia svobody voznositsia vvys'. Nasled'e otsov nashikh peredadim*

Ыйык сактап урпактарга берели.	Yiyk saktap urpaktarga bereli!	На благо народа потомкам своим.	Na blago naroda potomkam svoim.
CHORUS	CHORUS	CHORUS	CHORUS

English Translation

1

High mountains, valleys and fields
Are our native, holy land.
Our fathers lived amidst the Ala-Toe,
Always saving their motherland.

CHORUS

Come on, Kyrgyz people,
Come on to freedom!
Stand up and flourish!
Create your fortune!

2

We are open for freedom for ages.
Friendship and unity are in our hearts.
The land of Kyrgyzstan, our native state,
Shining in the rays of consent.

CHORUS

3

Dreams of the people came true,
And the flag of liberty is over us.
The heritage of our fathers we will
Pass to our sons for the benefit of people.

CHORUS

Kyrgyzstan

351

Laos

Sathalanalat Paxathipatai Paxaxon Lao

(Lao People's Democratic Republic)

Quick Country Facts

Location: Southeast Asia, Indochina Peninsula

Area: 91,429 sq. mi. (236,800 sq. km.)

Population (2000 est.): 5,777,180

Capital/Largest City: Vientiane (pop. 442,000)

Official Language: Lao

GDP/PPP: $9.2 billion, $1,630 per capita

Monetary Unit: Kip

Pheng Xat Lao

(Lao National Anthem)

Lyrics: Sisana Sisane (b. 1922). Music: Thongdy Sounthone Vichit (1905-1968). Adopted: 1947.

Historical Background

The music to the Laotian anthem was composed by Dr. Thongdy Sounthone Vichit in 1941. The original words adopted in 1947 were replaced in 1975 after the communists took control.

Lao Words (Transliteration)	English Translation
Xatlao tangtae dayma lao thookthuana xeutxoosootchay,	For all time the Lao people
Huamhaeng huamchit huamchay	have glorified their fatherland,
samakkhikan pen kamlang diao.	United in heart, spirit and vigor as one.
Detdiao phomkan kaona booxa xukiat khong lao,	Resolutely moving forwards,
Songseum xaysit pen chao	Respecting and increasing the dignity of the Lao people
laothook xonphao sameu pabkan.	And proclaiming the right to be their own masters.
Bo hay foong chackkaphat lae phuak	The Lao people of all origins are equal
khayxat khaomalob kuan,	And will no longer allow imperialists
Lao thangmuan xoo ekkalat itsalaphab khong xatlao vay,	and traitors to harm them.
Tatsin chay soo xing ao xay phaxat	The entire people will safeguard the independence

kaopay soo khuam vatthana.	And the freedom of the Lao nation. They are resolved to struggle for victory In order to lead the nation to prosperity.

Laos

354

phab khong xat - lao vay __, Tat - sin chay soo xing ao xay pha - xat kao - pay soo khuam vat - tha - na.

Latvia

Latvijas Republikā

(Republic of Latvia)

```
Quick Country Facts
Location: Eastern Europe, Baltic Sea
Area: 25,400 sq. mi. (64,589 sq. km.)
Population (2002 est.): 2,366,515
Capital/Largest City: Riga (pop. 874,000)
Official Language: Latvian
GDP/PPP: $20 billion, $8,300 per capita
Monetary Unit: Lats
```

Dievs, svētī Latviju

(God Bless Latvia)

Lyrics and Music: Karlis Baumanis (1834-1904). Adopted: 1873.

Historical Background[1]

The words and music to this national anthem were written by Karlis Baumanis (better known as Baumanu Karlis). The song first appeared in the second half of the nineteenth century, when the Latvian people were beginning to openly exhibit a strong sense of national pride and identity. Karlis Baumanis was the first Latvian composer to use the word "Latvia" in a song lyric. The concept of "Latvia" had only began to take shape in the minds of writers and activists and was used to describe all regions traditionally inhabited by Latvians. Although most Latvians did not yet dare dream of a sovereign state totally independent of the Tsarist Russian empire, the song served as a powerful catalyst for the emerging national consciousness. The use of the word "Latvia" in the song was an open challenge to the Tsarist regime that had little sympathy for national movements. Initially, Russian authorities forbade the use of that word in the title and text of the song and it was replaced by the word "Baltics."

The work was performed publicly in June of 1873 at the First Song Festival in Riga. It was first sung as a national anthem on 18 November 1918 at the proclamation of Latvia's independence. On 7 June 1920, it was officially proclaimed the national anthem of the Republic of Latvia.

Latvian Words	English Translation
Dievs, svētī Latviju,	Bless Latvia, O God,
Mūs' dārgo tēviju,	Our verdant native land sod,
Svētī jel Latviju,	Where Baltic heroes trod,
Ak, svētī jel to!	Keep her from harm!
(repeat stanza)	(repeat stanza)
Kur latvju meitas zied,	Our lovely daughters near.
Kur latvju dēli dzied,	Our singing sons appear,
Laid mums tur laimē diet,	May fortune smiling here
Mūs' Latvijā!	Grace Latvia!
(repeat stanza)	(repeat stanza)

Latvia

Laid mums tur lat - mē diet, Mūs' Lat - vi - jā _!

Lebanon

اللبنانيّة الجمهوريّة

Al Jumhuriyah al Lubnaniyah

République Libanaise

(Lebanese Republic)

Quick Country Facts

Location: West Asia, Middle East

Area: 4,015 sq. mi. (10,400 sq. km.)

Population (2002 est.): 3,677,780

Capital/Largest City: Beirut (pop. 1,100,000)

Official Languages: Arabic, French

GDP/PPP: $18.8 billion. $5,200 per capita

Monetary Unit: Lebanese Pound

النشيد الوطني اللبناني

An-Nashid Al-Watani Al-Lubnani

Hymne National Libanais

(Lebanese National Anthem)

Lyrics: Rashid Nakhlé (1873-1939). Music: Wadih Sabra (1876-1952). Adopted: 1927.

Historical Background

The Lebanese anthem was adopted on 12 July 1927.

Arabic Words	Arabic Words (Transliteration)	English Translation[1]
1	1	1
كلنا للوطن للعلى للعلم	*Kulluna lil-watan, lil'ula lil-'alam*	All for the country, for the glory, for the flag.
ملء عين الزّمن سيفنـا و القلـم	*Mil'u ayn az-zaman, saifuna wal-qalam*	From the beginning of centuries, our pencil and sword
سهلنا والجبل منبت للرّجال	*Sahluna wal-jabal, manbitun lir-rijal*	Our field and mountains are making the men,
قولنا والعمل في سبيل الكمال	*Qawluna wal-'amal fi sabil al-kamal*	Our word and work on the way of perfection,
كلّنا للوطن للعلى والعلم	*Kulluna lil-watan, lil'ula lil-'alam,*	All for the country, for the glory for the flag.
كلّنا للوطن	*Kulluna lil-watan*	
2	2	2
شيخنـا و الفتـى عند صوت الوطن	*Shaykhuna wal-fata, 'Inda sawt al-watan*	Young and old at the voice of the country,
أسد غاب متى ساورتنا الفتن	*Usdu ghaben mata, sawaratna al-fitan*	Lions of forest at the time of violation.
شرقنا قلبـه ابـدا لبنان	*Sharquna qalbuhu, abadan Lubnan*	Our east is its heart forever Lebanon,
صانـه ربـه لمدى الازمان	*Sanahu rabbuhu, li-mada al-azman*	Its God protects it all over the time,
كلّنا للوطن للعلى والعلم	*Kulluna lil-watan, lil'ula lil-'alam,*	All for the country, for the glory for the flag.
كلّنا للوطن	*Kulluna lil-watan*	
3	3	3
بحـره بـره درّة الشرقيـن	*Bahruhu barruhu, durratu-sharqayn*	Its sea, its land, are the pearl of the two orients.
رفـده بـرّه مالىء القطبين	*Ramzuhu birruhu, mali' al-qutbayn*	Its symbol, its charity, fill up the two poles,
اسمـه عـزّه منذ كان الجدود	*Ismuhu 'izzuhu, munzou kana al-judud*	Its name is its triumph since the time of our grandfathers,
مجـده ارزه رمزه للخلـود	*Majduhu arzuhu, ramzuhu lil-khulud*	Its glory is its cedars, its symbol is for the end of epochs.
كلّنا للوطن للعلى والعلم	*Kulluna lil-watan, lil'ula lil-'alam,*	All for the country, for the glory for the flag.
كلّنا للوطن	*Kulluna lil-watan*	

Lebanon

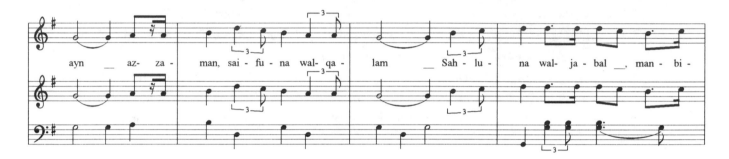

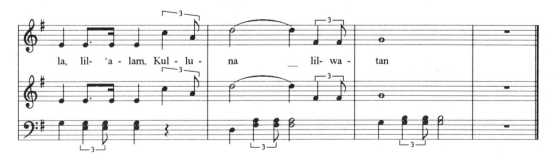

Lesotho

Muso oa Lesotho

Kingdom of Lesotho

```
                    Quick Country Facts
Location: Southern Africa
Area: 11,720 sq. mi. (30,355 sq. km.)
Population (2002 est.): 2,207,954
Capital/Largest City: Maseru (pop. 170,000)
Official Languages: Sesotho, English
GDP/PPP: $5.3 billion, $2,450 per capita
Monetary Unit: Loti
```

National Anthem

Lyrics: François Coillard (1834-1904). Music: Ferdinand-Samuel Laur (1791-1854). Adopted: 1967.

Historical Background

The words to this song were written by a French missionary in the nineteenth century.

Sesotho Words	English Translation
1	1
Lesotho fatse la bontat`a rona,	Lesotho, land of our fathers,
Har'a mafatse le letle ke lona.	You are the most beautiful country of all.
Ke moo re hlahileng,	You give us birth,
Ke moo re holileng,	In you we are reared
Rea la rata.	And you are dear to us.
2	2
Molimo ak`u boloke Lesotho,	Lord, we ask You to protect Lesotho.
U felise lintoa le matsoenyeho.	Keep us free from conflict and tribulation
Oho fatse lena,	Oh, land of mine,
La bontat`a rona,	Land of our fathers,
Le be le khotso.	May you have peace.

Lesotho

Le - so - tho fa - tse la bo - nta - t'a ro - na, Ha - r'a ma - fa - tse le le - tle ke lo - na.

Ke moo re hla - hi - leng, Ke moo re ho - li - leng, Re - a le ___ ra - ta ___.

Liberia

Republic of Liberia

```
┌─────────────────────────────────────────────┐
│              Quick Country Facts              │
│                                               │
│ Location: West Africa                         │
│ Area: 43,000 sq. mi. (111,370 sq. km.)        │
│ Population (2002 est.): 3,288,198             │
│ Capital/Largest City: Monrovia (pop. 1,000,000) │
│ Official Language: English                    │
│ GDP/PPP: $3.6 billion, $1,100 per capita      │
│ Monetary Unit: Liberian Dollar                │
└─────────────────────────────────────────────┘
```

All Hail, Liberia, Hail!

Lyrics: Daniel Bashiel Warner (1815-1880). Music: Olmstead Luca (1836-?). Adopted: 1847.

Historical Background

Daniel Balshiel Warner, who wrote the lyrics to the national anthem in 1847, later became the third president of Liberia, from 1864 to 1868. The song was adopted in the same year, after the Proclamation of Independence. Olmstead Luca composed the present music to the national anthem in 1860.

Words	
1	2
All hail, Liberia, hail!	All hail, Liberia, hail!
(repeat)	(repeat)
This glorious land of liberty	In union strong success is sure
Shall long be ours.	We cannot fail!
Though new her name,	With God above
Green be her fame,	Our rights to prove
And mighty be her powers,	We will o'er all prevail,
(repeat)	(repeat)
In joy and gladness	With heart and hand
With our hearts united,	Our country's cause defending
We'll shout the freedom	We'll meet the foe
Of a race benighted,	With valor unpretending.

Long live Liberia, happy land!	Long live Liberia, happy land!
A home of glorious liberty,	A home of glorious liberty,
By God's command!	By God's command!
(repeat previous two lines)	(repeat previous two lines)

Liberia

Liberia

ni - ted, We'll shout __ the free - dom Of a race be - night - ed, Long live Li - be - ria, hap - py

land __! A home of glo - rious li - ber - ty, By God's com - mand __! A home of glo - rious

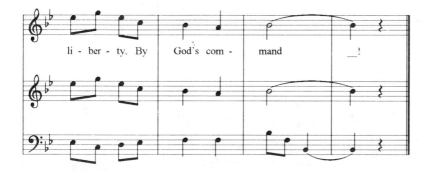

li - ber - ty, By God's com - mand __!

Libya

الجماهيرية العربية الليبية الشعبية الاشتراكية

al-Jamahiriyah al-Arabiya al-Libya al-Shsubabiya al-Ishtirakiya

(Great Socialist People's Libyan Arab Jamahiriya)

```
Quick Country Facts
Location: North Africa, Middle East
Area: 679,536 sq. mi. (1,759,540 sq. km.)
Population (2002 est.): 5,368,585
Capital/Largest City: Tripoli (pop. 591,062)
Official Language: Arabic
GDP/PPP: $40 billion, $7,600 per capita
Monetary Unit: Libyan Dinar
```

Allahu Akbar

(God Is Greatest)

Lyrics: Abdalla Shams el-Din (1921-1977). Music: Mahmoud el-Sherif (1912-1990). Adopted: 1969.

Historical Background

The Libyan anthem was adopted 1 September 1969.

Arabic Words (Transliteration)	English Translation
1	1
Allahu Akbar, Allahu Akbar	God is greatest!
Allahu Akbar Fauqua Kaidi Lmutadi	(repeat)
Alla hu Lilmazlumi Hairumu ayidi	He is above the plots of the aggressors,
(repeat previous two lines)	And He is the best helper of the oppressed.
Ana Bilyaqini Wabissilahi Saaftadi	With faith and with weapons I shall defend my country,
Baladi Wanuru L-haqqi Yastau Fi Yadi	And the light of truth will shine in my hand.
Qulu Mai, Qulu Mai	Sing with me!
Allahu Allahu Allahu Akbar	(repeat)

Allahu Fauqua L-mutadi!	God is greatest!
	(repeat)
	God, God, God is greatest!
	God is above the aggressors.
2	2
Ya Hadihi Ddunya Atilli Wa 'Smai	O world, look up and listen!
Gaisu L-aadi Ga'a Yabgi Masrai	The enemy's army is coming,
Bil-haqqi Saufa Fasaufa Afnihi Mai	Wishing to destroy me.
Qulu Mai L-wailu Lil-mustamiri	With truth and with my gun I shall repulse him.
Wa Llahu Fauqa L-gadiri L-mutagabbiri	And should I be killed,
Allahu Akbaru Ya Biladi Kabbiri	I would kill him with me.
Wahudi Binasiyati L-mugiri Wadammiri.	Sing with me—
	Woe to the imperialists!
	And God is above the treacherous tyrant.
	God is greatest!
	Therefore glorify Him, O my country,
	And seize the forehead of the tyrant
	And destroy him!

Libya

Al - la - hu   Ak - bar,   Al - la - hu   Ak - bar   Al - la - hu

Ak - bar Fau - qua Kai - di Lmu - - ta - di   Al - la - hu   Lil - maz - lu - mi Hai - rumu ay - - i -

di   Al - la - hu   Ak - bar Fau - qua Kai - di Lmu - - ta -   di   Al - la - hu

Lil - maz - lu - mi Hai - rumu ay - - i -   di   A - na Bil - ya - qini Wa - bis - si - lahi Saaf - ta -

di ___ Ba - ladi Wa - nu - ru L-haq - qi Yas - tau Fi Ya - di Qu - lu Ma - i, Qu - lu Ma -

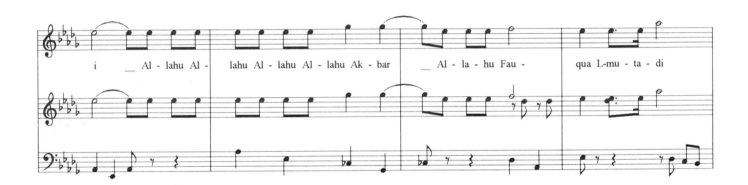

i ___ Al - lahu Al - lahu Al - lahu Al - lahu Ak - bar ___ Al - la - hu Fau - qua L-mu - ta - di

Liechtenstein

Fürstentum Liechtenstein

(Principality of Liechtenstein)

<table>
<tr><td>Quick Country Facts</td></tr>
<tr><td>Location: Western Europe, between Austria and Switzerland</td></tr>
<tr><td>Area: 61 sq. mi. (160 sq. km.)</td></tr>
<tr><td>Population (2002 est.): 32,842</td></tr>
<tr><td>Capital/Largest City: Vaduz (pop. 5,067)</td></tr>
<tr><td>Official Language: German</td></tr>
<tr><td>GDP/PPP: $730 million, $23,000 per capita</td></tr>
<tr><td>Monetary Unit: Swiss Franc</td></tr>
</table>

Liechtensteinische Landeshymne

(Liechtenstein National Anthem)

Lyrics: Jakob Josef Jauch (1802-1859). Adopted: 1951.

Historical Background[1]

No exact details have ever been found in the archives as to the origin of the national anthem. According to oral tradition, the anthem was composed in 1850 by a German clergyman named Jakob Josef Jauch, who lived in the commune of Balzers round about 1853-1863. The tune is that of the British national anthem, "God Save the King," composed by H. Carey. The original anthem consisting of five verses was amended and shortened in 1963 pursuant to a law approved by the Diet. Instead of "On the banks of German Rhine," the anthem now begins with "On the banks of the young Rhine." The original version recalls the fact that Liechtenstein is the last still existing representative of the former Holy Roman Empire of German Nations originally comprising 343 members.

German Words	English Translation[2]
1	1
Oben am jungen Rhein	High above the young Rhine
Lehnet sich Liechtenstein	Lies Liechtenstein, resting
An Alpenhöh'n.	On Alpine heights.

Dies liebe Heimatland,	This beloved homeland,
Das teure Vaterland,	Our dear fatherland
Hat Gottes weise Hand	Was chosen by God's wise hand
Für uns erseh'n.	Chosen for us.
2	2
Hoch lebe Liechtenstein	Long live Liechtenstein,
Blühend am jungen Rhein,	Flourishing on the young Rhine,
Glücklich und treu.	Happy and true!
Hoch leb' der Fürst vom Land,	Long live the country's prince,
Hoch unser Vaterland,	Long live our fatherland,
Durch Bruderliebe Band	Through the bond of brotherly love,
Vereint und frei.	United and free!

Liechtenstein

O - ben am jun - gen Rhein Leh - net sich Liech - ten - stein An Al - pen - höh'n Dies lie - be

Hei - mat - land, Das teu - re Va - ter - land, Hat Got - - tes __ wei - se Hand Für __ uns er - seh'n __

Lithuania

Lietuvos Respublika

(Republic of Lithuania)

```
Quick Country Facts
Location: Eastern Europe, Baltic Sea
Area: 25,212 sq. mi. (65,200 sq. km.)
Population (2000 est.): 3,601,138
Capital/Largest City: Vilnius (pop. 590,100)
Official Language: Lithuanian
GDP/PPP: $29.2 billion, $8,400 per capita
Monetary Unit: Litas
```

Tautiška giesmė

(State Anthem)

Lyrics and Music: Vincas Kudirka (1858-1899). Adopted: 1992.

Historical Background[1]

The lyrics and music to this song were written by journalist, writer and physician Vincas Kudirka, an active figure in the Lithuanian national movement of the late 19th century. The text first appeared in an underground Lithuanian magazine *Varpas* (The Bell) in 1898. "Tautiška giesmė" served as the anthem of the newly established Republic of Lithuania after World War I. Following the country's annexation by the Soviet Union, it was initially banned, but in 1944 it was proclaimed the anthem of the Lithuanian Soviet Socialist Republic (until 1950). During the years of occupation, people were persecuted for singing "Tautiška giesmė" (on some occasions, even when it was the official anthem of the Lithuanian SSR). It was openly sung again in the summer of 1988, and on 18 November of that year, it was readopted as the national anthem.

Lithuanian Words	English Translation[2]
Lietuva, tėvyne mūsų,	Lithuania, our native land
Tu didvyriu žeme,	You are the soil of our heroes
Iš praeities Tavo sūnūs	From their past your sons
Te stiprybę semia.	Will get their strength

Tegul Tavo vaikai eina Vien takais dorybės, Tegul dirba Tavo naudai Ir žmonių gėrybei.	May your children walk Only by the path of virtue May they work for your needs And good of your people
Tegul saulė Lietuvos Tamsumus prašalina, Ir šviesa ir tiesa Mūs žingsnius telydi.	May the Lithuanian sun Take away the darkness So that light and truth Follow our steps
Tegul meilė Lietuvos Dega mūsų širdyse, Vardan tos Lietuvos Vienybė težydi.	May the love for Lithuania Burn in our hearts So that Lithuanian unity Will blossom forever

Lithuania

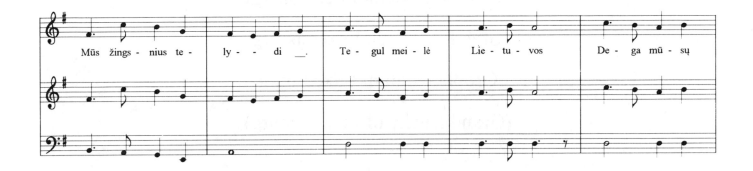

Mūs žings - nius te - ly - - di __. Te - gul mei - lė Lie - tu - vos De - ga mū - sų

šir - dy - se, Var - dan tos Lie - tu - vos Vie - ny - bė te - žy - - di __.

Luxembourg

Groussherzogtum Lëtzebuerg

Grand-duché de Luxembourg

Großherzogtum Luxemburg

(Grand Duchy of Luxembourg)

Quick Country Facts

Location: Western Europe

Area: 999 sq. mi. (2,586 sq. km.)

Population (2002 est.): 448,569

Capital/Largest City: Luxembourg (pop. 75,622)

Official Languages: Letzeburgesch, French, German

GDP/PPP: $20 billion, $44,000 per capita

Monetary Unit: Euro

Ons Heemecht

(Our Motherland)

Lyrics: Michel Lentz (1820-1893). Music: Jean-Antoine Zinnen (1827-1898). Adopted: 1895.

Historical Background[1]

This national anthem was written by poet Michel Lentz in 1859. Composer Jean-Antoine Zinnen put the words to music in 1864. The song was played for the first time in public during a grand ceremony at Ettelbruck that same year. Far from being a war hymn, like the "Marseillaise," the Luxembourg national anthem is a vibrant appeal to peace. The law of 17 June 1993, which amended the law of 23 June 1972, decreed that the first and last verses of "Ons Heemecht" are considered official.

Letzeburgesch Words	English Translation[2]
1	**1**
Wou d'Uelzecht durech d'Wisen zéit,	Where the Alzette slowly flows,
Duerch d'Fielsen d'Sauer brëcht.	The Sura plays wild pranks,
Wou d'Rief laanscht d'Musel dofteg bléit,	Where fragrant vineyards amply grow
Den Himmel Wäin ons mëcht.	On the Mosella's banks;
Dat as onst Land, fir dat mir géif,	There lies the land for which we would
Heinidden alles won.	Dare everything down here,
Onst Heemechtsland, dat mir sou déif	Our own, our native land which ranks
An onsen Hierzer dron.	Deeply in our hearts.
(repeat previous two lines)	(repeat previous two lines)
2	**2**
O Du do uewen, deem séng Hand	O Thou above whose powerful hand
Duurch d'Welt d'Natioune leet,	Makes States or lays them low,
Behitt Du d'Lëtzebuerger Land	Protect this Luxembourger land
Vru friemem joch a Leed!	From foreign yoke and woe.
Du hues ons all als Kanner schon	Your spirit of liberty bestow
De fräie Geescht jo gin.	On us now as of yore.
Looss viru blénken d'Frëiheetssonn,	Let Freedom's sun in glory glow
Déi mir sou laang gesin.	For now and evermore.
(repeat previous two lines)	(repeat previous two lines)

Luxembourg

Wou d'Uel - zecht du - rech d'Wi - sen zéit, Duerch d'Fiel - sen __ d'Sau - er brëcht __. Wou

d'Rief laanscht d'Mu - sel dof - teg bléit, Den Him - mel Wäin ons mëcht __. Dat as onst Land, fir

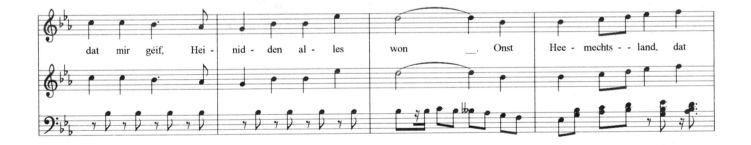

dat mir géif, Hei - nid - den al - les won __. Onst Hee - mechts - - land, dat

mir sou déif An on - sen Hier - zer dron __. Onst Hee - mechts - - land, dat

mir   sou déif An   on -   sen Hier - zer   dron __.

Macedonia

Република Македонија

Republika Makedonija

(Republic of Macedonia)

Quick Country Facts

Location: Eastern Europe, Balkan Peninsula

Area: 9,928 sq. mi. (25,333 sq. km.)

Population (2002 est.): 2,054,800

Capital/Largest City: Skopje (pop. 444,229)

Official Language: Macedonian

GDP/PPP: $10 billion, $5,000 per capita

Monetary Unit: Denar

Денес над Македонија се раѓа

Denes nad Makedonija se ragja

(Today above Macedonia)

Lyrics: Vlado Maleski (1919-1984). Music: Todor Skalovski (b. 1909). Adopted: 1992.

Historical Background[1]

    This national anthem was created in 1943 by Vlado Maleski, a poet from Struga. It was adopted as the anthem of the Republic of Macedonia upon its establishment after World War II. The song was later selected to be the anthem of the newly independent Republic of Macedonia in 1991.

Macedonian Words	Macedonian Words (Transliteration)	English Translation
1	1	1
Денес над Македонија се раѓа Ново сонце на слободата, Македонците се борат За своите правдини! (repeat previous two lines)	*Denes nad Makedonija se ragja* *novo sonce na slobodata* *Makedoncite se borat* *za svoite pravdini!* (repeat previous two lines)	Today above Macedonia, the new sun of liberty is born The Macedonians fight for their own rights! (repeat previous two lines)
2	2	2
Одново сега знамето се вее Над Крушевската Република Гоце Делчев, Питу Гули, Даме Груев, Сандански! (repeat previous two lines)	*Odnovo sega znameto se vee* *na Krushevskata Republika* *Goce Delchev, Pitu Guli* *Dame Gruev, Sandanski!* (repeat previous two lines)	For now on, the flag flies that the Krushevo Republic Goce Delchev, Pitu Guli Dame Gruev, Sandanski! (repeat previous two lines)
3	3	3
Горите македонски шумно псат Нови песни, нови весници Македонија слободна слободно живее! (repeat previous two lines)	*Gorite Makedonski shumno peat* *novi pesni, novi vesnici* *Makedonija slobodna* *slobodna zhivee!* (repeat previous two lines)	The Macedonian forests sing in one voice of new songs, of news that Macedonia is liberated and liberated it lives! (repeat previous two lines)

Macedonia

De - nes nad Ma - ke - do - ni - ja se ra - gja __ no - vo son - ce __ na slo -

bo - da - ta Ma - ke - don - ci - te se bo - rat __ za svoi - te prav - di - ni!

Ma - ke - don - ci - te se bo - rat za __ svoi - te prav - di - ni __ !

Madagascar

Repoblika n'i Madagaskar

République de Madagascar

(Republic of Madagascar)

```
+-------------------------------------------------------+
|                Quick Country Facts                     |
| Location: Southeast Africa, Indian Ocean               |
| Area: 226,660 sq. mi. (587,040 sq. km.)                |
| Population (2002 est.): 16,473,477                      |
| Capital/Largest City: Antananarivo (pop. 1,000,000)    |
| Official Languages: Malagasy, French                   |
| GDP/PPP: $14 billion, $870 per capita                  |
| Monetary Unit: Malagasy Franc                          |
+-------------------------------------------------------+
```

Ry Tanindrazanay Malala

(Our Beloved Country)

Lyrics: Pasteur Rahajason (1897-1971). Music: Norbert Raharisoa (d. 1964). Adopted: 1958.

Historical Background

This national anthem was written in 1958 and adopted that same year, after Madagascar achieved independence from France.

Malagasy Words	English Translation[1]
1	1
Ry Tanindrazanay malala ô!	O, our beloved fatherland,
Ry Madagasikara soa	O, fair Madagascar,
Ny fitiavanay anao tsy miala,	Our love will never decay,
Fa ho anao doria tokoa	But will last eternally.
CHORUS	CHORUS
Tahionao, ry Zanahary	O, Lord Creator, do Thou bless

Ity Nosin-dRazanay ity	This island of our fathers,
Hiadana sy ho finaritra He!	That she may be happy and prosperous
Sambatra tokoa izahay.	For our own satisfaction.
2	2
Ry Tanindrazanay malala ô!	O, our beloved fatherland,
Irinay mba hanompoana anao	Let us be thy servant
Ny tena sy fo fanahy anananay,	With body, heart and spirit
'Zay sarobidy sy mendrika tokoa.	In dear and worthy service.
CHORUS	CHORUS
3	3
Ry Tanindrazanay malala ô!	O, our beloved fatherland,
Irinay mba hitahiana anao,	May God bless thee,
Ka ilay Nahary izao tontolo izao	That created all lands;
No fototra ijoroan'ny satanao.	In order He maintains thee.
CHORUS	CHORUS

Madagascar

Ry Ta - ni - ndra - za - nay ma - la - la ô! Ry Ma - da - ga - si - ka - ra soa __ Ny

fi - tia - va - nay a - nao tsy mia - la, Fa ho a - nao ho a - na - o do - ria to - koa __ Ta -

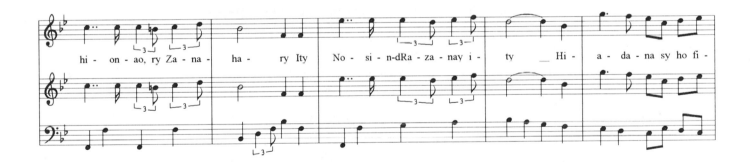

hi - on - ao, ry Za - na - ha - ry Ity No - si - n-dRa - za - nay i - ty __ Hi - a - da - na sy ho fi -

na - ri - tra He! Sa - mba - tra to - koa i - za - hay.

389

Malawi

Mfuko la Malawi

Republic of Malawi

Quick Country Facts

Location: Southeast Africa

Area: 45,747 sq. mi. (118,480 sq. km.)

Population (2002 est.): 10,701,824

Capital/Largest City: Lilongwe (pop. 260,000)

Official Language: Chichewa, English

GDP/PPP: $7 billion, $660 per capita

Monetary Unit: Kwacha

Mlungu Dalitsani Malawi

God Bless Our Land of Malawi

Lyrics and Music: Michael-Fredrick Paul Sauka (b. 1934). Adopted: 1964.

Historical Background

Michael-Fredrick Paul Sauka wrote the words and music to the song in 1964.

Chichewa Words	English Words
1	1
Mlungu dalitsani Malawi,	O God bless our land of Malawi,
Mumsunge m'mtendere.	Keep it a land of peace.
Gonjetsani adani onse,	Put down each and every enemy,
Njala, nthenda, nsanje.	Hunger, disease, envy.
Lunzitsani mitima yathu,	Join together all our hearts as one,
Kuti tisaope.	That we be free from fear.
Mdalitse Mtsogo leri na fe,	Bless our leader, each and every one,
Ndi Mai Malawi.	And Mother Malawi.

2	2
Malawi ndziko lokongola,	Our own Malawi, this land so fair,
La chonde ndi ufulu,	Fertile and brave and free.
Nyanja ndi mphepo ya m'mapiri,	With its lakes, refreshing mountain air,
Ndithudi tadala.	How greatly blest are we.
Zigwa, mapiri, nthaka, dzinthu,	Hills and valleys, soil so rich and rare,
N'mphatso zaulere.	Give us a bounty free.
Nkhalango, madambo abwino.	Wood and forest, plains so broad and fair,
Ngwokoma Malawi.	All-beauteous Malawi.
3	3
O! Ufulu tigwirizane,	Freedom ever, let us all unite
Kukweza Malawi.	To build up Malawi.
Ndi chikondi, khama, kumvera,	With our love, our zeal and loyalty,
Timutumikire.	Bringing our best to her.
Pa nkhondo nkana pa mtendere,	In time of war, or in time of peace,
Cholinga n'chimodzi.	One purpose and one goal.
Mai, bambo, tidzipereke,	Men and women serving selflessly
Pokweza Malawi.	In building Malawi.

Malawi

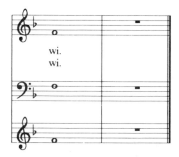

Malaysia

Persekutuan Tanah Malaysia

(Federation of Malaysia)

```
Quick Country Facts
Location: Southeast Asia
Area: 128,328 sq. mi. (329,750 sq. km.)
Population (2002 est.): 22,662,365
Capital/Largest City: Kuala Lumpur (pop. 1,145,000)
Official Language: Malay
GDP/PPP: $200 billion, $9,000 per capita
Monetary Unit: Ringgit
```

Negara Ku

(My Country)

Lyrics: Special committee. Music: Pierre Jean de Beranger (1780-1857). Adopted: 1957.

Historical Background[1]

The national anthem, whose tune has a romantic background that links it to the exile of Sultan Abdullah of Perak to the Seychelles by the British, was selected by a special committee headed by Malaysia's first prime minister, the late Tunku Abdul Rahman Putra Al-Haj, who was the Federation of Malaya's chief minister and minister of home affairs at the time. Initially, a world-wide contest was held for the composition of a national anthem for the Federation of Malaya. However, none of the entries, including those from distinguished composers of international standing, were found suitable. The final selection was made at a ceremony held at the police depot, Kuala Lumpur, on 5 August 1957.

The national anthem in fact is an adaptation of the Perak state anthem, which was selected on account of the traditional flavor of its melody. Between 1957 and 1963 the song served as the national anthem of the Federation of Malaya. With the formation of Malaysia in 1963, it was immediately adopted as the national anthem of the new federation. On 4 April 1968 the National Language Act, which makes any act of disrespect toward the national anthem a punishable offence, was gazetted. The honor of performing the national anthem is restricted to designated individuals.

During the 1992 National Day celebration, the national anthem was given a rather fast beat.

Malay Words	English Translation
Negara ku, tanah tumpahnya darahku,	My country, my native land.
Rakyat hidup bersatu dan maju,	The people living united and progressive,
Rahmat bahagia, Tuhan kurniakan,	May God bestow blessing and happiness
Raja kita selamat bertakhta.	May our ruler have a successful reign.
(repeat previous two lines)	(repeat previous two lines)

Malaysia

Maldives

Dhivehi Raajjeyge Jumhooriyyaa

(Republic of Maldives)

```
Quick Country Facts
Location: South Asia, Indian Ocean
Area: 115 sq. mi. (300 sq. km.)
Population (2002 est.): 320,165
Capital/Largest City: Male (pop. 82,973)
Official Language: Dhivehi
GDP/PPP: $1.2 million, $3,870 per capita
Monetary Unit: Maldivian Rufiyaa
```

National Anthem

Lyrics: Mohamed Jameel Didi (1915-1989). Music: Wannakuwattawaduge Don Amaradeva (b. 1927). Adopted: 1972.

Historical Background

Wannakuwattawaduge Don Amaradeva, a famous Sri Lankan composer and one of the pioneers in Sinhala music, wrote the tune for the Maldivian anthem in 1971.

Dhivehi Words (Transliteration)	English Translation
CHORUS	CHORUS
Qawmee mi ekuveri kan mathee	In National Unity we do salute our nation,
thibegen kureeme salaam.	In the National Language we do offer
Qawmee bahun gina heyo dhua'a	Our prayers and salute our nation.
kuramun kureeme salaam.	
1	1
Qawmee nishaan ah hurmathaa	We bow in respect to the emblem of our nation,
eku boa labaa thibegen	And salute the flag so exalted.
Audhaana kan libigen evaa	
dhidha ah kureeme salaam.	

CHORUS	CHORUS
2 *Nasraa naseebaa kaamiyaabu* *ge ramzakah himeney* *Fessa rathaai hudhaa ekee* *fenumun kureeme salaam.*	2 We salute the colors of our flag; Green, red, and white which symbolize Victory, blessing and success.
CHORUS	CHORUS

Maldives

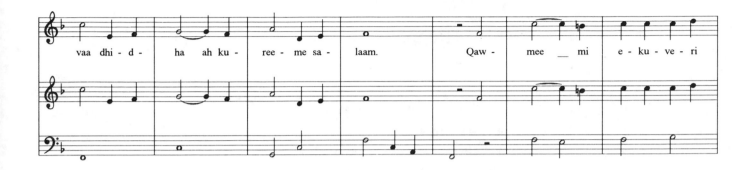

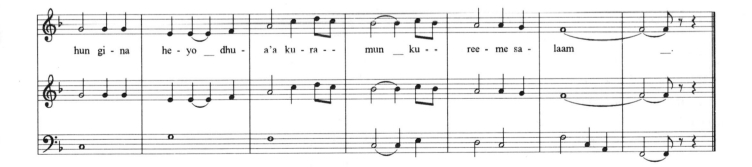

Mali

République du Mali

(Republic of Mali)

```
Quick Country Facts
Location: West Africa
Area: 478,819 sq. mi. (1,240,000 sq. km.)
Population (2002 est.): 11,340,480
Capital/Largest City: Bamako (pop. 746,000)
Official Language: French
GDP/PPP: $9.2 billion, $840 per capita
Monetary Unit: Franc CFA
```

Le Mali

(Mali)

Lyrics: Seydou Badian Kouyaté (b. 1928). Music: Banzoumana Sissoko (1890-1987). Adopted: 1962.

French Words	English Translation
1	1
A ton appel, Mali,	At your call, Mali,
Pour ta prospérité	So that you may prosper,
Fidèle à ton destin	Faithful to your destiny,
Nous serons tous unis,	We shall all be united,
Un peuple, un but, une foi.	One people, one goal, one faith
Pour une Afrique unie	For a united Africa.
Si l'ennemie découvre son front	If the enemy should show himself
Au dedans ou au dehors	Within or without,
Debout sur les remparts	On the ramparts,
Nous sommes résolus de mourir.	We are ready to stand and die.
CHORUS	CHORUS
Pour l'Afrique et pour toi, Mali	For Africa and for you, Mali,

Notre drapeau sera liberté.

Pour l'Afrique et pour toi, Mali

Notre combat sera unité.

O Mali d'aujourd'hui,

O Mali, de demain

Les champs fleurissent d'espérance,

Les cœurs vibrent de confidence.

2

L'Afrique se lève enfin

Saluons ce jour nouveau.

Saluons la liberté,

Marchons ver l'unité.

Dignité retrouvé

Soutient notre combat.

Fidèles à notre serment

De faire l'Afrique unie

Ensemble, debout mes frères

Tous au rendez-vous de l'honneur.

CHORUS

3

Debout, villes et campagnes,

Debout, femmes, jeunes et vieux

Pour la Patrie en marche

Vers l'avenir radieux

Pour notre dignité.

Renforçons bien nos rangs,

Pour le salut public

Forgeons le bien commun

Ensemble, au coude à coude

Faisons le sentier du bonheur.

CHORUS

4

La voie est dure, très dure

Qui mène au bonheur commun

Our banner shall be liberty.

For Africa and for you, Mali,

Our fight shall be for unity.

Oh, Mali of today,

Oh, Mali of tomorrow,

The fields are flowering with hope

And hearts are thrilling with confidence.

2

Africa is at last arising,

Let us greet this new day.

Let us greet freedom,

Let us march towards unity.

Refound dignity

Supports our struggle.

Faithful to our oath

To make a united Africa,

Together, arise, my brothers,

All to the place where honor calls.

CHORUS

3

Stand up, towns and countryside,

Stand up, women, stand up young and old,

For the Fatherland on the road

Towards a radiant future.

For the sake of our dignity

Let us strengthen our ranks;

For the public well-being

Let us forge the common good.

Together, shoulder to shoulder,

Let us work for happiness.

CHORUS

4

The road is hard, very hard,

That leads to common happiness.

Courage et dévouement,	Courage and devotion,
(repeat previous two lines)	Constant vigilance,
Vigilance à tout moment,	(repeat previous two lines)
Vérité des temps anciens,	Truth from olden times,
Vérité des tous les jours,	The truths of every day,
Le bonheur par le labeur	Happiness through effort
Fera la Mali de demain.	Will build the Mali of tomorrow.
CHORUS	CHORUS

Mali

A ton ap - pel, Ma - li, Pour ta pros - pé - ri - té Fi - dèle à ton des - tin Nous se - rons tous u -

nis, Un peuple, un but, u - ne foi. Pour une A - frique u - nie Si l'en - ne - mi dé - couvre son

front Au de - dans ou au de - hors De - bout sur les rem - parts Nous som - mes ré - so - lus de mou - rir.

Pour l'A - frique et pour toi, Ma - li No - tre dra - peau __ se - ra li - - ber - té.

Pour l'A- frique et pour toi Ma - li   No - tre com - bat   se - ra u - ni - té. O Ma - li, d'au - jour - d'hui, O Ma -

li,   de   de - main Les champs fleu -   ris - sent d'es - pé - ran - ce, Les   cœurs vi - brent de con - fiden -

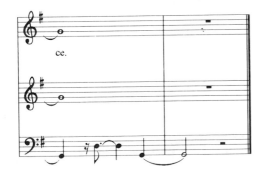

ce.

Malta

Repubblika ta Malta

Republic of Malta

> **Quick Country Facts**
>
> Location: Mediterranean Sea
> Area: 122 sq. mi. (316 sq. km.)
> Population (2002 est.): 397,499
> Capital: Valletta (pop. 9,183)
> Largest City: Sliema (pop. 13,541)
> Official Languages: Maltese, English
> GDP/PPP: $7 billion, $17,000 per capita
> Monetary Unit: Maltese Lira

Immu Malti

Hymn of Malta

Lyrics: Dun Karm Psaila (1871-1961). Music: Robert Samut (1870-1934). Adopted: 1945.

Historical Background[1]

In 1922, Dr. A. V. Laferla, Director of Primary Schools, obtained possession of a piece of music composed by Dr. Robert Samut. He handed it to Dun Karm Psaila, a well-known priest and poet, to write the lyrics for it as a school hymn. As Psaila began writing, he suddenly conceived the idea of writing a hymn in the form of a prayer to the Almighty. Psaila, who was later to become Malta's National Poet, wanted to bridge the gap existing between the political parties and to unite all with the strong ties of religion and patriotism. The "Immu Malti" was first played on 3 February 1923. In 1945 it was declared to be the official anthem of Malta.

Maltese Words	English Words[2]
1	1
Lil din l-art helwa, l-Omm li tatna isimha,	Guard her, O Lord, as ever Thou hast guarded
Hares Mulej, kif dejjem Int harist:	This motherland so dear whose name we bear!
Ftakar li lilha bl-oħla dawl libbist.	Keep her in mind whom Thou hast made so fair!

2	2
Aghti, kbir Alla, id-dehen lil min jahkimha,	May he who rules for wisdom be regarded,
Rodd il-hniena lis-sid, sahha 'l-haddiem:	In master mercy, strength in man increase!
Seddaq il-ghaqda fil-Maltin u s-sliem.	Confirm us all in unity and peace!

Malta

Lil ___ din l-art he - lwa ___ , l-Omm li tat - - na i - si - mha ___ ,
Guard ___ her, O Lord as ___ ev - er Thou ___ hast ___ guard - ed ___

Ha - res, Mu - lej ___ , kif dej - jem Int ha - rist ___: Ftak - kar li
This mo - ther - land ___ so dear whose name ___ we ___ bear ___! Keep her in

lil - ha bl- oh - la dawl ___ lib - bist ___:
mind ___ whom Thou hast made ___ so fair ___!

Marshall Islands

Republic of the Marshall Islands

Quick Country Facts

Location: Oceania, Pacific Ocean

Area: 70 sq. mi. (181.3 sq. km.)

Population (2002 est.): 73,630

Capital/Largest City: Majuro (pop. 20,000)

Official Languages: Marshallese, English

GDP/PPP: $115 million, $1,600 per capita

Monetary Unit: U.S. Dollar

Forever Marshall Islands

Lyrics and Music: Amata Kabua (b.1928)

Marshallese Words	English Words
Aelon eo ao ion lometo;	My island lies o'er the ocean;
Einwot wut ko loti ion dren elae;	Like a wreath of flowers upon the sea;
Kin meram in Mekar jen ijo ilan;	With a light of Mekar from far above;
Erreo an romak ioir kin meramin mour;	Shining with the brilliance of rays of life;.
Iltan pein Anij eweleo sim woj;	Our Father's wondrous creation;
Kejolit kij kin ijin jikir emol;	Bequeathed to us, our motherland;
Ijjamin Ilok jen in aolemo ran;	I'll never leave my dear home sweet home;
Anij an ro jemem	God of our forefathers
Wonakke im kej rammon Aelin kein am.	Protect and bless forever Marshall Islands.
(repeat previous five lines)	(repeat previous five lines)

Marshall Islands

Ae - lon __ eo ao __ ion lo - __ me - to __; Ein - wot wut __ ko loti __ ion dren __ e - lae __;
My is - __ land lies __ o'er the o - cean __; Like a wreath __ of flowers __ up - on __ the sea __;

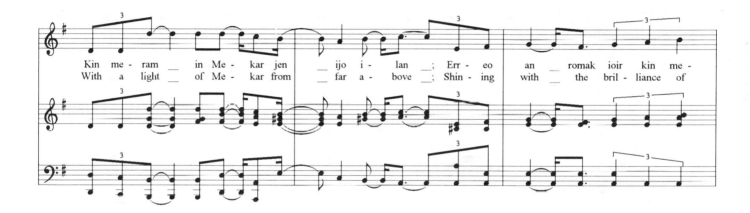

Kin me - ram __ in Me - kar jen __ ijo i - lan __; Err - eo __ an __ romak ioir kin me -
With a light __ of Me - kar from __ far a - bove __; Shin - ing with __ the bril - liance of

ram __ in mour __; Il - tan pein __ A - nij __ ewel - eo __ im woj __; Ke - jolit kij
rays of life __; Our __ Fa - ther's won - drous cre - a - tion __; Be - queathed to

kin ijin __ ji-kir __ e - mol __; Ij-ja-min __ i - lok __ jen in __ ao-le-mo-
__ us our __ mo - - ther - land __; I'll ne - ver leave __ my dear __ home __ sweet

__ ran __; An - ij an __ ro je-mem __ Wo-nak- __ ke im kej __ ram-mon Ae - -
home __; God of our fore-fa-thers __ Pro - tect __ and bless for - e - ver __ Mar - -

lin __ kein am __. Il - tan pein __ A - nij __ ewel - eo __ im woj __;
shall __ Is - lands __. Our __ Fa - ther's won - __ drous cre - a - tion __;

Ke - jolit kij kin ijin ji- __ kir e - mol __; Ij-ja- min __ I - lok jen in
Be - queathed __ to us __ our __ mo - ther - land __; I'll ne - ver leave my dear

Mauritania

Al-Jumhuriyah Al-Islamiyah Al-Muritaniyah

(Islamic Republic of Mauritania)

```
                    Quick Country Facts
Location: Northwest Africa
Area: 397,953 sq. mi. (1,030,700 sq. km.)
Population (2002 est.): 2,828,858
Capital/Largest City: Nouakchott (pop. 480,000)
Official Languages: Hassaniya Arabic, Wolof
GDP/PPP: $5 billion, $1,800 per capita
Monetary Unit: Ouguyia
```

National Anthem

Music: Tolia Nikiprowetzky (b. 1916). Adopted: 1960.

Historical Background

The Mauritanian anthem was composed by Tolia Nikiprowetzky, a prolific French musicologist and singer, as well as the president of the Mauritanian Society of Authors and Composers. There are no words to the song.

No Words

Mauritania

Mauritania

Mauritius

Republic of Mauritius

République de Maurice

Repiblik Morisiê

Quick Country Facts

Location: East Africa, Indian Ocean

Area: 787 sq. mi. (2040 sq. km.)

Population (2002 est.): 1,200,206

Capital/Largest City: Port Louis (pop. 134,516)

Languages: English, French, Creole

GDP/PPP: $12.9 billion, $10,800 per capita

Monetary Unit: Mauritian Rupee

Motherland

Lyrics: Jean Georges Prosper (b. 1933). Music: Philippe Gentil (b. 1928). Adopted: 1968.

Words

Glory to thee, motherland,

O motherland of mine.

Sweet is thy beauty,

Sweet is thy fragrance,

Around thee we gather

As one people,

As one nation,

For peace, justice and liberty.

Beloved country, may God bless thee

For ever and ever.

Mauritius

Glo - - ry to thee __, mo - ther- land, O mo - ther - land of mine __. Sweet is thy beau - ty, Sweet is

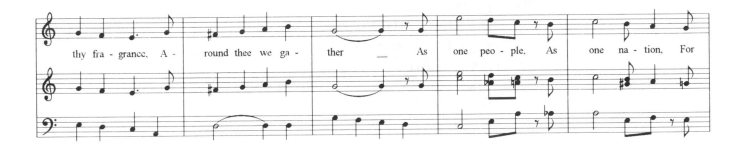

thy fra - grance, A - round thee we ga - ther __ As one peo - ple, As one na - tion, For

peace, jus - tice __ and li - ber - ty __. Be - - lov - ed coun - try, may God __ bless __ thee For

e - ver and e - - ver.

Mexico

Estados Unidos Mexicanos

(United Mexican States)

```
Quick Country Facts
Location: North America
Area: 761,600 sq. mi. (1,972,550 sq. km.)
Population (2002 est.): 100,400,165
Capital/Largest City: Mexico City (pop. 19,750,000)
Official Language: Spanish
GDP/PPP: $920 billion, $9,000 per capita
Monetary Unit: Peso
```

Himno Nacional Mexicano

(National Anthem of Mexico)

Lyrics: Francisco González Bocanegra (1824-1861). Music: Jaime Nunó (1824-1908). Adopted: 1854.

Historical Background[1]

The Mexican anthem was born out of a conception by General Antonio Lopez de Santa Anna, who felt that there should be "a truly patriotic song adopted by the Supreme Government as the National Anthem." His ideas were published in a literary journal on 12 November 1853. A competition for a national anthem was soon announced, and two separate commissions of writers and musicians were set up. The poet Francisco González Bocanegra won the contest for the lyrics, while Jaime Nunó's composition was selected for the music. Nunó was the director of military bands from Catalonia residing in Havana. He had come to Mexico at the request of Santa Anna. The song was first performed on the night of 15 September 1854 at the National Theatre. An Italian opera company directed by the teacher Juan Bottesini was put in charge of this task.

Spanish Words (First, Fifth, Sixth, and Tenth Verses, 10 Total)	English Translation
CHORUS	CHORUS
Mexicanos, al grito de guerra	Mexicans, at the cry of battle
El acero aprestad y el bridón,	Lend your swords and bridle;

Y retiemble en sus centros la tierra	And let the earth tremble at its centre
Al sonoro rugir del cañón.	Upon the roar of the cannon.
(repeat previous two lines)	(repeat previous two lines)

1

Ciña ¡oh PATRIA! tus sienes de oliva	Your forehead shall be girded, oh fatherland,
De la paz el arcángel divino,	With olive garlands by the divine archangel of peace,
Que en el cielo tu eterno destino	For in heaven your eternal destiny
Por el dedo de DIOS se escribió.	Has been written by the hand of God.
Más si osare un extraño enemigo	But should a foreign enemy
Profanar con su planta tu suelo,	Profane your land with his sole,
Piensa ¡oh PATRIA querida! que el cielo	Think, beloved fatherland, that heaven
Un soldado en cada hijo te dio.	Gave you a soldier in each son.

CHORUS

CHORUS

5

¡Guerra, guerra sin tregua al que intente	War, war without truce against who would attempt
De la PATRIA manchar los blasones!	To blemish the honor of the fatherland!
¡Guerra, guerra! los patrios pendones	War, war! The patriotic banners
En las olas de sangre empapad.	Saturate in waves of blood.
¡Guerra, guerra! En el monte, en el valle	War, war! On the mount, in the vale
Los cañones horrísonos truenen,	The terrifying cannon thunder
Y los ecos sonoros resuenen	And the echoes nobly resound
Con las voces de ¡unión! ¡libertad!	To the cries of union! liberty!

CHORUS

CHORUS

6

Antes, PATRIA, que inermes tus hijos	Fatherland, before your children become unarmed
Bajo el yugo su cuello dobleguen.	Beneath the yoke their necks in sway,
Tus campiñas con sangre se rieguen,	May your countryside be watered with blood,
Sobre sangre se estampe su pie;	On blood their feet trample.
Y sus templos, palacios y torres	And may your temples, palaces and towers
Se derrumben con hórrido estruendo,	Crumble in horrid crash,
Y sus ruinas existan diciendo:	And their ruins exist saying:
De mil héroes la PATRIA aquí fue.	The fatherland was made of one thousand heroes here.

CHORUS

CHORUS

10	10
¡PATRIA! ¡PATRIA! tus hijos te juran	Fatherland, fatherland, your children swear
Exhalar en tus aras su aliento,	To exhale their breath in your cause,
Si el clarín con su bélico acento	If the bugle in its belligerent tone
Los convoca á lidiar con valor.	Should call upon them to struggle with bravery.
¡Para ti las guirnaldas de oliva;	For you the olive garlands!
Un recuerdo para ellos de gloria!	For them a memory of glory!
¡Un laurel para ti, de victoria;	For you a laurel of victory!
Un sepulcro para ellos, de honor!	For them a tomb of honor!
CHORUS	CHORUS

Mexico

Me - xi - ca - nos al gri - to __ de guer - ra El a - ce - ro a - pre - stad y el bri - dón __, Y re -

tiem - ble en sus cen - tros la tier - ra __ Al so - no - ro ru - gir del __ ca - ñón __. Y re -

tiem - ble en sus cen - tros la tier - ra Al so - no - ro ru - gir del __ ca - ñón __. Ci - ña ¡oh

PA - TRIA! tus sie - nes de o - li - va De la paz __ el ar - cán - gel di - vi - no, Que en el

cie - lo tu e - ter - no des - ti - no ___ Por el de - - do de DIOS se es - cri - bió. Más si o -

sa - re un ex - tra - ño e - ne - mi - go ___ Pro - fa - nar ___ con su plan - ta tu sue - - lo, Pien - sa ¡oh

PA - TRIA que - ri - da! que el cie - - lo Un sol - da - do en ca - da hi - jo te dio. Un ___ sol -

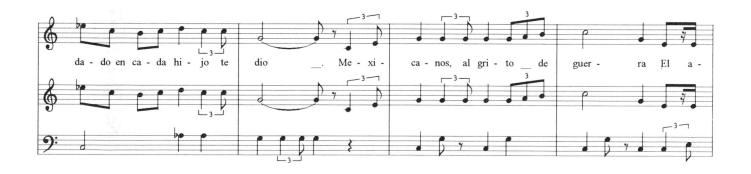

da - do en ca - da hi - jo te dio ___. Me - xi - ca - nos, al gri - to ___ de guer - ra El a -

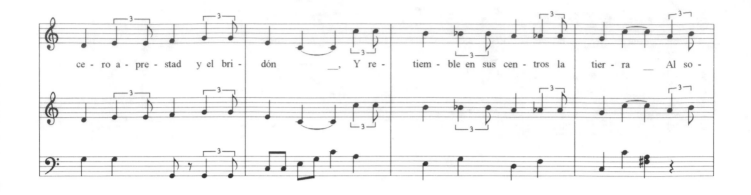

ce - ro a - pre - stad y el bri -   dón   _ , Y re -   tiem - ble en sus cen - tros la   tier - ra __   Al so -

no - ro ru - gir del __ ca -   ñón   __ . Y re -   tiem - ble en sus cen - tros la   tier - - ra Al so -

no - ro ru - gir del __ ca -   ñón   __ .

Micronesia

Federated States of Micronesia

Quick Country Facts

Location: Oceania, Pacific Ocean

Area: 271 sq. mi. (702 sq. km.)

Population (2002 est.): 135,869

Capital/Largest City: Palikir (pop. 9,900)

Official Language: English

GDP/PPP: $269 million, $2,000 per capita

Monetary Unit: U.S. Dollar

Patriots of Micronesia

Words			
1	CHORUS	2	3
We people of Micronesia	Make one nation	Our Ancestors made their	The world itself is an island
Exercise sov'reignty.	Of many isles,	homes here,	We seen from all nations.
Establish our constitution	Diversity of our cultures.	Displaced no other man,	Peace, friendship,
Of Federated States.	Our diff'rences	We who remain wish unity,	co-operation,
Affirm our common wish to	Will enrich us,	Been ruled we seek	Love and humanity.
live	Waters bring us	freedom,	With this constitution,
In peace and harmony.	All together.	Our days began when men	We now become proud
To preserve heritage of past	They don't sep'rate.	explored	guardian
And promise of future.	They sustain us.	Seas in rafts and canoes.	Of our beautiful islands.
	Our Islands	Our nation born when men	
	Our nation	voyaged	
	Get larger	The seas via the stars.	
	And make us stronger		
	And make us much	CHORUS	CHORUS
	stronger.		

Micronesia

We peo - ple of Mi - cro - ne - sia __ Ex - er - cise sov - 'reign - ty __ Es -

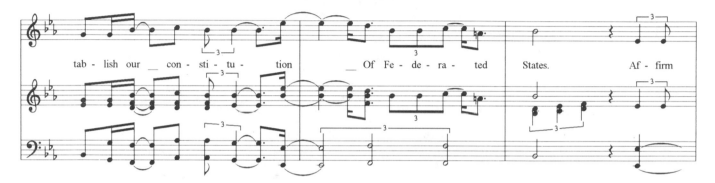

tab - lish our __ con - sti - tu - tion __ Of Fe - de - ra - ted States. __ Af - firm

our com - mon wish to __ live __ In __ peace and har - mo - ny __. To pre - serve he -

ri - tage of __ past And pro - mise of fu - ture __. Make one na - tion __ Of ma - ny isles, Di -

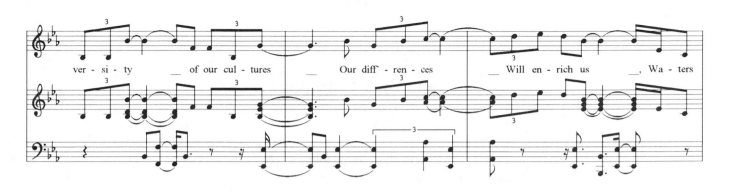

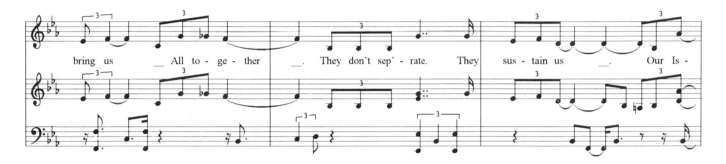

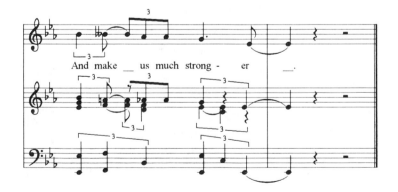

Moldova

Republica Moldova

(Republic of Moldova)

Quick Country Facts

Location: Eastern Europe

Area: 13,000 sq. mi. (33,843 sq. km.)

Population (2002 est.): 4,434,547

Capital/Largest City: Chisinau (pop. 676,700)

Official Language: Moldovan (Romanian)

GDP/PPP: $11 billion, $3,000 per capita

Monetary Unit: Moldovan Lem

Limba Noastră

Our Tongue

Lyrics: Alexei Mateevici (1888-1917). Music: Alexandru Cristi. Adopted: 1994.

Historical Background

Limba Noastră is a stirring hymn to the Moldovan (Romanian) language written by priest, poet, and publisher Alexei Mateevici.

Moldovan (Romanian) Words	English Translation
1	1
Limba noastră-i o comoară	A treasure is our tongue that surges
In adîncuri înfundată	From deep shadows of the past,
Un şirag de piatră rapă	Chain of precious stones that scattered
Pe moşie revărsată.	All over our ancient land.
Limba noastră-i foc ce arde	A burning flame is our tongue
Intr-un neam, ce fără veste	Amidst a people waking
S-a trezit din somn de moarte	From a deathly sleep, no warning,
Ca viteazul din poveste.	Like the brave man of the stories.
Limba noastră-i numai cîntec,	Our tongue is made of songs

Doina dorurilor noastre,	From our soul's deepest desires,
Roi de fulgere, ce spintec	Flash of lighting striking swiftly
Nouri negri, zări albastre.	Through dark clouds and blue horizons.

2

Limba noastră-i graiul pîinii,	Our tongue is the tongue of bread
Cînd de vînt se mișcă vara;	When the winds blow through the summer,
In rostirea ei bătrînii	Uttered by our forefathers who
Cu sudori sfințit-au țara.	Blessed the country through their labor.
Limba noastră-i frunză verde,	Our tongue is the greenest leaf
Zbuciumul din codrii veșnici,	Of the everlasting forests,
Nistrul lin, ce-n valuri pierde	Gentle river Nistru's ripples
Ai luceferilor sfeșnici.	Hiding starlight bright and shining.
Nu veți plînge-atunci amarnic,	Utter no more bitter cries now
Că vi-i limba prea săracă,	That your language is too poor,
Si-ți vedea, cît îi de darnic	And you will see with what abundance
Graiul țării noastre dragă.	Flow the words of our precious country.

3

Limba noastră-i vechi izvoade.	Our tongue is full of legends,
Povestiri din alte vremuri;	Stories from the days of old.
Și citindu-le 'nșirate, -	Reading one and then another
Te-nfiori adînc și tremuri.	Makes one shudder, tremble and moan.
Limba noastră îi aleasă	Our tongue is singled out
Să ridice slavă-n ceruri,	To lift praises up to heaven,
Să ne spiue-n hram și-acasă	Uttering with constant fervor
Veșnicele adevăruri.	Truths that never cease to beckon.
Limba noastră-i limba sfîntă,	Our tongue is more than holy,
Limba vechilor cazanii,	Words of homilies of old
Care o plîng ăi care o cîntă	Wept and sung perpetually
Pe la vatra lor țăranii.	In the homesteads of our folks.

4

Inviați-vă dar graiul,	Resurrect now this our language,
Ruginit de multă vreme,	Rusted through the years that have passed,
Ștergeți slinul, mucegaiul	Wipe off filth and mould that gathered
Al uitării 'n care geme.	When forgotten through our land.
Strîngeți piatra lucitoare	Gather now the sparkling stone,
Ce din soare se aprinde—	Catching bright light from the sun.

Şi-ţi avea în revărsare	You will see the endless flooding
Un potop nou de cuvinte.	Of new words that overflow.
Răsări-va o comoară	A treasure will spring up swiftly
In adîncuri înfundată,	From deep shadows of the past,
Un şirag de piatra rără	Chain of precious stones that scattered
Pe moşie revărsată.	All over our ancient land.

Moldova

Monaco

Principauté de Monaco

(Principality of Monaco)

```
Quick Country Facts
Location: Western Europe, French Mediterranean coast
Area: 0.73 sq. mi. (1.95 sq. km.)
Population (2002 est.): 31,987
Capital/Largest City: Monaco (pop. 30,400)
Official Language: French
GDP/PPP: $870 million, $27,000 per capita
Monetary Unit: French Franc
```

Hymne Monégasque

(Hymn of Monaco)

Lyrics: Théophile Bellando de Castro (1820-1903). Music: Charles Albrecht (1817-1895).

Historical Background

The music of the Monegasque anthem was composed by Charles Albrecht based on a traditional folk tune. This song was first performed in 1867.

French Words	English Translation
1	1
Principauté Monaco ma patrie,	Principality of Monaco, my country,
Oh! Combien Dieu est prodigue pour toi.	Oh! how God is lavish with you.
Ciel toujours pur, rives toujours fleuries,	An ever-clear sky, ever-blossoming shores,
Ton Souverain est plus aimé qu'un Roi.	Your sovereign is better liked than a king.
(repeat)	(repeat)
2	2
Fiers Compagnon de la Garde Civique,	Proud fellows of the civic guard,
Respectons tous la voix du Commandant.	Let us all listen to the commander's voice.

Suivons toujours notre bannière antique.	Let us always follow our ancient flag.
Le tambour bat, marchons tous en Avant.	Drums are beating, let us all march forward.
(repeat)	(repeat)
3	3
Oui, Monaco connut toujours des braves,	Yes, Monaco always had brave men.
Nous sommes tous leurs dignes descendants.	We all are their worthy descendants.
En aucun temps nous ne fûmes esclaves.	We never were slaves,
Et loin de nous, régnèrent les tyrans.	And far from us ruled the tyrants.
(repeat)	(repeat)
4	4
Que le nom d'un Prince plein de clémence	Let the name of a prince full of clemency
Soit répété par mille et mille chants.	Be repeated in thousands and thousands of songs.
Nous mourons tous pour sa propre défense,	We shall all die in his defense,
Mais après nous, combattrons nos enfants.	But after us, our children will fight.
(repeat)	(repeat)

Monaco

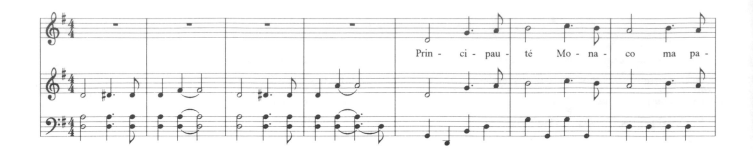

Prin - ci - pau - té Mo - na - co ma pa-

tri - e, Oh! Com - bien Dieu _ est pro - di - gue pour toi _. Ciel tou - jours

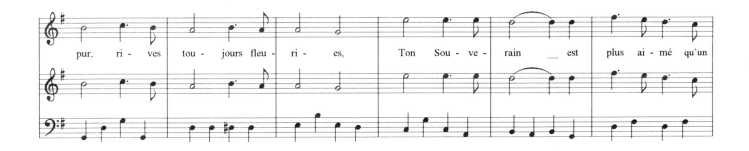

pur, ri - ves tou - jours fleu - ri - es, Ton Sou - ve - rain _ est plus ai - mé qu'un

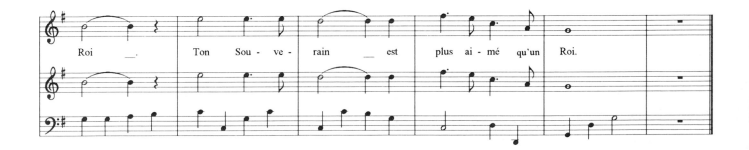

Roi _. Ton Sou - ve - rain _ est plus ai - mé qu'un Roi.

Mongolia

Монгол Улс

Mongol Uls

Quick Country Facts
Location: Central Asia
Area: 604,250 sq. mi. (1,565,000 sq. km.)
Population (2002 est.): 2,694,432
Capital/Largest City: Ulanbataar (pop. 619,000)
Official Language: Mongolian
GDP/PPP: $4.7 billion, $1,770 per capita
Monetary Unit: Tugrik

Монгол Улсын Тєрийн Дуулал

Mongol Ulsiin Teriin Duulal

(Mongol National Anthem)

Words: Tsendiin Damdinsuren (1908-1986). Music: Bilegiin Damdinsuren (1919-1991) and Luvsanjamts Murjorj (1915-1996). Adopted: 1950.

Historical Background

The music to the Mongolian national anthem was adopted in 1950. Author and scientist Tsendiin Damdinsuren wrote the lyrics in 1961. In 1991, after the country switched to a democratic system of government, the original words were modified and new words were written. Several paragraphs that glorified communism and contained references to the Soviet Union were deleted.

Mongolian Words (Transliteration)	English Translation
1	1
Dar khan manai khuvsgalt ulas	Our sacred revolutionary country
Dalaar mongolyn ariun golomtoo	Is the ancestral hearth of all Mongols,
Daisny khold khezeech orokhgui	No enemy will defeat us,
Dandaa enkhzhizh uurd monkhzhene.	And we will prosper for eternity.

CHORUS	CHORUS
Khamag delkhiin shudarga ulastai	Our country will strengthen relations
Khamtran negdsen egneeg bekhzhuulzhee	With all righteous countries of the world.
Khatan zorig bukhii chadlaaraa	And let us develop our beloved Mongolia
Khairtai mongol ornoo manduuliaa.	With all our will and might.
2	2
Zorigt mongolyin zoltoi arduud	The glorious people of the brave Mongolia
Zovlong tonilgozh zhargalyg edlev	Have defeated all sufferings, and gained happiness,
Zhargalyn tulkhuur khogzhliin tulguur	The key to delight, and the path to progress—
Zhavkhlant manai oron mandtugai.	Majestic Mongolia—our country, live forever!
CHORUS	CHORUS

Mongolia

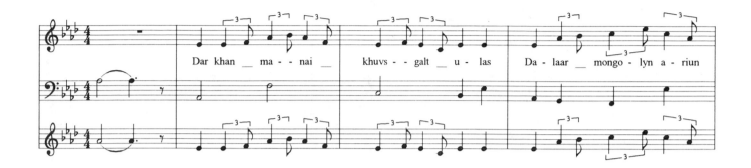

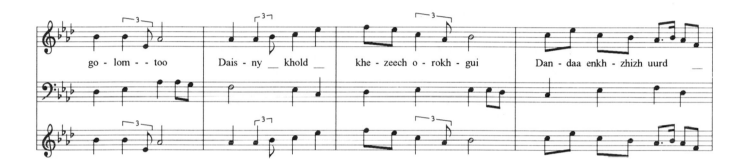

Khair - tai mon - gol or - noo man - duul - iaa ___.

Morocco

المملكة المغربية

Al-Mamlaka al-Maghribiya

Royaume du Maroc

(Kingdom of Morocco)

```
Quick Country Facts
Location: Northwest Africa
Area: 172,413 sq. mi. (446,550 sq. km.)
Population (2002 est.): 31,167,783
Capital: Rabat (pop. 1,220,000)
Largest City: Casablanca (pop. 2,943,000)
Official Languages: Arabic, French
GDP/PPP: $112 billion, $3,700 per capita
Monetary Unit: Dirham
```

النشيدالوطني

al-Nachid al-Watani

Hymne National

(National Anthem)

Lyrics: Ali Squalli Houssaini (b. 1932). Music: Léo Morgan (1919-1984).

Arabic Words	Arabic Words (Transliteration)	English Translation
منبت الاحرار	*Manbit Allahrah*	Fountain of freedom, source of light
مشرق الانوار	*Masriq Alanwar*	Where sovereignty and safety meet,
منتدى السؤدد وحماه	*Munta da Alsu'dad Wahamah*	Safety and sovereignty may you ever
دمت منتداه	*Dumt Muntadah Wahamah*	combine!
وحماه	*Isht Filawtan*	You have lived among nations with

437

عشت في الاوطان	*Lilala Unwan*	title sublime,
للعلى عنوان	*Mil'Kull Janaaan*	Filling each heart, sung by each
ملئ كل جنان	*Thikr Kull Lisan*	tongue,
دكرى كل لسان	*Bilrooh Biljasad*	Your champion has risen and
بالروح بالجسد	*Habba Fataak*	answered your call.
هب فتاك	*Labbaa Nidaak*	In my mouth and in my blood
لبى نيداك	*Fi Fammee Wa*	Your breezes have stirred both light
في فمي و في دمي	*Fi Dammee*	and fire.
هواك ثار نور وثار	*Hawaak Thar*	Up! my brethren, strive for the
اخوثي هيا	*Noor Wa Naar*	highest.
للعلى سعيا	*Ikhwatee Hayyaa*	We call to the world that we are here
نشنهد الدنيا	*Lilala Saayeea*	ready.
أنا هنا نحيا	*Nushid Addunya*	We salute as our emblem
بشعار	*Anna Huna Nuhayya*	God, homeland, and king.
الله	*Bisha'aar Allah*	
الوطن العلك	*AlWatan AlMalek.*	

Morocco

Man - bit Al - ah - - rah   Mas - riq Al - an - - war   Mun - ta da Al - su' - dad __ Wa - ha - mah

Dumt __ Mun - ta - dah Wa - ha - mah   Ish - t Fil - aw - - tan   Lil - a - la Un - wan

Mil' __ Kull Ja - na - aan   Thi - kr __ Kull Li - - san __   Bil - ro - - oh   Bil - ja - - sad

Hab - ba Fa - ta - ak   Lab - baa Ni - da - ak   Fi Fam - mee Wa   Fi Dam - mee Ha - waak Tha - - r

439

Noor Wa Naar __ Ikh - wa - tee Hay - - yaa Lil - a - la Saa - yee - a Nush - hid Ad - dun - -

ya An - na Hu - na __ Nu - hay - ya Bi - sha` - aar Al - lah Al - Wa - tan Al - Ma - lek.

Mozambique

República de Moçambique

(Republic of Mozambique)

Quick Country Facts

Location: Southeast Africa

Area: 303,073 sq. mi. (801,590 sq. km.)

Population (2002 est.): 19,607,519

Capital/Largest City: Maputo (pop. 1,095,300)

Official Language: Portuguese

GDP/PPP: $17.5 billion, $900 per capita

Monetary Unit: Metical

Hino Nacional

(National Anthem)

Lyrics and Music: Justino Sigaulane Chemane. Adopted: 1975.

Historical Background[1]

Since 1992, Mozambique has had a national anthem that consists of a tune, but no words. The main problem with the anthem is its first line—"Viva, viva a Frelimo" ("Long live, long live Frelimo")—felt to be inappropriate in a multiparty system. Frelimo stands for the Front for the Liberation of Mozambique, the former communists, which had been the only legal party in the country ever since its independence from Portugal.

The Assembly of the Republic on 27 April 1998 gave its go-ahead to a competition to rewrite the country's national anthem. The legislative body had previously decided to retain the current tune, and only alter the lyrics. But it modified that stance later, saying that the melody could be changed "slightly" to accommodate new lyrics. Writers of the new words should exalt "national unity, national independence and sovereignty, the heroism of the Mozambican people, work, equality amongst Mozambicans, and peace and internationalism."

However, discussion over the revision of the national anthem, as well as a new national flag, has stalled, and the current anthem and flag will remain the symbols of the country, at least for now.

Words Not in Use

Mozambique

Myanmar

Pyidaungzu Myanma Naingngandaw

(Union of Myanmar)

Quick Country Facts
Location: Southeast Asia, Indochina Peninsula
Area: 265,039 sq. mi. (678,500 sq. km.)
Population (2002 est.): 42,238,224
Capital/Largest City: Yangon (pop. 2,478,712)
Official Language: Burmese
GDP/PPP: $63 billion, $1,500 per capita
Monetary Unit: Kyat

National Anthem

Lyrics and Music: Saya Tin (1914-1947). Adopted: 1948.

Historical Background

Although Myanmar changed its name from Burma in 1989, the use of the latter term in the national anthem has not been altered.

Burmese Words (Transliteration)	English Translation
Gba majay Bma pyay	We shall always love Burma,
Dobo bwa myay si mo chi myano bey	Land of our forefathers.
(repeat previous two lines)	We fight and give our lives
Byay daungtsu go athe bay loo do ka kwe mlay.	For our union.
Da do byay da do myay way myay.	For her we responsibly shoulder the task,
Do byay do myay adjogo nyinya zwa do dudway.	Standing as one in duty to our precious land.
Taung saung ba tso lay do dawon bay apo dan myay.	

Myanmar

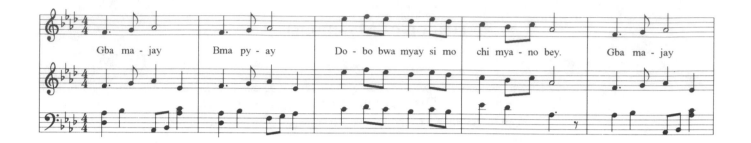

Gba ma - jay Bma py - ay Do - bo bwa myay si mo chi mya - no bey. Gba ma - jay

Bma py - ay Do - bo bwa myay si mo chi mya - no bey. Byay daung - tsu go athe bay loo

do ka kwe mlay. Da do byay da do myay do baing way myay. Do byay do myay

adjo - go nyi - nya zwa do dudway. Taung saung ba tso lay do da - won bay

444

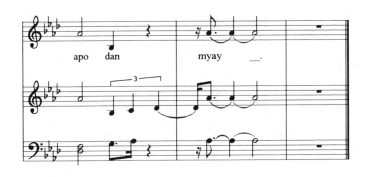

apo   dan   myay   __.

Namibia

Republic of Namibia

Quick Country Facts

Location: Southwest Africa

Area: 318,261 sq. mi. (825,418 sq. km.)

Population (2002 est.): 1,820,916

Capital/Largest City: Windhoek (pop. 161,000)

Official Language: English

GDP/PPP: $8.1 billion, $4,500 per capita

Monetary Unit: Namibian Dollar

Namibia Land of the Brave

Lyrics and Music: Axali Doeseb (b.1954). Adopted: 1991

Historical Background

The national anthem, "Namibia Land of the Brave," was written by Axali Doeseb after the country obtained independence in 1991.

Words	
VERSE	CHORUS
Namibia land of the brave,	Namibia our country
Freedom fight we have won	Namibia motherland
Glory to their bravery,	We love thee.
Whose blood waters our freedom.	
We give our love and loyalty	
Together in unity,	
Contrasting beautiful Namibia,	
Namibia our country.	
Beloved land of savannahs	
Hold high the banner of liberty.	

Namibia

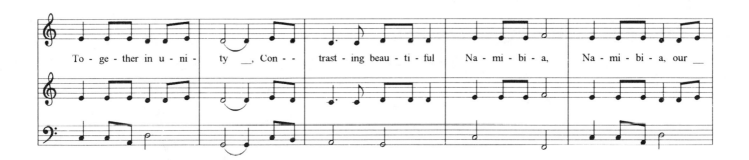

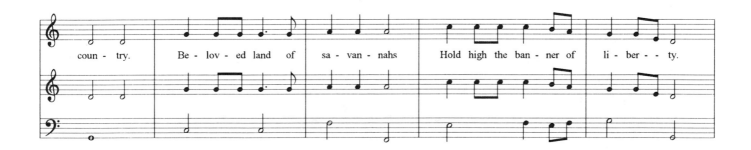

Nauru

Naoero

Republic of Nauru

```
┌─────────────────────────────────────────────┐
│            Quick Country Facts                │
│ Location: Oceania, Pacific Ocean              │
│ Area: 8.2 sq. mi. (21 sq. km.)                │
│ Population (2002 est.): 12,329                 │
│ Capital/Largest City: Yaren (pop. 559)        │
│ Official Languages: Nauruan, English          │
│ GDP/PPP: $60 million, $5,000 per capita       │
│ Monetary Unit: Australian Dollar              │
└─────────────────────────────────────────────┘
```

Nauru Bwiema

Nauru, Our Homeland

Lyrics: Collectively written. Music: Lawrence Henry Hicks (b. 1912). Adopted: 1968.

Nauruan Words	English Words
Nauru bwiema, ngabena ma auwe.	Nauru our homeland, the land we dearly love.
Ma dedaro bwe dogum, mo otata bet egom.	We all pray for you and we also praise your name.
Atsin ngago bwien okor, ama bagadugu	Since long ago you have been
Epoa ngabuna rı nan orre bet imur.	The home of our great forefathers
Ama memag ma nan epodan eredu won engiden,	And will be for generations yet to come.
Miyan aema ngeiyin ouge, Nauru eko dogin!	We all join in together and say;
	Nauru forevermore!

Nauru

Nau - ru __ bwi - e - ma __ , nga - ben - a ma au - we __ . Ma de - da - ro bwe do - gum, mo o -

ta - ta bet eg - om __ . A - - tsin nga - go bwi - - en o - kor, a - ma ba - ga - du - gu __ E -

po - a __ nga - - bu - na ri nan or - re bet i - mur __ . A - - ma me - mag ma nan e - po - dan

e - re - du won en - gi - den __ , Mi - - yan a - e - ma ngei - yin ou - ge __ , Nau - ru e - ko do -

gin   __!

Nepal

Nepal Adhirajya

(Kingdom of Nepal)

Quick Country Facts

Location: South Asia, Himalaya Mountains

Area: 54,463 sq. mi. (140,800 sq. km.)

Population (2000 est.): 25,873,917

Capital/Largest City: Kathmandu (pop. 535,000)

Official Language: Nepali

GDP/PPP: $35.6 billion, $1,400 per capita

Monetary Unit: Nepalese Rupee

Royal Salute

Lyrics: Chakrapani Chalise (1884-1959). Music: Bakhatbir Budhapirthi (1857-1920). Adopted: 1924.

Nepali Words (Transliteration)	English Translation (First Verse, 2 Total)
1	1
Shri man gumbhira nepali prachanda pratapi bhupati	May glory crown you, courageous sovereign,
Shri pach sarkar maharajadhiraja ko sada rahos unnati	You, the gallant Nepalese,
Rakhun chirayu ishale praja	Shri Pansh Maharajadhiraja, our glorious ruler,
Phailiyos pukaraun jaya premale	May he live for many years to come
Hami nepali bhai sarale.	And may the number of his subjects increase.
	Let every Nepalese sing this with joy.
2	
Bairi sara haraun shant houn sabai bighna vyatha,	
Gaun sara dinuyanle saharsha nathko sukirthi katha,	
Rakhaun shasana, bhari birtale,	
Nepal mathi sadhain nathko	
Shri hos thulo hami nepaliko.	

Nepal

Shri man gum - bhi - ra ne - pa - li pra - chan - da pra - ta - pi bhu - pa - ti Shri pach sar -

kar ma - ha - ra - ja - dhi - ra - ja ko sa - da ra - hos un - na - ti Ra - khun chi - ra - yu i - sha -

le pra - ja Phai - li - yos pu - ka - raun ja - ya pre - ma - le Ha - mi ne - pa - li bha - i __ sa -

ra - le __ .

The Netherlands

Koninkrijk der Nederlanden

(Kingdom of the Netherlands)

Wilhelmus van Nassouwe

(William of Nassau)

Lyrics: Attributed to Marnix van St. Aldegonde (c. 1538-1598). Music: Adriaen Valerius. Adopted: 1932.

Historical Background[1]

The "Wilhelmus" has been the official Dutch national anthem since 10 May 1932, when the Cabinet decided that it was to be played on all official occasions. Until then, the national anthem had been a setting by the composer J. W. Wilms, commissioned in 1815 on the foundation of the kingdom, of a poem by H. Tollens. This was called "Wiens Neerlands Bloed" ("Whose Dutch Blood"). Even before 1932, however, the "Wilhelmus" was often played or sung on official occasions, for example the investiture of Queen Wilhelmina in 1898.

The "Wilhelmus" has fifteen verses, the first and sixth of which are usually sung on national occasions. The first letters of all the verses strung together form an acrostic, WILLEM VAN NASSOV. The anthem was written during the Eighty Years' War as a tribute to Prince William I of Orange, the leader of the Dutch revolt against Spanish domination. The writer is generally considered to have been Philip van Marnix, Seigneur of Sint Aldegonde, secretary to the Prince. William of Orange, sometimes known as William the Silent, was the founder of the House of Orange-Nassau. The oldest known version of the melody of the Wilhelmus dates from 1574. It originated in France, probably during the siege of Chartres in 1568. The melody as used today was written down by Adriaen Valerius in 1626 in his collection

Nederlandtsche Gedenck-clanck, commissioned by the rhetoricians of Veere.

Old Dutch Words (First and Sixth Verses, 15 Total)	Modern Dutch Words (First and Sixth Verses, 15 Total)	English Translation (First and Sixth Verses, 15 Total) [2]
1	1	1
Wilhelmus van Nassouwe,	Wilhelmus van Nassouwe	William of Nassau, scion
Ben ick van Duytschen bloet.	Ben ik van Duitsen bloed,	Of a Dutch and ancient line,
Den Vaderlandt ghetrouwe,	Den vaderland getrouwe	I dedicate undying
Blijf ick tot inden doet:	Blijf ik tot in den dood;	Faith to this land of mine.
Een Prince van Oraengien	Een Prince van Oranjen	A prince I am, undaunted,
Ben ick vrij onverveert.	Ben ik, vrij onverveerd,	Of Orange, ever free,
Den Coninck van Hispaengien	Den Koning van Hispanjen	To the king of Spain I've granted
Heb ick altijt gheeert.	Heb ik altijd geeerd.	A lifelong loyalty.
6	6	6
Mijn Schild ende betrouwen	Mijn schild ende betrouwen	A shield and my reliance,
Sijt ghy, O Godt mijn Heer,	Zijt gij, o God mijn Heer,	O God, Thou ever wert.
Op u soo wil ick bouwen	Op u zo wil ik bouwen,	I'll trust unto Thy guidance.
Verlaet my nimmermeer:	Verlaat mij nimmermeer;	O leave me not ungirt.
Dat ick doch vroom mach blijven	Dat ik doch vroom mag blijven	That I may stay a pious
Uw dienaer taller stond,	Uw dienaar t'aller stond,	Servant of Thine for aye
Die Tyranny verdrijven,	Die tirannie verdrijven	And drive the plagues that try us
Die my mijn hert doorwondt.	Die mij mijn hert doorwondt.	And tyranny away.

The Netherlands

Wil - hel - mus van __ Nas - - sou - we, Ben ick van Duyt - - schen bloet __. Den
Wil - hel - mus van __ Nas - - sou - we Ben ick van Duit - - sen bloed __, Den

Va - der - landt __ ghe - - trou - we, Blijf ick tot in __ den doet __: Een __ Prin - ce van O -
va - der - land __ ge - - trou - we Blijf ik tot in __ den dood __; Een __ Prin - ce van O -

raen - gien Ben ick vrij on - ver - veert. Den Co - - nick van His - paen - gien Heb ick al - tijd ghe -
ran - jen Ben ik, vrij on - ver - veerd, Den Ko - - ning van His - pan - jen Heb ik al - tijd ge -

eert.
eerd.

New Zealand

Aotearoa

> **Quick Country Facts**
>
> Location: Oceania, Pacific Ocean
> Area: 103,884 sq. mi. (268,680 sq. km.)
> Population (2002 est.): 3,908,037
> Capital: Wellington (pop. 331,100)
> Largest City : Auckland (pop. 952,600)
> Official Languages: English, Maori
> GDP/PPP: $75.4 billion, $19,500 per capita
> Monetary Unit: New Zealand Dollar

God Defend New Zealand

Aotearoa

English Lyrics: Thomas Bracken (1843-1898). Maori Lyrics: Thomas Henry Smith (1824-1907). Music: John Joseph Woods (1849-1934). Adopted: 1977.

Historical Background[1]

In 1876 a prize of ten guineas was offered for the best musical setting for Thomas Bracken's poem "God Defend New Zealand." The prize was won by an Otago school teacher, John Joseph Woods. The anthem as we know it was first sung on Christmas Day 1876 in Dunedin by the Lydia Howarde Burlesque and Opera Buffe Troupe accompanied by the Royal Artillery Band. The first Maori translation was carried out at the request of Governor Sir George Grey in 1878. The translator was Thomas Henry Smith of Auckland, a judge in the Native Land Court.

In 1940, on the recommendation of the New Zealand Centennial Council, the anthem was declared New Zealand's national hymn. "God Save the Queen" remained the only national anthem until 1977, when the queen consented to giving "God Defend New Zealand" equal status with "God Save the Queen." There have been two further Maori translations of the anthem. The first was undertaken by Archdeacon Sir Kingi Ihaka, Ngati Kahu, in 1975, and a later version was the work of Maori Language Commissioner Professor Timoti S. Karetu.

English Words	Maori Words
1	**1**
God of nations at Thy feet	E Ihowā Atua,
In the bonds of love we meet,	O ngā iwi mātouā
Hear our voices, we entreat,	Āta whakarongona;
God defend our free land.	Me aroha noa
Guard Pacific's triple star,	Kia hua ko te pai;
From the shafts of strife and war,	Kia tau tō atawhai;
Make her praises heard afar,	Manaakitia mai
God defend New Zealand.	Aotearoa
2	**2**
Men of ev'ry creed and race	Ōna mano tangata
Gather here before Thy face,	Kiri whero, kiri mā,
Asking Thee to bless this place,	Iwi Māori Pākehā,
God defend our free land.	Repeke katoa,
From dissension, envy, hate,	Nei ka tono ko ngā hē
And corruption guard our state,	Māu e whakaahu kē,
Make our country good and great,	Kia ora mārire
God defend New Zealand.	Aotearoa
3	**3**
Peace, not war, shall be our boast,	Tōna mana kia tū!
But, should foes assail our coast,	Tōna kaha kia ū;
Make us then a mighty host,	Tōna rongo hei pakū
God defend our free land.	Ki te ao katoa
Lord of battles in thy might,	Aua rawa ngā whawhai
Put our enemies to flight,	Ngā tutū a tata mai;
Let our cause be just and right,	Kia tupu nui ai
God defend New Zealand.	Aotearoa
4	**4**
Let our love for Thee increase,	Waiha tona takiwā
May Thy blessings never cease,	Ko te ao mārama;
Give us plenty, give us peace,	Kia whiti tōna rā
God defend our free land.	Taiāwhio noa.
From dishonor and from shame	Ko te hae me te ngangau
Guard our country's spotless name	Meinga kia kore kau;

Crown her with immortal fame,	Waiho i te rongo mau
God defend New Zealand.	Aotearoa
5	5
May our mountains ever be	Tōna pai me toitū
Freedom's ramparts on the sea,	Tika rawa, ponu pū;
Make us faithful unto Thee,	Tōna noho, tana tū;
God defend our free land.	Iwi nō Ihowā.
Guide her in the nations' van,	Kaua mōna whakamā;
Preaching love and truth to man,	Kia hau te ingoa;
Working out Thy glorious plan,	Kia tū hei tauira;
God defend New Zealand.	Aotearoa

New Zealand (God Defend New Zealand)

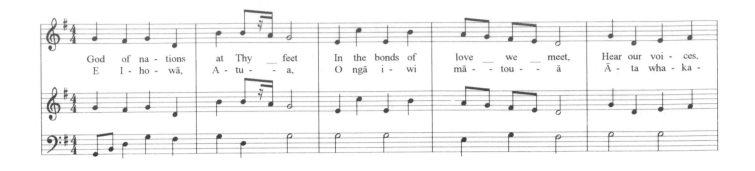

God of na - tions at Thy feet
In the bonds of love we meet,
Hear our voi - ces,
E I - ho - wā, A - tu - a, O ngā i - wi mā - tou - ā Ā - ta wha - ka -

we en - treat, God de - fend our free land. Guard Pa - ci - fic's tri - ple star,
ro - ngo - na; Me a - ro - ha no - a Ki - a hu - a ko te pai;

From the shafts of strife and war, Make her prais - es heard a - far, God de - fend New
Ki - a tau tō a - ta - whai; Ma - na - a - ki - ti - a mai A - o - te - a -

Zea - land
ro - a

460

God Save the Queen

Words and Music: Probably Henry Carey (1690-1743).

Historical Background

"God Save the Queen," the national anthem of the United Kingdom, was once sung in many parts of the earth, wherever British colonies existed. Today, it remains the second national anthem of New Zealand and the royal anthems of English-speaking states such as Australia and Canada.

Words

1

God save our gracious queen,

Long live our noble queen,

God save the queen!

Send her victorious,

Happy and glorious,

Long to reign over us;

God save the queen!

2

O Lord our God arise,

Scatter her enemies

And make them fall;

Confound their politics,

Frustrate their knavish tricks,

On Thee our hopes we fix,

Oh, save us all!

3

Thy choicest gifts in store

On her be pleased to pour;

Long may she reign;

May she defend our laws,

And ever give us cause

To sing with heart and voice,

God save the queen!

New Zealand (God Save the Queen)

God save our gra - cious queen, Long live our no - ble queen, God save the queen! Send her vic -

to - ri - ous, Hap - py and glo - ri - ous, Long to __ reign __ o - ver us; God __ save the queen __ !

Nicaragua

República de Nicaragua

(Republic of Nicaragua)

```
Quick Country Facts
Location: Central America
Area: 50,180 sq. mi. (129,494 sq. km.)
Population (2002 est.): 5,023,818
Capital/Largest City: Managua (pop. 974,000)
Official Language: Spanish
GDP/PPP: $12.3 billion, $2,500 per capita
Monetary Unit: Cordoba
```

Salve a Ti, Nicaragua

(Hail to You, Nicaragua)

Lyrics: Salóman Ibarra Mayorga (1890-1985). Lyrics: Luis Abraham Delgadillo (1887-1961). Adopted: 1939.

Historical Background

The music to the national anthem was adapted from an old anonymous liturgical psalm, composed during the final days of the colonial era. This portion of the anthem was adopted on 23 April 1918. The words were written by Salóman Ibarra Mayorga. They were significantly revised in 1939 and adopted by Executive Order No. 3 on 20 October of the same year.

Spanish Words	English Translation
¡Salve a ti, Nicaragua! en tu suelo	Hail to you, Nicaragua.
ya no ruge la voz del cañón	The cannon's voice no longer roars,
ni se tiñe con sangre de hermanos	Nor does the blood of our brothers
tu glorioso pendón bicolor.	Stain your glorious bicolored flag.
(repeat previous two lines)	(repeat previous two lines)
Brille hermosa la paz en tu cielo	Peace shines in beauty in your skies,
nada empañe tu gloria inmortal	Nothing dims your immortal glory,
que el trabajo es tu digno laurel	For work is what earns your laurels

| Y el honor es tu enseña triunfal, | And honor is your triumphal ensign, |
| es tu enseña triunfal. | Is your triumphal ensign. |

Nicaragua

¡Sal - ve a ti, Ni - ca - ra - gua! en tu sue - lo ya no ru - ge la

voz del cañ - ón ni se ti - ñe con san - gre de her - ma - nos tu glo -

rio - so pen - dón bi - co - lor, ni se ti - ñe con san - gre de her - ma - nos tu glo -

rio - so pen - dón bi - co - lor. Bri - lle her - mo - sa la paz en tu

cie - lo na - da em - pa - - ñe tu glo - ria in - mor - tal que el tra - ba - jo es tu dig - - no lau -

rel Y __ el ho - nor __ es tu en - se - ña tri - un - fal, es tu en - se - ña tri - un - fal.

Niger

République du Niger

(Republic of Niger)

La Nigerienne

(Song of Niger)

Lyrics: Maurice Albert Thiriet (1906-1969). Music: Robert Jacquet (1896-1976) and Nicolas Abel François Frionnet (b. 1911). Adopted: 1961.

Historical Background

The national anthem was adopted on 12 July 1961, just after Niger's independence from France.

French Words	English Translation
1	1
Auprès du grand Niger puissant	By the waters of the mighty Niger,
Qui rend la nature plus belle,	Which adds to the beauty of nature,
Soyons fiers et reconnaissants	Let us be proud and grateful
De notre liberté nouvelle.	For our new-won liberty.
Evitons les vaines querelles	Let us avoid vain quarrelling,
Afin d'épargner notre sang;	So that our blood may be spared,
Et que les glorieux accents	And may the glorious voice
De notre race sans tutelle	Of our race, free from tutelage,
S'élèvent dans un même élan	Rise unitedly, surging as from one man,

Jusqu'à ce ciel éblouissant
Où veille son âme éternelle
Qui fera le pays plus grand.

CHORUS
Debout Niger: Debout!
Que notre œuvre féconde
Rajeunisse le cœur de ce vieux continent,
Et que ce chant s'entende aux quatre coins du monde
Comme le cri d'un Peuple équitable et vaillant!
Debout Niger: Debout!
Sur le sol et sur l'onde,
Au rythme des tamtams, dans leur son grandissant,
Restons unis. toujours, et que chacun réponde
A ce noble avenir qui nous dit: En avant.

2
Nous retrouvons dans nos enfants
Toutes les vertus des Ancêtres:
Pour lutter dans tous les instants
Elles sont notre raison d'être.
Nous affrontons le fauve traître
A peine armés le plus souvent,
Voulant subsister dignement
Sans détruire pour nous repaître.
Dans la steppe où chacun ressent
La soif, dans le Sahel brûlant,
Marchons, sans défaillance, en maîtres
Magnanimes et vigilants.

CHORUS

To the dazzling skies above,
Where its eternal soul, watching over us,
Brings greatness to the country.

CHORUS
Arise, Niger, arise!
May our fruitful work
Rejuvenate the heart of this old continent,
And may this song resound around the world,
Like the cry of a just and valiant people.
Arise, Niger, arise! On land and river,
To the rhythm of the swelling drum-beats' sound,
May we ever be united and may each one of us
Answer the call of this noble future that says to us,
"Forward!"

2
We find again in our children
All the virtues of our ancestors.
Such virtues are our inspiration
For fighting at every moment.
We confront ferocious and treacherous animals
Often scarcely armed,
Seeking to live in dignity,
Not slaying with a lust to kill.
In the steppe where all feel thirst,
In the burning desert,
Let us march tirelessly forward
As magnanimous and vigilant masters.

CHORUS

Niger

Au - près du grand Ni -

ger puis - sant Qui rend la na - tu - re plus bel - le, So - yons fiers et re - con - nais - sants

De no - tre li - ber - té nou - vel - le. E - vi - tons les vai - nes que - rel - les A - fin d'é - par -

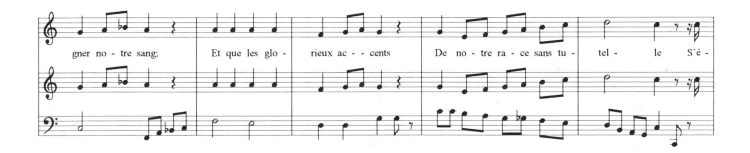

gner no - tre sang; Et que les glo - rieux ac - cents De no - tre ra - ce sans tu - tel - le S'é -

469

lèvent dans un mê - me é - lan   Jus - qu'à ce ciel é - blou - is - sant   Où

veil - le son âme é - ter - nel - le __ Qui fe - ra le pa - ys plus   grand.   De - bout Ni - ger: De -

bout __!   Que notre œuvre fé - con - de   Rajeu - nis - se le   cœur de ce   vieux con - ti - nent __, Et

que ce chant   s'entende   aux qua - tre coins du   mon - de Com - me le cri d'un   Peuple équi - table et vail -

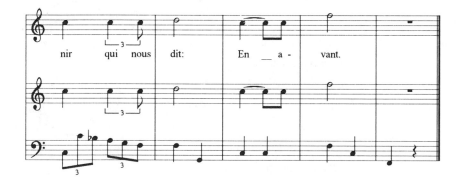

Nigeria

Federal Republic of Nigeria

Quick Country Facts
Location: West Africa
Area: 356,700 sq. mi. (923,768 sq. km.)
Population (2002 est.): 129,934,911
Capital: Abuja (pop. 339,000)
Largest City: Lagos (pop. 13,050,000)
Official Language: English
GDP/PPP: $105.9 billion, $840 per capita
Monetary Unit: Naira

Arise, O Compatriots

Lyrics: Collectively written. Music: Benedict Elide Odiase (b. 1934). Adopted: 1978.

Historical Background[1]

The former national anthem, adopted at independence in 1960, was replaced on 1 October 1978, by the current one. The music was composed by Benedict Elide Odiase, director of music of the Nigerian Police Band. The final words of the national anthem were formed from the entries of the best five picks: John A. Ilechukwu, Eme Etim Akpan, B. A. Ogunnaike, Sotu Omoigui, and P. O. Aderibigbe. A total of 1,499 entries were submitted in a competition organized by the National Publicity Committee on the Draft Constitution/Return to Civilian Rule.

Words	
1	2
Arise. O compatriots.	O God of creation,
Nigeria's call obey	Direct our noble cause;
To serve our fatherland	Guide thou our leaders right:
With love and strength and faith.	Help our youth the truth to know,
The labors of our heroes past	In love and honesty to grow,
Shall never be in vain,	And living just and true,
To serve with heart and might	Great lofty heights attain,
One nation bound in freedom, peace and unity.	To build a nation where peace and justice reign.

Nigeria

A - rise, O Com - pa - triots __, Ni - ge - ria's call o - bey __ To serve our fa - ther -

land __ With love and strength and faith __. The la - bor of our he - roes past Shall ne - ver be in

vain __, To serve with heart and might __ One na - tion bound __ in free - dom __, peace and u - ni -

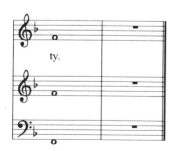

ty.

Norway

Kongeriket Norge

(Kingdom of Norway)

```
Quick Country Facts
Location: Northern Europe, Scandinavia
Area: 125,049 sq. mi. (324,220 sq. km.)
Population (2002 est.): 4,525,116
Capital/Largest City: Oslo (pop. 483,401)
Official Languages: Bokmål and Nynorsk Norwegian
GDP/PPP: $143 billion, $31,800 per capita
Monetary Unit: Krone
```

Ja, Vi Elsker Dette Landet

(Yes, We Love This Land)

Lyrics: Bjørnstjerne Bjørnson (1832-1910).   Music: Rikard Nordraak (1842-1866).

Historical Background[1]

In 1864, Bjørnstjerne Bjørnson completed the lyrics of the Norwegian national anthem, "Ja, Vi Elsker Dette Landet" ("Yes, We Love This Land"). It was written for the 50th anniversary of the constitution. Some say the song was sung for the first time at Eidsvoll on 17 May 1864, while others claim it was in front of the palace in Christiania (Oslo). Regardless of where it was first heard, it caught on quickly and soon became very popular. It became a part of the reading books in schools all over the country and was sung by the children in the children's parades organized by Bjørnson on every 17 May. Rikard Nordraak composed the music to the national anthem. He was Bjørnson's cousin and put music to several of Bjørnson's poems, but composing the music to the national anthem is what gained him the most fame and recognition.

Norwegian Words (First, Seventh, and Eighth Verses, 8 Total)	English Translation (First, Seventh, and Eighth Verses, 8 Total) [2]
1	1
Ja, vi elsker dette landet,	Norway, thine is our devotion.
som det stiger frem,	Land of hearth and home,
furet, værbitt, over vannet,	Rising storm-scarr'd from the ocean,
med de tusen hjem.	Where the breakers foam.
Elsker, elsker det og tenker	Oft to thee our thoughts are wending,
på vår far og mor	Land that gave us birth,
og den saganatt som senker	And to saga nights still sending
drømmer på vår jord.	Dreams upon our earth.
(repeat previous two lines)	(repeat previous two lines)
7	7
Norske mann I hus og hytte,	Men of Norway be your dwelling,
takk din store Gud!	Cottage, house or farm
Landet ville han beskytte	Praise the Lord who all compelling
skjønt det mørkt så ut.	Sav'd our land from harm
Alt hva fedrene har kjempet,	Not the valor of a father
mødrene har grett,	On the battlefield
har den Herre stille lempet,	Nor a mother's tears, but rather
så vi vant vår rett.	God our vict'ry sealed.
(repeat previous two lines)	(repeat previous two lines)
8	8
Ja, vi elsker dette landet,	Norway, thine is our devotion.
som det stiger frem,	Land of hearth and home,
furet, værbitt, over vannet,	Rising storm-scarr'd from the ocean,
med de tusen hjem.	Where the breakers foam.
og som fedres kamp har hevet	As our fathers' vict'ry gave it
det av nød til seier,	Peace for one and all,
også vi, nar det blir krevet,	We shall rally, too, to save it
for dets fred slår leir.	When we hear the call,
(repeat previous two lines)	(repeat previous two lines)

Norway

Ja, vi el - sker det - te lan - det, som det sti - ger frem, fu - ret, vær - bitt, o - ver van - net

med de tu - sen hjem. El - sker, el - sker det og ten - ker på vår far og mor ___ og den

sa - ga - natt som sen - ker drøm - mer på vår jord. og den sa - ga - natt som sen - ker, sen - ker

drøm - mer på vår jord.

Oman

سلطنة عمان

Saltanaat al-'Umman

(Sultanate of Oman)

Quick Country Facts
Location: West Asia, Arabian Peninsula
Area: 82,030 sq. mi. (212,460 sq. km.)
Population (2002 est.): 2,713,462
Capital/Largest City: Muscat (pop. 350,000)
Official Language: Arabic
GDP/PPP: $21.5 billion, $8,200 per capita
Monetary Unit: Omani Rial

Nashid as-Salaam as-Sultani

(Sultan's National Anthem)

Adopted: 1972.

Arabic Words (Transliteration)	English Translation
Ya Rabbana Ehfid Lana Jalalat Al Sultan	O Lord, protect for us our majesty the sultan
Waashabi Fee Al'wtan	And the people in our land,
Bialeizy Walaman.	With honor and peace.
Walyadum Muoayadda,	May he live long, strong and supported,
Aahilan Momajjada;	Glorified be his leadership.
Bilnufoosi Yuftda.	For him we shall lay down our lives.
(repeat previous three lines)	(repeat previous three lines)
Ya Oman, Nahnoo Min Ahd Il Nabi	O Oman, since the time of the Prophet
Awfiya Min K'ram Al Arabi.	We are a dedicated people

Abshiry Qaboos Jaa *Faltubarakhu 'I Sama.*	Amongst the noblest Arabs. Be happy! Qaboos has come With the blessing of Heaven.
Waasidy Waltoq 'hi Bilduoaa.	Be cheerful and commend him To the protection of our prayers.

Oman

Bil - nu - foo - si Yuf - t - da __ . Wa - lya - dum Muoay - ad - da, Aa - hi - lan Momaj - ja - da;

Bil - nu - foo - si Yuf - t - da __ . Ya O - man, Nah - noo Min Ahd Il Na - bi __

A - w - fiya Min K`- ram Al A - ra - bi __ . Ab - shi - ry Qaboos Ja - a

Faltu - bara - khu 'I - Sa - ma. Waa - si - dy Wal - to - q'hi Bil - duo - aa.

Pakistan

Islam-i Jamhuriya-e Pakistan

(Islamic Republic of Pakistan)

Quick Country Facts

Location: Southwest Asia, Near East

Area: 310,400 sq. mi. (803,940 sq. km.)

Population (2002 est.): 147,663,429

Capital: Islamabad (pop. 201,000)

Largest City: Karachi (pop. 12,100,000)

Official Languages: Urdu, English

GDP/PPP: $299 billion, $2,100 per capita

Monetary Unit: Pakistan Rupee

Tarana

(National Anthem)

Lyrics: Abu-al-Asar Hafeez Jullandhuri (1900-1982). Music: Ahmed Gulamali Chagla (1902-1953). Adopted: 1954.

Historical Background[1]

The national anthem of Pakistan is a harmonious rendering of a three-stanza composition with a tune based on eastern music but arranged in such a manner that it can be easily played by foreign bands. It was adopted in August 1954. An open competition was held among all highly competitive entries, and the entry of Abu-al-Asar Hafeez Jallundhuri was approved by the jury. The national anthem of Pakistan is one of the most prestigious ones in the world and is very short. Its duration is only one minute and eight seconds.

Urdu Words (Transliteration)	English Translation[2]
Pak sarzameen shad bad Kishwar-e-Haseen shad bad	Blessed be the sacred land,
Tou Nishaan-e-Azm-e-aali shan Arz-e-Pakistan	Happy be the bounteous realm,
Markaz-e-yaqeen Shad bad	Symbol of high resolve, land of Pakistan.
	Blessed be thou citadel of faith.

Pak sarzameen ka nizaam	The order of this sacred land
Qouwat-e-Akhouwat-e-Awam	Is the might of the brotherhood of the people.
Qaum mulk saltanat Painda tabinda bad	May the nation, the country, and the state.
Shad bad Manzil-e-murad	
Parcham-e-Sitara-o-Hilal	Shine in glory everlasting.
Rahbar-e-Tarakkeey-o-Kamal	Blessed be the goal of our ambition.
Tarjumaan-e-mazee-shaan-e-Hal	This flag of the crescent and the star
Jan-e-Istaqbal	Leads the way to progress and perfection,
Saaya-e-Khuda-e-zuljalal	Interpreter of our past, glory of our present,
	Inspiration of our future,
	Symbol of Almighty's protection.

Pakistan

Pak sar - za - meen shad bad _ Kish - wa - r-e- Ha - seen shad _ bad _

Tou Ni - shaa - n-e- Az - m-e- aa - li shan Ar - z-e- Pak - is - tan Mar - ka - z-e- ya - qeen Shad _ bad _

Pak sar - za - meen ka ni - zaam _ Qou - wa - t-e- A - khou - wa - t-e- A - wam

Qaum mulk sal - ta - nat Pain - da ta - bin - da bad Shad bad _ Man - zi - l-e- mu - rad _

483

Palau

Belu'u era Belau

Republic of Palau

Quick Country Facts

Location: Oceania, Pacific Ocean

Area: 177 sq. mi. (458 sq. km.)

Population (2002 est.): 19,409

Capital/Largest City: Koror (pop. 12,299)

Languages: Palauan, English

GDP/PPP: $174 million, $9,900 per capita

Monetary Unit: U.S. Dollar

National Anthem

Lyrics: Written Collectively. Music: Ymesei O. Ezekiel (1926-1984). Adopted: 1980.

Palauan Words	English Translation (First Verse, 4 Total)
1	1
Belau loba klisiich er a kelulul,	Palau is coming forth with strength and power,
El dimia ngarngii ra rechuodelmei	By her old ways abides still every hour.
Meng mengel uoluu er a chimol beluu,	One country, safe, secure, one government
El ngar cheungel a rirch lomke sang.	Under the glowing, floating soft light stands.
2	
Bo dole ketek a kerruul er a belluad,	
Lolab a blakelreng ma duchelreng.	
Belau a chotil a klengar re kid,	
Mebo dorurtabedul msa klisichel.	
3	
Bod kai ue reke dchim lokiu a reng,	
E dongedmokel ra dimla koted.	
Lomcheliu a rengrdel ma klebkellel,	

Lokiu a budch ma beltikelreng.

4
Dios mo mek ngel tengat ra Be lumam,
El dimla dikesam ra rechuodelmei,
Beskemam a klisicham ma llemeltam,
Lorrurt a klungiolam elmo ch'rechar.

Palau

Be - lau lo - ba kli - siich er a kelu - lul __, El di - mia ngar - ngii ra re - chuo - del -

mei __ Meng __ me - ngel uoluu er a chi - mol be - luu __, El ngar cheu - ngel a rir - ch

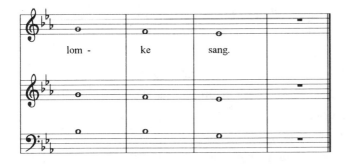

lom - ke sang.

Palestine

دولة الفلسطيني

Daulat Al-Falasteen

(State of Palestine)

```
Quick Country Facts
Location: West Asia, Middle East
Area: 4,320 sq. mi. (12,000 sq. km.)
Population (2000 est.): 5,060,000
Capital/Largest City: Al-Qouds (Jerusalem, pop. 550,590)
Languages: Arabic, Hebrew, English
GDP/PPP: $1.1 billion, $1,000 per capita
Monetary Units: Israeli Shekel, Jordanian Dinar, U.S.
Dollar
```

فدائي

Biladi

(My Homeland)

Arabic Words	English Translation[1]
فدائي فدائي فدائي يا أرض الجدود	My country, my country
فدائي فدائي فدائي يا شعبي يا شعب الخلود	My country, the land of my grandfathers
بعزمي و ناري و بركان ثاري	My country, my country
و أشواق دمي لأرضي و داري	My country, my nation, the nation of eternity
صعدت الجبال و خضت النضال	With my determination, my fire and the volcano of my
قهرت المحال حطمت القيود	revenge
فدائي فدائي فدائي يا أرضي يا أرض الجدود	The longing of my blood for my land and home
بعصف الرياح و نار السلاح	I have climbed the mountains and fought the wars
و إصرار شعبي لخوض الكفاح	I have conquered the impossible, and crossed the borders
فلسطين داري فلسطين ناري	My country, my country, the nation of eternity

فلسطين ثاري و أرض الصمود	With the resolve of the winds and the fire of the guns
فدائي فدائي فدائي يا أرضي يا أرض الجدود	And the determination of my nation in the land of struggle
بحق القسم تحت ظل العلم	Palestine is my home, Palestine is my fire,
بأرضي و شعبي و نار الألم	Palestine is my revenge and the eternal land
سأحيا فدائي و أمضي فدائي	My country, my country, the nation of eternity
و أقضي فدائي إلى أن أعود	I swear under the shade of the flag
فدائي فدائي فدائي يا ارضي يا أرض الجدود	To my land and nation, and the fire of pain
	I will live as a guerrilla, I will go on as guerrilla,
	I will expire as guerrilla until I return
	My country, my country, the nation of eternity.

Music Sheet Not Available

Panama

República de Panamá

(Republic of Panama)

Quick Country Facts

Location: Central America

Area: 29,761 sq. mi. (78,200 sq. km.)

Population (2002 est.): 2,882,329

Capital/Largest City: Panama City (pop. 450,668)

Official Language: Spanish

GDP/PPP: $16.9 billion, $5,900 per capita

Monetary Unit: Balboa

Himno Istmeño

(Isthmus Anthem)

Lyrics: Jerónimo de la Ossa (1847-1907). Music: Santos Jorge (1870-1941). Adopted: 1925.

Historical Background

The music to the Panamanian anthem was composed in 1904 by Santos Jorge, a Spanish national who served as director of the Republican Band at the time. That same year, the poet Jerónimo de la Ossa wrote the words at the request of Jorge. The song was approved by Law 30 of 1906 and adopted by Law 28 of 1941.

Spanish Words	English Translation
CHORUS	CHORUS
Alcanzamos por fin la victoria	At last we reached victory
En el campo feliz de la unión;	In the joyous field of the union;
Con ardientes fulgores de gloria	With ardent fires of glory
Se ilumina la nueva nación.	A new nation is illuminated.
(repeat previous two lines)	(repeat previous two lines)
1	1
Es preciso cubrir con un velo	It is necessary to cover with a veil

Del pasado el calvario y la cruz;
Y que adorne el azul de tu cielo
De concordia la espléndida luz.
El progreso acaricia tus lares.
Al compás de sublime canción,
Ves rugir a tus pies ambos mares
Quedan rumbo a tu noble misión.

CHORUS

2
En tu suelo cubierto de flores
A los besos del tibio terral,
Terminaron guerreros fragores;
Sólo reina el amor fraternal.
Adelante la pica y la pala,
Al trabajo sin más dilación,
Y seremos así prez y gala
De este mundo feraz de Colón.

CHORUS

The past times of Calvary and cross;
Let now the blue skies be adorned
With the splendid light of concord.
Progress now caresses your path.
To the rhythm of a sublime song,
You see both your seas roar at your feet
Giving you a path to your noble mission.

CHORUS

2
In your soil covered with flowers
To the kisses of the warm earth,
Warrior roars have ceased;
Only fraternal love reigns.
Ahead the shovel and pick,
At work without any more dilation,
and we will be as such at work and gala
Of this fruitful world of Columbus.

CHORUS

Panama

Al - can - za - mos por fin __ la vic - to - ria En el cam - po fe - liz de la u - nión; Con ar -

dien - tes ful - go - res de glo - ria Se ilu - mi - na la nue - va na - ción ___. Con ar -

dien - tes ful - go - res de glo - ria Se ilu - mi - na la nue - va na - ción. Es pre -

ci - so cu - brir con un ve - lo Del pa - sa - do el cal - va - rio y la cruz __; Y que a -

dien - tes ful - go - res de glo - ria Se ilu - mi - na la nue - - va na - ción ___. Con ar -

dien - tes ful - go - res de glo - ria Se ilu - mi - na la nue - - va na - ción.

Papua New Guinea

Independent State of Papua New Guinea

Papua Niugini

Quick Country Facts

Location: Oceania, Eastern New Guinea

Area: 178,704 sq. mi. (462,840 sq. km.)

Population (2002 est.): 5,172,033

Capital/Largest City: Port Moresby (pop. 250,000)

Languages: English, Tok Pisin

GDP/PPP: $12.2 billion, $2,400 per capita

Monetary Unit: Kina

O Arise All You Sons

Lyrics and Music: Thomas Shacklady (b. 1917). Adopted: 1975.

Words	
1	2
O arise all you sons of this land,	Now give thanks to the good Lord above
Let us sing of our joy to be free,	For His kindness, His wisdom and love
Praising God and rejoicing to be	For this land of our fathers so free,
Papua New Guinea.	Papua New Guinea.
CHORUS 1	CHORUS 2
Shout our name from the mountains to seas	Shout again for the whole world to hear
Papua New Guinea;	Papua New Guinea;
Let us raise our voices and proclaim	We're independent and we're free,
Papua New Guinea.	Papua New Guinea.

Papua New Guinea

O a- rise all you sons of this land ___, Let us sing of our joy to be free ___, Prais - ing

God and re - joic - ing to be ___ Pa - pu - a New Gui - nea ___. Shout our name from the moun - tains to

seas ___ Pa - pu - a ___ New Gui - nea ___; Let us raise our voi - ces and pro - claim ___ Pa - pu -

a ___ New Gui - nea ___.

Paraguay

República del Paraguay

(Republic of Paraguay)

Quick Country Facts

Location: South America

Area: 157,047 sq. mi. (406,750 sq. km.)

Population (2002 est.): 5,884,491

Capital/Largest City: Asunción (pop. 502,426)

Official Language: Spanish

GDP/PPP: $26.2 billion, $4,600 capita

Monetary Unit: Guaraní

Himno Nacional

(National Anthem)

Lyrics: Francisco Esteban Acuña de Figueroa (1791-1862). Music: Francisco José Debali (1791-1859), Francés Dupuy (1813-1861), or Louis Cavedagni (d. 1916). Adopted: 1846.

Historical Background

The Paraguayan anthem was adopted in 1846 and declared official in 1934.

Spanish Words (First Verse, 7 Total)	English Translation (First Verse, 7 Total)
1	1
A los pueblos de América infausto,	For three centuries a reign oppressed
Tres centurias un cetro oprimió,	The unhappy peoples of America,
Mas un día soberbia surgiendo,	But one day, their anger aroused, they said:
¡Basta! dijo, y el cetro rompió.	"An end to this!" and broke the reign.
Nuestros padres lidiando grandiosos,	Our forefathers, fighting magnificently,
Ilustraron su gloria marcial;	Displayed their immortal glory,
Y trozada la augusta diadema,	And when the august diadem was shattered,
Enalzaron el gorro triunfal	They raised the triumphal cap of liberty.
(repeat previous two lines)	(repeat previous two lines)

CHORUS	CHORUS
¡Paraguayos, República o Muerte!	Paraguayans, Republic or death!
Nuestro brío nos dio libertad;	It was our strength that gave us our final liberty.
Ni opresores, ni siervos, alientan.	Neither tyrants nor slaves can continue,
Donde reina unión, e igualdad.	Where unity and equality reign,
(repeat previous two lines)	(repeat previous two lines)
Unión, e igualdad.	Where unity and equality reign.
(repeat)	(repeat)

Paraguay

A los pue - blos de A - mé - ri - ca in - faus - - to, Tres cen - tu - rias un __

ce - tro o - pri - mió, Mas un dí - a so - ber - bia sur - gien - -

do, ¡Ba - sta! di - jo, y el ce - - tro rom - pió. Nue - stros

pa - dres li - dian - - do gran - dio - - sos, I - lus - tra - - ron su

glo - ria mar - ci - al; Y tro - - za - - da la au - gus - ta dia - de -

ma, E - - nal - za - ron el gor - - ro triun - fal Y tro - - za - - da la au -

gus - - ta dia - de - ma, E - - nal - za - - ron el gor - - ro triun - fal

¡Pa - ra - gua - yos, Re - pú - bli - ca o Muer - te ___! Nue - stro brí - o nos dio ___ li - ber -

tad ____; Ni o - pre - so - res, ni sier - vos, a - lien - tan ___, Don - de re - i - na u - nión, e i - gual -

dad ____. Ni o - pre - so - res, ni sier - vos, a - lien - tan ___, Don - de re - i - na u - nión e i - gual -

dad. U - nión e i - gual - dad. U - nión e i - gual - dad ____.

Peru

República del Perú

(Republic of Peru)

Quick Country Facts
Location: South America
Area: 496,222 sq. mi. (1,285,220 sq. km.)
Population (2002 est.): 27,949,639
Capital/Largest City: Lima (pop. 7,450,000)
Official Languages: Spanish, Quecha
GDP/PPP: $132 billion, $4,800 per capita
Monetary Unit: Nuevo Sol

Himno Nacional

(National Anthem)

Lyrics: José de la Torre Ugarte (1786-1831). Music: José Bernardo Alzedo (1788-1878). Adopted: 1913.

Historical Background

Once the Protectorate was established after the country's independence, General José de San Martín called a contest to establish the national anthem as a symbol of sovereignty. The winning piece was written by José Bernardo Alzedo (music) and José de la Torre Ugarte (words). The anthem, considered one of the most beautiful in the world, was sung for the first time in the Principal Theatre of Lima on the night of 24 September 1821 by Rosa Merino de Arenas and was chosen as Peru's national anthem on 15 April 1822. In 1869, Claudio Rebagliati made a few revisions to the original lyrics and rewrote some lines. The anthem was adopted officially in 1913.

Spanish Words (First Verse, 6 Total)	English Translation (First Verse, 6 Total)
CHORUS	CHORUS
Somos libres, seámoslo siempre, seámoslo siempre	We are free; let us always be so, let us always be so
Y antes niegues sus luces sus luces sus luces el sol,	Let the sun rather deny its deny its light
Que faltemos al voto solemne	Than that we should fail the solemn vow
Que la patria al Eterno elevó.	Which our country raised to God
(repeat previous two lines three times)	(repeat previous two lines three times)

502

1	1
Largo tiempo, el peruano oprimido	For a long time the Peruvian, oppressed,
la ominosa cadena arrastró	Dragged the ominous chain;
condenado a cruel servidumbre largo tiempo,	Condemned to cruel serfdom,
largo tiempo, largo tiempo en silencio gimió.	For a long time, for a long time,
Mas apenas el grito sagrado	for a long time he moaned in silence.
¡Libertad! en sus costas se oyó,	But as soon as the sacred cry of
la indolencia de esclavo sacude, la humillada,	Freedom! was heard on his coasts.
la humillada, la humillada cerviz levantó.	He shook off the indolence of the slave,
la humillada, cerviz levantó, cerviz levantó.	He raised his humiliated,
	his humiliated, his humiliated head.
	He raised, he raised his humiliated head.
CHORUS	CHORUS

Peru

lem - ne   Que __ la   pa - tria al E - ter - - no e - le - vó __. Lar - go   tiem - po el pe - rua - no o - pri - -

mi - - do la o - mi - no - sa ca - de - na arras - - tró __ con - de - na - do a cruel ser - vi -

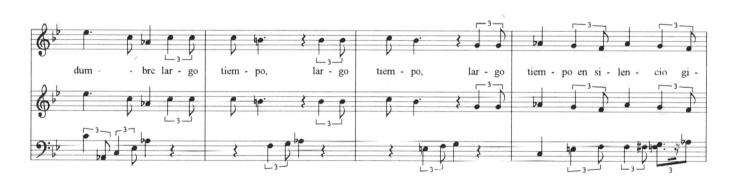

dum - - bre lar - go   tiem - po,   lar - go   tiem - po,   lar - go   tiem - po en si - len - cio gi -

mió __. Mas a - pe - nas el gri - to sa - gra - do   ¡Li - ber - tad! en sus cos - - tas __

se o - yó, la in - do - len - cia de es - cla - - vo sa - cu - de, la hu - mi - lla - da, la hu - mi -

lla - da, la hu - mi - lla - da cer - viz le - van - tó. la hu - mi - lla - da cer - viz __ le - van -

tó, cer - viz __ le - van - tó __. So - mos lib - res, se - á - mos - lo siem - pre, se - á - mos - lo

siem - pre __, Y an - tes nie - gues sus lu - ces sus lu - ces sus lu - ces el sol __, Que fal -

te - mos al vo - - to so - lem - ne ___ Que la pa - tria al E - ter - no e - le - vó ___. Que fal -

te - mos al vo - - to so - lem - ne Que la pa - tria al E - ter - - no e - le - vó ___. Que fal -

te - mos al vo - - to so - lem - ne Que __ la pa - tria al E - ter - - no e - le - vó ___.

The Philippines

Republik ng Pilipinas

Republic of the Philippines

Quick Country Facts
Location: Southeast Asia
Area: 115,830 sq. mi. (300,000 sq. km.)
Population (2002 est.): 84,525,639
Capital/Largest City: Manila (pop. 13,450,000)
Official Languages: Filipino, English
GDP/PPP: $335 billion, $4,000 per capita
Monetary Unit: Peso

Pambangsang Awit ng Pilipinas

Marcha Nacional Filipina

(Philippine National March)

Filipino Lyrics: Felipe Padilla de Leon (1912-1992). Spanish Lyrics: José Palma. Music: Julian Felipe (1861-1944). Adopted: 1935.

Historical Background[1]

The Philippine national anthem is a product of revolution, a response to the need of the revolutionary times that gave birth to it. And this need arose in 1898, when the revolution against Spain was in its second year and a Filipino victory was in sight. General Emilio Aguinaldo astutely recognized the need for national symbols to rally the nation against the enemy.

On 5 June 1898, he commissioned Julian Felipe, a Cavite pianist and composer, to work on a march for the revolutionists. Felipe worked on the assignment for six days and on 11 June, sitting in front of a piano in the Aguinaldo living room, played his music before the president and his lieutenants. Named by Felipe the "Marcha Filipino Magdalo" (after Aguinaldo's nom de guerre and his faction in the Katipunan), the music was adopted on the spot and renamed the "Marcha Nacional Filipina" ("Philippine National March").

The national anthem was heard publicly for the first time on 12 June 1898, when, standing on the balcony of his Kawit mansion, Aguinaldo proclaimed Asia's first independent republic before a cheering throng. Two rallying symbols were presented to the infant nation that day. Also displayed for the first time was the national flag, unfurled to the stirring strains of the *marcha nacional* played by the band of San Francisco de Malabon (now Heneral Trias) whose members had learned the music the day before.

But still without words, Felipe's music was simply a march. It could not be sung. The need for lyrics was just as great as there was for the music. In December 1898, the Philippines was ceded by Spain to the United States in the Treaty of Paris. Having thrown off Spanish rule, the Filipinos found themselves under new colonial masters, the Americans. In February of 1899, the Filipino-American War erupted. The defiant lyrics to march the stirring strains of Felipe were supplied by José Palma, a 23-year-old soldier who was as adept with the pen as he was with the sword. He wrote a poem entitled "Filipinas" and this was wed to the Felipe composition.

The anthem was readily taken by the young nation at war. But on 23 March 1901, the war with America ground to a halt with the capture of Aguinaldo in Palanan, Isabela. The first half of the century were years of humiliation for the Filipinos. The American administrators discouraged the singing of the anthem. Nevertheless, in the 1920s, Palma's original Spanish lyrics underwent several English and Tagalog translations. The most popular were the following versions, one in English by Camilo Osias and M. A. L. Lane and one in Tagalog. In 1956, a new version penned by the Surian ng Wikang Pambansa (Institute of National Language) was adopted.

Filipino Words	Spanish Words	English Translation[2]
Bayang Magiliw, Perlas ng Silanganan Alab ng Puso sa dibdib mo'y buhay	Tierra adorada, Hija del Sol de Oriente, Su fuego ardiente En ti latiendo está.	Land of the morning Child of the sun returning With fervor burning Thee do our souls adore.
Lupang Hinirang, Duyan ka ng magiting, Sa manlulupig di ka pasisiil.	Patria de Amores, Del heróismo cuna, Los invasores No te holláran jamás.	Land dear and holy Cradle of noble heroes Ne'er shall invaders Trample thy sacred shore.
Sa dagat at bundok, Sa simoy at sa langit mong bughaw, May dilag ang tula At awit sa paglayang minamahal.	En tus azul cielo, en tus auras, En tus montes y en tu mar Esplende y late el poema De tu amada libertad.	O'er within thy skies and through thy clouds And o'er thy hills and seas, Do we behold the radiance feel the throb of glorious liberty.
Ang kislap ng watawat mo'y Tagumpay na nagniningning; Ang bituin at araw niya Kailan pa ma'y di magdidilim.	Tu pabellón, que en las lides La Victoria iluminó, No verá nunca apagados Sus estrellas y su sol.	Thy banner dear to all our hearts thy sun and stars alight. Never shall its shining rays Be dimmed by tyrants' might.
Lupa ng araw, ng luwalhati't pagsinta,	Tierra de dichas, de sol y amores,	O beautiful land of love,

| Buhay ay langit sa piling mo;
Aming ligaya na pag may mang-aapi
Ang mamatay nang dahil sa iyo.
(repeat first two stanzas) | En tu regazo dulce es vivir,
Es una gloria para tus hijos,
Cuando te ofenden, por ti morir.
(repeat first two stanzas) | O land of life,
In thine embrace
'Tis rapture to lie.
But it is glory ever
when thou art wronged
for us, thy sons, to suffer and die.
(repeat first two stanzas) |

The Philippines

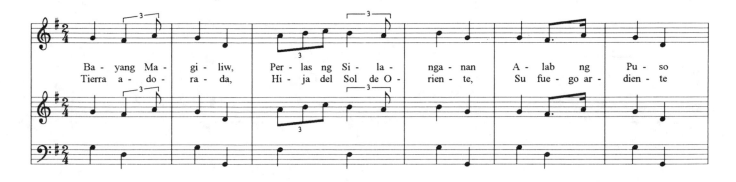

Ba - yang Ma - gi - liw, Per - las ng Si - la - nga - nan A - lab ng Pu - so
Tierra a - do - ra - da, Hi - ja del Sol de O - rien - te, Su fue - go ar - dien - te

sa dib - dib mo'y bu - hay ___ Lu - pang Hi - ni - rang, Du - yan ka ng ma - gi - ting,
En ti la - tien - do es - tá ___. Pa - tria de A - mo - res, Del he - ró - is - mo cu - na,

Sa man - lu - lu - pig di ka pa - si - si - il. Sa da - gat at bun - dok, Sa si - moy, at sa
Los in - va - so - res No te hol - lá - ran ja - más. En tus a - zul cie - lo, en tus au - ras En

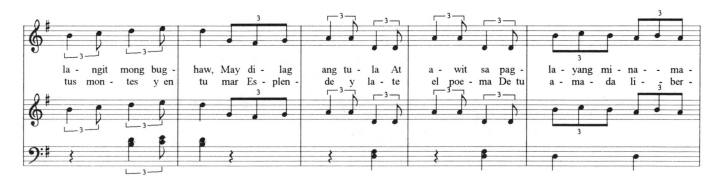

la - ngit mong bug - haw, May di - lag ang tu - la At a - wit sa pag - la - yang mi - na - ma -
tus mon - tes y en tu mar Es - plen - de y la - te el poe - ma De tu a - ma - da li - ber -

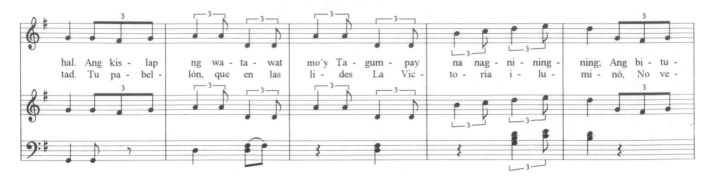

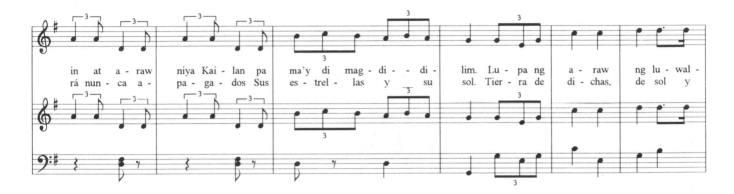

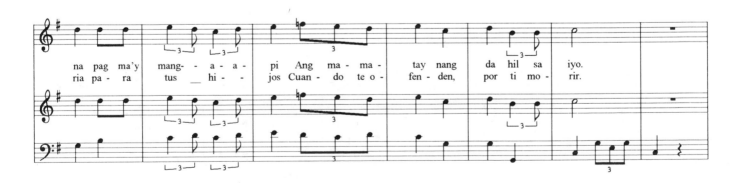

Ba - yang Ma - gi - liw, Per - las ng Si - la - nga - nan A - lab ng Pu - so
Tierra a - do - ra - da, Hi - ja del Sol de O - rien - te, Su fue - go ar - dien - te

sa dib - dib mo'y bu - hay Lu - pang Hi - ni - rang, Du - yan ka ng ma - gi - ting,
En ti la - tien - do está Pa - tria de A - mo - res, Del he - ró - is - mo cu - na,

Sa man - lu - lu - pig di ka pa - si - si - il
Los in - va - so - res No te hol - lá - ran ja - más

Poland

Rzeczpospolita Polska

(Republic of Poland)

<table>
<tr><td colspan="2" align="center">Quick Country Facts</td></tr>
<tr><td>Location: Eastern Europe</td></tr>
<tr><td>Area: 120,727 sq. mi. (312,685 sq. km.)</td></tr>
<tr><td>Population (2002 est.): 38,625,478</td></tr>
<tr><td>Capital/Largest City: Warsaw (pop. 1,642,700)</td></tr>
<tr><td>Official Language: Polish</td></tr>
<tr><td>GDP/PPP: $368.1 billion, $9,500 per capita</td></tr>
<tr><td>Monetary Unit: Zloty</td></tr>
</table>

Mazurek Dąbrowskiego

(Dąbrowski's Mazurka)

Lyrics: Jósef Wybicki (1747-1822). Music: Michal Kleofas Ogiński (1765-1833). Adopted: 1927.

Historical Background[1]

In 1797 General Józef Wybicki, who was a member of the Polish troops that served Napoleon in Italy and Spain, penned a song to bid farewell to the departing Polish army. The Polish Legion, led by General Dąbrowski, had hoped to come with the Napoleonic troops "from Italy to Poland" to liberate their country, and the Mazurka's text made this hope explicit. The troops fought and won with Napoleon, and a short-lived "Duchy of Warsaw" was born from this hope, only to die in 1815 for the next 100 years. The first line of the text states that "Poland is not dead, as long as we live" and Poles continued to sing these words through the 19th century while struggling for their country's reemergence. Thus, Napoleon Bonaparte became immortalized in Poland's national anthem.

Another unusual fact relates to the anthem's music, the traditional melody of a swift mazurka. In the 19th century a variant of this mazurka became a pan-Slavonic hymn, "Hey Slovane," which in 1945 was declared the national anthem of Yugoslavia. Now of course, it no longer serves this function. It is interesting to notice that the two melodies are virtually indistinguishable except for the first three notes.

The "Dąbrowski's Mazurka" was declared the official anthem of the country in 1926 after Józef Piłsudski took control of the country. Poland had been independent since 1918, and had no official anthem for the first eight years of its existence. The valiant "Mazurka" became a winner in a competition for the position of the national anthem with several other revered songs.

Polish Words	English Translation[2]
1	1
Jeszcze Polska nie zginęła	Poland has not yet succumbed.
Kiedy my żyjemy,	As long as we remain,
Co na obca przemoc wzięła,	What the foe by force has seized,
Szablą odbierzemy.	Sword in hand we'll gain.
CHORUS	CHORUS
Marsz, marsz, Dąbrowski,	March! March, Dąbrowski!
Z ziemi włoskiej do Polski	March from Italy to Poland!
Za twoim przewodem,	Under your command
Złączym się z narodem.	We shall reach our land.
(repeat chorus)	(repeat chorus)
2	2
Przejdziem Wisłę, Przejdziem Wartę,	Cross the Vistula and Warta
Będziem Polakami,	And Poles we shall be;
Dał na przykład Bonaparte,	We've been shown by Bonaparte
Jak zwyciężać mamy.	Ways to victory.
CHORUS	CHORUS
3	3
Jak Czarniecki do Poznania,	As Czarniecki Poznan town regains,
Po szwedzkim zaborze,	Fighting with the Swede,
Dla ojczyzny ratowania,	To free our fatherland from chains.
Wrócim się przez morze.	We shall return by sea.
CHORUS	CHORUS
4	4
Już tam ojciec do swej Basi,	Father, in tears, says to his Basia:
Mówi zapłakany,	"Just listen,
Słuchaj jeno pano nasi	It seems that our people
Biją w tarabany.	Are beating the drums."
CHORUS	CHORUS

Poland

Jesz - cze Pol - ska nie zgi - nę - - ła __ Kie - dy my __ ży - je - my, Co na ob - ca

prze - moc wzię - - ła __, Szab - lą od - bie - rze - my __. Marsz, marsz __, Dą - brow - - ski,

Z zie - mi wło - skiej do Pol - ski Za two - im __ prze - wo - - dem, Złą - czym się __ z na -

ro - dem.

Portugal

República Portuguesa

(Republic of Portugal)

Quick Country Facts

Location: Western Europe, Iberian Peninsula

Area: 36,090 sq. mi. (92,391 sq. km.)

Population (2002 est.): 10,084,245

Capital/Largest City: Lisbon (pop. 677,790)

Official Language: Portuguese

GDP/PPP: $182 billion, $18,000 per capita

Monetary Unit: Euro

A Portuguesa

(In the Portuguese Way)

Lyrics: Henrique Lopes de Mendonça (1856-1931). Music: Alfredo Keil (1850-1907). Adopted: 1910.

Historical Background[1]

During the monarchy, the concept of the Portuguese nation was based on the power of the king. There was no notion of a national anthem, and for this reason musical pieces with public or official character were identified with the reigning monarch. In this context, in 1826, the "Patriotic Hymn," written by Antonio Marcos Portugal, was considered a national anthem. This anthem was inspired by the final part of the cantata La Speranza o sia L'Augurio Felice, composed and offered to Prince-Regent Dom Joao when he was with the Court of Brazil, which was presented at the Sao Carlos Theater in Lisbon on 13 May 1809 to celebrate his birthday. The lyrics of the "Patriotic Hymn" had different versions depending on the circumstances and events of the era, naturally becoming generalized and national because of its pleasant martial expression, which rallied Portuguese spirits, inviting them to continue with heroic actions. With the return of the king to the country, in 1821, the same author dedicated a poem to him that, when sung with the music of the hymn, spread rapidly and came to be solemnly intoned.

Meanwhile, following the revolution of 1820, on 22 September 1822, the First Liberal Portuguese Constitution was approved, sworn by D. Joao VI. D. Pedro, then prince regent in Brazil, composed the "Imperial and Constitutional Hymn," dedicated to the constitution. After the death of the King, and with the rise to the throne of D. Pedro, he presented to the Portuguese a Constitutional Charter. The hymn he had written spread with the official denomination of the "Hymn of the Charter," being considered officially as the national anthem and therefore obligatory at all public ceremonies, after May 1834. Using the music of the "Hymn of the Charter," various works of public nature were composed or dedicated to important events and personalities, identifying it completely with political and social life of the last seventy years of the monarchy in Portugal.

At the end of the nineteenth century, "A Portuguesa," a vibrant and stirring march, with strong patriotic sentiment, by affirming the independence it represented and the enthusiasm it drew out, became naturally and on its own merits, a national symbol. The "Hymn," meanwhile, which had been conceived to unite the Portuguese around a common sentiment, because it was sung by the revolutionaries of 31 January 1891, was downplayed by the monarchs and its performance was prohibited at official and ceremonial events. With the installation of the Republic in 1910, "A Portuguesa" flowered spontaneously again with popular voice, being sung and played in the streets of Lisbon. The same Constitutional Assembly of 19 June 1911 that approved the national flag proclaimed "A Portuguesa" as the national anthem. This meant that the composition written by Alfredo Keil and Henrique Lopes de Mendonça became official; it was an extraordinarily happy alliance of music and poetry that was able, in 1890, to successfully interpret the patriotic sentiment of revolt against the English Ultimatum, imposed in humiliating and arrogant terms against Portugal.

In 1956, there were a number of variations of the anthem, not just in its melodic line but also in the instrumentation, especially for a band. Recognizing this, the government named a commission charged with determining the official version of "A Portuguesa." This commission prepared a proposal that, approved by the Council of Ministers on 16 July 1957, remains in effect to this day.

The anthem is officially played at national civil and military ceremonies where praise is given to the nation, the national flag or the President of the Republic. In addition, its performance is obligatory whenever a foreign head of state is officially received on national territory after hearing the anthem of the represented country.

Portuguese Words	English Translation
VERSE	VERSE
Heróis do mar, nobre Povo,	Heroes of the sea, noble race,
Nação valente, imortal	Valiant and immortal nation,
Levantai hoje de novo,	Now is the hour to raise up on high once more
O esplendor de Portugal!	Portugal's splendor.
Entre as brumas da memória,	From out of the mists of memory,
Ó pátria sente-se a voz	Oh Homeland, we hear the voices
Dos teus egrégios avós	Of your great forefathers
Que há-de guiar-te à vitória.	That shall lead you on to victory!
CHORUS	CHORUS
Às armas! Às armas!	To arms, to arms
Sobre a terra, sobre o mar!	On land and sea!
Às armas! Às armas!	To arms, to arms
Pela Pátria lutar!	To fight for our homeland!
Contra os canhões marchar, marchar!	To march against the enemy guns!

Portugal

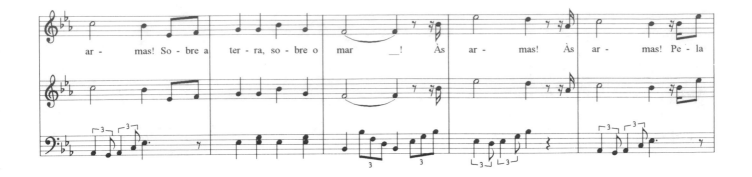

ar - mas! So - bre a ter - ra, so - bre o mar ___! Às ar - mas! Às ar - mas! Pe - la

Pá - tria lu - tar ___! Con - tra os ca - nhões mar - char, mar - char!

Qatar

دولة قطر

Dawlatu Qatar

(State of Qatar)

Quick Country Facts

Location: West Asia, Arabian Peninsula

Area: 4,468 sq. mi. (11,437 sq. km.)

Population (2002 est.): 793,341

Capital/Largest City: Doha (pop.300,000)

Official Language: Arabic

GDP/PPP: $16.3 billion, $21,200 per capita

Monetary Unit: Qatari Riyal

النشيد لقطر

Al-Nasheed al-Qatar

(Qatari National Anthem)

Adopted: 1996.

Historical Background

The original Qatari anthem was adopted in 1954 and had no lyrics. It was replaced by a new song with both words and music on 7 December 1996.

Arabic Words	English Translation
قسما بمن رفع السماء	I swear by he
قسما بمن نشر الضياء	Who lifted the sky and spread the light
قطر ستبقى حرة	Qatar will remain free,
تسمو بروح الفداء	Rising high by the spirits of the faithful
سيروا على نهج الأولى	Move along on the plain road of the ancestors
وعلى ضياء الأنبياء	And on the lights of the prophets

قطر بقلبي سيرة	Qatar, in my heart,
عز وأمجاد الإباء	Is the story of glory and the forefathers` honor
قطر الرجال الأولين	Qatar of forefathers,
حماتنا يوم النداء	Who were our defenders at war,
وحمائم يوم السلام	Who were pigeons at peace
جوارح يوم الفداء	And predators on the day of redemption.

Qatar

523

Qatar

Romania

România

```
┌─────────────────────────────────────────────────┐
│              Quick Country Facts                │
│  Location: Eastern Europe                       │
│  Area: 91,700 sq. mi. (237,500 sq. km.)         │
│  Population (2002 est.): 22,317,730             │
│  Capital/Largest City: Bucharest (pop. 2,351,000) │
│  Official Language: Romanian                    │
│  GDP/PPP: $152.7 billion, $6,800 per capita     │
│  Monetary Unit: Leu                             │
└─────────────────────────────────────────────────┘
```

Deşteaptă-te, române

(Awaken Thee, Romanian)

Lyrics: Andrei Mureşanu (1816-1863). Music: Anton Pann (1796-1854). Adopted: 1990.

Historical Background[1]

The lyrics of the national anthem belong to Andrei Mureşanu, a Romantic poet, journalist, translator, a genuine tribune of the times marked by the 1848 Revolution. The music was composed by Anton Pann, a poet and ethnographer, a man of great culture, a singer, and author of music textbooks.

Andrei Muresanu's poem "Un răsunet," written and published during the 1848 Revolution, found the adequate music within a few days, as the anthem was sung for the first time on 29 June 1848 at Râmnicu Vâlcea (in Wallachia the revolution had broken out on 11 June). The poem became an anthem under the title "Deşteaptă-te române" ("Awaken Thee, Romanian") and spontaneously earned recognition owing to its energetic and mobilizing message.

Since 1848 "Deşteaptă-te române" has been a song dear to the Romanians, giving them courage in the crucial moments, during the Independence War (1877-1878), just as during World War I. In the moments of crisis after 23 August 1944 when, after the state coup, Romania turned against Hitler's Germany and then participated in the war along with the Allies, this anthem was spontaneously sung by everyone and was aired on the national radio, keeping the whole country on alert. The same happened on 22 December 1989, at the time of the anti-Communist revolution; the anthem rose from the streets, accompanying huge masses of people, dispelling the fear of death and uniting a whole people in the lofty feelings of the moment. Thus, its institution as a state anthem came by itself, upon the tremendous pressure of the demonstrators.

The message of the anthem "Deşteaptă-te române" is social and national at the same time; social because it imposes a permanent state of vigil meant to secure the passing to a new world; national because it gears this awakening to the historical tradition. The anthem proposes that sublime "now or never," present in all national anthems from the paion with which the Greeks fought at Marathon and Salamina to the French revolutionary "Marseillaise." The invocation of the national fate is the peak a people can reach in its soaring toward the divine. This "now or never" historically calls upon all vital energies and mobilizes to the full. Romania's national anthem has several stanzas, of which the four are sung on ceremonial occasions.

Romanian Words (First, Second, Fourth, and Eleventh Verses, 11 Total)	English Translation (First, Second, Fourth, and Eleventh Verses, 11 Total) [2]
1	1
Deşteaptă-te, romane, din somnul cel de moarte,	Awaken thee, Romanian, shake off the deadly slumber
În care te-adânciră barbarii de tirani,	The scourge of inauspicious barbarian tyrannies
Barbarii de tirani,	Barbarian tyrannies
Acum ori niciodată croieşte-ţi altă soarte,	And now or never to a bright horizon clamber
La care să se-nchine şi cruzii tăi duşmani.	That shall to shame put all your nocuous enemies.
Şi cruzii tăi duşmani.	All your nocuous enemies.
(repeat previous three lines)	(repeat previous three lines)
2	2
Acum ori niciodată să dăm dovezi în lume	It's now or never to the world we readily proclaim
Că-n aste mâni mai curge un sânge de roman,	In our veins throbs and ancestry of Roman
Şi că-n a noastre piepturi păstrăm cu fală-un nume	And in our hearts for ever we glorify a name
Triumfător în lupte, un nume de Traian.	Resounding of battle, the name of gallant Trajan.
4	4
Priviţi, măreţe umbre, Mihai, Ştefan, Corvine,	Do look imperial shadows, Michael, Stephen, Corvinus
Româna naţiune, ai voştri strănepoţi,	At the Romanian nation, your mighty progeny
Cu braţele armate, cu focul vostru-n vine,	With arms like steel and hearts of fire impetuous
Viaţa-n libertate ori moarte strigă toţi.	It's either free or dead, that's what they all decree.
11	11
Preoţi, cu crucea-n frunte căci oastea e creştină,	Priests, rise the cross, this Christian army's liberating
Deviza-i libertate şi scopul ei preasfânt.	The word is freedom, no less sacred is the end
Murim mai bine-n luptă, cu glorie deplină,	We'd rather die in battle, in elevated glory
Decât să fim sclavi iarăşi în vechiul nost'pământ.	Than live again enslaved on our ancestral land.

Romania

Deş - teap - tă - te, ro - mâ - ne, din som - nul cel de moar - - te, În ca - re te - a - dân -

ci - ră bar - ba - rii de ti - rani __ bar - ba - rii __ de ti - rani __ A - cum ori nici - o -

da - tă cro - ieş - te - ţi al - tă soar - - te, La ca - re să __ se - n - chi - ne __ şi

cru - zii tăi duş - mani __ şi cru - zii tăi duş - mani __ A - cum ori nici - o -

da - tă cro - ieş - te-ţi al - tă soar - te. La ca - re să se-n - chi - ne şi

cru - zii tăi duş - mani şi cru - zii tăi duş - mani.

Russia

Российская Федерациа

Rossiyskaya Federatsiya

(Russian Federation)

```
┌─────────────────────────────────────────────────────┐
│                Quick Country Facts                    │
│  Location: Eastern Europe, Central and Northeast Asia │
│  Area: 6,592,800 sq. mi. (17,075,200 sq. km.)        │
│  Population (2002 est.): 144,978,573                  │
│  Capital/Largest City: Moscow (pop. 13,200,000)      │
│  Official Language: Russian                           │
│  GDP/PPP: $1.27 trillion, $8,800 per capita          │
│  Monetary Unit: Ruble                                 │
└─────────────────────────────────────────────────────┘
```

Государственный гимн Российской Федерации

Gosudarctvenniy gimn Rossiyskoy Federatsii

(National Anthem of the Russian Federation)

Lyrics: Sergei Vladimirovich Mikhalov (b. 1913). Music: Alexandr Vasilievich Alexandrov (1883-1946). Adopted: 2000.

Historical Background[1]

A new Russian national anthem was adopted on 20 December 2000 by decree of President Vladimir Putin. Its tune is the same as that of the old USSR anthem. New lyrics were written the following year by Sergei Vladimirovich Mikhalov, who also authored the words to the former Soviet song.

The issue of national symbols had been left unsettled since Russia became an independent nation in 1991. At the beginning of the 1990s former President Boris Yeltsin proclaimed a flag, emblem and anthem of the new state: the tricolored flag of the Romanovs's czarist empire, a two-headed golden eagle, and the music of the nineteenth-century composer Mikhail Glinka. These symbols were never approved by the Russian parliament, dominated by the communists. They rejected the czar's emblem and flag, so according to the Russian constitution these were never legal. What is more, rumor has it that the wrong piece of music became the anthem. Yeltsin, when signing the decree, had a different

Glinka composition in mind than the one that was accepted, which had no lyrics.

When taking over, Putin announced the integration of society around new symbols. As he said prior to a meeting of the Duma which was dedicated to these issues, "Russia should refer to different periods of its history, czarist as well as Soviet. The seventy years of the Soviet Union brought good and bad, but we cannot erase the life of our fathers."

The will of society confirmed Putin's choice. According to the allegedly objective Foundation of Public Opinion Research 49 percent of Russians want the return of the former Soviet anthem with new words. Only 13 percent wish Glinka's music to remain the country's most important song. The czarist anthem "Bozhe Tsarya Khrani" ("Lord, Protect the Czar") and a song from the times of World War II, "Vstavay Strana Ogromnaya" ("Rise Great Country") were also taken into account.

Russian Words	Russian Words (Transliteration)	English Translation[2]
1	1	1
Россия—священная наша держава,	*Rossiya svyaschennaya nasha dyerzhava*	Russia, our holy country!
Россия—любимая наша страна.	*Rossiya lyubimaya nasha strana*	Russia, our beloved country!
Могучая воля, великая слава—	*Moguchaya volya vyelikaya slava*	A mighty will, a great glory,
Твое достоянье на все времена!	*Tvoyo dostoyan'ye na vsya vryemyena!*	Are your inheritance for all time!
CHORUS	CHORUS	CHORUS
Славься, Отечество наше свободное,	*Slav'sya Otechestvo, nashe svobodnoye*	Be glorious, our free fatherland!
Братских народов союз вековой,	*Bratskikh narodov soyuz vyekovoy*	Eternal union of fraternal peoples,
Предками данная мудрость народная!	*Predkami dannaya mudrost' narodnaya*	Common wisdom given by our forebears,
Славься, страна! Мы гордимся тобой!	*Slav'sya strana my gordimsya toboy!*	Be glorious, our country! We are proud of you!
2	2	2
От южных морей до полярного края	*Ot yuzhnykh morey do polyarnogo kraya*	From the southern seas to the polar region
Раскинулись наши леса и поля.	*Raskinulis' nashi lesa i polya*	Spread our forests and fields.
Одна ты на свете! Одна ты такая—	*Odna ty na svete odna ty takaya*	You are unique in the world, inimitable,
Хранимая Богом родная земля!	*Khranimaya bogom rodnaya zyemlya!*	Native land protected by God!
CHORUS	CHORUS	CHORUS

3	3	3
Широкий простор для мечты и для жизни Грядущие нам открывают года. Нам силу дает наша верность Отчизне. Так было, так есть и так будет всегда!	*Shirokiy prostor dlya mechty i dlya zhizni* *Gryaduschiye nam otkryvayut goda* *Nam silu dayot nasha vernost' Otchiznye* *Tak bylo, tak yest' i tak budet vsyegda!*	Wide spaces for dreams and for living Are opened for us by the coming years Faithfulness to our country gives us strength Thus it was, so it is and always will be!
CHORUS	CHORUS	CHORUS

Russia

Ros- si - ya svya- schen- na - ya na - sha dyer- zha- va Ros- si - ya lyu- bi - ma - ya

na - sha stra- na __ Mo- gu- cha- ya vol- ya vye- li- ka- ya sla - va Tvo- yo dos- to- an'- ye na

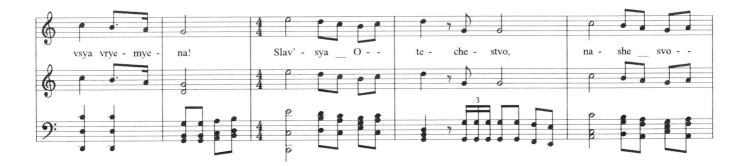

vsya vrye- mye - na! Slav'- sya __ O- te- che- stvo, na- she __ svo-

bod- no- ye Bra- tskikh na- ro- dov so- yuz vye- ko- voy Pred- ka - mi __

dan - na - ya   Mu - - drost' __ na - rod - na - ya   Slav' - sya stra - na my gor - dim - sya to -

boy __ !

Rwanda

Repubulika y'u Rwanda

République Rwandaise

Republic of Rwanda

```
Quick Country Facts
Location: East Central Africa
Area: 10,169 sq. mi. (26,338 sq. km.)
Population (2002 est.): 7,398,074
Capital/Largest City: Kigali (pop. 232,733)
Languages: Kinyarwanda, French, English
GDP/PPP: $7.2 billion, $1,000 per capita
Monetary Unit: Rwanda Franc
```

Historical Background[1]

Rwanda's government unveiled a new flag and national anthem on 31 December 2001 as part of its drive to promote national unity and reconciliation after the 1994 genocide. The new national anthem will refer to the Rwandans as one people, rather than to Tutsi, Hutu, and Twa. Many believe the old anthem—adapted from a traditional folk tune thirty years ago—glorified the Hutu as they fought to throw off Tutsi oppression. The overthrow of the monarchy in 1959 was accompanied by widespread massacres of Tutsi and the flight into exile of countless others.

Legislation providing for the new flag and the new anthem was passed in the late 1990s. The government then organized a nationwide competition, asking Rwandans to design their flag and compose lyrics and music for the anthem.

Anthem Not Available

Saint Kitts and Nevis

Federation of Saint Kitts and Nevis

Quick Country Facts

Location: North America, Caribbean Sea

Area: 100 sq. mi. (261 sq. km.)

Population (2002 est.): 38,736

Capital/Largest City: Basseterre (pop. 19,000)

Official Language: English

GDP/PPP: $339 million, $8,700 per capita

Monetary Unit: East Caribbean Dollar

National Anthem

Lyrics and Music: Kenrick Anderson Georges (b. 1955). Adopted: 1983.

Words

O land of beauty!

Our country where peace abounds,

Thy children stand free

On the strength of will and love.

With God in all our struggles,

Saint Kitts and Nevis be

A nation bound together

With a common destiny.

As stalwarts we stand,

For justice and liberty,

With wisdom and truth

We will serve and honor thee.

No sword nor spear can conquer,

For God will sure defend.

His blessings shall for ever to posterity extend.

Saint Kitts and Nevis

O land of beau - ty! Our coun - try where peace a - bounds, Thy chil - dren stand __ free __ On the

strength of will and love __ . With God in all our strug - gles Saint Kitts and Ne - vis be

__ A na - tion bound to - ge - ther With a com - mon des - ti - ny __. As stal - warts we stand

__, For just - ice and li - ber - ty, With wis - dom and __ truth __ We will serve and hon -

or thee __. No sword nor spear can con - quer, For God will sure de - fend __. His bless - ings shall for e - -

ver To pos - ter - i - ty ex - tend __.

Saint Lucia

Quick Country Facts

Location: North America, Caribbean Sea

Area: 238 sq. mi. (616 sq. km.)

Population (2002 est.): 160,145

Capital/Largest City: Castries (pop. 13,600)

Official Language: English

GDP/PPP: $700 million, $4,400 per capita

Monetary Unit: East Caribbean Dollar

Sons and Daughters of Saint Lucia

Lyrics: Charles Jesse (1897-1985). Music: Leton Felix Thomas (b. 1926). Adopted: 1967.

Historical Background

The national anthem of Saint Lucia was adopted when the country achieved commonwealth status in 1967 and upon complete independence in 1979.

Words		
1	2	3
Sons and daughters of St. Lucia,	Gone the times when nations battled	May the good Lord bless our island,
Love the land that gave us birth,	For this Helen of the West,	Guard her sons from woe and harm!
Land of beaches, hills and valleys,	Gone the days when strife and discord	May our people live united,
Fairest isle of all the earth.	Dimmed her children's toil and rest.	Strong in soul and strong in arm!
Wheresoever you may roam,	Dawns at last a brighter day,	Justice, truth, and charity,
Love, oh love your island home.	Stretches out a glad new way.	Our ideal for ever be!

Saint Lucia

Sons and daugh - ters of Saint Lu - cia, Love the land that gave us birth, Land of bea - ches,

hills and val - leys, Fair - est isle of __ all the earth. Where - so - ev - er you may roam __,

Love, oh __ love your is - land home __.

Saint Vincent and the Grenadines

```
┌─────────────────────────────────────────────┐
│            Quick Country Facts                │
│  Location: North America, Caribbean Sea       │
│  Area: 150 sq. mi. (389 sq. km.)             │
│  Population (2002 est.): 116,394              │
│  Capital/Largest City: Kingstown (pop. 15,466)│
│  Official Language: English                   │
│  GDP/PPP: $339 million, $2,900 per capita     │
│  Monetary Unit: East Caribbean Dollar         │
└─────────────────────────────────────────────┘
```

National Anthem

Lyrics: Phyllis Joyce McClean Punnett (b.1917). Music: Joel Bertram Miguel (b.1938). Adopted: 1969.

Historical Background

The national anthem of Saint Vincent and the Grenadines was adopted when the country achieved commonwealth status in 1969 and upon complete independence in 1979.

Words		
1	2	3
Saint Vincent! Land so beautiful,	Hairoun! Our fair and blessed isle,	Our little sister islands are
With joyful hearts we pledge to thee	Your mountains high, so clear and green,	Those gems, the lovely Grenadines,
Our loyalty and love, and vow	Are home to me, though I may stray,	Upon their seas and golden sands
To keep you ever free.	A haven, calm, serene.	The sunshine ever beams.
CHORUS	CHORUS	CHORUS
Whate'er the future brings,		
Our faith will see us through.		
May peace reign from shore to shore,		
And God bless and keep us true.		

Saint Vincent and the Grenadines

Saint Vin - cent! Land so beau - ti - ful, With joy - ful hearts we pledge to thee Our loy - al - ty and

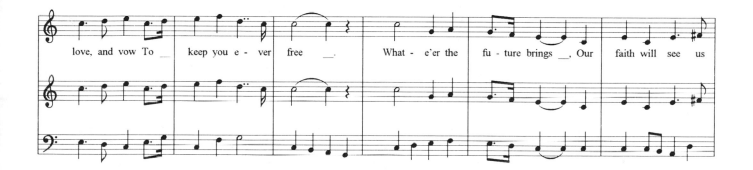

love, and vow To __ keep you e - ver free __. What - e'er the fu - ture brings __, Our faith will see us

through __. May peace reign from shore __ to shore __, And God bless and keep us true.

Samoa

Malo Sa'oloto Tuto'atasi o Samoa

Independent State of Samoa

Quick Country Facts
Location: Oceania, Pacific Ocean
Area: 1,093 sq. mi. (2,944 sq. km.)
Population (2002 est.): 178,631
Capital/Largest City: Apia (pop. 32,859)
Official Languages: Samoan, English
GDP/PPP: $618 million, $3,500 per capita
Monetary Unit: Tala

The Banner of Freedom

Lyrics and Music: Sauni Iiga Kuresa (1900-1978). Adopted: 1962.

Historical Background

Originally written and composed in 1948 by Sauni Iiga Kuresa, the Samoan anthem was adopted fourteen years later.

Samoan Words	English Translation
Samoa, tula`i ma sisi ia lau fu'a, lou pale lea;	Samoa, arise and raise your banner that is your crown!
(repeat)	Oh! see and behold the stars on the waving banner!
Vaai i na fetu o loo ua agiagia ai;	They are a sign that Samoa is able to lead.
Le faailoga lea o Iesu namaliu ai mo Samoa Oi!	Oh! Samoa, hold fast
Samoa e, uu mau lau pule ia faavavau.	Your freedom for ever!
`Aua e te fefe, o le Atua lo ta fa`a vae	Do not be afraid; as you are founded on God;
O lota Sa`o lotoga,	Our treasured precious liberty.
Samoa, tula`i, ia agiagia lau	Samoa, arise and wave
Fu`a lou pale lea.	Your banner that is your crown!

Samoa

Sa - moa __, tu - la'i __ ma si - si ia lau fu'a __, lou pa - le le - a; Sa -

moa __, tu - la'i __ ma si - si ia lau fu'a __, lou pa - le le - a; Va - ai i na fe -

tu o loo ua a - gia - gi - a ai __; Le fa - ai - lo - ga lea o Ie - su na - ma - liu ai mo Sa -

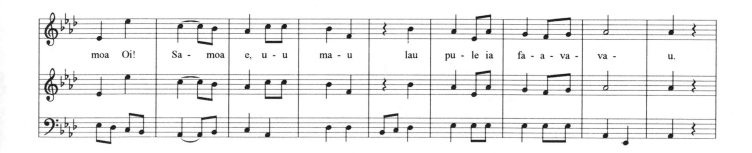

moa Oi! Sa - moa e, u - u ma - u lau pu - le ia fa - a - va - va - u.

'Au - a e te   fe - fe, o le   Atua   lo ta fa'a   vae __ O   lo - ta   Sa'o lo -   to -   ga,   Sa-

moa __, tu - la'i __, ia   a - gia -   gia lau   Fu'a __ lou   pa - le   le -   a.

San Marino

Repubblica di San Marino

Republic of San Marino

```
┌─────────────────────────────────────────────┐
│            Quick Country Facts                │
│ Location: Western Europe, Italian peninsula   │
│ Area: 23.4 sq. mi. (61.2 sq. km.)            │
│ Population (2002 est.): 27,730               │
│ Capital/Largest City: San Marino (pop. 2,397)│
│ Official Language: Italian                    │
│ GDP/PPP: $940 million, $34,600 per capita    │
│ Monetary Unit: Italian Lira                  │
└─────────────────────────────────────────────┘
```

Inno Nazionale

(National Anthem)

Music: Ferderico Consolo (1841-1906). Adopted: 1894.

Historical Background

Based on a tenth century chorale, this anthem was adopted in 1894. Although several poets, including the Italian Giosué Carducci, have written verses to the song, it remains officially without words.

No Words

San Marino

São Tomé and Príncipe

República Democrática de São Tomé e Príncipe

(Democratic Republic of São Tomé and Príncipe)

> **Quick Country Facts**
>
> Location: West Africa, Gulf of Guinea
>
> Area: 370 sq. mi. (1,001 sq. km.)
>
> Population (2002 est.): 170,372
>
> Capital/Largest City: São Tomé (pop. 43,420)
>
> Official Language: Portuguese
>
> GDP/PPP: $189 million, $1,200 per capita
>
> Monetary Unit: Dobra

Hino Nacional de São Tomé e Príncipe

(National Anthem of São Tomé and Príncipe)

Lyrics: Alda Neves da Graça do Espirito Santo (b. 1926). Music: Manuel dos Santos Barreto de Sousa e Almeida (b. 1933)

Portuguese Words	English Translation
CHORUS 1	CHORUS 1
Independência total	Total independence,
Glorioso canto do povo	Glorious song of the people,
Independência total	Total independence,
Hino sagrado combate	Sacred hymn of combat.
Dinamismo	Dynamism
Na luta nacional	In the national struggle,
Juramento eterno	Eternal oath
No país soberano	To the sovereign country
De São Tomé e Príncipe	Of São Tomé and Príncipe.

1

Guerrilheiro da guerra sem armas na mão

Chama viva na alma do povo

Congregando os filhos das ilhas

Em redor da Patria Imortal

Independência total, total e completa

Construindo no progresso e na paz

A Nação mais ditosa da terra

Com os braços heróicos do povo

CHORUS 2

Independência total

Glorioso canto do povo

Independência total

Hino sagrado combate

2

Trabalhando, lutando e vencendo

Caminhamos a passos gigantes

Na cruzada dos povos africanos

Hasteando a bandeira nacional

Voz do povo, presente, presente em conjunto

Vibra rijo no coro da esperança

Ser herói na hora do perigo

Ser herói no ressurgir do país

CHORUS 1

1

Warriors in the war without weapons,

Live flame in the soul of the people,

Congregating the sons of the islands

Around the immortal fatherland.

Total independence, total and complete,

Building, in progress and peace,

With the heroic hands of the people,

The happiest nation on earth.

CHORUS 2

Total independence,

Glorious song of the people,

Total independence,

Sacred hymn of combat.

2

Working, struggling, struggling and conquering,

We go ahead with giant steps

In the crusade of the African peoples,

Raising the national flag.

Voice of the people, present, present and united,

Strong beat in the heart of hope

To be a hero in the hour of peril,

A hero of the Nation's resurgence.

CHORUS 1

São Tomé and Príncipe

Saudi Arabia

المملكة العربية السعودية

al Mamlakah al Arabiyah as Saudiyah

(Kingdom of Saudi Arabia)

Quick Country Facts

Location: West Asia, Arabian Peninsula

Area: 865,000 sq. mi. (1,960,582 sq. km.)

Population (2002 est.): 23,513,330

Capital/Largest City: Riyadh (pop. 3,000,000)

Official Language: Arabic

GDP/PPP: $241 billion, $10,600 per capita

Monetary Unit: Riyal

An-Nashid al-Watani

National Anthem

Lyrics: Ibrahim Khafaji (b. 1935). Music: Abdul Rahman al-Khateeb (b. 1923). Adopted: 1950.

Historical Background

The Saudi national anthem was first performed in 1947.

Arabic Words (Transliteration)	English Translation
Sarei Lil Majd Walulya	Hasten to glory and supremacy!
Majjedi Le Khaleg Assama	Glorify the Creator of the heavens
(repeat previous two lines)	(repeat previous two lines)
Warfai El Khaffag Akhdar	And raise the green, fluttering flag,
Yahmil Annoor al mosattar	Carrying the emblem of light!
Raddedy Allah Wakbar	Repeat—God is greatest!
Yamawteni Mawtenii Gad	O my country, my country, may you always live,
Isht Fakhr Al Moslemeen	The glory of all Muslims!
Aash Al Maleek Lelalam Walwatan.	Long live the king, for the flag and the country!

Saudi Arabia

lam Wal - wa - tan.

Senegal

République du Sénégal

Sounougal

(Republic of Senegal)

<table>
<tr><td colspan="1">Quick Country Facts</td></tr>
<tr><td>Location: West Africa</td></tr>
<tr><td>Area: 75,954 sq. mi. (196,190 sq. km.)</td></tr>
<tr><td>Population (2002 est.): 10,589,571</td></tr>
<tr><td>Capital/Largest City: Dakar (pop. 1,729,823)</td></tr>
<tr><td>Languages: French, Wolof</td></tr>
<tr><td>GDP/PPP: $16.2 billion, $1,580 per capita</td></tr>
<tr><td>Monetary Unit: Franc CFA</td></tr>
</table>

Un peuple, un but, une foi

(One People, One Goal, One Faith)

Lyrics: Léopold Sédar Senghor (1906-2001). Music: Herbert Pepper (b. 1912). Adopted: 1960.

Historical Background

This national anthem was written by former President and statesman Léopold Sédar Senghor, who passed away in December 2001. The composer, French ethnomusicologist Herbert Pepper, wrote numerous works of original African tunes. One of his works also became the national anthem of the Central African Republic.

French Words	English Translation
1	1
Pincez tous vos coras, frappez vos balafons	Sound, all of you, your Koras, beat the drums,
Le lion rouge a rugi. Le dompteur de la brousse	The red lion has roared, the tamer of the bush
D'un bond s'est élancé dissipant les ténèbres	With one leap has rushed forward, scattering the gloom.
Soleil sur nos terreurs, soleil sur notre espoir.	Light on our terrors, light on our hopes.
Debout frères voici l'Afrique rassemblée.	Arise, brothers, Africa behold united!

CHORUS

Fibres de mon cœur vert épaule contre épaule

Mes plus que frères. O Sénégalais, debout !

Unissons la mer et les sources, unissons

La steppe et la forêt.

Salut Afrique mère.

2

Sénégal, toi le fils de l'écume du lion,

Toi surgi de la nuit au galop des chevaux,

Rends-nous, oh! rends-nous l'honneur de nos Ancêtres

Splendides comme l'ébène et forts comme le muscle !

Nous disons droits—l'épée n'a pas une bavure.

CHORUS

3

Sénégal, nous faisons nôtre ton grand dessein :

Rassembler les poussins à l'abri des milans

Pour en faire, de l'est à l'ouest, du nord au sud,

Dressé, un même peuple, un peuple sans couture,

Mais un peuple tourné vers tous les vents du monde.

CHORUS

4

Sénégal, comme toi, tous nos héros,

Nous serons durs, sans haine et les deux bras ouverts,

L'épée, nous la mettrons dans la paix du fourreau,

Car notre travail sera notre arme et la parole.

Le Bantou est un frère, et l'Arabe et le Blanc.

CHORUS

CHORUS

Fibers of my green heart.

Shoulder to shoulder, O people of Senegal,

More than brothers to me, arise!

Unite the sea and the springs,

Unite the steppe and the forest!

Hail, mother Africa!

2

Senegal, thou son of the lion

Arise in the night with great speed,

Restore, oh, restore to us the honor of our ancestors,

Magnificent as ebony and strong as muscles!

We are a straight people—the sword has no fault.

CHORUS

3

Senegal, we make your great design our own:

To gather the chicks, sheltering thcm from kites,

To make from them, from East to West, from North to South,

A people rising as one, in seamless unity,

Yet a people facing all the winds of the earth.

CHORUS

4

Senegal, like thee, likc all our hcrocs,

We will be stern without hatred, and with open arms.

The sword we will put peacefully in its sheath,

For work and words will be our weapon.

The Bantu is our brother, the Arab, and the White man too.

CHORUS

5	5
Mais que si l'ennemi incendie nos frontières	But if the enemy violates our frontiers,
Nous soyons tous dressés et les armes au poing :	We will all be ready, weapons in our hands;
Un peuple dans sa foi défiant tous les malheurs ;	A people in its faith defying all evil;
Les jeunes et les vieux, les hommes et les femmes.	Young and old, men and women,
La mort, oui! Nous disons la mort mais pas la honte.	Death, yes! but not dishonor.
CHORUS	CHORUS

Senegal

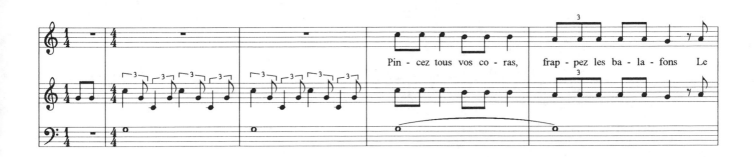

Pin - cez tous vos co - ras, frap - pez les ba - la - fons Le

lion rouge a ru - gi. Le domp - teur de la brousse D'un bond s'est é - lan - cé dis - si - pant les tén - è - bres So -

leil sur nos ter - reurs, so - leil sur notre es - poir. De - bout frè - res voi - ci l'A - fri - que ras - sem - blée.

Fi - bres de mon cœur vert é - pau - le contre é - pau - le Mes plus que frères. O Sé - né - ga - lais, de - bout!

U – nis – sons la mer et les   sour – ces, u – nis – sons La   steppe et la fo – rêt.   Sa – lut A – fri – que mère.

Seychelles

Republik Sesel

République des Seychelles

Republic of Seychelles

Quick Country Facts

Location: Oceania, Pacific Ocean

Area: 175 sq. mi. (455 sq. km.)

Population (2002 est.): 80,098

Capital/Largest City: Victoria (pop. 25,000)

Languages: Seselwa, French, English

GDP/PPP: $605 million, $7,600 per capita

Monetary Unit: Seychelles Rupee

Koste Seselwa

(Come Together Seychellois!)

Lyrics: David François Marc André (b. 1958). Music: George Charles Robert Payet (b. 1959). Adopted: 1996.

Historical Background

The new national anthem gives thanks to God for the harmony, love, and peace reigning in the Seychelles. It replaced the former anthem in 1996.

Seselwa Words	English Translation
Sesel ou menm nou sel patri	Seychelles you are our only motherland
Kot nou viv dan larmoni	Where we live in harmony,
Lazwa, lanmour ek lape	Joy, love and peace
Nou remersye Bondye	We give thanks to God
Preserv labote nou pei	Preserve the beauty of our country
Larises nou losean	The richness of our ocean
En leritaz byen presye	A precious heritage

Pour boner nou zanfan	For the future of our children
Reste touzour dan linite	Let us always be united
Fer monte nou paviyon	As we hoist our flag
Ansanm pou tou leternite	Together, for all eternity
Koste Seselwa!	Come together Seychellois!

Seychelles

Se - sel ou menm nou sel pa - tri __ Kot nou viv dan lar - mo - ni __ La - zwa, lan - mour ek

la - pe Nou re - mer - sye Bon - dye __ Prezerv la - bo - te nou pe - i __ La - ri - ses nou lo - se -

an __ En le - ri - taz byen pre - sye Pour bo - ner nou zan - fan __ Res - te tou - zour dan li - ni -

te Fer mon - te nou pa - vi - yon __ An - sanm pour tou le - ter - ni - te

561

Kos - te Se - sel - wa ___!

Sierra Leone

Republic of Sierra Leone

```
┌─────────────────────────────────────────────┐
│            Quick Country Facts                │
│ Location: West Africa                         │
│ Area: 27,925 sq. mi. (71,740 sq. km.)         │
│ Population (2002 est.): 5,614,743             │
│ Capital/Largest City: Freetown (pop. 1,300,000) │
│ Official Language: English                    │
│ GDP/PPP: $2.7 billion, $500 per capita        │
│ Monetary Unit: Leone                          │
└─────────────────────────────────────────────┘
```

National Anthem

Lyrics: Clifford Nelson Fyle (b. 1933). Music: John Joseph Akar (1927-1975). Adopted: 1961.

Words		
1	2	3
High we exalt thee, realm of the free;	One with a faith that wisdom inspires,	Knowledge and truth our forefathers spread,
Great is the love we have for thee;	One with a zeal that never tires;	Mighty the nations whom they led;
Firmly united ever we stand,	Ever we seek to honor thy name,	Mighty they made thee, so too may we
Singing thy praise, O native land.	Ours is the labor, thine the fame.	Show forth the good that is ever in thee.
We raise up our hearts and our voices on high,	We pray that no harm on thy children may fall,	We pledge our devotion, our strength and our might,
The hills and the valleys reecho our cry;	That blessing and peace may descend on us all;	Thy cause to defend and to stand for thy right;
Blessing and peace be ever thine own,	So may we serve thee ever alone,	All that we have be ever thine own,
Land that we love, our Sierra Leone.	Land that we love, our Sierra Leone.	Land that we love, our Sierra Leone.

Sierra Leone

High we ex - alt __ thee, realm of the free; Great is the love __ we have for __ thee;

Firm - ly u - nit - - ed e - ver we stand, Sing - ing thy praise __, O __ nat - ive __ land. We

raise up our hearts and our voic - es on high, The hills and the val - leys re - e - cho our cry;

Bless - ing and peace __ be e - ver thine own, Land that we love __, our __ Sier - ra Le - one.

Singapore

Republik Singapura

Republic of Singapore

新加坡共和国

Xinjiapo Gongheguo

Singapore Kudiyarasu

```
Quick Country Facts
Location: Southeast Asia
Area: 252.9 sq. mi. (692.7 sq. km.)
Population (2002 est.): 4,452,732
Capital/Largest City: Singapore (pop. 3,044,000)
Official Languages: Malay, Mandarin Chinese, English,
Tamil
GDP/PPP: $106.3 billion, $24,700 per capita
Monetary Unit: Singapore Dollar
```

Majulah Singapura!

May Singapore Progress!

Lyrics and Music: Zubir Said (1907-1987). Adopted: 1959.

Historical Background[1]

The national anthem was written in the wake of nationalism during 1956-1957. Its composer, the late Encik Zubir Said, had written it on the basis of two words, "Majulah Singapura" or "Onward Singapore." The patriotic song was first performed by the Singapore Chamber Ensemble on the occasion of the opening of the newly renovated Victoria Theater. It was launched on 3 December 1959 together with the national flag and the state crest, at the installation of the new Head of State, Yang di-Pertuan Negara, at the City Hall steps. Upon independence in 1965, "Majulah Singapura" was adopted as the republic's national anthem. A grander and more inspiring arrangement of the song was launched on 19 January 2001. The new recording comes with a revised English version of the lyrics so that the meaning of the anthem can be better understood. Guidelines for the singing and playing of the national anthem have also been relaxed to encourage the singing of the anthem at all events of national significance.

Malay Words	English Words[2]
Mari kita rakyat Singapura,	Come, fellow Singaporeans,
Sama-sama menuju bahagia,	Let us progress towards happiness together.
Cita-cita kita yang mulia,	May our noble aspiration bring
Berjaya Singapura.	Singapore success.
Marilah kita bersatu,	Come, let us unite
Dengan semangat yang baru,	In a new spirit.
Semua kita berseru,	Let our voices soar as one.
Majulah Singapura!	Onward Singapore!
(repeat)	(repeat)

Singapore

ra ____!   Ma - ju - lah __ Si - nga - pu - ra ____!

Slovakia

Slovenská republika

(Republic of Slovakia)

Quick Country Facts

Location: Central Europe

Area: 18,917 sq. mi. (48,845 sq. km.)

Population (2002 est.): 5,422,366

Capital/Largest City: Bratislava (pop. 446,600)

Official Language: Slovak

GDP/PPP: $66 billion, $12,200 per capita

Monetary Unit: Koruna

Nad Tatrou sa blýska

(Lightning over the Tatras)

Words: Janko Matúška (1821-1877).

Historical Background[1]

The score for "Lightning over the Tatras," the Slovak national anthem, was written in 1884 during a trip by students of Bratislava's Evangelical Grammar School to Levoca in support of Ludovít Štúr. The author, Janko Matúška, set his words to the Slovak folk song "A Well She Dug" and the work became the favorite song of Štúr's young followers. It was circulated in hand-written copies and is found in many manuscript song collections.

Based on a popular melody and written in standard Slovak, it became known across the nation and was adopted by the Slovak volunteers of 1848, who printed it as a pamphlet. In December 1918 the first stanza became part of the national anthem of the Czechoslovak Republic and since 1 January 1993 the first two stanzas have constituted the national anthem of the independent Slovak Republic.

Slovak Words	English Translation
1	**1**
Nad Tatrou sa blýska, hromy divo bijú,	Lightning flashes over the Tatra, the thunder pounds
(repeat)	wildly,
Zastavme ich, bratia,	(repeat)
ved''sa ony stratia, Slováci ožijú.	Let them pause, brothers, they will surely disappear.
(repeat previous two lines)	The Slovaks will revive.
	(repeat previous two lines)
2	**2**
To Slovensko naše posiaľ tvrdo spalo,	This Slovakia of ours has been fast asleep until now.
(repeat)	(repeat)
ale blesky hromu vzbudzujú ho k tomu,	But the thunder and lightning
aby sa prebralo.	Are encouraging it to come alive,
(repeat previous two lines)	(repeat previous two lines)

Slovakia

Nad Ta - trou sa blý - ska, hro - my di - vo bi - jú, Nad Ta - trou sa blý - ska, hro - my di - vo bi - jú,

Za - stav - me ich, bra - tia, ved' sa o - ny stra - tia, Slo - vá - ci o - ži - jú. Za - stav - me ich, bra - tia,

ved' sa o - ny stra - tia, Slo - vá - ci o - ži - jú

Slovenia

Republika Slovenija

(Republic of Slovenia)

Quick Country Facts

Location: East Central Europe

Area: 7,819 sq. mi. (20,273 sq. km.)

Population (2002 est.): 1,932,917

Capital/Largest City: Ljubljana (pop. 330,000)

Official Language: Slovenian

GDP/PPP: $36 billion, $18,000 per capita

Monetary Unit: Slovenian Tolar

Zdravljica

(The Toast)

Lyrics: France Prešeren (1800-1849). Music: Stanko Premrl (1880-1965). Adopted: 1989.

Historical Background[1]

France Prešeren is Slovenia's greatest and most celebrated poet. The national awards for culture bear his name and are awarded on the National Day of Culture (8 February), an official holiday. A widely renowned figure of European Romanticism, Prešeren established through his prodigious work a focus for Slovenia's first national program. "Zdravljica" represents the peak of Prešeren's political poetry. It was written in autumn 1844, removed from the manuscript of the collection of poems Poezije (1847) by the censors, and published on 26 April 1848 in the newspaper *Novice* after the collapse of Metternich's absolutism and the termination of censorship.

Its dominant idea, a radical demand for freedom of the Slovenian nation, arises from the humanistic vision of equality and friendly coexistence of all nations, and every person's right to independence. It originates from the concepts of the French Revolution of equality, freedom, and brotherhood, which were adjusted to the basic political needs of the Slovenian people at the time of the "Spring of Nations" and concerned their independence. However, Prešeren's "Marseillaise" reaches beyond the nature of a political manifesto and bears a strong note of intimate humanity.

In the history of constituting the Slovenian nation Prešeren's "Zdravljica" was of extreme conceptual significance. It became particularly topical during the occupation and National Liberation Struggle from 1941 to 1945, and in the period of what was called the "Slovenian Spring" in the eighties when it started to be sung as the national anthem on state holidays and major public events.

"Zdravljica" was proclaimed the new Slovenian anthem on 27 September 1989 when the Slovenian Assembly adopted the Amendments to the Slovenian Constitution. The Law on the National Anthem of the Republic of Slovenia adopted on 29 March 1990 specified the seventh stanza set to the music of Stanko Premrl as the actual anthem. Following the independence of Slovenia, the National Assembly adopted (in 1994) the law governing the official crest, the national flag and the anthem of the Republic of Slovenia.

Slovenian Words	English Translation[2]
Žive naj vsi narodi	God's blessing on all nations,
ki hrepene dočakat' dan,	Who long and work for that bright day,
da koder sonce hodi,	When o'er earth's habitation
prepir iz sveta bo pregnan,	No war, no strife shall hold its sway;
da rojak	Who long to see
prost bo vsak,	That all man free
ne vrag, le sosed bo mejak!	No more shall foes, but neighbors be.
da rojak	Who long to see
prost bo vsak,	That all man free
ne vrag, le sosed bo	No more shall foes, but
ne vrag, le sosed bo mejak!	No more shall foes, but neighbors be.

Slovenia

Solomon Islands

God Save Our Solomon Islands

Lyrics and Music: Panapasa Balekana (b. 1929). Adopted: 1978.

Words

God save our Solomon Islands from shore to shore.

Bless all her people and her lands

With Your protecting hands.

Joy, peace, progress and prosperity;

That men should brothers be, make nations see.

Our Solomon Islands, Our Solomon Islands,

Our nation, Solomon Islands,

Stands for evermore.

Solomon Islands

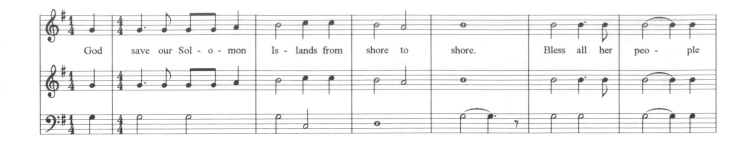

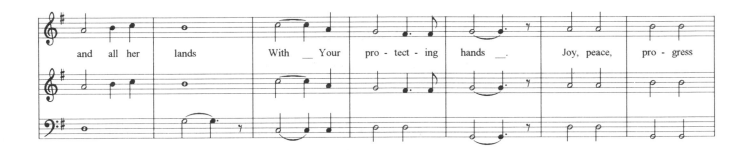

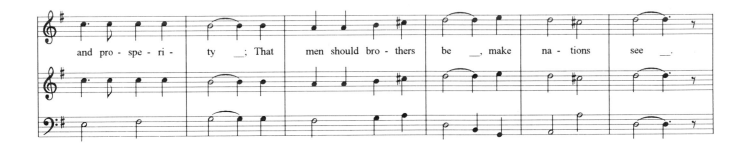

Is - lands, Stands for e - ver - more.

Somalia

Al Jumhouriya As-Somalya al-Dimocradia

(Democratic Republic of Somalia)

```
Quick Country Facts
Location: East Africa
Area: 246,199 sq. mi. (637,657 sq. km.)
Population (2002 est.): 7,753,310
Capital/Largest City: Mogadishu (pop. 900,000)
Official Languages: Somali, Arabic
GDP/PPP: $4.1 billion, $550 per capita
Monetary Unit: Somali Shilling
```

National Anthem

Historical Background[1]

In 2000, after ten years of anarchy and civil war, Somalia finally received a somewhat stable democratic government. A new anthem was adopted that, unlike the previous one, has lyrics.

Anthem Unavailable

South Africa

Republic of South Africa

Republiek van Suid-Afrika

Quick Country Facts

Location: Southern Africa

Area: 471,440 sq. mi. (1,219,912 sq. km.)

Population (2002 est.): 43,647,658

Capitals: Pretoria (pop. 1,080,187), Cape Town (pop. 2,350,157), Bloemfontein (pop. 700,325)

Largest City: Johannesburg (pop. 5,700,000)

Official Languages: English, Afrikaans, Ndebele, Sesotho sa Leboa, Sesotho, Swati, Xitsonga, Setswana, Tshivenda, Xhosa, Zulu

GDP/PPP: $412 billion, $9,400 per capita

Monetary Unit: Rand

National Anthem of South Africa

Lyrics: Enoch Mankayi Sontonga (1860-1904) and Cornelius Jacob Langenhoven (1873-1932). Music: Enoch Mankayi Sontonga (1860-1904) and Marthinus Lourens de Villiers (1885-1977). Adopted: 1995.

Historical Background[1]

A proclamation issued by the (then) state president on 20 April 1994 in terms of the provisions of Section 248(1) together with Section 2 of the *Constitution of the Republic of South Africa*, No. 200 of 1993, stated that the Republic of South Africa would have two national anthems. They were "Nkosi Sikelel' iAfrika" and "The Call of South Africa" ("Die Stem van Suid-Afrika"). In terms of Section 4 of the *Constitution of South Africa*, 1996 (Act 108 of 1996) and following a proclamation in the *Government Gazette* No. 18341 (dated 10 October 1997), a shortened, combined version of "Nkosi Sikelel' iAfrika" and "The Call of South Africa" is now the national anthem of South Africa.

"Die Stem van Suid-Afrika" is a poem written by Cornelius Jacob Langenhoven in May 1918. The music was composed by the Reverend Marthinus Lourens de Villiers in 1921. The South African Broadcasting Corporation played both "God Save the King" and "Die Stem" to close their daily broadcasts and the public became familiar with it. It was first sung publicly at the official hoisting of the national flag in Cape Town on 31 May 1928, but it was not until 2 May 1957 that the government made the announcement that "Die Stem" had been accepted as the official national anthem of

South Africa. In the same year, the government also acquired the copyright and this was confirmed by Act of Parliament in 1959. In 1952 the official English version of the national anthem, the "Call of South Africa," was accepted for official use.

"Nkosi Sikelel' iAfrika" was composed in 1897 by Enoch Sontonga, a Methodist mission school teacher. The words of the first stanza were originally written in Xhosa as a hymn. Seven additional stanzas in Xhosa were later added by the poet Samuel Mqhayi. A Sesotho version was published by Moses Mphahlele in 1942. "Nkosi Sikelel' iAfrika" was popularized at concerts held in Johannesburg by Reverend J. L. Dube's Ohlange Zulu Choir. It became a popular church hymn that was later adopted as an anthem at political meetings. It was sung as an act of defiance during the apartheid years. The first stanza is generally sung in Xhosa or Zulu followed by the Sesotho version. Apparently there is no standard version or translations of "Nkosi" and the words vary from place to place and from occasion to occasion.

Words (Xhosa, Sesotho, Afrikaans, English)	English Translation
Nkosi sikelel' iAfrika,	Lord, bless Africa,
Maluphakanyisw' uphondo lwayo.	May her spirit rise high up.
Yizwa imithandazo yethu,	Hear thou our prayers,
Nkosi sikelela, thina lusapho lwayo.	Lord bless us, your family.
Morena boloka setjhaba sa heso,	Descend, O Spirit,
O fedise dintwa la matshwenyeho,	Save our nation.
O se boloke, o se boloke setjhaba sa heso.	End all wars and strife,
Setjhaba sa South Afrika, South Afrika.	Bless South Africa, South Africa.
Uit die blou van onse hemel.	Ringing out from our blue heavens,
Uit die diepte van ons see.	From our deep seas breaking round;
Oor ons ewige gebergtes.	Over everlasting mountains
Waar die kranse antwoord gee.	Where the echoing crags resound.
Sounds the call to come together,	Sounds the call to come together,
And united we shall stand.	And united we shall stand.
Let us live and strive for freedom	Let us live and strive for freedom
In South Africa our land!	In South Africa our land!

South Africa

sa   South Af - ri - ka,   South Af - ri - ka __. Uit die   blou van on - se   he - mel. Uit die   diep - te __ van ons

see __. Oor ons   e - wi - ge ge -   berg - tes. Waar die   kran - se __ ant - woord   ge __. Sounds the

call to come to -   ge - ther, And u -   ni - ted we shall   stand __. Let us   live and strive for   free - dom in South

Af - ri - ca our   land __!

Spain

Reino de España

(Kingdom of Spain)

Marcha Real

(Royal March)

Adopted: 1942.

Historical Background[1]

Spain's national anthem is one of the oldest in Europe. Its origins are unknown. The music was found in a document dated in the year 1761, the "Libro de Ordenanza de los toques militares de la Infantería Española"—the Spanish Infantry's book of regulation bugle calls—by Manuel de Espinosa. The anthem appears there with the title "March of the Grenadiers," already then with the mention "unknown author." A long time before, the King's Grenadiers engaged in battle and marched past the Royal Family in tune with their "March." Some historians stress the similarities of the March with military airs from the time of Emperor Charles I of Spain and V of Germany, or his son's Felipe—Philip—II (sixteenth century).

King Carlos III declared on 3 September 1770 the "Marcha Granadera" as the "Honor March," making official the traditional custom of playing it at public and ceremonial events. In a short time, and without any specific law declaring it so, Spaniards regarded "La Marcha Granadera" as their national anthem and called it "La Marcha Real," or "The Royal March," because it was always played at public events in presence of the king, the queen, or the Prince of Asturias, the official title of Spain's Crown Prince.

"La Marcha Real" has always been the Spanish national anthem except for the period of the Second Republic (1931-1939), when the "Himno de Riego" was adopted. This was a march of the National Militia Battalions from the early nineteenth century. After the Civil War, Franco declared "La Marcha Real" again as the anthem but retained its old title "La Marcha Granadera." In October 1997 a Royal Decree was promulgated regulating the official use of the "Marcha Real," both for its long or complete version and for its short one. A partition was officially promulgated after its adoption by the Royal Academy of Fine Arts, in which the musical tones from the eighteenth century are recovered and brought out.

"La Marcha Real" is one of the few national anthems which has only a tune, but no lyrics. During the reign of Alfonso XIII a poem was written to be used as lyrics of the anthem, but this was neither officially recognized nor did it catch on in people's traditions. During Franco's dictature (1939-1975), the anthem was sometimes sung with the lyrics written by poet José María Pemán. These lyrics were never officially recognized, however.

No Words

Spain

Spain

Sri Lanka

Shri Lanka Prajatantrika Samajavadi Janarajaya

Ilangai Jananayaka Socialisa Kudiarasu

(Democratic Socialist Republic of Sri Lanka)

Quick Country Facts

Location: South Asia, Indian Ocean

Area: 25,332 sq. mi. (65,610 sq. km.)

Population (2002 est.): 19,576,783

Capitals: Colombo (pop. 1,994,000), Sri Jayawardenepura Kotte (pop. 107,000)

Largest City: Colombo

Official Languages: Sinhala, Tamil

GDP/PPP: $62.7 billion, $3,250 per capita

Monetary Unit: Sri Lanka Rupee

Sri Lanka Matha

Sri Lanka Thaaye

(Mother Sri Lanka)

Lyrics and Music: Ananda Samarakone (1911-1962). Adopted: 1952.

Historical Background[1]

After gaining independence from foreign rule the people of Sri Lanka were kindled with patriotic feeling.

On the recommendation of the Sri Lanka Gandharva Sabha, a competition to select a national anthem was conducted in January 1948. The winning entry, Ananda Samarakoon's composition "Namo Namo Matha," was chosen as the national anthem on 22 November 1951. The main theme of the anthem is to instill honor and respect to the Motherland and create national development through unity.

During the early 1950s there was a controversy about the national anthem. A defect was found in the lyrics, and the opening words were changed to "Sri Lanka Matha—Apa Sri Lanka." The first rendering of the national anthem was made on Independence Day, 4 February 1952, by a group of 500 students from Musaeus College, Colombo, and broadcast over the radio.

The National Anthem is incorporated into section 7, third schedule of the *Constitution of the Democratic Socialist Republic of Sri Lanka.*

Sinhala Words (Transliteration)	Tamil Words (Transliteration, First Verse, 2 Total)	English Translation
1	1	1
Sri Lanka Matha	*Sri Lanka Thaaye, nam Sri Lanka,*	Mother Lanka we worship Thee!
Apa Sri Lanka	*Namo Namo Namo*	Plenteous in prosperity, Thou,
Namo Namo Namo	*Namo Thaaye.*	Beauteous in grace and love,
Namo Matha	*Nallelil poli Seeranee,*	Laden with grain and luscious fruit,
Sundara siri barani surandi athi soba	*Nalangal yaavum Niraivaan mani*	And fragrant flowers of radiant hue,
mana Lanka	*Lanka*	Giver of life and all good things,
Dhanya dhanaya neka mal palathuru	*Gnaalam puhala vala vayal nathi*	Our land of joy and victory,
piri jaya bhoomiya Ramya	*malai malar narum solai kol Lanka.*	Receive our grateful praise sublime,
Apa hata sapa siri setha sadhana	*Namathuru puhalidam ena olir vaai,*	Lanka! we worship Thee!
jeevanaye matha	*namathuyire Thaaye!*	
Piliganumana apa bhakthi pooja	*Namathalai ninathadi mail vyththome*	
Namo Namo Matha	*Namo Namo Thaaye.*	
Apa Sri Lanka	*Nam Sri Lanka,*	
Namo Namo Namo	*Namo Namo Namo*	
Namo Matha	*Namo Thaaye.*	
2		2
Obave apa vidya		Thou gavest us knowledge and truth,
Obamaya apa sathya		Thou art our strength
Obave apa shakthi		And inward faith.
Apa hada thula bhakthi		Our light divine and sentient being,
Oba apa aloke		Breath of life and liberation,
Apage anu prane		Inspire us forever.
Oba apa jeevanave		In wisdom and strength renewed,
Apa mukthiya obave		Ill-will, hatred, strife all ended,
Nava jeevana demine nithina apa		In love enfolded, a mighty nation,
pubudu karan matha		Marching onward,
Gnana veerya vadawamina ragana		All as children of one mother,
yanu mana jaya bhoomi kara		Leads us, mother, to fullest freedom.
Eka mawakage daru kala bawina		
Yamu yamu wee nopama		
Prema wada sama bheda dhurarada		

Namo Namo Matha Apa Sri Lanka Namo Namo Namo Namo Matha		

Sri Lanka

Sri Lan - ka Ma - - tha ___ A - pa Sri ___ Lan - -
Sri Lan - ka Thaa - - ye ___, nam ___ Sri ___ Lan -

ka Na - mo Na - mo Na - mo Na - mo Ma - - tha Sun - da - ra si - ri ba - ra -
ka, Na - mo Na - mo Na - mo Na - mo Thaa - - ye. Nall - el - il po - li See - ra -

ni su - ran - di a - thi so - - ba ma - ma - na Lan - - ka ___
nee, Na - lan - gal yaa - vum Ni - rai - vaan ni Lan - - ka ___

Dhan - - ya dhan - a - ya ne - ka mal pa - la - thu - ru pi - ri ja - ya bhoom - i - ya Ram - -
Gnaa - - lam pu - ha - la va - la va - yal na - thi ma - lai ma - lar na - rum so - lai kol Lan -

Sudan

جمهورية السودان

Jumhuriyat as-Sudan

(Republic of the Sudan)

Nahnu Djundullah

(Army of God)

Lyrics: Ahmad Muhammed Salih (1896-1971). Music: Ahmad Murjan (1905-1974). Adopted: 1956.

Arabic Words (Transliteration)	English Translation
Nahnu Djundullah Djundulwatan.	We are the army of God and of our land,
In Da A Da Il Fida Lam Nakhun.	We shall never fail when called to sacrifice.
Natahaddal Maut Endalmihan.	Whether braving death, hardship or pain,
Nashta Ril Madjd Bi Aghlathaman.	We give our lives as the price of glory.
Hathihil Ard Lana! Falyaish Sudanuna,	May this our land, Sudan, live long,
Alaman Bayn Al Umam.	Showing all nations the way.
Ya Benissudan, Hatharamzukum;	Sons of the Sudan, summoned now to serve,
Yah Miluleb, Wa Yahmi Ardakum.	Shoulder the task of preserving our country.

Sudan

Suriname

Republiek Suriname

(Republic of Suriname)

```
Quick Country Facts
Location: Northeast South America
Area: 63,251 sq. mi. (163,270 sq. km.)
Population (2002 est.): 436,494
Capital/Largest City: Paramaribo (pop. 200,970)
Official Languages: Dutch, Sranan Togo
GDP/PPP: $1.5 billion, $3,500 per capita
Monetary Unit: Suriname Guilder
```

Volkslied

(National Anthem)

Dutch Lyrics: Cornelis Atses Hoekstra. Sranan Togo Lyrics: Henry F. de Ziel (1916-1975). Music: Johannes Corstianus de Puy (1835-1924). Adopted: 1954.

Historical Background

The music to the national anthem of Suriname was composed by a Frisian, Johannes Corstianus de Puy, in 1876. Lutheran minister Cornelis Hoekstra wrote the Dutch words to the song in 1893. That same year, Sranan Togo words were added by Tresofa, the pseudonymn for Henry F. de Ziel. The anthem today consists of the Dutch first verse and the second verse in Sranan Togo. Usually, the latter is sung most of the time.

Words (Dutch, Sranan Togo)	English Translation
1	1
God zij met ons Suriname	God be with our Suriname
Hij verhef ons heerlijk land	May He glorify our beautiful land
Hoe wij hier ook samen kwamen	However we came together here
Aan zijn grond zijn wij verpand	We are pledged to your soil
Werkend houden w'in gedachten	As we work, let us remember
Recht en waarheid maken vrij	That justice and truth make us free

Al wat goed is te betrachten	Practicing all that is good
Dat geeft aan ons land waardij.	Will make our country a worthy land.
2	2
Opo kondreman oen opo!	Rise country men, rise
Sranan gron e kari oen	The soil of Suriname is calling you
Wans operata komopo	Where ever our ancestors came from
Wi moe seti kondre boen	We should take care of our country
Stre de f'stre wi no sa frede	We are not afraid to fight
Gado de wi fesi man	God is our leader
Eri libi te na dede	Our whole life until our death
Wi sa fcti gi Sranan.	We will fight for Suriname.

Suriname

God zij met ons Suri- na- me Hij ver- hef ons heer- lijk land ___ Hoe wij
O- po kon- dre- man oen o- po! Sra- nan gron e ka- ri oen ___ Wans o-

hier ook sa- men kwa- men Aan zijn grond zijn wij ver- pand ___ Wer- kend hou- den w'in ge-
pe- ra- ta ko- mo- po Wi moe se- ti kon- dre boen ___ Stre de f'stre wi no sa

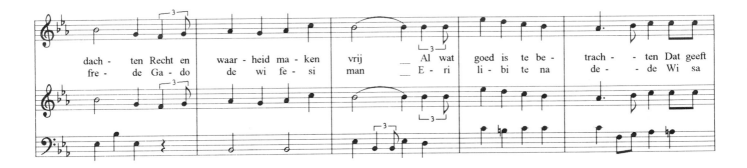

dach- ten Recht en waar- heid ma- ken vrij ___ Al wat goed is te be- trach- ten Dat geeft
fre- de Ga- do de wi fe- si man ___ E- ri li- bi te na de- de Wi sa

aan ons land waar- dij ___.
fe- ti gi Sra- nan ___.

Swaziland

Umbuso wakaNgwane

Kingdom of Swaziland

Quick Country Facts

Location: Southern Africa, surrounded by South Africa

Area: 6,704 sq. mi. (17,363 sq. km.)

Population (2002 est.): 1,123,605

Capital/Largest City: Mbabane (pop. 47,020)

Official Languages: Swazi, English

GDP/PPP: $4.6 billion, $4,200 per capita

Monetary Unit: Lilageni

Ingoma Yesive

National Anthem

Lyrics: Andrease Enoke Fanyana Simelane (b. 1934). Music: David Kenneth Rycroft (b. 1924). Adopted: 1968.

Historical Background

The music to the Swazi anthem was composed by musicologist and linguist Professor David Rycroft.

Swazi Words	English Words
Nkulunkulu	O Lord our God, bestower of the blessings of the Swazi;
Mnikati wetibusiso TeMaSwati,	We give Thee thanks for all our good fortune;
Siyatibonga tonkhe tinhlanhla,	We offer thanks and praise for our king;
Sibonga iNgwenyama yetfu,	And for our fair land, its hills and rivers;
Live netintsaba nemifula.	The Blessings be on all rulers of our Country;
Busisa tiphatsimandla takaNgwane	Might and power are Thine alone;
Nguwe wedvwa Somandla wetfu;	We pray Thee to grant us wisdom without deceit or malice.
Sinike kuhlanipha	Establish and fortify us, Lord Eternal.
Lokungena bucili	
Simise usicinise,	
Simakadze!	

597

Swaziland

Nku - lu - nku - lu Mni - ka - ti we - ti - bu - si - so Te - Ma - Swa - ti, Si - ya - ti -

bo - nga to - nkhe ti - nhla - nhla, Si - bo - nga i - Ngwe - nya - ma ye - tfu, Li - ve

ne - ti - ntsa - ba ne - mi - fu - la. Bu - si - sa ti - pha - tsi - ma - ndla ta - ka Ngwane ___ Ngu - we

we - dvwa So - ma - ndla we - tfu; Si - ni - - ke ku - hla - - ni - pha Lo -

ku - nge - na __ bu - ci - - li Si - mi - - se u - si - ci - ni - - se, Si - ma - ka -

dze __ !

Sweden

Konungariket Sverige

(Kingdom of Sweden)

Quick Country Facts

Location: Western Europe, Scandinavia

Area: 173,800 sq. mi. (449,964 sq. km.)

Population (2002 est.): 8,876,744

Capital/Largest City: Stockholm (pop. 703,627)

Official Language: Swedish

GDP/PPP: $227.4 billion, $25,400 per capita

Monetary Unit: Krona

Du Gamla Du Fria

(Thou Ancient, Thou Free)

Lyrics: Richard Dybeck (1811-1877).

Historical Background[1]

The Swedish national anthem "Du Gamla Du Fria" was originally a folk song from the county of Västmanland in central Sweden. It was called "As I Ride through the Twelve Mile Forest." Rewritten in 1844 by the Swede Richard Dybeck, it was not at all intended to be a national anthem. Neither does the song relate specifically to the country of Sweden but pays homage to all of the Nordic countries, with a strong feeling of patriotism toward the Nordic environment.

"Du Gamla Du Fria" was publicly performed for the first time by an opera singer at a music evening arranged by Dybeck in Stockholm. It was accepted by the public with standing ovation. "Du Gamla Du Fria" gradually obtained the character of a patriotic hymn and in the 1890s was unofficially accepted as Sweden's national anthem.

Swedish Words (First and Second Verses, 4 Total)	English Translation (First and Second Verses, 4 Total) [2]
1	**1**
Du gamla, du fria, du fjällhöga Nord	Ye free, ancient country
du tysta, du glädjerika sköna!	Ye high mountained north
Jag hälsar dig vänaste land uppå jord,	Ye silent and free
din sol, din himmel, dina ängder gröna,	and so delightful
(repeat previous two lines)	We greet you as loveliest
	land upon earth
	Your shining sun, your sky
	Your pastures green
	(repeat previous two lines)
2	**2**
Du tronar på minnen från fornstora dar,	You rest on your memories
då ärat ditt namn flög över jorden.	of days great and past
Jag vet att du är och du blir vad du var.	When all round the world
Ja, jag vill leva, jag vill dö i Norden!	your name was honored
(repeat previous two lines)	I know that you'll always remain
	the way you were
	In my own Nordic land
	I'll live forever
	(repeat previous two lines)

Sweden

Du gam - la, du fri - a, du fjäll - hö - ga Nord du tys - ta, du gläd - je - ri - ka skö - na! Jag

häl - sar dig vä - nas - te land __ up - på jord, din sol, din him - mel, di - na äng - der grö - na, din

sol, din him - mel, di - na äng - der grö - na.

Switzerland

Confoederatio Helvetica

(Swiss Confederation)

```
Quick Country Facts
Location: Central Europe
Area: 15,941 sq. mi. (41,290 sq. km.)
Population (2002 est.): 7,301,994
Capital: Bern (pop. 129,423)
Largest City: Zurich (pop. 343,045)
Official Languages: German, French, Italian, Romansh
GDP/PPP: $231 billion, $31,700 per capita
Monetary Unit: Swiss Franc
```

Schweizer Psalm

Cantique Suisse

Salmo Svizzero

Psalm Svizzer

(Swiss Psalm)

German Lyrics: Leonhard Widmer (1809-1867). French Lyrics: Charles Chatelanat (1833-1907). Italian Lyrics: Camillo Valsangiacomo (1898-1978). Romansh Lyrics: Gion Antoni Bühler (1825-1897). Music: Father Alberich Zwyssig (1808-1854). Adopted: 1965.

Historical Background[1]

In the summer of 1841, Alberich Zwyssig, a priest and composer from Uri, was visiting his brother at St. Carl, a magnificent patrician's house at the gates of Zug, when he received mail from Leonhard Widmer, a music publisher, journalist, and lyricist from Zurich. The mail contained a patriotic poem that Widmer had written and wanted set to music. Zwyssig chose to use a hymn that he had composed to the psalm "Diligam te Domine" ("I Will Love Thee, O Lord") for an ordination service in 1835 when he was music director at the monastery in Wettingen. He worked on his adaptation until late autumn. Finally, on the evening of St. Cecilia's Day, Monday, 22 November 1841 in the first-floor study at St. Carl overlooking the lake and the city, Zwyssig rehearsed his "Schweizerpsalm" ("Swiss Psalm") for the first time with four residents of Zug.

In 1843, the new patriotic song appeared in the celebration brochure of the Zurich Zofinger marking the anniversary of Zurich's membership into the Swiss Confederation in 1351. (The Zofinger association is the oldest Swiss student fraternity.) It was also performed at the National Singing Festival in the same year, where it was received with acclaim by the audience. The "Swiss Psalm" was soon performed by male choirs throughout Switzerland (thanks to translations) and was frequently sung at patriotic celebrations.

Numerous attempts were made between 1894 and 1953 to have it declared the Swiss national anthem, but they were consistently turned down by the Swiss government for the reason that a national anthem should not be selected by government decree but by popular opinion. In fact, there was another song that was used for official political and military occasions at that time which was equally popular. "Rufst Du mein Vaterland" ("When My Fatherland Calls") was sung to the same melody as "God save the King (Queen)," which occasionally led to embarrassing situations as international contacts increased during the course of the twentieth century. It was for this reason that the Swiss government declared the "Swiss Psalm," a fully and unmistakably Swiss creation, the provisional Swiss national anthem in 1961. Following a three-year trial period twelve cantons (or states) voted in favor of the "Swiss Psalm," seven requested an extension of the trial period, and no less than six rejected it as the official national anthem. In spite of these mixed reactions, the "Swiss Psalm" was confirmed (provisionally) as the Swiss national anthem in 1965. The provisional clause was abandoned ten years later, but without official ratification as the national anthem. A number of other suggestions for a national anthem were made in the years that followed, none of which, however, earned nearly as many votes as the "Swiss Psalm."

Finally, on 1 April 1981, the "Swiss Psalm" was officially declared the Swiss national anthem, a purely Swiss song, dignified and ceremonial, the kind of national anthem that the majority of citizens would like to have.

German Words	French Words	Romansh Words
1	1	1
Trittst im Morgenrot daher,	Sur nos monts, quand le soleil	En l'aurora la damaun
She'ich dich im Strahlenmeer,	Annonce un brillant réveil,	ta salida il carstgaun,
Dich, du Hocherhabener, Herrlicher!	Et prédit d'un plus beau jour le retour,	spiert etern dominatur, Tutpussent!
Wenn der Alpen Firn sich rötet,	Les beautés de la patrie	Cur ch'ils munts straglischan sura,
Betet, freie Schweizer, betet!	Parlent à l'âme attendrie;	ura liber Svizzer, ura.
Eure fromme Seele ahnt	Au ciel montent plus joyeux,	Mia olma senta ferm,
(repeat)	(repeat)	(repeat)
Gott im hehren Vaterland,	Les accents d'un cœur pieux,	Dieu en tschiel, il bab etern.
Gott, den Herrn, im hehren Vaterland.	Les accents émus d'un cœur pieux.	Dieu en tschiel, il bab, il bab etern.
2	2	2
Kommst im Abendglühn daher,	Lorsqu'un doux rayon du soir	Er la saira en splendur da las stailas en l'azur
Find'ich dich im Sternenheer,	Joue encore dans le bois noir,	
Dich, du Menschenfreundlicher,	Le cœur se sent plus heureux près de	tai chattain nus, creatur, Tutpussent!

Liebender!

In des Himmels lichten Räumen

Kann ich froh und selig träumen!

Denn die fromme Seele ahnt

(repeat)

Gott im hehren Vaterland,

Gott, den Herrn, im hehren Vaterland.

3

Ziehst im Nebelflor daher,

Such'ich dich im Wolkenmeer,

Dich, du Unergründlicher, Ewiger!

Aus dem grauen Luftgebilde

Bricht die Sonne klar und milde,

Und die fromme Seele ahnt

(repeat)

Gott im hehren Vaterland,

Gott, den Herrn, im hehren Vaterland.

4

Fährst im wilden Sturm daher,

Bist du selbst uns Hort und Wehr,

Du, allmächtig Waltender, Rettender!

In Gewitternacht und Grauen

Lasst uns kindlich ihm vertrauen!

Ja, die fromme Seele ahnt,

(repeat)

Gott im hehren Vaterland,

Gott, den Herrn, im hehren Vaterland.

Dieu

Loin des vain bruits de la plaine

L'âme en paix est plus sereine;

Au ciel montent plus joyeux,

(repeat)

Les accents d'un cœur pieux,

Les accents émus d'un cœur pieux.

3

Lorsque dans la sombre nuit

La foudre éclate avec bruit,

Notre cœur pressent encore le Dieu

fort.

Dans l'orage et la détresse,

Il est notre forteresse.

Offrons-lui des cœurs pieux

(repeat)

Dieu nous bénira des cieux,

Dieu nous bénira du haut des cieux.

4

Des grand monts vient le secours,

Suisse! espère en Dieu toujours!

Garde la foi des aïeux, vis comme

eux!

Sur l'autel de la patrie

Mets tes biens, ton cœur, ta vie!

C'est le trésor précieux

(repeat)

Que Dieu nous bénira des cieux,

Que Dieu nous bénira du haut des

cieux.

Cur ch'il firmament sclerescha en

noss cors

fidanza crescha.

Mia olma senta ferm,

(repeat)

Dieu en tschiel, il bab etern.

Dieu en tschiel, il bab, il bab etern.

3

Ti a nus es er preschent

en il stgir dal firmament,

ti inperscrutabel spiert, Tutpussent!

Tschiel e terra t'obedeschan

vents e nivels secundeschan.

Mia olma senta ferm,

(repeat)

Dieu en tschiel, il bab etern.

Dieu en tschiel, il bab, il bab etern.

4

Cur la furia da l'orcan

fa tremblar il cor uman

alur das ti a nus vigur, Tutpussent!

Ed en temporal sgarschaivel stas ti

franc a nus fidaivel.

Mia olma senta ferm,

(repeat)

Dieu en tschiel, il bab etern.

Dieu en tschiel, il bab, il bab etern.

Italian Words	English Translation[2]
1	1
Quando bionda aurora	When the morning skies grow red
Il mattin c'indora,	And o'er us their radiance shed,
L'alma mia t'adora	Thou, O Lord, appeareth in their light.
Re del Ciel.	When the Alps glow bright with splendor,

Quando l'alpe già rosseggia
A pregare allor t'atteggia,
In favor del patrio suol,
(repeat)
Cittadino Dio lo vuol,
Cittadino Dio, sì Dio lo vuol.

2

Se di nubi un velo
M'asconde il tuo cielo,
Pel tuo raggio anelo,
Dio d'amor!
Fuga o sole quei vapori
E mi rendi i tuoi favori
Di mia patria deh, pietà!
(repeat)
Brilla, o sol die verità,
Brilla sol, o sol di verità!

3

Tu mi sei vicino,
Splendi nel mattino,
Segni il mio cammino,
Con bontà.
O Signore, quando è sera,
Mi rivolgo a Te in preghiera,
Penso al bene che mi fai,
Alla terra che mi dai.
Splenda a noi la tua bontà,
Dona pace e libertà.

Pray to God, to Him surrender,
For you feel and understand,
(repeat)
That He dwelleth in this land.
(repeat)

2

In the sunset Thou art nigh
And beyond the starry sky,
Thou, O loving Father, ever near.
When to Heaven we are departing,
Joy and bliss Thou'lt be imparting,
For we feel and understand
(repeat)
That Thou dwellest in this land.
(repeat)

3

When dark clouds enshroud the hills
And gray mist the valley fills,
Yet Thou art not hidden from Thy sons.
Pierce the gloom in which we cower
With Thy sunshine's cleansing power
Then we'll feel and understand
(repeat)
That God dwelleth in this land.
(repeat)

Switzerland

Trittst im Mor - gen - rot da - her __, She' ich dich im Strah - len - meer,
Sur nos monts, quand le so - leil An - nonce un bril - lant ré - veil,
En l'au - ro - ra la da - maun __ ta sa - li - da il carst - gaun,
Quan - do bion - da au - ro - ra __ Il mat - tin c'in - - do - ra,

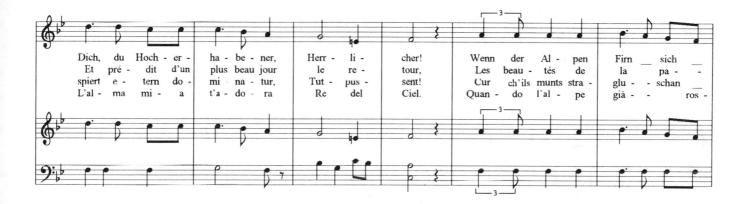

Dich, du Hoch - er - ha - be - ner, Herr - li - cher! Wenn der Al - pen Firn __ sich
Et pré - dit d'un plus beau jour le re - tour, Les beau - tés de la pa -
spiert e - tern do - mi - na - tur, Tut - pus - sent! Cur ch'ils munts stra - glu - schan __
L'al - ma mi - a t'a - do - ra Re del Ciel. Quan - do l'al - pe già - - ros -

rö - tet __, Be - tet, frei - e Schwei - - zer, be - tet __! Eu - re from - me
tri - e __ Par - lent à l'âme at - - ten - dri - - e __; Au ciel mon - tent
su - ra __, u - ra li - ber Svi - - zzer, u - ra __. Mi - a ol - ma
se - gia __ A pre - ga - re al - - lor t'at - teg - gia __, In fa - vor del

See - le ahnt   Eu - re from - me   See - le ahnt __   Gott im heh - ren   Va - ter - land __,
plus joy - eux,   Au ciel mon - tent   plus joy - eux __,   Les ac - cents d'un   cœur pi - eux __.
sen - ta ferm,   Mi - a ol - ma   sen - ta ferm __   Dieu en tschiel, il   bab e - tern __.
pa - trio suol,   In fa - vor del   pa - trio suol __,   Cit - ta - di - no   Dio lo vuol __,

Gott,   den Herrn, im   heh - ren   Va -   -   ter -   land.
Les   ac - cents é -   mus d'un   cœur   pi -   eux.
Dieu   en tschiel, il   bab, il   bab   e -   tern.
Cit -   ta - di - no   Dio, si   Dio   lo   vuol.

Syria

الجمهورية العربية السورية

Al-Jumhuriyya al-'Arabiyya as-Suriyya

Syrian Arab Republic

```
Quick Country Facts
Location: West Asia, Middle East
Area: 71,498 sq. mi. (185,180 sq. km.)
Population (2002 est.): 17,195,814
Capital: Damascus (pop. 1,549,932)
Largest City: Aleppo (pop. 1,591,400)
Official Language: Arabic
GDP/PPP: $54.2 billion, $3,200 per capita
Monetary Unit: Syrian Pound
```

النشيد الوطني الشوري

An-Nashid as-Suri

(Syrian National Anthem)

Lyrics: Khalil Mardam Bey (1895-1959). Music: Mohammad Salim Flayfel (1899-1986). Adopted: 1936.

Arabic Words (First Two Verses, 4 Total)	Arabic Words (Transliteration, First Two Verses, 4 Total)	English Translation (First Two Verses, 4 Total)
1 حماة الديار عليكم سلام أبت أن تذلّ النفوسُ الكرام عرينُ العروبة بيتٌ حرام وعرشُ الشموس حمىّ لا يُضام	1 *Homatal diyari 'alaikum salam* *abat an tathilla nufousul kiram* *areenul urubati baytun haram* *wa arshu shumusi himan la* *Yudham*	1 Defenders of the realm, Peace on you; Our proud spirits will Not be subdued. The adobe of Arabism, A hallowed sanctuary; The seat of the stars,

		An inviolable preserve.
2	2	2
ربوعُ الشام بروجُ العَلا	*Rubu'u ashaami buroujul ala*	Syria's plains are
تحاكي السماءَ بعالي السنا	*tuhaki sama'a bi ali ssana*	Towers in the heights,
(repeat previous two lines)	(repeat previous two lines)	Resembling the sky
فأرضٌ زهت بالشموس الوضاء	*fa'ardhun zahat bi shumusil widha*	Above the clouds.
سماءٌ لعمُرك أو كالسما	*sama'un laumroka am kassama*	(repeat previous four lines)
		A land resplendent
		With brilliant suns,
		Becoming another sky,
		Or almost a sky.

Syria

bi a - li - s - sa - na   fa - 'ar - dhun za - hat   bi shum - usi - l wid - ha   sa - ma - 'un laum - ro - ka

am kas - sa - ma

Tajikistan

Jumhurii Todhzikiston

(Republic of Tajikistan)

Quick Country Facts
Quick Country Facts
Location: Central Asia
Area: 55,300 sq. mi. (143,100 sq. km.)
Population (2002 est.): 6,719,567
Capital/Largest City: Dushanbe (pop. 524,000)
Official Language: Tajik
GDP/PPP: $7.5 billion, $1,140 per capita
Monetary Unit: Somoni

National Anthem

Lyrics: Gulnazar Keldi. Music: Suleiman Yudakov (b. 1916). Adopted: 1991.

Historical Background

The anthem of Tajikistan was officially adopted upon 1991 independence and is unchanged from the anthem used when it was a Soviet republic. Suleiman Yudakov also wrote the first opera that was performed in Central Asia.

Words Not Available

Tajikistan

Tanzania

Jamhuri ya Mwungano wa Tanzania

United Republic of Tanzania

Quick Country Facts

Location: East Africa

Area: 364,879 sq. mi. (945,087 sq. km.)

Population (2002 est.): 37,187,939

Capitals: Dar es Salaam (pop. 1,360,850), Dodoma (pop. 45,807)

Largest City : Dar es Salaam

Official Languages: Kiswahili, English

GDP/PPP: $22.1 billion, $610 per capita

Monetary Unit: Tanzanian Shilling

Mungu Ibariki Afrika

God Bless Africa

Lyrics: Group of citizens. Music: Mankayi Enoch Sontonga (1860-1904). Adopted: 1961.

Historical Background

The words to this anthem were written collectively to the adapted music of "Nkosi sikelel' iAfrika," originally composed by Enoch Sontonga. That same year, 1961, it was adopted as the national anthem of Tanganyika. After Zanzibar united with Tanganyika in 1964, the song was adopted as the anthem of the newly formed state of Tanzania.

Kiswahili Words	English Words
1	1
Mungu ibariki Afrika.	God bless Africa.
Wabariki viongozi wake.	Bless its leaders.
Hekima Umoja na	Let wisdom, unity, and
Amani hizi ni ngao zetu	Peace be the shield of
Afrika na watu wake.	Africa and its people.

CHORUS 1	CHORUS 1
Ibariki Afrika	Bless Africa,
(repeat)	(repeat)
Tubariki watoto wa Afrika.	Bless the children of Africa.
2	2
Mungu ibariki Tanzania.	God bless Tanzania.
Dumisha uhuru na umoja	Grant eternal freedom and unity
Wake kwa waume na watoto.	To its sons and daughters.
Mungu ibariki Tanzania na watu wake.	God bless Tanzania and its people.
CHORUS 2	CHORUS 2
Ibariki Tanzania	Bless Tanzania,
(repeat)	(repeat)
Tubariki watoto wa tanzania.	Bless the children of Tanzania.

Tanzania

Thailand

ประเทศ

Prathet Thai

(Kingdom of Thailand)

Quick Country Facts

Location: Southeast Asia, Indochina Peninsula

Area: 198,455 sq. mi. (514,000 sq. km.)

Population (2002 est.): 61,354,402

Capital/Largest City: Bangkok (pop. 7,200,000)

Official Language: Thai

GDP/PPP: $410 billion, $6,600 per capita

Monetary Unit: Baht

เพลงชาติ

Pleng Chart

(National Anthem)

Lyrics: Luang Saranuprabhandh (1896-1954). Music: Phra Jenduriyang (1883-1968). Adopted: 1939.

Historical Background[1]

The national anthem is played on all ceremonial occasions, before performances (such as at the cinema), and while the Thai flag is being raised and lowered each day at 8:00 and 18:00 every day. At these times, it is accepted behavior to stand to attention.

The music to the national anthem was composed by Professor Phra Jenduriyang in 1932 (the year the constitutional monarchy was adopted), while the lyrics presently used were written in 1939 by Colonel Luang Saranuprabhandh.

Thai Words	Thai Words (Transliteration)	English Translation[2]
ประเทศไทยรวมเลือดเนื้อชาติเชื้อไทย	*Pra thet thai ruam nu'a chat chu'a thai*	Thailand embraces in its bosom
อยู่ดำรงคงไว้ได้ทั้งมวล		All people of Thai blood.
ไทยนี้รักสงบแต่ถึงรบไม่ขลาด	*Pen pra cha rat pha thai kho'ng thai thuk suan*	Every inch of Thailand
สละเลือดทุกหยาดเป็นชาติพลี		belongs to the Thais.
เป็นประชารัฐไผทของไทยทุกส่วน	*Yu dam rong khong wai dai thang muan*	It has long maintained its sovereignty
ด้วยไทยล้วนหมายรักสามัคคี		because the Thais have always been
เอกราชจะไม่ให้ใครข่มขี่	*Duay thai luan mai rak sa mak*	united.
เถลิงประเทศชาติไทยทวีมีชัย ชโย	*khi Thai ni rak sa ngop*	The Thai people are peace-loving
	tae thu'ng rop mai khalt	But there are no cowards at war.
	Ek ka rat ha mai hai khrai khom khi	They shall allow no one
	Sa la luat thuk yat pen chat phli	To rob them of their independence.
	Tha loeng pra thet chat thai tha wi mi chat chai yo.	Nor shall they suffer tyranny.
		All Thais are ready to give up
		Every drop of blood for the nation's
		Safety, freedom and progress.

Thailand

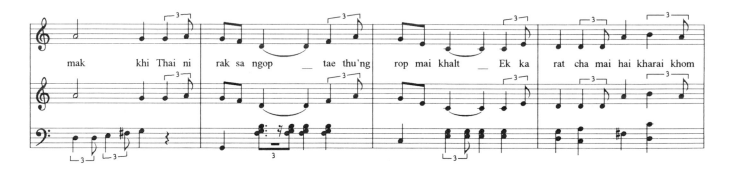

Togo

République Togolais

(Republic of Togo)

```
Quick Country Facts

Location: West Africa
Area: 21,925 sq. mi. (56,785 sq. km.)
Population (2002 est.): 5,285,501
Capital/Largest City: Lomé (pop. 366,476)
Official Language: French
GDP/PPP: $7.6 billion, $1,500 per capita
Monetary Unit: Franc CFA
```

Salut à toi, pays de nos aïeux

(Hail to thee, land of our forefathers)

Lyrics and Music: Alex Casimir-Dosseh (b. 1923). Adopted: 1960.

Historical Background

Adopted upon independence from France in 1960, the Togolese national anthem was replaced in 1979 and restored in 1991.

French Words	English Translation
1	1
Salut à toi, pays de nos aïeux!	Hail to thee, land of our forefathers,
Toi qui les rendais forts, paisibles et joyeux,	Thou who made them strong, peaceful and happy,
Cultivant vertu, vaillance	Men who for posterity cultivated virtue and bravery.
Pour la postérité.	Even if tyrants shall come, thy heart yearns towards
Que viennent les tyrans, ton coeur soupire vers la liberté.	freedom.
Togo, debout! Luttons sans défaillance,	Togo arise! Let us struggle without faltering.
Vainquons ou mourons, mais dans la dignité.	Victory or death, but dignity.
Grand Dieu, Toi seul nous as exaltés	God almighty, Thou alone hast made Togo prosper.
Du Togo pour la prospérité,	People of Togo arise! Let us build the nation.

Togolais, viens! Bâtissons la Cité!	
2	**2**
Dans l'unité nous voulons te servir,	To serve thee in unity is the most burning desire of our hearts.
C'est bien là de nos cœurs le plus ardent désir.	
Clamons fort notre devise	Let us shout aloud our motto
Que rien ne peut ternir.	That nothing can tarnish.
Seuls artisans de ton bonheur ainsi que de ton avenir,	We the only builders of thy happiness and of thy future,
Brisons partout les chaînes, la traîtrise	Everywhere let us break chains and treachery,
Et nous te jurons toujours fidélité	And we swear to thee for ever faith, love, service, untiring zeal,
Et aimer, servir, se dépasser,	
Faire encore de toi sans nous lasser	To make thee yet, beloved Togo, a golden example for humanity.
Togo Chéri, l'Or de l'Humanité.	

Togo

Sa - lut à toi, pa - ys de nos aï - - eux __! Toi qui les ren - dais forts __, pai - si - bles et joy - eux __, Cul -

ti - vant __ ver - tu, vail - lan - ce __ Pour la pos - té - ri - té. Que __ vien - nent

les ty - rans __, ton cœur sou - pi - re vers la li - ber - té __. To - go, de - bout __! Lut - tons sans

dé - fail - lan - ce, Vain - quons ou mou - rons, mais dans la di - gni - té __. Grand Dieu, Toi seul nous as ex - al - tés

Du To - go __ pour la pros - pé - ri - té, To - go - lais, viens! Bâ - tis - sons la __ Ci - té __!

Tonga

Pule'anga Tonga

Kingdom of Tonga

```
Quick Country Facts
Location: Oceania, Pacific Ocean
Area: 290 sq. mi. (748 sq. km.)
Population (2002 est.): 106,137
Capital/Largest City: Nuku'alofa (pop. 34,000)
Official Languages: Tongan, English
GDP/PPP: $225 million, $2,200 per capita
Monetary Unit: Pa'anga
```

National Anthem

Lyrics: Prince Tevita 'Unga (d. 1879).

Historical Background[1]

The actual word text was composed and set by the late Crown Prince Tevita 'Unga, son and heir of King George Tupou I, who died in 1879. The melody is of unknown origin and provided by Reverend Shirley Baker. The first reported singing of this national anthem dates back to July 1874, but it was probably in use earlier.

Tongan Words	English Words
'E 'Otua Mafimafi,	Oh Almighty God above,
Ko ho mau 'Eiki koe,	Thou art our Lord and sure defense,
Ko Koe ko e falala'anga,	In our goodness we do trust Thee
Mo e 'ofa ki Tonga:	And our Tonga Thou dost love;
'Afio hifo 'emau lotu	Hear our prayer, for though unseen
'A ia 'oku mau fai ni,	We know that Thou hast blessed our land;
Mo ke tali homau loto	Grant our earnest supplication,
'O malu'i 'a Tupou.	Guard and save Tupou our King.

Tonga

Trinidad and Tobago

Republic of Trinidad and Tobago

Quick Country Facts

Location: North America, Caribbean Sea

Area: 1,980 sq. mi. (5,128 sq. km.)

Population (2002 est.): 1,163,724

Capital/Largest City: Port-of-Spain (pop. 52,451)

Official Language: English

GDP/PPP: $10.6 billion, $9,000 per capita

Monetary Unit: Trinidad and Tobago Dollar

National Anthem

Lyrics and Music: Patrick Stanislaus Castagne (b. 1916). Adopted: 1962.

Historical Background

Patrick Stanislaus Castagne composed the words and music of the national anthem in 1962.

Words

Forged from the love of liberty, in the fires of hope and prayer,

With boundless faith in our destiny, we solemnly declare:

Side by side we stand, islands of the blue Caribbean Sea.

This our native land, we pledge our lives to thee.

Here ev'ry creed and race find an equal place,

And may God bless our nation.

(repeat previous two lines)

Trinidad and Tobago

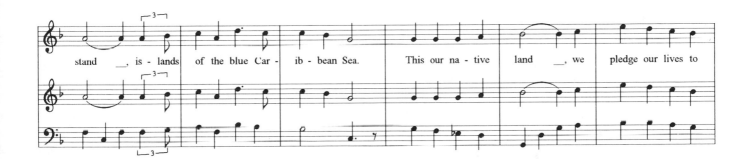

creed and race find an   e -   qual   place,   And may God   bless   our na - tion

Tunisia

'Al-Jumhuriyya Tunisiyya

République Tunisienne

(Tunisian Republic)

Quick Country Facts
Location: North Africa, Middle East
Area: 63,170 sq. mi. (163,610 sq. km.)
Population (2002 est.): 9,815,644
Capital/Largest City: Tunis (pop. 887,800)
Official Languages: Arabic, French
GDP/PPP: $64.5 billion, $6,600 per capita
Monetary Unit: Tunisian Dinar

Himat Al Hima

(Defenders of the Homeland)

Lyrics: Mustafa Sadik Al-Rafii (1880-1937) and Aboul Kacem Chabbi (1909-1934). Music: Mohamed Abdel Wahab (1915-1991). Adopted: 1987.

Historical Background

"Himat Al Hima" was adopted in 1987, replacing "Ala Khallidi" ("Oh Make Eternal"). Composer Mohamed Abdel Wahab also wrote the music to the national anthem of the United Arab Emirates.

Arabic Words (Transliteration)	English Translation
Humata 'L-hima Ya Humata 'L-hima	O defenders of the homeland!
Halummu, Halummu, Li-majdi 'Z-zaman	Rally around to the glory of our time!
Laqad Sarakhat Fil-'uruqi 'D-dima	The blood surges in our veins,
Namutu, Namutu, Wa-yahya 'L-watan	We die for the sake of our land.
Li-tadwi 'S-samawatu Bira 'diha	Let the heavens roar with thunder.
Li-tarmi 'S-sawa'iqu Niranaha	Let thunderbolts rain with fire.
Ila 'Izzi Tunis Ila Majdiha	Men and youth of Tunisia,

Rijala L-biladi Wa-shubbanaha	Rise up for her might and glory.
Fala Asha Fi Tunisa Man Khanaha	No place for traitors in Tunisia,
Wa-la Asha Man Laysa Min Jundiha	Only for those who defend her!
Namutu Wa-nahya 'Ala 'Ahdiha	We live and die loyal to Tunisia,
Hayata 'L-kirami Wa-mawta 'L-'izam.	A life of dignity and a death of glory.

Tunisia

Turkey

Türkiye Cumhuriyeti

(Republic of Turkey)

Quick Country Facts

Location: Southwest Asia, Southeast Europe

Area: 300,947 sq. mi. (780,580 sq. km.)

Population (2002 est.): 67,308,928

Capital: Ankara (pop. 2,890,025)

Largest City: Istanbul (pop. 10,250,000)

Official Language: Turkish

GDP/PPP: $468 billion, $7,000 per capita

Monetary Unit: Turkish Lira

İstiklal Marşi

(March of Independence)

Lyrics: Mehmet Akif Ersoy (1873-1936). Music: Zeki Üngör (1880-1958). Adopted: 1921.

Historical Background[1]

The "İstiklal Marşi" ("Independence March") was officially adopted as Turkey's national anthem on 12 March 1921. Seven hundred twenty-four poems were submitted to a competition organized to find and select the most suitable original composition for this march, and a poem written by Mehmet Akif Ersoy was adopted unanimously by the Turkish Grand National Assembly. Twenty-four composers participated in another competition arranged for the selection of a musical composition for the national anthem. The Council, which was only able to convene in 1924 due to the War of Independence, adopted the music composed by Ali Rifat Çagatay. The words of the national anthem were sung to it for eight years. Thereafter, the music of the national anthem was changed to an arrangement written by Zeki Üngör, conductor of the Presidential Symphonic Orchestra, and the words have been sung to this accompaniment ever since.

Turkish Words (First Two Verses, 10 Total)	English Translation (First Two Verses, 10 Total)
1	**1**
Korkma Sönmez bu şafaklarda yüzen al sancak,	Fear not and be not dismayed,
Sönmeden yurdumun üstünde tüten en son ocak,	This crimson flag will never fade
O benim milletimin yıldızıdır parlayacak,	It is the last hearth that's burning for my nation and
O benimdir o benim milletimindir ancak!	We know for sure that it will never fail.
	It is my nation's star that ever forth will shine.
	It is nation's star and it is mine.
2	**2**
Çatma, kurban olayım çehreni ey nazlı hilâl;	Frown not, fair crescent, for I
Kahramân ırkıma birgül, ne bu şiddet, bu celâl!	Am ready even to die for thee.
Sana olmaz dökülen kanlarımız sonra helâl.	Smile now upon my heroic nation, leave this anger,
Hakkıdır hakka tapan milletimin istiklal.	Lest the blood shed for the unblessed be,
	Freedom's the right of this my nation,
	Yes, freedom for us who worship God and seek what's right.

Turkey

Turkmenistan

Quick Country Facts

Location: Central Asia

Area: 188,500 sq. mi. (488,100 sq. km.)

Population (2002 est.): 4,688,963

Capital/Largest City: Ashgabat (pop. 518,000)

Official Language: Turkmen

GDP/PPP: $21.5 billion, $4,700 per capita

Monetary Unit: Manat

Independent, Neutral, Turkmenistan State Anthem

Music: Veli Mukhatov (b. 1916). Adopted: 1997.

Historical Background

This anthem was adopted in 1997, replacing the previous one, which had been adopted during the Soviet era.

Words Not Available

Turkmenistan

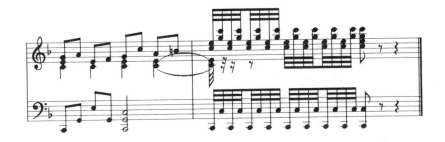

Tuvalu

Fakavae Aliki-Malo i Tuvalu

Constitutional Monarchy of Tuvalu

Quick Country Facts

Location: Oceania, Pacific Ocean

Area: 10 sq. mi. (26 sq. km.)

Population (2002 est.): 11,146

Capital/Largest City: Fongafale (pop. 3,839)

Official Languages: Tuvaluan, English

GDP/PPP: $12.2 million, $1,100 per capita

Monetary Units: Tuvaluan Dollar, Australian Dollar

Tuvalu mo te Atua

Tuvalu for the Almighty

Lyrics and Music: Afaese Manoa (b. 1942). Adopted: 1978.

Tuvaluan Words	English Words
1	1
"Tuvalu mo te Atua"	"Tuvalu for the Almighty"
Ko te Fakavae sili,	Are the words we hold most dear;
Ko te alu foki tena,	For as people or as leaders
O te manuia katoa;	Of Tuvalu we all share
Loto lasi o fai,	In the knowledge that God
Tou malo saoloto;	Ever rules in heav'n above,
Fusi ake katoa	And that we in this land
Ki te loto alofa;	Are united in His love.
Kae amo fakatasi	We build on a sure foundation
Ate atu fenua.	When we trust in God's great law;
"Tuvalu mo te Atua"	"Tuvalu for the Almighty"
Ki te se gata mai!	Be our song for evermore!

2	2
Tuku atu tau pulega	Let us trust our lives henceforward
Ki te pule mai luga,	To the King to whom we pray,
Kilo tonu ki ou mua	With our eyes fixed firmly on Him
Me ko ia e tautai.	He is showing us the way.
"Pule tasi mo ia"	"May we reign with Him in glory"
Ki te se gata mai,	Be our song for evermore,
Ko tena mana	for His almighty power
Ko tou malosi tena.	Is our strength from shore to shore.
Pati lima kae kalaga	Shout aloud in jubilation
Ulufonu ki te tupu.	To the King whom we adore.
"Tuvalu ko tu saoloto"	"Tuvalu free and united"
Ki te se gata mai.	Be our song for evermore!

Tuvalu

Tuvalu

te A - tu - a" Ki te se ga - ta ma - i _!
the Al - migh - ty" Be our song for e - ver - more _!

Uganda

Republic of Uganda

```
Quick Country Facts
Location: East Africa
Area: 91,459 sq. mi. (236,040 sq. km.)
Population (2002 est.): 24,699,073
Capital/Largest City: Kampala (pop. 773,463)
Official Language: English
GDP/PPP: $29 billion, $1,200 per capita
Monetary Unit: Ugandan Shilling
```

Pearl of Africa

Lyrics and Music: George Wilberforce Kakoma (b. 1923). Adopted: 1962.

Words		
1	2	3
Oh Uganda! may God uphold thee,	Oh Uganda! the land of freedom.	Oh Uganda! the land that feeds us
We lay our future in thy hand.	Our love and labor we give,	By sun and fertile soil grown.
United, free, for liberty	And with neighbors all at our	For our own dear land we'll always
Together we always stand.	country's call	stand:
	In peace and friendship we'll live.	The pearl of Africa's crown.

Uganda

Oh U - gan - da! may God up - hold thee, We lay our fu - ture in thy hand __. U - ni - ted, free, for

lib - er - ty To - ge - ther we'll al - ways stand __.

Ukraine

Україна

Ukrayina

Quick Country Facts

Location: Southeastern Europe

Area: 233,000 sq. mi. (603,700 sq. km.)

Population (2002 est.): 48,396,470

Capital/Largest City: Kyiv (pop. 2,637,000)

Official Language: Ukrainian

GDP/PPP: $205 billion, $4,200 per capita

Monetary Unit: Hryvnia

Ще не вмерла Україна

Shche Ne Vmerla Ukrayina

(Ukraine Is Not Yet Dead)

Lyrics: Pavlo Chubynsky (1839-1884). Music: Mykhailo Verbytsky (1815-1870). Adopted: 1917.

Historical Background[1]

In 1992 the Ukrainian Parliament chose as the national anthem music composed in 1863 by Mykhailo Verbytsky, a western Ukrainian composer and Catholic priest. Verbytsky wrote the score originally as a solo song and later for orchestra to accompany a patriotic poem written in 1862 by Pavlo Chubynsky, a prominent ethnographer in the Kyiv region.

In his poem "Shche Ne Vmerla Ukrayina" (which means "Ukraine is Not Yet Dead"), Chubynsky expresses the mixture of hope and desperation felt by Ukrainians over their continuous struggle to rule their own land. Both the melody and lyrics were similar to Polish and Serbian anthems. The song was widely sung around the country as the "Hymn to Ukraine." In 1917 it became the anthem of the short-lived Ukrainian National Republic, but during the Soviet era it was replaced.

Over time there have been numerous changes and additions to Chubynsky's original words. Following independence, however, the Ukrainian government did not adopt any of the versions as the official anthem lyrics because they were considered dated. A commission sponsored several contests for new lyrics, but results have not been fruitful, so the music continues to be associated with Chubynsky's poem. Three stanzas are in circulation, with only slight variations among the lyrics.

Ukrainian Words	Ukrainian Words (Transliteration)	English Translation[2]
1	1	1
Ще не вмерла Україна, ні слава, ні воля,	*Shche ne vmerla Ukrayina, i slava, i vola,*	Ukraine has not perished, neither her glory, nor freedom,
Ще нам, браття-українці, усміхнеця доля.	*Shche nam brattia molodii Usmikhnet dola:*	Upon us, fellow—Ukrainians, fate shall smile once more.
Згинуть наші воріженьки, як роса на сонці.	*Zkhynut'nashi vorozhen'ky, Yak rossa na sonci,*	Our enemies will vanish, like dew in the morning sun,
Заживемо і ми, браття, у своїй сторонці.	*Zapanuyem i my, brattia, U svoii storonci.*	And we too shall dwell, brothers, in a free land of our own.
CHORUS	CHORUS	CHORUS
Душу й тіло ми положим за нашу сободу	*Dushu, tilo my polozhym Za nashu svobodu*	We'll lay down our souls and bodies to attain our freedom,
І покажем, що ми, браття, козацького роду.	*I pokazhem, shcho my, brattia, Kozackoho rodu.*	And we'll show that we, brothers, are of the Kozak nation.
(repeat chorus)	(repeat chorus)	(repeat chorus)
2	2	2
Станем браття, всі за волю, від Сяну до Дону	*Stanem, bratt'a v biy krivavyi vid Syanu do Donu*	We'll stand together for freedom, from the Sian to the Don,
Вріднім краю панувати не дамо ні кому.	*V ridnim krayu panuvaty ne damo nikomu*	We will not allow others to rule in our motherland.
Чорне море ще всміхнеця, дід Дніпро зрадіє,	*Chorne morye sche smikhnet's'a did Dnipro zradiye*	The Black Sea will smile and grandfather Dnipro will rejoice,
Ще на нашій Україні доленька доспіє.	*Sche u Nashiy Ukrayini dolen'ka naspiye!*	For in our own Ukraine fortune shall flourish again.
CHORUS	CHORUS	CHORUS
3	3	3
А завзятта праця щира свого ще докаже,	*A zavzyattya pracya shira svoho sche dokazhe*	Our persistence and our sincere toils will be rewarded,
Ще ся вомі в Україні піснь гучна розляже.	*Sche s'a voli v Ukrayini pisn' huchna 'rozl'azhe*	And freedom's song will resound throughout all of Ukraine.
За Карпати відібється, згомонить	*Za Karpatt'a vidob'yet's'a zhomonyt'*	Echoing off the Carpathians, and

степами, України слава стане поміж гародами. CHORUS	*stepamy* *Ukrayini slavo stane pomizh vorohami!* CHORUS	rumbling across the steppes, Ukraine's fame and glory will be known among all nations. CHORUS

Ukraine

I po - ka - zhem, shcho my, brat - - tia, Ko - zac - ko - ho ro - du. Du - shu, ti - lo

my po - lo - - zhym Za na - shu svo - bo - - du I po - ka - zhem, shcho my, brat - - tia,

Ko - zac - ko - ho ro - du.

United Arab Emirates

المتحدة دولة الإمارات العربية

Dawlat Al-Imarat al'-Arabiyyah al-Muttahida

Quick Country Facts

Location: West Asia, Arabian Peninsula

Area: 32,375 sq. mi. (82,880 sq. km.)

Population (2002 est.): 2,445,989

Capital/Largest City: Abu Dhabi (pop. 363,432)

Official Languages: Arabic, English

GDP/PPP: $51 billion, $21,100 per capita

Monetary Unit: UAE Dirham

National Anthem

Music: Mohamed Abdel Wahab (1915-1991). Adopted: 1971

Historical Background

Composer Mohamed Abdel Wahab also wrote the music to the national anthem of Tunisia. The anthem is without words.

No Words

United Arab Emirates

United Kingdom

United Kingdom of Great Britain and Northern Ireland

Quick Country Facts

Location: Western Europe, British Isles

Area: 94,247 sq. mi. (244,820 sq. km.)

Population (2002 est.): 59,778,002

Capital/Largest City: London (pop. 11,800,000)

Official Language: English

GDP/PPP: $1.52 trillion, $25,300 per capita

Monetary Unit: Pound Sterling

God Save the Queen

Words and Music: Probably Henry Carey (1690-1743).

Historical Background[1]

Though usually attributed to Arne, there is good ground for believing it is really the work of Henry Carey, a singer and composer. It is said to have been written sometime between 1736 and 1740 but was first heard in public at a dinner in 1740 to celebrate the taking of Portobello by Admiral Vernon. Carey sang it as his own composition. The oldest copy is in "Harmonia Anglicana" of 1743, to which Carey was one of the chief contributors.

Several similar earlier airs exist in a manuscript of 1619 attributed to Dr. John Bull, an organist in the Chapel Royal during the reign of James I. In the same book is a song called "God Save the King," but the music is different. The Scots claim it is based on an old carol of 1611 called "Remember O Thou Man" or "Franklyn Is Fled Away" of 1669. It has also been traced to Purcell in 1696. As a phrase from the Coverdale Bible of 1535, "God Save the King" was used as a naval watchword to which the countersign was "Long to reign over us."

For a long time the song was used as an expression of personal loyalty to the king and in translation it was used in Prussia, Denmark, and in Russia until 1833 when Tsar Nicholas commissioned a new version. The tune has also been used in Sweden, Switzerland, Liechtenstein, and the United States. "God Save the Queen" is sung in the United Kingdom as a matter of tradition. It has never been proclaimed the national anthem by an act of parliament or a royal proclamation.

Words

1	2	3
God save our gracious queen,	O Lord our God arise,	Thy choicest gifts in store
Long live our noble queen,	Scatter her enemies	On her be pleased to pour;
God save the queen!	And make them fall;	Long may she reign;
Send her victorious,	Confound their politics,	May she defend our laws,
Happy and glorious,	Frustrate their knavish tricks,	And ever give us cause
Long to reign over us;	On Thee our hopes we fix,	To sing with heart and voice,
God save the queen!	Oh, save us all!	God save the queen!

United Kingdom

God save our gra - cious queen, Long live our no - ble queen, God save the queen! Send her vic -

to - ri - ous, Hap - py and glo - ri - ous, Long to __ reign __ o - ver us; God __ save the queen __!

United States

United States of America

Quick Country Facts

Location: North America

Area: 3,297,226 sq. mi. (9,158,960 sq. km.)

Population (2002 est.): 280,562,489

Capital: Washington (pop. 606,900)

Largest City: New York (pop. 20,250,000)

Languages: English, Spanish

GDP/PPP: $10.082 trillion, $36,300 per capita

Monetary Unit: U.S. Dollar

The Star-Spangled Banner

Lyrics: Francis Scott Key (1779-1843). Adopted: 1931.

Historical Background[1]

"The Star-Spangled Banner" was born out of the emotions experienced by Francis Scott Key as he watched the bombardment of Fort McHenry during the War of 1812 against Great Britain. Key's poem, the "Defense of Fort McHenry," came to be sung to the tune of a pre-existing song, "To Anacreon in Heaven," the melody of which is attributed to Englishman John Stafford Smith. The first musical edition was published by Benjamin Carr of Baltimore and titled "The Star-Spangled Banner." With the passage of time the song grew in popularity, and in 1931 an act of Congress made it the official national anthem.

Words	
1	2
Oh, say, can you see, by the dawn's early light,	On the shore, dimly seen thro' the mists of the deep,
What so proudly we hail'd at the twilight's last gleaming?	Where the foe's haughty host in dread silence reposes,
Whose broad stripes and bright stars, thro' the perilous fight,	What is that which the breeze, o'er the towering steep,
O'er the ramparts we watch'd, were so gallantly streaming?	As it fitfully blows half conceals, half discloses?
And the rocket's red glare, the bombs bursting in air	Now it catches the gleam of the morning's first beam,
Gave proof thro' the night that our flag was still there.	In full glory reflected now shines in the stream;
	'Tis the Star-Spangled Banner, O long may it wave
	O'er the land of the free and the home of the brave.

Oh, say, does that Star-Spangled Banner yet wave
O'er the land of the free and the home of the brave?

3

And where is that band who so vauntingly swore
That the havoc of war and the battle's confusion
A home and a country should leave us no more?
Their blood has wiped out their foul footstep's pollution.
No refuge could save the hireling and slave
From the terror of flight, or the gloom of the grave:
And the star-spangled banner in triumph doth wave
O'er the land of the free and the home of the brave.

4

Oh, thus be it ever when free men shall stand
Between their loved homes and the war's desolation!
Blest with vict'ry and peace, may the heav'n rescued land
Praise the Pow'r that hath made and preserved us a nation!
Then conquer we must, when our cause it is just,
And this be our motto, "In God is our trust"
And the Star-Spangled Banner in triumph shall wave
O'er the land of the free and the home of the brave!

United States

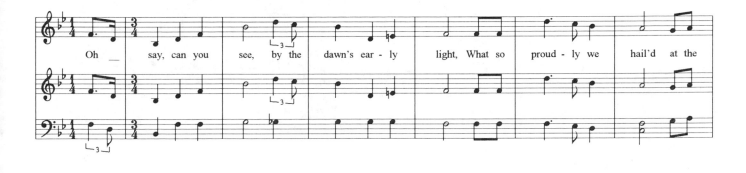

Oh __ say, can you see, by the dawn's ear - ly light, What so proud - ly we hail'd at the

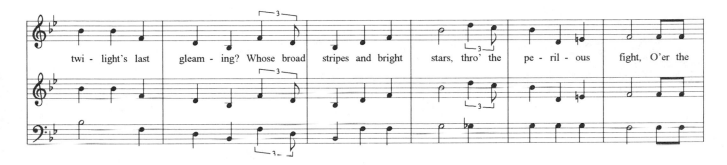

twi - light's last gleam - ing? Whose broad stripes and bright stars, thro' the pe - ril - ous fight, O'er the

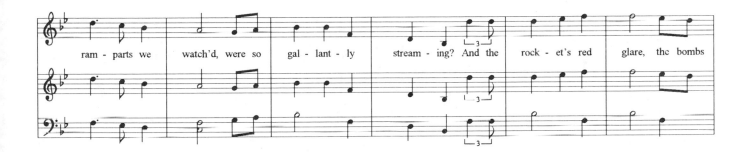

ram - parts we watch'd, were so gal - lant - ly stream - ing? And the rock - et's red glare, the bombs

burst - ing in air Gave proof thro' the night that our flag was still there. Oh, say, does that __

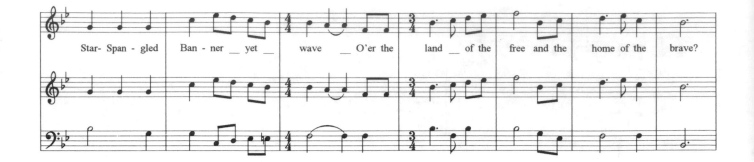

Star- Span - gled   Ban - ner __ yet __   wave __ O'er the   land __ of the   free and the   home of the   brave?

Uruguay

República Oriental del Uruguay

(Oriental Republic of Uruguay)

Quick Country Facts

Location: South America

Area: 68,040 sq. mi. (176,220 sq. km.)

Population (2002 est.): 3,386,575

Capital/Largest City: Montevideo (pop. 1,330,440)

Official Language: Spanish

GDP/PPP: $31 billion, $9,200 per capita

Monetary Unit: Peso

Himno Nacional

(National Anthem)

Lyrics: Francisco Esteban Acuña de Figueroa (1791-1862). Music: Francisco José Debali (1791-1859). Adopted: 1845.

Historical Background

This national anthem was approved by the decrees of 8 July 1833, 12 July 1845, 25 July 1848, and 26 July 1848. The arrangement and instrumentation of the song were standardized through the resolution of 20 May 1938. These changes were made by composers Gerardo Grasso and Benone Calcavecchia. Francisco Esteban de Figueroa and Francisco José Debali also wrote and composed the national anthem of Paraguay, respectively.

Spanish Words (First Verse, 11 Total)	English Translation (First Verse, 11 Total)
CHORUS	CHORUS
¡Orientales, la patria o la tumba!	Eastern landsmen, our country or the tomb!
¡Libertad o con gloria morir!	Freedom, or with glory to die!
(repeat previous two lines)	(repeat previous two lines)
Es el voto que el alma pronuncia	This is the vow that our souls take
Y que heroicos sabremos cumplir,	And which we know how, courageously, to fulfill,
(repeat previous two lines)	(repeat previous two lines)

que sabremos cumplir,	Know how to fulfill.
Es el voto que el alma pronuncia	This is the vow that our souls take
Y que heroicos sabremos cumplir,	And which we know how, courageously, to fulfill,
que sabremos cumplir,	Know how to fulfill
(repeat)	(repeat)
sabremos cumplir.	Know how to fulfill.
(repeat two times)	(repeat two times)
1	1
¡Libertad, libertad, Orientales!,	Freedom, freedom, eastern landsmen,
este grito a la Patria salvó	This cry saved our country,
que a sus bravos en fieras batallas,	Inflaming its brave men
de entusiasmo sublime inflamó.	With enthusiasm in fierce battles.
De este don sacrosanto la gloria	We merited the glory of this sacred gift.
merecimos ¡Tiranos temblad!	Let tyrants tremble!
¡Tiranos temblad! ¡Tiranos temblad!	(repeat previous two lines three times)
¡Libertad en la lid clamaremos	Ah, in the fight we shall clamor for freedom
Y muriendo también libertad!	And, dying, still cry for it.
(repeat previous two lines)	(repeat previous two lines)
y muriendo también libertad!	And, dying, still cry for it,
también libertad!	Still cry for it.
(repeat)	(repeat)

Uruguay

¡O - rien - ta - les, la pa - tria o la tum - ba! ¡Li - ber - tad, o con glo - ria mo -

rir! ¡O - rien - ta - les, la pa - tria o la tum - ba! ¡Li - ber - tad o con glo - ria mo - rir! Es el

vo - to que el al - ma pro - nun - cia Y que he - ro - i - cos sa - bre - mos cum - plir, Es el

vo - to que el al - ma pro - nun - cia Y que he - roi - cos sa - bre - mos cum - plir, que sa -

bre - mos cum - plir, Es el vo - to que el al - ma pro - nun - cia Y que he -

roi - cos sa - bre - mos cum - plir, que sa - bre - mos cum - plir

sa - bre - mos cum - plir. sa - bre - mos cum - plir, sa - bre - mos cum - plir.

¡Li - ber - tad, li - ber - tad, O - rien - ta - les!, es - te gri - to a la Pa - tria sal -

vó que a sus bra - vos en fie - ras ba - ta - llas, de en - tu - sias - mo su - bli - me in - fla -

mó. De es - te don sa - cro - san - to la glo - ria me - re - ci - mos ¡Ti - ra - nos tem -

blad! ¡Ti - ra - nos tem - blad! ¡Ti - ra - nos tem - blad! ¡Li - ber - tad en la lid cla - ma -

re - mos Y mu - rien - do tam - bién li - ber - tad! ¡Li - ber - tad en la lid cla - ma -

re -   mos __ Y   mu - -   rien -   do tam - bién   li - ber -   tad!   __ y   mu - -

rien -   do tam - bién __ li - ber -   tad!   tam - bién li - ber -   tad!

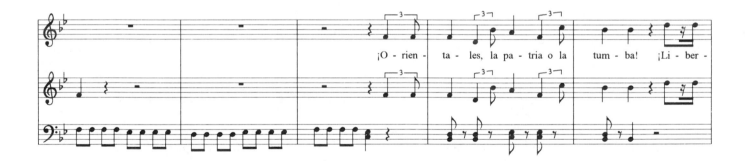

¡O - rien -   ta - les, la pa - tria o la   tum - ba! ¡Li - ber -

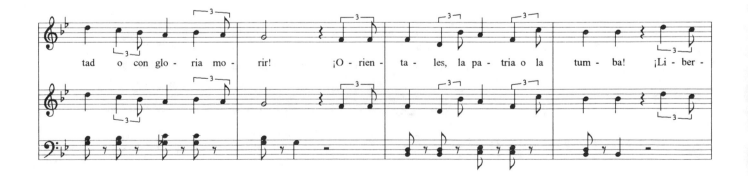

tad   o con glo - ria mo -   rir!   ¡O - rien -   ta - les, la pa - tria o la   tum - ba! ¡Li - ber -

Uzbekistan

Ўзбекистон Республикаси

Uzbekiston Respublikasi

(Republic of Uzbekistan)

Quick Country Facts

Location: Central Asia

Area: 172,700 sq. mi. (447,400 sq. km.)

Population (2002 est.): 25,563,441

Capital/Largest City: Toshkent (pop. 2,106,000)

Official Language: Uzbek

GDP/PPP: $62 billion, $2,500 per capita

Monetary Unit: Sum

National Anthem

Words: Abdulla Aripov (b. 1941). Music: Mutal Burkhanov (b. 1916). Adopted: 1992.

Historical Background

For two years, many poets and composers took part in the creation of the national anthem. The joint work of Abdulla Aripov, the People's Poet of Uzbekistan, and Mutal Burkhanov, the People's Artist of Uzbekistan, was voted the best by the session of the Oliy Majlis (Parliament) of the Republic of Uzbekistan on 10 December 1992.

The creators of the anthem said that it should sound solemn, embodying and glorifying the people. Therefore, the melodies and rhythms from the imperishable legacy of the Shashmaqom musical art of the East was used in the anthem.

Uzbek Words	Uzbek Words (Transliteration)	English Translation
1	1	1
Серкуяш, хур олкам, елга бахт нажат	*Serquyash, hur olkam, elga bakht najat*	My country, sunny and free, salvation to your people
Сен ўзинг достларин ёлдашб мэрибан!	*Sen ozing dostlarin yoldash, mehriban!*	You are a warmhearted companion to the friends
Яшнагай та абад илму фан, ижад,	*Yashnagay ta abad ilmu fan, ijad,*	Flourish eternally with knowledge and inventions,
Шухратинг парласин таки бар жан!	*Shukhrating parlasin taki bar jahn!*	

		May your fame shine as long as the world exists!
CHORUS Алтин бу вадийлар—Ђан Ўзбекистан, Аждадлар мардана руҳи сенга яр! Улуғ халқ қудрати ёш упган заман, Аламни маҳлия айлаган лияр!	CHORUS *Altin bu vadiylar—jan Ozbekistan,* *Ajdadlar mardana ruhi senga yar!* *Ulugh khalq qudrati josh urgan zaman,* *Alamni mahliya aylagan diyar!*	CHORUS These golden valleys—dear Uzbekistan, Manly spirit of ancestors is companion to you! When the great power of people became exuberant You are the country that amazes the world!
2 Бағри кенг Ўзбекнинг очмас иймани, Еркин, яш авладдар сенга зор қанат! Истиклал машь али, тинчлик пасбани, Хақсевар ана юрт, мангу бол абад!	2 *Baghri keng ozbekning ochmas iymani.* *Erkin, yash avladlar senga zor qanat!* *Istiqlal mash' ali, tinchlik pasbani,* *Khaqsevar ana yurt, mangu bol abad!*	2 Belief of generous Uzbck does not die out, Free, young children are a strong wing for you! The torch of independence, guardian of peace, Motherland, be eternally prosperous!
CHORUS	CHORUS	CHORUS

Uzbekistan

Vanuatu

Republic of Vanuatu

République de Vanuatu

Ripablik Blong Vanuatu

Quick Country Facts

Location: Oceania, Pacific Ocean

Area: 5,700 sq. mi. (12,200 sq. km.)

Population (2002 est.): 196,178

Capital/Largest City: Port Vila (pop. 26,100)

Official Languages: English, French, Bislama

GDP/PPP: $257 million, $1,300 per capita

Monetary Unit: Vatu

Yumi, Yumi, Yumi

(We, We, We)

Lyrics and Music: François Vincent (b. 1955). Adopted: 1980.

Bislama Words	English Translation
CHORUS	CHORUS
Yumi, Yumi, Yumi i glat blong talem se,	We are happy to proclaim
Yumi, Yumi, Yumi i man blong Vanuatu!	We are the People of Vanuatu!
1	1
God i givim ples ia long yumi,	God has given us this land;
Yumi glat tumas long hem,	This gives us great cause for rejoicing.
Yumi strong moyumi fri long hem,	We are strong, we are free in this land;
Yumi brata evriwan!	We are all brothers.
CHORUS	CHORUS

2

Plante fasin blong bifo i stap,
Plante fasin blong tedei,
Be yumi i olsem wan nomo,
Hemia fasin blong yumi!

CHORUS

3

Yumi save plante wok i stap,
Long ol aelan blong yumi,
God i help em yumi evriwan,
Hemi papa blong yumi,

CHORUS

2

We have many traditions
And we are finding new ways.
Now we shall be one People,
We shall be united for ever.

CHORUS

3

We know there is much work to be done
On all our islands.
May God, our Father, help us!

CHORUS

Vanuatu

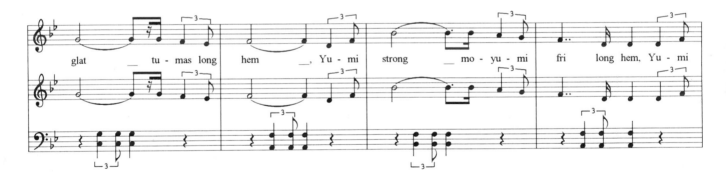

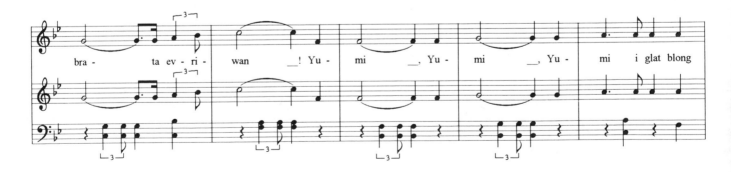

Vatican City

Santa Sede

(The Holy See)

Quick Country Facts

Location: Western Europe, surrounded by Rome, Italy

Area: 0.17 sq. mi. (0.44 sq. km.)

Population (2000 est.): 900

Official Languages: Latin, Italian

Budget: $175.5 million

Monetary Unit: Italian Lira

Inno e Marcia Pontificale

(Hymn and Pontifical March)

Lyrics: Antonio Allegra (1905-1969). Music: Charles Gounod (1818-1893). Adopted: 1950.

Italian Words	English Translation
INNO	HYMN
Roma immortale di Martiri e di Santi,	O Rome immortal, city of martyrs and saints,
Roma immortale accogli i nostri canti:	O immortal Rome, accept our praises.
Gloria nei cieli a Dio nostro Signore,	Glory in the heavens to God our Lord
Pace ai Fedeti, di Cristo nell'amore.	And peace to men who love Christ!
A Te veniamo, Angelico Pastore,	To you we come, angelic Pastor,
In Te vediamo il mite Redentore,	In you we see the gentle Redeemer.
Erede Santo di vera e santa Fede;	You are the holy heir of our faith,
Conforto e vanto a chi combatte e crede,	You are the comfort and the refuge of those who believe and fight.
Non prevarranno la forza ed il terrore,	Force and terror will not prevail,
Ma regneranno la Verità, l'Amore.	But truth and love will reign.
MARCIA PONTIFICALE	PONTIFICAL MARCH
Salve Salve Roma, patria eterna di memorie,	Hail, O Rome,

Cantano le tue glorie mille palme e mille altari.	Eternal abode of memories;
Roma degli apostoli, Madre guida dei Rendenti,	A thousand palms and thousand altars
Roma luce delle genti, il mondo spera in te!	Sing your praises.
Salve Salve Roma, la tua luce non tramonta,	O city of the Apostles,
Vince l'odio e l'onta lo splendor di tua beltà.	Mother and guide of the elect,
Roma degli Apostoli, Madre e guida dei Redenti,	Light of the nations,
Roma luce delle genti, il mondo spera in te!	And hope of the world!
	Hail, O Rome!
	Your light will never fade;
	the splendor of your beauty
	Disperses hatred and shame.
	O city of the Apostles,
	Mother and guide of the elect,
	Light of the nations,
	And hope of the world!

Vatican City

Ro - ma im - mor - ta - le di Mar - ti - ri e di San - ti, Ro - ma im - mor - ta - le ac -
co - gli i nos - tri can - ti: Glo - ria nei cie - li a Dio nos - tro Si - gno - re,
Pa - ce ai Fe - de - ti, di Cri - sto nel - l'a - mo - re. A __ Te ve - nia - mo, An -

ge - li - co Pa - sto - re, In __ Te ve - dia - mo il __ mi - te Re - den -

po - sto - li,   Ma - dre e gui - da dei Re - den - ti,   Roma   lu - ce del - le   gen - ti, il

mon - do spe - ra in   te   !   Sal - ve Sal - ve   Ro - ma,   la tua   lu - ce non tra -

mon - ta,   Vin - ce l'o - dio e   l'on - ta lo splen - dor di   tua bel - tà   .

Ro - ma de - gli A -   po - sto - li,   Ma - dre e gui - da dei Re - den - ti,   Ro - ma lu - ce del - le

gen - ti, il   mon - do spe - ra in   te   !

Venezuela

República Bolivariana de Venezuela

(Bolivarian Republic of Venezuela)

Quick Country Facts

Location: South America

Area: 352,143 sq. mi. (912,050 sq. km.)

Population (2002 est.): 24,287,670

Capital/Largest City: Caracas (pop. 2,784,042)

Official Language: Spanish

GDP/PPP: $146.2 billion, $6,100 per capita

Monetary Unit: Bolivar

Gloria al Bravo Pueblo

(Glory to the Brave People)

Lyrics: Vincente Salias (1786-1814). Music: Juan José Landaeta (1780-1814). Adopted: 1881

Historical Background

The Venezuelan national anthem was adopted on 25 May 1881 by Antonio Guzmán Blanco, former President of the Republic. Written by Juan Landaeta around 1810, the purpose was to remind the future generations of Venezuelans of their successful struggle for national emancipation. It had already been a popular patriotic song sung by the people of Greater Colombia during their fight for independence from Spain.

Spanish Words	English Translation
CHORUS	CHORUS
Gloria al bravo pueblo	Glory to the brave nation
que el yugo lanzó	Which shook off the yoke,
la ley respetando, la virtud y honor.	Respecting law, virtue, and honor.
(repeat chorus)	(repeat chorus)
1	1
¡Abajo cadenas!	"Off with the chains! Off with the chains!"

(repeat)

gritaba el Señor

(repeat)

y el pobre en su choza

libertad pidió

A este santo nombre

tembló de pavor

el vil egoísmo

que otra vez triunfó.

A este santo nombre

(repeat)

tembló de pavor

el vil egoísmo

que otra vez triunfó.

(repeat previous two lines)

CHORUS

2

Gritemos con brío:

(repeat)

¡Muera la opresión!

(repeat)

Compatriotas fieles,

la fuerza es la unión;

y desde el Empíreo

el Supremo Autor,

un sublime aliento

al pueblo infundió.

y desde el Empíreo

(repeat)

el Supremo Autor,

un sublime aliento

al pueblo infundió.

(repeat previous two lines)

CHORUS

Cried the Lord, cried the Lord,

And the poor man in his hovel

Implored freedom.

At this holy name, there trembled

The vile selfishness that had triumphed,

At this holy name, at this holy name

There trembled

The vile selfishness that had triumphed,

(repeat)

CHORUS

2

Let's cry out aloud, let's cry out aloud:

Down with oppression! Down with oppression!

Faithful countrymen, your strength

Lies in your unity;

And from the heavens, and from the heavens

The supreme Creator

Breathed a sublime spirit into the nation.

And from the heavens the supreme Creator

Breathed a sublime spirit into the nation.

(repeat)

CHORUS

3	3
Unida con lazos	United by bonds, united by bonds
(repeat)	Made by heaven, made by heaven
que el cielo formó	All America exists
(repeat)	as a Nation;
la América toda	And if tyranny raises its voice,
existe en nación.	Follow the example given by Caracas.
Y si el despotismo	And if tyranny, if tyranny
levanta la voz	Raises its voice,
seguid el ejemplo	Follow the example given by Caracas.
que Caracas dio.	(repeat)
Y si el despotismo	
(repeat)	
levanta la voz	
seguid el ejemplo	
que Caracas dio.	
(repeat previous two lines)	
CHORUS	CHORUS

Venezuela

Glo - ria al bra - vo pue - blo que el yu - go lan - zó __ la ley res - pe - tan - do, la vir - tud y ho -

nor __. Glo - ria al bra - vo pue - blo que el yu - go lan - zó __ ia ley res - pe - tan - do,

la vir - tud y ho - nor __. ¡A - ba - jo ca - de - nas! ¡A - ba - jo ca - de - nas! gri - ta - ba el Se -

ñor __ gri - ta - ba el Se - ñor __ y el po - bre en su cho - za li - ber - tad pi - dió

tan - do,   la vir - tud y ho -   nor.

Vietnam

Cộng hoà xã hội chủ nghĩa Việt Nam

(Socialist Republic of Vietnam)

Quick Country Facts

Location: Southeast Asia, Indochina Peninsula

Area: 127,246 sq. mi. (329,560 sq. km.)

Population (2002 est.): 81,098,416

Capital: Hanoi (pop. 1,073,760)

Largest City: Ho Chi Minh City (pop. 3,015,743)

Official Language: Vietnamese

GDP/PPP: $168.1 billion, $2,100 per capita

Monetary Unit: Dong

Tiến quân ca

(March to the Front)

Lyrics and Music: Nguyen Van Cao (1923-1995). Adopted: 1946.

Historical Background[1]

Late composer Nguyen Van Cao was born in Vu Ban (Nam Dinh province) on 11 November 1923 and died on 10 July 1995. He made great contributions to the fields of music, poetry and painting and was presented the Ho Chi Minh Prize in 1996 by the government of Vietnam. He was the composer of "Tien Quan Ca" ("March to the Front"), which was later selected as the Vietnamese national anthem.

In the middle of 1944, Van Cao joined the operations at the Viet Minh front (the League for the Independence of Vietnam) in Haiphong. By the end of the year, he worked for *Doc Lap* (Independence) newspaper—the organ of the Democratic Party behind the Viet Minh front. During this time, he began to develop the idea of the song. The composer's autograph that remains in Van Cao's selected song book, published in 1993 by the Music Publishing House, says that "in November 1944, I wrote 'Tien Quan Ca' myself on a stone printing slab on the first literature and art page of *Doc Lap* newspaper that remains the handwriting of a mere apprentice. A month later, when the newspaper was issued, I returned from a printing office. Crossing a small street (now Mai Hac De Street), I suddenly heard the sound of a mandolin from a balcony. There was someone practicing the 'Tien Quan Ca.' I stopped and felt moved. The emotion that came to me was more significant than all of my songs performed at theatres earlier."

On 14 August 1945, at the Tan Trao National Congress in Tuyen Quang province, the provisional government selected "Tien Quan Ca" as the national anthem. During the days of the general uprising from 17-19 August 1945, the song was sung in marching demonstrations and meetings of the revolutionary public in Hanoi. The Fourth Rank soldiers from the Dong Trieu military zone along the operation roads to liberate Haiphong also sung this song loudly. Following was Saigon and other localities nationwide that were heard resounding with "Tien Quan Ca," and the song became a part of history.

The immortal song has gone together with each section of the national revolutionary road for more than the past half a century. It has contributed to encouraging and stimulating the armed forces and people in the cause of national liberation and reconstruction.

Vietnamese Words	English Translation[2]
1	1
Đoàn quân Việt Nam đi	Soldiers of Vietnam, we go forward,
Chung lòng cứu quốc	With the one will to save our fatherland,
Bước chân dồn vang trên đường gập ghềnh xa	Our hurried steps are sounding
Cờ in máu chiến thắng vang hồn nước,	On the long and arduous road.
Súng ngoài xa chen khúc quân hành ca.	Our flag, red with the blood of victory,
Đường vinh quang xây xác quân thù,	Bears the spirit of our country.
Thắng gian lao cùng nhau lập chiến khu.	The distant rumbling of the guns mingles with our
Vì nhân dân chiến đấu không ngừng,	marching song.
Tiến mau ra xa trường,	The path to glory passes over the bodies of our foes.
Tiến lên, cùng tiến lên.	Overcoming all hardships, together we build our resistance
Nước non Việt Nam ta vững bền.	bases.
	Ceaselessly for the people's cause let us struggle,
	Let us hasten to the battlefield!
	Forward! All together advancing!
	Our Vietnam is strong, eternal.
2	2
Đoàn quân Việt Nam đi	Soldiers of Vietnam, we go forward!
Sao vàng phấp phới	The gold star of our flag in the wind
Dắt giống nòi quê hương qua nơi lầm than	Leading our people, our native land,
Cùng chung sức phấn đấu xây đời mới,	Out of misery and suffering.
Đứng đều lên gông xích ta đập tan.	Let us join our efforts in the fight
Từ bao lâu ta nuốt căm hờn,	For the building of a new life.
Quyết hy sinh đời ta tươi thắm hơn.	Let us stand up and break our chains.
Vì nhân dân chiến đấu không ngừng,	For too long have we swallowed our hatred.
Tiến mau ra xa trường,	Let us keep ready for all sacrifices and our life will be
Tiến lên, cùng tiến lên.	radiant.

Nước non Việt Nam ta vững bền.	Ceaselessly for the people's cause let us struggle,
	Let us hasten to the battlefield!
	Forward! All together advancing!

Vietnam

Yemen

الجمهورية اليمنية

al-Jumhuriyah al-Yamaniyah

(Republic of Yemen)

```
Quick Country Facts
Location: West Asia, Arabian Peninsula
Area: 203,850 sq. mi. (527,970 sq. km.)
Population (2002 est.): 18,701,257
Capital: Sana'a (pop. 972,011)
Largest City: Tiaz (pop. 2,205,947)
Official Language: Arabic
GDP/PPP: $14.8 billion, $820 per capita
Monetary Units: Rial
```

United Republic

Lyrics: Abdulla Abdul Wahab Noman (1916-1982). Music: Ayob Tarish (b. 1943). Adopted: 1990.

Historical Background

Originally the anthem of South Yemen, "United Republic" was adopted in 1990, when the two Yemens merged.

Arabic Words	Arabic Words (Transliteration, First Verse, 2 Total)	English Translation (First Verse, 2 Total)
VERSES	1	1
رددية واعيدي واعيدي رددي ايتها الدنيا نشيدي	*Raddidi Ayyatuha 'D-dunya Nashidi*	Repeat, O World, my song. Echo it over and over again.
وامنحيه حللا من ضو عيدي واذكري في فرحتي	*Raddidihi Wa-a 'idi Wa-a idi*	Remember, through my joy, each
كل شهيد	*Wa 'Dhkuri Fi Farhati Kulla*	martyr.
رددي ايتها الدنيا نشيدي رددي ايتها الدنيا نشيدي	*Shahidi*	Clothe him with the shining
سوف نحمي كل ما بين يدينا من جلالك يابلادي	*Wa 'Mnahihi Hullalan Min Daw'i*	mantles
نحن ابناء واحفاد رجالك	*Idi*	Of our festival.
كل صخرة في جبالك كل ذرة في رمالك وسيبقى	*Raddidi Ayyatuha 'D-dunya*	Repeat, O World, my song.
خالد الضوء على كل المسالك		

689

حقنا جاء من امجاد ماضيك المثيرة ملكنا	Nashidi	In faith and love I am part of
انها ملك امانينا الكبيرة	'Ishtu Imani Wa-hubbi Umamiyya	mankind.
رددي ايتها الدنيا نشيدي رددي ايتها الدنيا نشيدي	Wa-masiri Fawqa Darbi Arabiyya	An Arab I am in all my life.
انت عهد عالق في كل ذمة وحدتي	Wa-sayabqa Nabdu Qalbi	My heart beats in tune with
وحدتي يانشيدا رائعا يملاء نفسي	Yamaniyya	Yemen.
اخلدي خافقة في كل قمة رايتي	Lan Tara 'D-dunya Ala Ardi	No foreigner shall dominate over
رايتي يا نسيجا حكته من كل شمس	Wasiyya.	Yemen.
واذخريني لك يا اكرم امه امتي		
امتي امنحيني الباس يامصدر باسي		
ومسيري فوق دربي عربيا عشت ايماني وحبي		
سرمديا		
لن ترى الدنيا على ارضي وصيا وسيبقى نبض		
قلبي يمنيا		
رددبه واعيدي واعيدي رددي ايتها الدنيا نشيدي		
وامنحيه حللا من ضوء عيدي واذكري في فرحتي		
كل شهيد		
رددي ايتها الدنيا نشيدي رددي اتها الدنيا نشيدي		

Yemen

Zambia

Republic of Zambia

Quick Country Facts

Location: South-central Africa

Area: 290,586 sq. mi. (752,614 sq. km.)

Population (2002 est.): 9,959,037

Capital/Largest City: Lusaka (pop. 1,800,000)

Official Language: English

GDP/PPP: $8.5 billion, $870 per capita

Monetary Unit: Kwacha

Stand and Sing of Zambia

Lumbanyeni Zambia

Lyrics: Collectively Written. Music: Mankayi Enoch Sontonga (1860-1904). Adopted: 1964.

Historical Background[1]

The tune of the Zambian national anthem was taken from a song called "Nkosi Sikelele Africa," composed by a South African, Mankayi Enoch Sontonga, in 1897. The anthem expresses freedom, unity, hard work, and respect for God. Sang in official occasions, the song takes Zambians back in time to when the country was granted independence.

English Words	Bemba Words
1	1
Stand and sing of Zambia, proud and free,	Lumbanyeni Zambia, no kwanga,
Land of work and joy in unity,	Ne cilumba twange tuumfwane,
Victors in the struggle for the right,	Mpalume sha bulwi twa cine,
We have won freedom's fight.	Twaliilubula.
All one, strong and free.	Twikatane bonse.
2	2
Africa is our own motherland,	Bonse tuli bana ba Africa,
Fashion'd with and blessed by God's good hand,	Uwasenaminwa na Lesa,
Let us all her people join as one,	Nomba bonse twendele pamo,

Brothers under the sun.	Twaliilubula.
All one, strong and free.	Twikatane bonse.
3	3
One land and one nation is our cry,	Fwe lukuta lwa Zambia lonse,
Dignity and peace 'neath Zambia's sky,	Twikatane tubyo mutende,
Like our noble eagle in its flight,	Pamo nga lubambe mu mulu,
Zambia, praise to thee.	Lumbanyeni Zambia.
All one, strong and free.	Twikatane bonse.
CHORUS	CHORUS
Praise be to God.	Lumbanyeni,
Praise be, praise be, praise be,	Lesa, Lesa, wesu,
Bless our great nation,	Apale calo,
Zambia, Zambia, Zambia.	Zambia, Zambia, Zambia.
Free men we stand	Fwe bantungwa
Under the flag of our land.	Mu luunga lwa calo.
Zambia, praise to thee!	Lumbanyeni Zambia.
All one, strong and free.	Twikatane bonse.

Zambia

Stand and sing of Zam - bia, proud and free, Land of work and joy in u - ni - ty,
A - fri - ca is our own mo - ther - land, Fash - ion'd with and blessed by God's good hand,
Lu - mba - nye - ni Za - mbia, no kwang - ga, Ne ci - lum - ba twa - nge tu - umfwa - ne,
Bon - se tu - li ba - na ba A - fri - ca, U - wa - se - na - min - wa na Le - sa,

Vic - tors in the strug - gle for __ the right, We have won free - - dom's fight. All one,
Let us all her peo - ple join __ as one, Bro - thers un - der the sun. All one,
Mpa - lu - me sha bul - wi twa __ ci - ne, Twa - li - i - lu - bu - la. Twi - ka -
Nom - ba bon - se twe - nde - le __ pa - mo, Twa - li - i - lu - bu - la. Twi - ka -

strong __ and free. One land and one na - tion is our cry, Dig - ni - ty and peace 'neath
strong __ and free. Fwe lu - ku - ta lwa Za - mbia lon - se, Twi - ka - ta - ne tu - byo
ta - ne bon - se.
ta - ne bon - se.

Zam - bia's sky, Like our no - ble ea - gle in __ its flight, Zam - bia, praise __ to thee.
mu - ten - de, Pa - mo nga lu - ba - mbe mu __ mu - lu, Lu - mba - nye - ni Zam - bia.

694

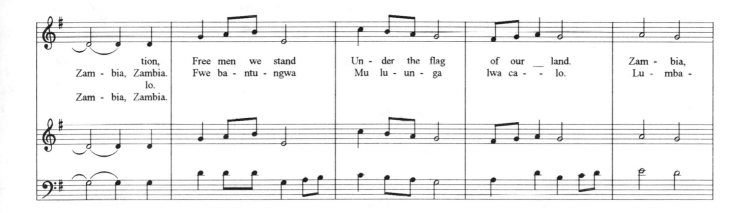

Zimbabwe

Republic of Zimbabwe

```
Quick Country Facts
Location: South-central Africa
Area: 150,698 sq. mi. (390,580 sq. km.)
Population (2002 est.): 11,376,676
Capital/Largest City: Harare (pop. 1,184,169)
Official Language: English
GDP/PPP: $28 billion, $2,450 per capita
Monetary Unit: Zimbabwean Dollar
```

Blessed be the Land of Zimbabwe

Ngaikomborerwe Nyika yeZimbabwe

Kalibusisiwe Ilizwe leZimbabwe

Lyrics: Soloman M. Mutswairo (b. 1924). Music: Fred Lecture Changundega (b. 1954). Adopted: 1994.

Historical Background[1]

Since independence, Zimbabwe had been using the "Ishe Komborera Africa" theme as its national anthem. Over the years the country looked for a truly Zimbabwean song that would take into account the country's history and the aspirations of its peoples.

Poets, artists, musicians, and ordinary people were asked to come up with the music and lyrics for a new national anthem. The winning entry was a song written by Professor Soloman M. Mutswairo and composed by Fred Lecture Changundega. It was launched in March 1994.

English Words	Shona Words	Ndebele Words
1	1	1
O lift high the banner, the flag of Zimbabwe	Simudzai mureza wedu weZimbabwe	Phakamisan iflegi yethu yeZimbabwe
The symbol of freedom proclaiming victory;	Yakazvarwa nomoto wechimurenga;	Eyazalwa yimpi yenkululeko;
	Neropa zhinji ramagamba	Legaz' elinengi lamaqhawe ethu
	Tiidzivirire kumhandu dzose;	Silivikele ezithan izonke;
We praise our heroes' sacrifice,	Ngaikomborerwe nyika yeZimbabwe	Kalibusisiwe ilizwe leZimbabwe.

And vow to keep our land from foes; And may the Almighty protect and bless our land.		
2 O lovely Zimbabwe, so wondrously adorned With mountains, and rivers cascading, flowing free; May rain abound, and fertile fields; May we be fed, our labor blessed; And may the Almighty protect and bless our land.	2 Tarisai Zimbabwe nyika yakashongedzwa Namakomo, nehova, zvinoyevedza Mvura ngainaye, minda ipe mbesa Vashandi vatuswe, ruzhinji rugutswe; Ngaikomborerwe nyika yeZimbabwe.	2 Khangelan' iZimbabwe yon' ihlotshiwe Ngezintaba lang' miful' ebukekayo, Izulu kaline, izilimo zande; Iz' sebenzi zenam', abantu basuthe; Kalibusisiwe ilizwe leZimbabwe.
3 O God, we beseech Thee to bless our native land; The land of our fathers bestowed upon us all; From Zambezi to Limpopo May leaders be exemplary; And may the Almighty protect and bless our land.	3 Mwari ropafadzai nyika yeZimbabwe Nyika yamadzitateguru edu tose; Kubva Zambezi kusvika Limpopo, Navatungamiri vave nenduramo; Ngaikomborerwe nyika yeZimbabwe.	3 Nkosi busis' ilizwe lethu leZimbabwe Ilizwe labokhokho bethu thina sonke; Kusuk' cZambezi kusiy' eLimpopo Abakhokheli babe lobuqotho; Kalibusisiwe ilizwe leZimbabwe.

Zimbabwe

O __ lift high the banner, the flag of __ Zi-mba-bwe __ The __ sym-bol of
Si - mu- dza-i mu- re-za we- du we- Zi- mba- bwe Ya-ka- zva- rwa no-
Pha- ka- mi-san i- fle-gi ye- thu ye- Zi- mba- bwe E-ya- za- lwa

free-dom pro - claim- ing __ vic-to- ry __; We praise our he-roes' __
mo - to we- chi-mu-re - nga __; Ne- ro-pa zhi-nji __
yi- mpi ye- nku-lu-le- ko __; Le- gaz' e- li- ne-ngi la-

sac-ri-fice, And __ vow to __ keep our land __ from __ foes; And __ may the Al-
ra-ma-ga-mba Ti - i- dzi- vi- ri- re ku-mha-ndu dzo-se; Nga- i-ko-mbo-
ma-qha-we e- thu Si- li- vi-ke- le e- zi-the-ni-zo-nke; Ka- li-bu-

migh-ty pro- tect and __ bless our land __.
re- rwe nyi- ka ye- Zi- mba- bwe __.
si- swe i- li- zwe le- Zi- mba- bwe __.

Notes

Unless mentioned below, transliterations and English translations of the anthems are provided with permission from David Kendall.

Albania

    1. Berishaj, Antoni, and Lushi, Uk, "Anthem." *Albanian.com*. 1998. www.albanian.com/main/countries/albania/general/anthem.html (6 July 2001).

    2. See above.

Andorra

    1. Embassy of the Principality of Andorra in Brussels, Belgium.

    2. See above.

Antigua and Barbuda

    1. Charisma, "Antigua Net. Antigua!" 1997. www.antiguanet.net/disclaimer.htm (5 June 2001).

Armenia

    1. Translated by Makrouhie Maljian.

Australia

    1. National Australia Day Council, "About Australia: National Anthem." www.nadc.com.au/aboutaust/anthem.html (2 July 2001).

Austria

    1. Austrian Press and Information Service, Washington, D.C.

Azerbaijan

    1. Azerbaijan International, "Azerbaijan National Hymn." 2002. www.azer.com/aiweb/categories/music/AudioPages/NationalAnthem/hymn_independence.html (5 September 2002)

Bangladesh

    1. Translated by Professor Syed Ali Ahsan.

Barbados

    1. Barbados Government Information Service.

Belarus

    1. Jan Zaprudnik. *Historical Dictionary of Belarus* (Lanham, Md.: Scarecrow Press, 1998), p.161.

Brazil

    1. Cultura Brasileira, "The National Symbols of Brazil." www.culturabrasil.pro.br/simbolospatrios.htm (5 September 2002).

    2. See above.

Bulgaria

    1. Special thanks to David Kendall.

    2. *O pismeneh*, "Anthem of the Republic of Bulgaria." 1998. www.kirildouhalov.net/republic/anthem.html. (5 September 2002).

Canada

    1. Government of Canada.

Cape Verde

    1. Presidency of the Republic of Cape Verde.

China

    1. *People's Daily* English Edition.

    2. See above.

China, Republic of

    1. Government Information Office, Republic of China.

Costa Rica

    1. Costa Rica Web, "National Anthem." 1996.
www.costarica.com/culture/national-symbols/national-anthem.html (5 September 2002).

    2. See above.

Croatia

    1. Croatia Net, "Croatian Anthem." 1996. www.croatia.net/anthem/ (5 September 2002).

    2. Translated by Profikon.

Cyprus

    1. Special thanks to P. Kritidis.

    2. Translated by Sir Rudyard Kipling.

Czech Republic

    1. Musica Bona, "Frantisek Skroup." 2000. www.musicabona.com/cdall1/skroup01.html (5 September 2002).

Denmark

    1. Royal Danish Embassy in Washington, D.C.

    2. See above.

    3. See above.

    4. See above.

Egypt

    1. Egypt State Information Service.

    2. See above.

Eritrea

    1. Special thanks to Mebrat Tzehaie.

Estonia

    1. Office of the President of the Republic of Estonia.

    2. Translated by Jenny Wahl.

Finland

    1. Virtual Finland, "Finnish National Anthem." 1999. virtual.finland.fi/finfo/english/maamme.html (5 September 2002).

    2. See above.

France

1. Embassy of the French Republic in Canberra, Australia.

Germany

1. Brandenburg Historica, "Deutschland, Deutschland über alles." 1996. www.brandenburghistorica.com/page5.html (5 September 2002).

2. See above.

Greece

1. Special thanks to Mr. P. Kritidis.

2. Translated by Sir Rudyard Kipling.

Haiti

1. Site Kreyol, "History." 2002. www.sitekreyol.com/National_Anthem.htm (5 September 2002).

2. Haitian Student Association of the University of Florida.

Hungary

1. Embassy of the Republic of Hungary in Zagreb, Croatia.

2. Translated by William N. Loew.

Iceland

1. Prime Minister's Office, Government of the Republic of Iceland.

2. See above.

India

1. Prime Minister's Office of India.

2. Translated by Rabindranath Tagore.

Indonesia

1. Embassy of the Republic of Indonesia in Prague, Czech Republic.

2. See above.

Iraq

1. Radio Free Europe.

Ireland

1. Department of the Taoiseach, Government of the Republic of Ireland.

Israel

1. Our Jerusalem, "The History of 'Hatikva': Israel's National Anthem." 2001. www.ourjerusalem.com/history/story/history20010501a.html (5 September 2002).

2. Israel Science and Technology Homepage, "National Anthem of Israel." 1999. www.science.co.il/Israel-anthem.asp (5 September 2002).

Italy

1. Italian Cultural Institute of Washington, D.C.

2. See above.

Japan

1. Ministry of Foreign Affairs, Japan.

2. Translated by Basil H. Chamberlain.

Korea, North

    1. Korean Central News Agency.

Korea, South

    1. Korean Cultural Service, Embassy of the Republic of Korea in Washington, D.C.

    2. See above.

Kuwait

    1. Special thanks to the Kuwait Information Office.

    2. See above.

Latvia

    1. The Latvian Institute.

Lebanon

    1. Special thanks to Yesser Kadado.

Liechtenstein

    1. Fürstentum Liechtenstein, "The national anthem." www.liechtenstein.li (5 September 2002).

    2. See above.

Lithuania

    1. Embassy of the Republic of Lithuania, Washington, D.C.

    2. See above.

Luxembourg

    1. Government of the Grand Duchy of Luxembourg.

    2. See above.

Macedonia

    1. Presidency of the Republic of Macedonia.

Madagascar

    1. Embassy of the Republic of Madagascar, Washington, D.C.

Malaysia

    1. Embassy of Malaysia in Seoul, Korea.

Malta

    1. Department of Information, Government of Malta.

    2. See above.

Mexico

    1. Inside Mexico. "Mexico's National Anthem." www.inside-mexico.com/anthem.htm (5 September 2002).

Mozambique

    1. Mozambique News Agency, London, UK.

The Netherlands

    1. Royal Netherlands Embassy in Belgrade, Serbia and Montenegro.

    2. See above.

New Zealand

    1. Ministry for Culture and Heritage, Government of New Zealand.

Nigeria

    1. Embassy of the Federal Republic of Nigeria in Washington, D.C.

Norway

    1. Stavanger Web, "17th of May in Norway." www.stavanger-web.com/17may/ (5 September 2002).

    2. See above.

Pakistan

    1. Pakistan News Service.

    2. See above.

Palestine

    1. Palestine History, "Palestine Flag and Anthem." www.palestinehistory.com/anthem.htm (5 September 2002).

The Philippines

    1. Special thanks to Rogelio A. Santos.

    2. Translated by Camilo Osias and A. L. Lang.

Poland

    1. Department of Polish Music, University of Southern California.

    2. See above.

Portugal

    1. Presidency of the Portuguese Republic.

Romania

    1. Presidency of Romania.

    2. Embassy of Romania in Canberra, Australia.

Russia

    1. *Warsaw Voice*.

    2. Russian Legacy, "Anthem of the Russian Federation." 2001. www.russianlegacy.com/en/go_to/anthem.htm (5 September 2002).

Rwanda

    1. British Broadcasting Corporation.

Singapore

    1. Ministry of Communication, Information, and the Arts, Republic of Singapore.

    2. See above.

Slovakia

    1. Slovakia.org, "Slovak National Anthem." www.slovakia.org/sk-anthem.htm (5 September 2002).

Slovenia

    1. Government of the Republic of Slovenia.

    2. See above.

Somalia

    1. Special thanks to David Kendall.

South Africa

    1. Government of the Republic of South Africa.

Spain

1. Special thanks to Julio Rancel.

Sri Lanka

1. Council for Information Technology, Sri Lanka.

Sweden

1. AT&T Jens Virtual Classroom, "Swedish National Anthem History." www.jp.kids-commons.net/vc96/vc-05/indexb.htm (5 September 2002).

2. AT&T Jens Virtual Classroom, "Swedish National Anthem. Lyrics." www.jp.kids-commons.net/vc96/vc-05/indexc.htm (5 September 2002).

Switzerland

1. Federal Authorities of the Swiss Confederation.

Thailand

1. Sawadee Thailand, "National Symbols." 1999. www.sawadeethailand.com/about/flag/flag.html (5 September 2002).

2. See above.

Tonga

1. Prime Minister's Office, Kingdom of Tonga.

Turkey

1. Ministry of Foreign Affairs, Republic of Turkey.

Ukraine

1. Linda Hodges and George Chumak. *The Language and Travel Guide to Ukraine* (New York: Hippocrene, 2000).

2. Translated by Ihor Slabicky.

United Kingdom

1. Government of Canada.

United States

1. Embassy of the United States of America in Stockholm, Sweden.

Vietnam

1. Embassy of the Socialist Republic of Vietnam in Washington, D.C.

2. See above.

Zambia

1. Zambia Information Desk, "Our National Identity: National Anthem." 2001. www.zambiainfodesk.com/zambiathecountry/zambia-anthem.html (5 September 2002).

Zimbabwe

1. Ecoweb. 2001. www.ecoweb.co.zw/education/zim_anthem.asp (5 September 2002).